The Spice Lover's Guide to

HERBS & SPICES

Tony Hill

WILEY

JOHN WILEY & SONS, INC.

For Mom, Hobbes, and Cat (There's salmon in it for all of you)

Originally published in hardcover as *The Contemporary Encyclopedia of Herbs & Spices: Seasonings for the Global Kitchen*.
Published by arrangement with Tony Hill and becker&mayer!, Ltd. www.beckermayer.com.
Published by John Wiley & Sons, Inc., Hoboken, New Jersey
Published simultaneously in Canada

For general information on our other products and services or for technical support, please contact our Customer Care Department within the United States at 800–762-2974, outside the United States at (317)572–3993 or fax (317)572–4002.

Wiley also publishes its books in a variety of electronic formats. Some content that appears in print may not be available in electronic books. For more information about Wiley products, visit our web site at www.wiley.com.

Library of Congress Cataloging–in–Publication Data:
Hill, Tony
    The spice lover's guide to herbs and spices / by Tony Hill.
        p.   cm.
    Includes bibliographical references and index.
    ISBN-13: 978-0-764-59739-8 (pbk.)
    ISBN-10: 0-764-59739-6 (pbk.)
    ISBN-13: 978-0-471-21423-6 (cloth)
    ISBN-10: 0-471-21423-X (cloth)
    1. Cookery (Herbs)   2. Herbs   I. Title.

    TX819.H4H55 2005
    641.6'57—dc22   2005041622

Interior photography: WKDG Partners
Book design: Richard Oriolo
Cover design: Jeff Faust

Printed in the United States of America

10 9 8 7 6 5 4 3

CONTENTS

Every culture in the world uses herbs and spices to enliven food and to create the culinary signature of its native land. Select seeds, leaves, roots, bark, flowers, and pods provide the special notes cooks summon up to make dishes sing. Combinations of seasonings create indelible patterns of taste tied to specific cuisines. Cumin and cilantro, for example, blend in a Latin beat. Ginger and star anise proclaim an Asian accent. And saffron and *pimentón* speak of Spain.

Because dining has become so global, with many cuisines fused to startling effect, herbs and spices are more sought after than ever before. Cooks have become culinary adventurers, bravely seeking out new foods from all over the globe. Foreign travel has introduced an incredible diversity of flavors, which, back home, dominate the contemporary dining experience. Star chefs, always on the lookout for the next hot trend, constantly experiment with exotic herbs, spices, and rubs. They mix their own blends, and like white-coated chemists, steep fragrant oils in glass jars, seeking yet another potent elixir to thrill their customers' ever more sophisticated palates.

With all this experience comes a vast array of new ingredients. Cooks want to re-create the flavors of India, Thailand, and the Middle East. Where the spice rack once stood neatly stocked with European herbs and sweet spices—basil, rosemary, oregano, thyme, cinnamon, cloves—it now bulges with containers of less familiar items: fenugreek, *tabil*, lemongrass, and *kaffir* lime leaves. Luckily for the cook, the availability of these items has increased exponentially along with the demand.

I've been a world traveler most of my adult life. Returning home from each trip, my bags laden with packets, jars, and bags of fragrant spices and other pungent ingredients, I would be compelled to re-create the exciting tastes I found abroad. What came next was an odyssey of discovery. Inspired by the romance of the past, I became a spice merchant, a modern-day Marco Polo of sorts, tramping all over the world in search of adventure and the knowledge that goes with the territory.

The history of the spice trade is filled with adventure, romance, and much peril. As early as the second century B.C., spices were the exclusive provenance of kings and the wealthy merchant class. Overland trade routes from Asian plantations to European cities financed empires perched along the way. More than five centuries ago, wars were waged over cargoes of cloves from the Banda Islands of Indonesia, and the English and Portuguese dueled over trading rights to nutmeg. And Malacca (Singapore today), a port poised at the gateway to the oceanic routes to Europe, was conquered some eleven times in two hundred years. It was the extraordinary profits from spice commerce that prodded Magellan, funded by the queen of Spain, to try so desperately to discover a way to sail around the globe.

Great caravans laden with cinnamon and peppercorns trekked across Asian deserts, unloading their precious wares in the port of Constantinople. From there, sailing ships carried the cargoes across the Mediterranean Sea to Venice, at that time the spice-trade capital of the world, where they commanded the most outrageous prices Europe had to offer. Andean chiles and Caribbean allspice were deposited right next to Aztec gold in the treasure vaults of Spanish conquistadores.

Marco Polo himself was motivated to travel to the East, lured in part by profits from the spice trade. Old World trading centers such as Istanbul became melting pots of culture and status, just as their kitchens blended spices and herbs in culinary masterpieces laced with the essence of far-flung cuisines.

The spice trade today continues to encircle the globe. I've followed the same paths of discovery and adventure—alas, without a sailing ship or a great Spanish queen as financial backer. Mastering the finesse of spicing techniques has been my goal. After years of roasting coriander, sifting rosemary, and grinding curry blends, I now happily offer my own considerable number of the "tricks of the trade."

In fact, *The Contemporary Encyclopedia of Herbs & Spices* presents more than 125 pure herbs and spices, plus dozens of interesting blends. Here are botanical facts, information on buying and storing, and, most important, cooking uses for each listing. Recipes to accompany unusual seasonings pepper the book. Photographs help to identify all the herbs and spices as well as provide a glimpse into fields and harvests.

Some people seem intimidated by more complex spice combinations, choosing to take a simpler approach, and that is fine too. There is no need to spend hours making Indonesian *sambal goreng* to benefit from a knowledge of spices. Imagine a simple perfect, sweet, garden-ripe sliced tomato. Add a tiny dusting of Tellicherry peppercorn and a pinch of French sea salt, and that tomato is transformed into a culinary epiphany. Even the casual condiment user can vastly improve his or her dining experience by following the spice basics included here.

The section on spice blends will help you re-create the flavors remembered from visits to the Caribbean, Russia, the Middle East, Africa, Asia, and beyond. Armed with knowledge from these pages, you can make the same journey to the Old World by seasoning in the fashion developed locally over the centuries. This is not to discourage experimentation at the stove. But traditions evolved for a reason—the food tasted good that way. Only by knowing the "old" ways of spicing can you create "new" options for yourself.

I've been lucky enough to learn these flavor patterns directly from the cultures that created them. My work has given me access to the paprika fields of Hungary for authentic goulash, the saffron plantations of La Mancha for a fragrant paella, and the chile markets of the Andes for a properly spiced Peruvian stew, to name a few. These are places that have elevated their indigenous foods to cultural-icon status. Generations of home cooks and chefs have worked to perfect these recipes, all the while relying on local ingredients, not the least of which are spices and herbs.

It is my hope that this book will inspire you to seek out the incredibly diverse varieties of herbs and spices available to everyone today. With each entry, I've sought to provide history, horticulture, tradition, and techniques, along with my own first encounters with the particular seasoning. Whether you are looking for a way to perk up an old meat loaf standby or the secrets of an authentic Indonesian rijsttafel, my intent is to reveal the fascinating international world of flavors that offers adventure in the kitchen and ongoing delight at the table.

Tony Hill
Seattle, Washington, USA

ACKNOWLEDGMENTS

The number of people it takes to coalesce an idea floating around in a spice merchant's mind into a finished book is astounding. The process, when successful, is akin to a minor miracle, and this example is no exception. From the first moment when Susanne DeGalan walked into my shop to propose the idea of a book until the last stroke of the editorial staff at Wiley, I've been incredibly lucky to have consummate professionals keeping me on the precarious path to successful publishing.

While the list is long and could not hope to be complete, I have to point out some of those without whom the book you're now holding would still be merely an idea. Susan Wyler, my lead editor at Wiley, whose experience and candor has pushed me to be better, gently guided me through the murky waters of the book world. My agents at Becker & Mayer, most notably Heather ("Rockstar") Dalglish and Ben Raker, have been unfaltering in their support throughout the entire process. Freelance editors Judith Sutton and Justin Schwartz along with the entire staff at Wiley, including Monique Calello and Jeff Faust, have all focused their talents on my work and tirelessly labored to make the raw stream of composition from my pen into something the rest of the world could understand. To all these people, I thank you.

The list of chefs, researchers, and industry leaders who have contributed ideas, tested recipes, and simply been kind enough to talk to me about their chosen profession is a long list in itself but must absolutely include Brian Scheeser, Chris Keff, Brian Poor, Dino Batali, Jason Chen, Danielle Custer, Tom Douglas, Nimal Fernando, Joseph Jimenez de Jimenez, Jerry Traunfeld, and most definitely my entire crew at World Spice. It goes without saying that all my customers, who I really regard more as friends, have also made this effort possible.

Of course the demands of writing a book take their toll on an author's free time, and all my friends who've heard "I can't, I'm working on the book," as an answer for the past three years will now have to begin asking me to be social again. I thank them for their patience. Nia, who has waited in Wales for my schedule to clear, will most certainly no longer take my excuses, and so to her I promise to begin building chicken coops as soon as she desires.

All About Seasonings for the Global Kitchen

Herbs and Spices Defined

SPICES AND HERBS FOR THE CULINARY world are harvested from the entire spectrum of plant species. Most commonly the seeds and leaves of these botanical treasures are used to impart flavor, but barks, roots, nuts, flowers, and berries also have much to offer, depending on which plant you have before you. What just about all these species, in their many forms, have in common is a unique pungency compared with other crops. A spice or herb destined for the kitchen is likely to have a strong signature not duplicated elsewhere.

Occasionally, however, the selection of species is only part of the process. It can be what occurs after harvest that situates the basic plant firmly in the spice category. The gentle roasting of saffron to intensify its flavor, the drying of peppercorn berries into black or white varieties, and the curing of raw green vanilla beans into a usable form are all prime examples of how other hands make those tastes into what we know in the kitchen.

In the spice world, many parts of the same plant may be used for culinary purposes. Seeds, buds, barks, roots, stems, flowers, and a variety of other forms can all be pressed into service in the kitchen, frequently with very different results. Generally speaking, seeds and barks tend toward the lowest common denominator of a given species' flavor, whereas leaf and bud forms typically have a brighter characteristic. There is some intrinsic logic at work here if you think of the former as the "older growth" of a plant and the latter as the "new growth," with all its spring energy pumped into propagating itself in the plant world.

A perfect example of this same plant/different parts approach is coriander, or cilantro, and it makes for some confusion in the kitchen with regard to the name game played by cooks around the world. In America, the seed form is known as coriander and the leaf form, usually, as cilantro. In Europe, "cilantro" is typically dropped and a recipe will call for coriander leaf, coriander seed, or even, perhaps, fresh coriander, meaning the green leafy parts with stems intact. Southeast Asia will call on both, or even the root of the same plant, and, to confuse you completely, may ask for all three in the same recipe, interchanging the names or muddling them all together with local dialects.

Buying Herbs and Spices

WHEN YOU'RE SELECTING HERBS AND SPICES for your own pantry, there is no better way to judge character than with your senses of taste and smell. Buying spices and herbs should be a tactile experience, not just pulling a jar from a shelf. The pungency native to the product should be readily evident. Whole spices, almost always a better choice than preground, can be gently rubbed between fingers to reveal their fragrant oils and, ultimately, their flavor potential. Mixed spice blends can be tasted on the tip of the tongue to see if each layer of flavor is present. And herbs can be smelled to see if there is the fresh quality you'd expect in leaves just cut from the plant.

However, a few warnings are in order for the informed spice consumer. Every industry has its deep, dark secrets. For the spice trade in America, this dirty laundry takes the form of overall homogenization of selection, extended warehousing time, and filler and chemicals in the blends. The motive in almost all cases is a simple one: profit.

Mainstream supply lines have evolved to offer only the simplest and, subsequently, cheapest-to-procure products. Certainly this is obvious when looking for exotica like *mahleb* or grains of paradise at your local supermarket, but it extends into old familiar spices like oregano and basil too: whatever was cheapest on the world market when the buyer went looking is typically what's offered. The answer: seek out several regional sources and use the taste test to decide which is best for your cuisine. The subtle yet important difference between oregano cultivated in the Mediterranean versus that from California may be just the edge that takes your tomato sauce to the next level. Or your taste buds may find that the savory Spanish paprika works better than the sweeter Hungarian in your barbecue rub.

After you've done the math for price and formula, your next hurdle comes with the status quo in distribution. As many as twenty sets of hands may have touched the product from harvest to your stockpot. Generally, the price doubles at each step of the supply line, with farmers, packers, cleaners, importers, exporters, and retail merchants all adding to the final tab. With even a short turnover at each stage in the best-case scenario, the time adds up to some significant pages of the calendar and, subsequently, loss of flavor, despite the most modern packing and drying techniques. The only solution is to buy fresh products in small amounts and use them up as quickly as possible. You'd never eat a three-month-old peach, so why should you settle for two-year-old pepper?

Try as they might, the lads at the grocery just can't seem to sell spices as quickly as they'd like. While restocking should result in the freshest products on the shelves, more often than not older jars languish in the spice rack—and "too good to be true" pricing on massive tubs at warehouse shopping clubs usually are. Because spices are typically potent flavorings to begin with, there's usually at least *some* flavor left months or even years after packing. But the little bits of taste lingering behind are pale imitations of the flavors that were once present.

I can describe to people an original flavor profile of a spice with, say, ten distinct characteristics included. Over time, the top and bottom notes will dissipate, leaving only perhaps the middle five or six. The argument most often put forward is "just use more of the older stuff," but you never reclaim those lost bits, you just get more of that center, less-interesting flavor. With that in mind, refreshing your spices every six to eight months is a wise idea if you want to enjoy the original complexity. Ground samples hold steady for even less time, while some whole seeds and nuts might last longer. Keep in mind that I frequently hear "I can never go back to Brand X" in the spice store, so my suspicion is that once you seek out the best quality, you won't have a hard time convincing yourself to stay at the peak of freshness. (When refresh time does come around at my house, I grab the potatoes and make a huge pot of catchall spiced soup with my aging samples.) And, of course, grinding spices yourself or hand rubbing your dried herbs only when you need them is the best method if you want to preserve these flavor intricacies.

Examples that deserve particular mention include the lemony high of coriander, the wonderfully complex nose of nutmeg, and the peppery punch of fresh cardamom. All of these will evaporate within days of grinding, and thus these spices merit special care, yet you see ground versions of all of them offered at retail at ridiculous prices in bottles that may have been sealed months or even years earlier. Get them whole for home grinding, and quiz your merchant as to their harvest time when you do so. Being as reasonable as the hemisphere you call home will allow, be an informed buyer who uses his or her own taste buds to decide.

Another potential problem lies in a practice that has recently gained popularity, namely "bulk bin" purchasing. It started years ago in natural food co-ops and the like, and you can now walk into better grocery stores and culinary shops to find large bins of spices and herbs. The most attractive factor of this scenario is typically price, as the retailer has been able to reduce the supply line by a step or two by forgoing fancy packaging. But let the buyer beware from a freshness perspective. I always ask myself (and then the store manager), "How often do you see these bins empty?" And are they being stored in the light or next to the takeaway-meal warming lights? As alluring as a large tub of paprika at $10 a pound can be for some cooks, don't be tempted to buy in bulk until you've tasted and cooked with a small sample to prove its freshness and ultimate worth.

Spice blends deserve a special mention. The equation that introduces fillers into things like chili and curry powder hinges on a few simple facts. Fillers like salt, cornstarch, and flour cost relatively little, say $2 or $3 a pound at most. With the average price of a spice mix in the $25-per-pound range, you see the obvious room for profit-margin padding. Add cheap preservatives and "flow enhancers" to keep things pouring smoothly from the bottle, and you see that the main flavor constituents, the spices themselves, start to get pushed to the side.

The recipe's integrity may also be compromised by way of tilting toward cheaper, less flavorful spices in the mix. While turmeric is integral to any decent Indian curry powder recipe, it shouldn't make up seventy percent of the blend. Unfortunately, its low price on the world market lands it in a prominent position in many of the commercially prepared powders. Other examples, like garlic salt with three-quarters salt and chili powder half made of corn flour, readily come to mind.

This is not to say that you shouldn't have any salt, sugar, or other nonspice components in your blends. Rather, it's simply to point you toward watching how much of these ingredients make it into any particular mix and realizing what price you pay for them. I'm the first to add sugar to my barbecue rubs and salt to my pickling solutions, but it's my hand that does the adding and, moreover, it's usually an interesting raw sugar or mineral-rich sea salt that I grab, so I'm also adding some higher level of flavor to the dish. (The last time I used plain iodized salt at my house was in a feeble attempt to de-ice the sidewalk, and even then I discovered there were better products for the job.)

Stocking the Spice Rack

SEVERAL YEARS AGO, I FOUND THAT there was great demand for a definitive list of essential herbs and spices in the kitchen. Something to provide the catchall inventory for someone moving into a new house or a newlywed couple's first kitchen seemed to be the logic behind lots of the requests. At first this seemed like a good idea, a par list of sorts that you shouldn't leave home without, so to speak. It continued to seem that way until I sat down to try and make such a list.

The ancient herbs and spices that reside in prepackaged spice racks, I'm convinced, are simply there for color—and sometimes they don't even provide that. If you happen to like the hardware of such devices and they give you airtight conditions, by all means buy them, but please make your first task to dump the flavorless dust out of each jar and refill them with fresh. I began looking more closely at these kits to find out what apparently represented the flavor pulse of the masses. Eventually I decided that there is no consensus.

I doubt, in fact, that any single list could address a range of opinion, so I will give you a theory before I tell you my own personal choices. The idea is that you should buy what you plan to cook with in, say, a month. If you're in an Indian mood, curries, peppercorns, and fenugreek leaf are in order. If it's Latin you crave, load up on chiles, cumin, and Mexican oregano. After a few months of this, you'll discover that you have a taste for a few specifics that cross all cuisines. Those should be the ones that make it on to your list on a permanent basis. Everything else should be considered a short-term visitor and, as such, not stocked in any significant quantity.

So here is the solid answer for those of you who must have specifics or who plan on giving a selection of herbs and spices as a wedding gift and have nowhere to start. Everyone uses peppercorns and sea salts, so they easily make the list. Paprika, cumin, basil, oregano, sage, rosemary, dried garlic, cassia-cinnamon, cloves, fennel, ginger, a reasonable chili powder, and a simple curry powder round out my choices for the must-haves. With these choices, I can make or fake something like 80 percent of the dishes in my own repertoire. Truth be told, however, my last count of spice jars in the kitchen sat somewhere around eighty-five—but it's important to note that most of them were almost empty.

Naming Confusion

I FREQUENTLY DESCRIBE MY JOB AS a global treasure hunt. Not only are herbs and spices far-flung across the globe, but they frequently hide behind aliases that make them harder to spot in a crowd. Customers come to my doorstep trying to track down some seemingly obscure spice from the last time they went on holiday. The local dialect they heard sounds impressively exotic, but often once the translation comes through, it turns out they have some of this or that growing in their own backyard. The first step to finding a "new" spice is to find out as many of its names as possible.

In addition, blended spices can often be confused with pure spices. Perhaps the most glaring example of this is curry, commonly thought of as a single spice when, in fact, it is a blend of several pure spices. If you find you can't locate an exotic spice, check to see if perhaps it is in fact a blend of spices and herbs. Often a blend has become so ubiquitous in an area that even the locals consider it a single spice.

Regional Differences Among Herb and Spice Sources

WHEN YOU CONSIDER THAT EVERY CUISINE in the world uses some form of spice, and, further, that every country in the world produces something in the herb and spice genre, you realize that the marketplace is vast and somewhat convoluted. Peppercorns, for example, come from a mere handful of producing countries, but they manage to make their way into 95 percent of the world's kitchens. Knowing how this intriguing supply and demand relationship works can help a cook choose better sources.

In the wine trade, the different characteristics of each region, each field, and even each row of grapes are embraced and celebrated as part of the beauty of a natural product. The same idea applies to all sorts of foods, not the least of which are herbs and spices. Growing conditions affect any crop, and since herbs and spices are typically intense versions of plants, they reflect trends and changes in climate and become potent distillations of variations in any particular region. Spring crops may have more new growth character, fall crops may be more fully developed. Herbs grown in an irrigated desert will taste different from those cultivated on a rainy coast. These are the differences the cook should want to understand.

While there is no one rule that can be applied, tastings from various regions can tell you a lot about the range an herb or spice may be able to achieve. For example, basil from Californian fields will taste sweeter than the crop in Egypt, but the latter will have more intensity because of the stress the plant endures under irrigation. Both have their merits, and only the cook can decide which is best for his or her kitchen or, more specifically, for a particular dish.

Harvesting itself can be done in several fashions, but in this age-old business, gathering, sorting, and processing are still most frequently done by hand for the vast majority of crops. Certainly there is large-scale production of spices like coriander and mustard seeds, harvested almost completely by modern machine techniques, but simple hand picking and air-drying is more common in the countries that produce the most varied number of species. India and China are notable examples, where you can still see tarps laden with ginger or chiles drying in the sun, collected by an army of independent workers. What the modern day has brought to these practices is better quality control and machine-assisted sorting and packaging.

Whether the crops are formally cultivated or harvested from the wild, they have all had to begin to conform to safety standards of the West. Machines to clean and sift products are manyfold and range from simple wire screens in wooden frames to laser-imaging equipment that can recognize the difference between a peppercorn and a rock. And purity standards are being put in place to assure the consumer that these are international norms rather than arbitrary guidelines.

Note: You'll notice that I refer to a few herb and spice plants as "wild-crafted." This is a term that means much less than organized cultivation but more than "wild-harvested," which would be closer to simple foraging. Mushrooms are a good example; wild species aren't "planted" but the "in-the-wild" conditions that make them thrive are encouraged and developed as much as possible without interfering with the process that makes growing possible. It's a fine line, but some species resist higher levels of interference by man.

The Mystical Spice Markets of the Middle East

THERE ARE SOME VERY IMPRESSIVE SPICE markets on the face of the planet, most notably the ones in the Middle East, in ancient cities like Istanbul. While these bazaars bring together some of the world's most impressive arrays of spices and are certainly worth the visit, cook-travelers should remember that there, as in other lo-cales around the globe, not all the products you see are grown locally. It's easy to get caught up in the romance of the marketplace, but merchants there are forced to import products just like those in London or Los Angeles, and what is offered may not always be the freshest or best value.

What these marketplaces do have is the benefit of their location on historic trade routes. That alone is worth a trip just for the education aspects, even if global ship-ping systems may have rendered what was once a serious freshness advantage almost no advantage at all. Buy what is locally produced for the best flavors, and get as close to the source as possible. Load up your luggage with a few select products, and save the big shopping spree for rugs and *kilims*.

THE ART OF THE BARTER

One of the things that first struck me when I began traveling the markets of the world is that no price is fixed. From the bazaars of Istanbul to the open-air kiosks of Oax-aca, the art of haggle is a refined and sought-after skill. If you're a good negotiator, not only do you get a better price, but you gain the respect it takes to get a better qual-ity of product as well.

Another skill when making the buying rounds is not so obvious to the casual traveler: it's the age-old art of barter. Long before currency standards and commodi-ties exchanges, there was barter. A brick of tea in Nepal could get you a yak, a cow, or, with the proper negotiations, a mate! In my mind, the best barter environment can be seen at the merchants' stalls, among the merchants and farmers themselves, before the day's commerce begins. A cheese farmer will bring an extra-special round from his private stock because the chile farmer brought him prime ancho pods the day before. An enterprising greens grower may barter some of his wares to the spice merchant, who makes the perfect vinaigrette seasoning. If they find an olive oil producer, a food partnership is formed around the infallible principle of fresh and available.

In my shop below the century-old Pike Place Market in Seattle, such bartering happens every day. My salmon spice rub finds its way to the fishmongers upstairs and, in turn, fresh-smoked Copper River salmon is always in my fridge. One such gentleman of the trading inclination came to me on a winter afternoon with a proposition: a recipe in exchange for a vanilla bean. I somewhat reluctantly agreed, partly out of curiosity and partly because the beans were plentiful and cheap that year. What I got for my trouble was a superb coffee liqueur recipe (see page 328), and what ensued was an addictive relationship between my taste buds and this smooth liquor. That's a fair trade, if you ask me.

In the Kitchen and Garden

HOW TO STORE HERBS AND SPICES

FOR STORAGE, AN AIRTIGHT CONTAINER IN a cool, dark place (not above the stove—even if the rack looks so nice there) is best. But avoid the refrigerator or freezer: cold temperatures will actually leach out the essential oils that give flavor. Glass or ceramic containers are better to my mind despite the popularity of tins for the same use. Spices tend to pick up metallic flavors from the latter unless they are made of the highest-quality stainless steel. And be sure to use only tightly sealed containers, not those with porous cork lids or seals. Dense composite cork or, better yet, lids with rubber gaskets will preserve the most flavor.

Grinding spices fresh is a must, of course, and only what will be used immediately should ever be processed. With herbs, you may want to simply hand rub the leaves—that is, to take a measure in the palm of your hand and rub with your other into smaller pieces. I do this over a plate just to be sure that any stray stems or large pieces don't slip through. This helps release the essential flavor oils just as mill grinding does for hard seeds or barks but leaves you some degree of pleasing texture that you can then add to your pot.

Speaking of storage, the unfortunate reality is that some plants simply lose all their flavor when dried. It may be the drying process itself that extracts the oils prematurely, or it may be the subsequent cutting and grinding that spells the demise of flavor. Chopping or grinding exposes more surface area to the elements and thus the volatile flavor compounds evaporate, leaving behind, in some cases, nothing more than brown powder.

For my tastes, cilantro, parsley, and curry leaf hold little more than color, if that, in dry forms, and should be sought only in fresh produce–quality forms and used as such. However, if you simply must try to preserve them, try blending them to a paste with a small amount of water or oil. Freeze the paste in ice cube trays, then store the cubes in an airtight freezer container. It's not a perfect solution, but it's better than doing without or having to make a last-minute trip to the market when you find yourself facing an herb shortage.

HOW TO GRIND SPICES

My customers frequently ask me, "How do I grind spices at home?" Although I've tried everything from antique cast-iron grain mills to smashing two bricks together, there is still no better way in my mind than a small electric coffee mill. While this method may seem old hat to you, a few decades of experience has taught me certain tricks to the method. The coffee mills work with a blade-type grinder; i.e., the blade spins at high rotation and cuts the seeds, berries, and the like down to size. Because the speed is so high, small amounts of spices, anything less than a few teaspoons, will fly around the top of the grinder. But simply grinding more spices in a batch will fix this problem—or you can "borrow" some other dry ingredients from your recipe to bulk up the sample. This higher volume will weigh down the spices, causing them to hit the grinding blades better.

The other thing to watch out for with this technique is stripping out the relatively inexpensive blade from its spindle. A chunk of anything wedged under the blade will rip the nut (typically plastic) holding the blade, and then it's time to go to the coffee mill store again. You can easily prevent this from happening, however, simply by holding the entire mill, lid on, spices inside, upside down before turning it on. This allows the blades to get up to speed and have a running start at the grind. You'll still dispatch a mill every few years with normal home use, but they have become so inexpensive that it's worth the price. At last count, I had about eight in my kitchen, marked with a variety of inscriptions like "sweet stuff," "herbs only," and "anything with chile" to keep the flavors segregated and reduce the need for cleaning. If your kitchen budget or real estate constrains the number you care to have on hand, grind a bit of dry rice or bread crumbs in the mill between particularly disparate flavors as a fast cleaning method.

Mortars and pestles certainly have a place in the modern kitchen. While they may be less efficient than electric mills, they can give interesting textures based on the cook's ability and persistence with the pestle. They can also work well for spices if the amount needed is tiny or if you're incorporating wet or fresh ingredients into a mix. The curries of Southeast Asia are normally pounded into a paste with tall narrow pestles being "thrown down" into a mortar filled with cumin and coriander seeds, fresh cilantro, garlic cloves, and kaffir leaves.

Look for rough-bottomed mortars whose abrasive qualities will help in the grinding. Experiment with both wooden and stone versions of each utensil to see which works best with your ingredients. For example, I prefer all stone when grinding fresh herbs with oils, but I like a wooden pestle in ceramic when grinding hard seeds. Each material will give different results. Just like electric mills, mortars and pestles will retain some character of what's ground within them. Rather than risk leaving soap residue from washing, I grind some inert ingredients like dry rice or bread to pick up the bulk of any remaining oils. Better still, I have the luxury of several mortars labeled variously for each general category of spice: chiles, mints, etc.

Note, however, that when a fully integrated flavor is desired, electric mills should be used. I've also found that a grinding of mixed spices can marry the flavors together better, even if the components were preground.

TOASTING SPICES

Toasting spices is a technique seen in every culture across the globe, and while it's a fabulous way to jump-start or even alter flavors, it may not be something you want to apply wholesale to every recipe. Think about the process as in general cooking, where the application of heat causes volatile oils to come out more quickly and, in some cases, chemically change into something different. The lessons to apply to vegetables and meats can also be taken to the spice rack.

The way I decide is half experimental and half theoretical. With the latter, I think in terms of what cooking method I plan on using. Is it a long, slow stewing, where the flavors will have plenty of opportunity to release, or is it a relatively rapid sauté, where the flavor needs a bit of a head start on the rest of the dish? Will the seasoning for my heavy root vegetables benefit from a deep roast, while my delicate spring vegetables prefer a lighter toasting?

Then, of course, there are cases like avocado leaf, for example, where you *need* the toasting stage to change the flavor into a usable form. Or perhaps it's a seed that is too hard to open and release flavor without the heat, as is the case with nigella.

At the other extreme, there are spices that will be ruined if direct heat is applied, whether it's a case of truly burning the spice to ruin or just completely vaporizing the character out of the spice, or cases where the other ingredients are needed to buffer the heat and act as a medium to hold the flavors. Almost all herbs and most spices that come preground fall into this "do not toast" character.

Two methods of toasting will serve almost every instance you find in the kitchen. The first is simply to add the spices to a dry pan or skillet set over medium heat, and shake or toss them almost constantly to avoid scorching or burning and to yield even results. Alternately, a baking sheet with a nice high rim to hold the spices in check works well, either in a low oven for long, slow toasting or under the broiler for rapid roasting. Just be sure to watch or monitor the progress carefully in each instance, as you can go from roasted to burnt in a matter of seconds. And once the spices are as lightly or heavily toasted as you desire, remove them from the pan or baking sheet so they don't scorch or burn from the "carryover" heat.

RECONSTITUTING DRIED SPICES AND HERBS

When cooking with a dried spice or herb, your task is to release its flavor into your dish. Sometimes the cooking process benefits from a helping hand, by reconstituting, or soaking the spice or herb in liquid, before beginning. Some seasonings, such as dried chiles, are soaked in water first, until their flesh is soft; then they are blended into a sauce or paste. Other spices have oil-soluble components, which can only be drawn out in oil. Sometimes the process is a short ten-minute affair, as with saffron; other times the desired result is accomplished only with an overnight steeping, as with hard fenugreek seeds.

When using the technique, you will often want to reserve the liquid itself, as it will hold a significant amount of flavor. And, whenever practical, slightly warmed liquid can be used to accelerate the process.

An interesting twist is to use fruit juice as the liquid, especially with hot spices like chiles, mustards, and wasabi. The heat-sweet combo can add wonderful balance to sauces and condiments.

AROMATIC INFUSIONS FOR FULLER FLAVOR PROFILES

I learned a trick in beer brewing that has served me well with herbs and spices in stocks and soups. In brewing, a recipe will call for a measure of "boiling" hops and a measure of "finishing" hops, the former for depth of flavor and the latter primarily for aromatic effect. The "boiling" hops are added early for the full duration of the cooking process and the "finishing" only in the last few minutes of cooking.

The same idea works with almost all herbs and with particularly volatile spices. There are certainly flavors imparted into a dish with a lengthy cooking time, but these are frequently at the cost of some of the more delicate aromatics. Adding a second measure of the same herb or spice later gives you the best of both worlds. In particularly aromatic or volatile cases, such as delicate chervil or pungent lemongrass, you may even want it only as a garnish, with the carryover heat of the dish bringing the aromatic to the lucky diner. Fresh or dried herbs added in an initial sweating of ingredients often need an extra measure added when the cooking is almost finished.

An especially good example of this is chives. They're so delicate and wonderfully "green" in flavor that you want to get some sense of that into a soup. I add them by the handful to my favorite leek and potato soup recipe at the beginning, but I always reserve some for the table to bring that fresh grass character, which couldn't possibly survive twenty minutes on the stovetop, up to the front of the palate.

Remember, a large part of what you taste is what you smell.

SMOKING WITH HERBS AND SPICES

I've been known to barbecue when others are putting on their parkas. Actually, I've been known to start the barbecue pit in the dead of winter seven nights a week. "Addiction" is probably too mild a term.

"Barbecue" here means the real thing, slow, low-heat cooking (see Barbecue Rubs, pages 337–343), and one of the wonderful parts of tending a fire for hours on end is that you have plenty of free time to think of odd ways to introduce flavor. Since my trusty barbecue pit sits conveniently close to a spice warehouse, I've had the opportunity to test all manner of things in the fire beyond the conventional hickory chips and mesquite logs.

Any spent herb stems, especially rosemary and thyme, burn with a strong aroma that can flavor anything on the grill. Cardamom, or more specifically just the husks that held the seeds, can add a pleasantly camphorous sweetness. Black cardamom pods naturally taste of smoke, but their husks can impart a subtle difference to the smoker. Cassia and cinnamon sticks, cloves, and star anise can all be burned with wonderfully aromatic results. Granted, they can become costly when used for smoking purposes, but lower-quality supplies, even surplus inventories from spice traders, can make it a more reasonable endeavor.

Actually, almost any part of a spice or herb that is considered waste in the kitchen can be saved and dried for the fire. As with wood, you'll want to soak your desired flavor in water to restrict its burning and to slowly infuse the taste via smoke.

Smoky Herbs and Spices Masquerading as Meats

Speaking of smoke, certain herbs and spices, especially fleshy chiles and coarse salts, carry smoked flavors very well. Most people's palates will read a smoked flavor as something akin to meat—and these smoky tastes can be lifesavers when you're trying to cut back on meat in your diet or when it's too cold outside to fire up the grill. And vegetarians and vegans can appreciate the deep, dark, satisfying tastes normally known to come from a smoked ham hock—for example, via a large chile, a head of garlic, or a batch of coarse sea salt that's had a trip through the smoker.

Pimentón, the smoked paprika of Spain, has long been used to give the impression of hours over the coals in dishes like paella, but it can be borrowed just as easily for vegetable stews and the like.

MAKING YOUR OWN EXTRACTS AND LIQUEURS

If you want to make your own extracts, time is your best friend. I almost always use pure grain alcohol instead of vodka or brandy to give the cleanest flavors. If pure grain alcohol isn't available, the highest-proof grain vodka is the best choice, though I don't recommend the substitution in my homemade coffee liqueur (page 328). There are some specialty liqueur recipes that will call for more flavorful bases, like brandy, even Cognac, but the technique for all is the same.

The "cold" processes will preserve the most flavor but also take the most time on the shelf for aging. Typically, they need a minimum of three months, but, thankfully, most will not spoil and can only benefit from more time to infuse. "Hot" processes will infuse faster but vaporize more character in the beginning.

A good rule of thumb for all is twenty parts liquor to one part spice. In the case of homemade vanilla extract, that equates to roughly one bean per pint. This can be increased to taste, but know that it is possible to have too much of a good thing. With an overgenerous six beans per pint, you'll get a bitter, overpowering flavor, so lighten up on your measurement if you get unpleasant harshness.

I've noticed that these flavors tend to oxidize quickly, so when starting your extracts, fill the bottle completely to minimize air space. I use old wine bottles and corks when first preparing extracts. Then, after opening, any reasonable method of reducing oxidation, from vacuum pumps to simple airtight seals, should be employed to maintain the flavor.

EXOTIC HERB VARIETALS AND A USEFUL HOME GARDEN

Almost all of the leaf herbs discussed in this text, beginning with basil, have odd variations that hold interest for the cook. And, as with basil, there are numerous sub-varieties found in today's greenhouses and nurseries that aren't cultivated commercially for the food trade. Typically it's a matter of production costs, minimal demand, and/or simple volume economics. Species that produce higher volumes make more sense for commercial growers, whose eyes are set upon profit figures rather than dinner parties. The home gardener is therefore called upon to bring these back into the kitchen.

For my own garden, I cultivate nearly year-round and include as essential basil, oregano, marjoram, rosemary, sage, chives, and thyme. Each year I'll select new variations to attempt, knowing that in the worst-case scenario, I'll get at least a few pickings to make the effort worthwhile. In the best case, I'll have a viable plant for several years to come. Plant and seed co-ops in your own microclimate should be a good source of information and starts and should be explored for your own herb treasures.

HERBS AND SPICES

AJWAIN

ALTERNATE NAMES Ajowan, Bishop's weed, Carom, Ethiopian cumin

BOTANICAL NAMES OF CULINARY SPECIES *Trachyspermum ammi, Carum ajowan*

PLANT FAMILY Parsley (*Umbelliferae*)

COUNTRY/REGION OF BOTANICAL ORIGIN India

MAJOR COUNTRIES/REGIONS OF CULTIVATION North Africa, India, Pakistan

SEASON OF HARVEST Late summer into fall

PARTS USED Seeds

COLOR Pale brown-yellow

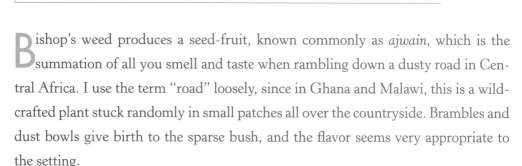

Bishop's weed produces a seed-fruit, known commonly as *ajwain*, which is the summation of all you smell and taste when rambling down a dusty road in Central Africa. I use the term "road" loosely, since in Ghana and Malawi, this is a wild-crafted plant stuck randomly in small patches all over the countryside. Brambles and dust bowls give birth to the sparse bush, and the flavor seems very appropriate to the setting.

Imagine the bitter of celery seed coupled with roasted caraway and cumin, and you're on the path toward ajwain's taste. It has a musty, dark aroma, almost akin to tar, when uncooked, which can be a brilliant foil to sweet soups and nut-milk stews. Considering that its main flavor compound is thymol, the same as in thyme, it's not surprising that a certain amount of herbaceous character peeks around the savory edges. The instensity of flavor can be a bit strong for all but the most adventurous palates, so be cautious. This seed will tilt your palate toward the acrid if you're not light-handed with the amount you add to a recipe.

In fresh batches of the seeds, there should be some distinct brown-yellow tones rather than a more spotty bleached look, which would be a sign of old age. Ajwain can be found as processed commercially bleached seeds that show a consistently lighter color, but this practice doesn't seem to be commonplace or to have much impact on the flavor, perhaps only a slight mellowing that can easily be accomplished with a quick toasting at home. There is frequently a small hairlike "tail" in the seed, which should not be cause for worry. The seed tends to be stubby and not as elongated as, say, cumin or fennel, but is of a similar ridged shape.

India is another ajwain producer of note. The seed has its botanical origins in the Indian subcontinent and is still cultivated widely in most provinces. It has made its way into vegetarian and Ayurvedic cuisine because of its rumored healing properties. There are also antigaseous effects, which is convenient, since lentils and beans are the perfect carriers for its intense flavor. Anything in the vegetable world that needs a touch of savory humility can benefit from ajwain in small doses.

Savory doughs in India are flavored with ajwain and made into everything from naan to poppadams. The baking or frying process tends to pop open the flavor from the seeds and temper bitter components of the flavor. Look for it in several of the more savory spice mixes of India like *chat* or *kala masala,* where they begin with an initial toasting. A friend who has dubbed herself the "cracker queen" adds ajwain to one version served with a sweet caramelized onion soup, for the perfect balance.

The classic Central African treatment of "groundnut" (peanut) soup must have a dose of lightly toasted ajwain, else the dish becomes sickly sweet. Whether added pure or as an ingredient in other blends like *berberé,* the flavor will ground the palate on the savory end of the spectrum. After accidentally making a batch of soup without the spice, I was amazed at how the ajwain brought balance back to taste buds that were on the brink of sweet overload from the peanut and coconut milk.

Beyond Africa and India, cultivation of the seed is sporadic at best, a contributing factor to its near nonexistence on traditional grocery shelves of the West. Significant cultivation is maintained for the essential oil trade, however, as it's a major source of natural thymol, and that has kept the seed commonly available on a commercial level and in its producing countries all over the Middle East.

West African Groundnut Soup

Peanuts are a New World crop that changed the face of cuisine in Africa when they came back across the ocean with the Spanish *conquistadores* and, later on, slave-trading ships returning home. On that continent, they are commonly called groundnuts and are a vital protein and flavor source, whether used whole, as a paste, or processed for their oil. They are also the base for a sweet-savory soup that's served as comfort food across North and Central Africa but has integrated itself most notably into the culinary lexicon of Ghana.

The soup is sometimes little more than crushed peanuts stewed in milk, sometimes a more elaborate affair with meat, tomatoes, and complex spicing. I've seen examples that use flaked fish, shrimp, or goat, but here I use chicken, as is commonly the custom. In Africa, they would tend to add whole chicken pieces, including bones and skin, but I've removed those for Western sensitivities. Adventurous cooks should experiment, as the recipe works well in all permutations, including vegetarian.

I got the beginnings of this version of the recipe from a spice-trading friend who travels all over West Africa. As you might expect, it includes some of the spices he happens to sell to me, namely grains of paradise and ajwain, the former lending peppery heat and the latter adding a savory, bittering character. **SERVES 4 TO 6**

3 tablespoons unsalted butter

1 onion, finely chopped

1 tablespoon finely ground grains of paradise

2 teaspoons ground ajwain

1 pound boneless, skinless chicken thighs, cut into 1½-inch pieces

3 cups chicken stock

¾ cup peanut butter (any style)

¼ cup finely chopped peanuts

2 tomatoes, seeded and finely diced

⅔ cup coconut milk

Coarse sea salt

2 tablespoons chopped fresh cilantro

3 tablespoons freshly ground *tabil* (page 394)

Melt the butter in a medium pot over medium-high heat. Add the onion and cook, stirring, until translucent, about 3 minutes. Add the spices and stir to coat the onion. Add the chicken and cook, stirring frequently, until lightly browned, 5 to 7 minutes. Pour in the chicken stock and bring to a boil, scraping up any brown bits from the bottom of the pot. Then add the remaining stock. Add the peanut butter, peanuts, tomatoes, coconut milk, and enough water to cover by 1 inch. Bring to a boil, reduce the heat, and simmer, partially covered, for 25 minutes. Season with salt to taste.

Ladle the soup into bowls and garnish with cilantro. Pass the *tabil* at the table, to be stirred in by each guest to his or her preference of heat.

ALTERNATE NAMES **Allspice berries, Jamaica pepper, Myrtle pepper, Pimento, *Pimenta* (Spanish), West Indian bay (leaves)**

CULINARY SPECIES BOTANICAL NAME ***Pimenta dioica***

PLANT FAMILY **Myrtle (*Myrtaceae*)**

COUNTRY/REGION OF BOTANICAL ORIGIN **West Indies**

COUNTRIES/REGIONS OF CULTIVATION **Jamaica, Caribbean, tropical South America**

SEASON OF HARVEST **Year-round**

PARTS USED **Berries, Leaves (rarely)**

COLOR **Deep brown**

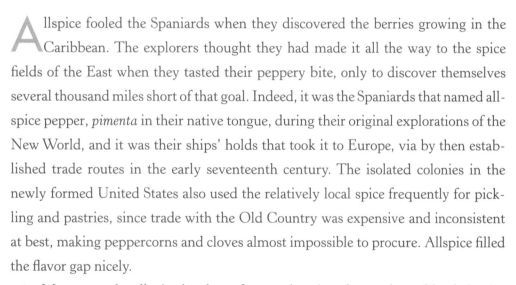

Allspice fooled the Spaniards when they discovered the berries growing in the Caribbean. The explorers thought they had made it all the way to the spice fields of the East when they tasted their peppery bite, only to discover themselves several thousand miles short of that goal. Indeed, it was the Spaniards that named allspice pepper, *pimenta* in their native tongue, during their original explorations of the New World, and it was their ships' holds that took it to Europe, via by then established trade routes in the early seventeenth century. The isolated colonies in the newly formed United States also used the relatively local spice frequently for pickling and pastries, since trade with the Old Country was expensive and inconsistent at best, making peppercorns and cloves almost impossible to procure. Allspice filled the flavor gap nicely.

More recently, allspice has been frequently misunderstood as a blended spice mixture. The fruit of a native Caribbean evergreen, the berries are round, moderately wrinkled, and slightly larger than peppercorns. Dried, they have a deep brown character and remind the palate of cloves in taste, although not quite as intense, and they wake the taste buds with a heat and sharpness of flavor. Despite efforts to cultivate it elsewhere, production plantings of allspice have remained primarily in the Caribbean and Central America.

The tall evergreen trees can produce for several decades after an initial infancy of seven years, with male and female specimens being interplanted. The berries in the wild will mature to a darker blue color if left on the tree, but they lose their potency in the process, so most are harvested unripe and sun-dried to the familiar brown tone until the seeds rattle quietly inside. Growing in clusters on the tree after a flowering of tiny white blossoms, the berries are gathered by hand, and the perfume of the harvest season permeates the air with an intoxicating aroma akin to sweet anise, pepper, and baking pumpkin pies of the American holiday season. Large black drying blocks the size of small houses are set among the hillsides to take full advantage of the local sun to concentrate the flavors. A particularly old farmer told me once that the sun was Jamaica's most important energy source, "as it dries the berries and bakes the tourists."

The best-quality allspice certainly comes from the island countries of the Caribbean, with Jamaica being the leader and the spice a source of national pride there: local officials would convince you that the manufacture and regulation of farming practices comprise the most important platform of any government agenda. Everything from moisture content standards to penalties for theft of harvesting tools is laid out in detail. Berries from mainland productions from Mexico through Central America are also found on the world market, but they are considered of generally lower quality—and the offerings are sometimes even diluted with the berries of a similar myrtle species. Confirm your source as Caribbean, and look for solidly brown berries with no dusty residue or significant number of broken specimens. They become more brittle as they dry beyond useful life and thus will have lower concentrations of the desirable oils.

Mulling, a common technique of infusing spices into wine or cider, calls upon allspice in harmony with other potent flavors like cardamom or citrus peel to enhance warming drinks on cold winter days. Gentle heating of the lightly crushed spices for twenty minutes will impart the spice character without overwhelming the beverage beyond drinkability.

One of the more uncommon concoctions made with allspice is the old Mayan preparation of cacao bean, the source of our modern chocolate, where it was blended with myriad other ingredients including annatto, canela, and even chile. But allspice can impart its own brand of warming heat to your own favorite mug of cocoa. Remembering that cloves weren't readily available in the New World, you'll see allspice called for in many similar applications as it developed along flavor lines parallel to those that made cloves so popular.

More commonly in the Caribbean, you see the peppery heat of allspice in curries and marinades. Its crossover of heat and sweet is famous in jerk rubs for meats slow-roasted over open fires, served with the starchy vegetables popular to the area like plantain and sweet potato. The spice is sometimes called West Indies bay, and the fresh, waxy leaves of the tree are used to perfume fish and meats, but dried versions lose their fragrance—so the practice is limited to local plantations and restaurants. More famously, classic "bay rum" aftershave uses the leaves as an aroma base that is reminiscent of a stroll through the mature allspice groves.

Perhaps because of the plant's reluctance to propagate in the Old World, there you find the spice emerging first in the cuisines that had reasonable access to the West Indies. Coastal Africa traders and British Empire conquerors brought the berries back home, and they stayed local to those areas without spreading much farther across the globe. Even today, distribution, from both a cultivation and a culinary perspective, is limited mainly to the Western Hemisphere. Elsewhere allspice is frequently overshadowed by cloves and peppercorns. Those cuisines outside its native lands that have embraced the potency make the best use of it in pickles, pastries, and condiments where stronger flavors are important: logical if you consider that the reality of global logistics dictates that potency has better shelf life than the more delicate perfume of the local crop. Two unexpected users of allspice are the pickled herring and ketchup industries! Not two flavors I'd care to try together, but you can certainly taste the allspice signature in each.

Yucatán Chicken Rojo

Rojo simply means "red" in Spanish. Rubs from the Yucatán peninsula take their ruddy color from the South American native annatto, a seed with a strong red pigment that happens to have a wonderful flavor in the bargain. In this recipe, I stew the chicken with the spices to gain the full benefit, rather than simply rubbing them on and grilling, also a valid technique. **SERVES 4**

CHICKEN

One 4½-pound chicken, cut into serving pieces, rinsed, and patted dry

2 tablespoons corn oil

¼ cup freshly ground Yucatán Rojo Rub (page 360)

1 green bell pepper, coarsely chopped

1 onion, coarsely chopped

1 carrot, sliced

1 celery stalk, coarsely chopped

2 tablespoons olive oil

1 cup dry red wine

2 tablespoons smoked Spanish paprika (*pimentón*)

RICE

2 cups chicken stock

15 saffron threads

¼ cup finely diced pimientos

10 allspice berries, finely ground

Coarse sea salt

2 cups long-grain white rice

Preheat the oven to 350°F. Toss the chicken pieces with the corn oil to coat. Dust with the rojo rub, rubbing it in well.

In a large skillet, cook the vegetables briefly in olive oil over high heat, stirring, just until slightly softened, about 3 minutes. Using a slotted spoon, transfer the vegetables to a Dutch oven or similar heavy ovenproof pot. Brown the chicken pieces briefly in the oil remaining and transfer to the Dutch oven. Pour the wine into the pan and bring to a boil, scraping up the browned bits, and add to Dutch oven.

Add enough water to cover the chicken, tightly cover the pot, and bake for 1½ hours or until the chicken is very tender and almost falling from the bone.

Meanwhile, make the rice: combine the broth, 2 cups of water, the saffron, pimientos, allspice, and salt in a medium saucepan and bring to a simmer. Stir in the rice, cover, reduce the heat to very low, and cook until the rice is tender and almost all the liquid is absorbed, 18 to 20 minutes. Let stand for 5 minutes, then fluff the rice with a fork. Cover, and keep warm.

Transfer the chicken pieces to a serving platter. Add the smoked paprika to the sauce and puree with an immersion blender in the pot until smooth, or in a regular blender or food processor. Serve the chicken with the rice, passing the sauce on the side.

AMCHOOR

ALTERNATE NAMES **Amchur, Mango powder**

BOTANICAL NAME OF CULINARY SPECIES *Mangifera indica*

PLANT FAMILY **Cashew (*Anacardiaceae*)**

COUNTRY/REGION OF BOTANICAL ORIGIN **Southeast Asia**

MAJOR COUNTRIES/REGIONS OF CULTIVATION **Widely across tropical climates, Middle East**

SEASON OF HARVEST **Year-round**

PARTS USED **Fruits (unripe)**

COLOR **Pale yellow-green**

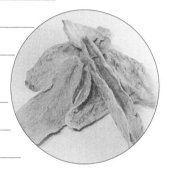

In the Middle East, India, and the tropics, mangoes are plentiful. They easily became the target of cooks seeking a sour character in their cuisine. It seems that someone got the idea to take the unripe fruit, dry it in the sun, and grind it into a powder for cooking purposes. This was the birth of *amchoor*, the tart, greenish yellow powder called for in Indian chutneys and masalas.

The important point here is that the mango is completely unripe. Green in color, it's like an underripe pear in consistency crossed with a new-crop Granny Smith apple in flavor. It's completely unlike the ripe fruit, which may be called for in the same chutney recipes, and only hints at the ripe fruit's sweetness.

Vegetarian cuisine in India uses the powder to add brightness to root vegetables and curries, and the Ayurvedic disciplines call for it as an all-purpose flavor enhancer, much as the West would use salt. It's also used as a meat tenderizer, either by coating the meat directly or marinating it in a paste made of *amchoor* and water overnight. My experiments show that this is appropriate only for stronger-flavored meats like lamb and even then only with the less interesting cuts, as the sour flavors can be intense and overpowering.

For quality, look for deeper yellow tones, not a pale, sandy hue, which indicates stale powder. The latter will offer only the jaw-locking tart without any of the balancing sweetness found in the fresher product. For best results, it's actually very easy to make your own amchoor if green unripe mangoes can be found. Slice and dry it in a low oven or in the sun, and grind the pieces as needed.

Pumpkin and Lentils with Black Masala

So-called black *masalas* take their name not only from the black ingredients but also from the toasting techniques used to make them (see page 12). *Kala Masala* makes use of *amchoor's* tart bite to balance the heavier roasted flavors and works well to unify this recipe. To stand up to such deep flavors, I take pumpkin and similarly roast it with other vegetables, blooming the flavor with a rather sinister charring. **SERVES 6**

1 pound cut-up fresh pumpkin, or butternut squash, peeled and cut into 1-inch pieces

2 tablespoons safflower oil

2 large tomatoes, seeded and diced

3 cups chicken stock

2 *kokum* skins (see page 197), or 20 dried cranberries

3 tablespoons freshly ground *Kala Masala* (page 389)

1 cup black lentils (sometimes called beluga lentils), picked over, soaked in water to cover for 1 hour, and drained

2 teaspoons fine sea salt

1 jalapeño chile, seeded and diced (optional)

Preheat the broiler. Toss the pumpkin with oil and place in a single layer on a baking sheet. Broil 4 inches from the heat, shaking the pan occasionally to prevent sticking, until the edges begin to char, 5 to 8 minutes. Set aside. Spread the tomatoes in a single layer in a baking sheet and broil, stirring occasionally, until the edges begin to char, 3 to 5 minutes.

Bring the chicken stock to a low simmer in a medium saucepan. Add the *kokum* skins and simmer for 15 minutes.

Strain the stock into a small pot. Add the *masala*, roasted vegetables, lentils, salt, and chile, if using. Simmer until the lentils are tender and most of the liquid is absorbed, 30 to 40 minutes.

ANGELICA

ALTERNATE NAMES **Angel's root, Holy Ghost root, Wild celery**

BOTANICAL NAMES OF CULINARY SPECIES *Angelica archangelica* **(garden varieties),** *Angelica atropurpurea* **(North American wild),** *Angelica sylvestris* **(European wild)**

PLANT FAMILY **Parsley (*Umbelliferae*)**

COUNTRY/REGION OF BOTANICAL ORIGIN **Northern Europe**

MAJOR COUNTRIES/REGIONS OF CULTIVATION **Northern Europe, North America, Russia**

SEASONS OF HARVEST **Spring and summer**

PARTS USED **Stalks, Leaves, Roots, Seeds (rarely)**

COLORS **Green (leaves), Greenish-red (stalks), Light brown (roots and seeds)**

When I first smelled a jar of angelica root in a medicinal herbalist's shop, the aromas of fennel and sage came to me so clearly that I thought I had opened a container of sausage. Fortunately, the shopkeeper had a fine herb garden out back that let me sample all that this plant had to offer.

Quite the showstopper in a garden when it's in flower, the plant can grow to up to seven feet in height and explode with a regular fireworks display of a flower head. A round umbel of tiny purple flowers comes after two years, leaving behind small yellowish seeds before the plant expires. The foliage is a wide green leaf with a serrated edge, and the roots are remarkably shallow for a plant of such great height.

All the parts of the plant are used in a plethora of legendary medicinal uses. Everything from colic to blindness was supposedly cured with a dose of some part or another, and even today, it is touted as a cure-all. For the cooks among us, however, the tall stalks are what should be harvested first. Tubular and ridged like celery stalks, they impart a similar flavor. More delicate than the root of the plant I first smelled, they have sweetness along the lines of anise but still with hints of the characteristic fennel flavor.

I had a call from a pastry chef friend wanting to experiment with the stalks in an ice cream, but what she was after is a common preparation—angelica stalks cut and candied in simple syrup. Frequently dyed an artificial green, candied angelica has a sweetness that is a bit overpowering and seems to obscure the lovely flavors found in the fresh.

Popular with Scandinavians, the fresh stalks are commonly served as a vegetable, simply blanched or steamed and served with butter. As a rare delicacy, the seeds are harvested and ground to flavor simple meat pies made with root vegetables. The meat takes on that sage and fennel aroma found in the roots, but without the accompanying bitterness.

Some wild species of angelica are found in Europe and America and give similar taste profiles. The herbalist friend, in fact, happened to have three species growing side by side and on tasting, the wild versions had a decidedly more bitter flavor and aroma. For the cook, I'd suggest sticking with the garden varieties.

That same herbalist, whom I've dubbed my "angelica queen," was kind enough to sit me down to a cup of tea made with roots she had dried in years past and served some savory scones made with angelica leaves, dried cranberries, and cloves. For dinner, we had fish poached with the leaves and allspice, a recipe from her Icelandic grandmother—no doubt the woman who had taught her all about this wonderfully heady and spectacularly beautiful plant. Since angelica is rarely sold fresh, I'll try to talk her into sharing some seeds with me next planting season.

ANISE, BROWN

ALTERNATE NAMES **Aniseed, White anise**

BOTANICAL NAME OF CULINARY SPECIES *Pimpinella anisum*

PLANT FAMILY **Parsley (*Umbelliferae*)**

COUNTRY/REGION OF BOTANICAL ORIGIN **Persia**

MAJOR COUNTRIES/REGIONS OF CULTIVATION **Turkey, Spain, Egypt, Mediterranean, Central America**

SEASONS **Late summer**

PARTS USED **Seeds, Leaves (rarely)**

COLOR **Light brown**

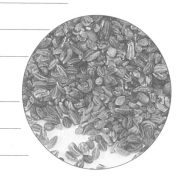

Perhaps anise is familiar to you only by way of the poor aging biscotti that live in plastic cages at coffee shops. They beg to be released by some unsuspecting bleary-eyed latte drinker in a moment of early morning sleep deprivation. If that is indeed your only knowledge of anise, it really is time for you to wake up.

The seeds themselves are tiny, about half the size of cumin or caraway but of the same familiar ridged shape seen in many related plants. They should be a brownish yellow hue and not have a dusty aroma or appearance. A recently opened jar of anise will first tantalize with licorice scent and then quickly move to surprising sweetness in the nose. A quick sample shouldn't have too much bitterness—the last flavor to remain in an older batch. Like ajwain, the seeds frequently have bits of stem left on that look like little tails. I prefer a more cleaned version, because those hairlike filaments can be a detraction if the seeds are used whole, as in many baking recipes. Pay the slightly higher price for the "fancy" grades that have been cleaned of this chaff.

Sweet applications of anise range all the way back to the Roman Empire, when rations of hardtack for the soldiers was heavily spiced with anise and fennel. The Romans so loved the sweet fennel-meets-licorice tastes that they even used anise seed as payment of taxes in the plant's native growing regions of the Eastern

Mediterranean, Turkey, and the Middle East. Perhaps it was more than just the taste, though; the Romans believed the seeds to be mild digestive aids—with all the lavish feasts they were holding in those days, a bit of assistance was probably welcomed with open togas.

Later, in European circles, the monks of the Pyrenees began to produce anise-flavored liquors similar to anisette and sambuca, potent distillations that take the normally mild licorice flavor to almost unbearable intensity. The French quickly found a taste for them, not just as aperitifs, but also in the classic stews and stocks of the region. Perhaps the most popular of these liquors today are ouzo, the Greek combination of anise and barley, and pastis, the French interpretation, both potent intoxicants classically mixed with a small amount of water. Ouzo takes on the flavors of the sea during a stage that soaks the anise and barley in the ocean for a few hours, but the spice is still dominant, making the liquor a valuable tool in the kitchen for everything from sauces to marinades.

In India, seeds of the *jeera* family, which includes anise, fennel, and cumin, are sugar-coated and served at the end of meals as both digestive aids and breath fresheners. After a properly spice-heated *vindaloo*, the seeds can take on an almost wintergreen character, which soothes the taste buds.

In Italy, you'll discover that anise's sweet connotations are married with tomato in classic marinara sauces. The combination of anise, garlic, and peppercorn seems to be the spice balance within most of these creations, imparting sweet, savory, and heat respectively in a delicate balancing act. Some cooks will toast the seeds while infusing garlic into olive oil as a start, while others simply grind them and add to the simmering pot, knowing that hours on the stove will draw out all the flavor of the seeds.

I had a customer come into my store one afternoon and hurl a flat, crackerlike disk in my direction. "Can you help me make this taste like something?" he bellowed. A quick interrogation told me that I was holding a *pizzelle*, the hard Italian cookie made on a special waffle iron, this one flavored almost exclusively with anise seed. It turned out the guy had learned to make them back in Philadelphia and had started a small bakery producing these treats exclusively "to get some decent flavor with my coffee. Anything's better than those dead biscotti they sell." I solved his problem with a fresher source of anise, which gave him the sweet flavor he was looking for.

No discussion of anise would be complete without a nod to proper biscotti. Italians have populated the pastry shelves of their coffee counters with the hardened cookie-meets-biscuit treats for ages. Theirs are a far cry from the mass-produced versions seen as just a profitable sideline in the American coffee industry. Perhaps it's an homage of sorts back to the Roman era, but since then, the Italian versions have matured into complex sweets flavored with everything from lemon to chocolate but always with a base of anise in the mix. I think that the deep roast of Italian coffee needs the lift from the sweet seeds, and perhaps the coffee roasters of America could take a cue from the Italians here. Lose the stale, uninteresting stuff sold ubiquitously in the States and make a fresh batch thick with the heady licorice perfume of anise.

ANISE, BLACK

ALTERNATE NAME	*Anice nero* (Italian)
BOTANICAL NAME OF CULINARY SPECIES	*Pimpinella anisum, spp. Nero*
PLANT FAMILY	Parsley (*Umbelliferae*)
COUNTRY/REGION OF BOTANICAL ORIGIN	Italy
MAJOR COUNTRIES/REGIONS OF CULTIVATION	Italy
SEASON OF HARVEST	Late summer
PARTS USED	Seeds
COLOR	Jet black

Imagine a charming elderly Italian grandmother coming into your store and depositing a tiny bag on your counter holding roughly twenty seeds within. Then imagine this same sweet character telling you in no uncertain terms that this is the only *real* anise and that you had better find some fast if you want to be taken seriously. Oh, the life of a spice merchant.

This was exactly how my quest for the elusive black anise started some years ago. I had heard of the species but never actually seen any. My new Italian "teacher" explained to me that it came from the southern parts of the "Old Country" and was the only way one could make biscotti traditionally. Inquiries to Sicily and the Amalfi Coast proved unsuccessful, until I got a visit from an Italian farmer friend late one summer. This farmer-turned-merchant had only a few ounces and told me, "*Nessuno più*": no more from his annual crop. Further investigations revealed to me that it is strictly a micro-crop and each family produces just a bit, mostly for their own consumption.

The grandmother was correct in her estimation of flavor, however, with the jet-black species being noticeably sweeter and less bitter than the more commonplace brown varieties. Even in Italy it's held for special occasions, reserved for holiday pastries and only the highest-quality sauce.

ANNATTO

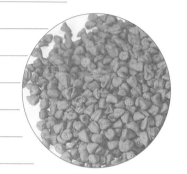

ALTERNATE NAMES Achiote, Lipstick tree (cosmetic uses), *Urucum* (Brazil)

BOTANICAL NAME OF CULINARY SPECIES *Bixa orellana*

PLANT FAMILY Annatto (*Bixaceae*)

COUNTRY/REGION OF BOTANICAL ORIGIN South America

MAJOR COUNTRIES/REGIONS OF CULTIVATION Brazil, Philippines

SEASON OF HARVEST Year-round

PARTS USED Seeds

COLOR Bright brick red

Annatto is one of those spices that everyone has consumed but almost no one knows by name. If you're a fan of South and Central American cuisine, it will pay for you to introduce yourself the next chance you get.

The tiny red seeds look something akin to miniature lava rocks and have a unique flavor profile often described as earthen and sharp. Perhaps where most have consumed them, however, is as a coloring agent in commercially prepared foods like "brick" Cheddar cheese. The seeds impart such a significant yellow-orange color that foods made with annatto are often wrongly assumed to contain saffron or turmeric. A friend from Norway once asked me, "Why is your butter so yellow?" It seemed an odd question until I realized that annatto, and the color it gives foods in its native Western hemisphere, is much less common elsewhere.

The shrublike plant holds yet another oddity in its appearance. It produces heart-shaped pods, in groups of ten to fifteen, roughly the size of baseballs and covered in spiked quills. Inside the pod is a webbing of material that holds the seeds. When I first saw the plant, it looked as if nature was telling me to stay away, but, thankfully, the local South American guides knew it was safe to approach. In fact, its origins in South American and Mexican cooking can be traced back to early Mayan and Aztec civilizations, when, it is believed, it started out as a ceremonial pigment and only later made the transition to culinary use in everything from stews to chocolate drinks.

While the seeds can be ground directly, it's just as common to cook them in oil and use this infusion with the gritty seeds strained out. Add 1 cup of seeds to 4 cups of mild oil; canola and peanut both work well. Gently heat the oil and seeds, stirring constantly, for up to 10 minutes. Allow to cool, then strain the mix and store as you would any oil. The yellow liquid is easily added to rice dishes and the like, used to start stocks and sauce bases, or simply drizzled as a condiment at the table.

If you do use the whole seeds, take care to grind them completely to a fine powder, or you'll add an unpleasant gritty texture to your dishes. Sometimes, in fact, this can be accomplished only with commercial processes, but a fine sifting usually serves the purpose well. Home grinding preserves more of the delicate aroma, making it well worth the effort, but some applications require the flour consistency, which can be attained only by industrial equipment.

Achiote paste is a common preparation of annatto seeds, easily found in Latin American markets and some supermarkets. It is simply a paste made of the ground seeds mixed with oil, though some more elaborate versions add garlic, chiles, and/or salt. All are typically strained to be smooth, so there's no texture problem as there sometimes can be with the freshly ground seeds. Mixing them with oil to a paste consistency also allows some better development of flavor, but it does shorten the shelf life of the already mild flavor. Always check pastes for a brilliant red color and a dry, savory aroma, something like bay and juniper blended together.

Throughout annatto's habitat, it seems that meat—pork, chicken, and even fish—all have become local favorites when colored and flavored with the seeds. Latin American meat stews from Peru, Venezuela, and Guatemala all use annatto liberally, as do Southeast Asian and Pacific Island dishes along the same themes. The doses used here provide much more than simple coloring and truly impart earthy flavors that read well on the palate with acids like tomato, vinegar, and citrus. A curious use of the seeds' coloring ability is to add a small handful of whole seeds to a pot of eggs when hard-boiling them. As the eggs jiggle up and down in the pan with the seeds resting at the bottom, they gain a speckled appearance that can make for bewildered looks at the breakfast table.

One special dish that features annatto's flavor is an oiled snapper preparation given to me by a hotel chef on the Baja peninsula (see the recipe below). Local farmers had brought him seedpods, and he mistakenly sautéed them as a vegetable. Realizing his mistake, his indigenous staff helped the newcomer by rescuing the flavored oil from the pan, straining the whole lot, and tossing in fillets of the fresh catch of the day. It's ridiculously easy, but the uniqueness of the spice adds an unmistakable color and what I'd describe as a mild buzz on the taste buds. Even the completely uninitiated can't make a mistake with this preparation.

Annatto-oiled Snapper

Annatto has a unique "electric" quality that can brighten any number of dishes. Here it's both dusted on the fish and infused into the oil, which not only tastes great but colors the fish a brilliant yellow red. Take care to arrange the plates as described below, and you're bound to get rave reviews at the table. **SERVES 4**

Four 6-ounce skinless snapper fillets, 1½ inches thick

Juice of 2 limes

1 cup julienned celery root (celeriac)

1 cup julienned carrots

2 garlic cloves, minced

Coarse sea salt

Freshly ground black pepper

2 teaspoons ground annatto

1½ cups dry white wine

2 tablespoons Annatto Oil (recipe follows)

Place the fillets in a shallow baking dish, and pour the lime juice over them. Cover and refrigerate, turning occasionally, for at least 30 minutes but no more than 2 hours.

Preheat the oven to 350°F. Remove the fillets from the baking dish and toss the celery roots, carrots, and garlic with the lime juice in the dish. Dust the fillets with salt and pepper on both sides and place on top of the vegetables. Dust the top of the fillets with the powdered annatto and pour the wine around the fish.

Bake for 12 minutes, or until the fish is just opaque throughout. Remove and allow to stand for 10 minutes.

Heat a large skillet over medium-high heat until hot. Add the annatto oil, and immediately place the fillets in the pan to sear on one side only, at most 2 minutes. Transfer the fillets to a cutting board and cut them in half. Arrange on warmed plates, half seared side down, and the other half seared side up. Drizzle any oil from the pan over the fillets, and arrange the vegetables around them.

NOTE: The juices from the baking dish can be enriched with an herb butter and reduced for a simple sauce, if desired.

Annatto Oil

MAKES 2 CUPS

¼ cup annatto seeds
2 cups canola oil

Combine the seeds and oil in a heavy saucepan, and heat over medium heat until the oil is warm. Reduce the heat to low and let infuse for 2 minutes longer. Remove from the heat and let stand for at least 30 minutes. Strain the oil. It will keep for up to 2 weeks, covered and refrigerated.

ARROWROOT

ALTERNATE NAME **Arrowroot flour**

BOTANICAL NAME OF CULINARY SPECIES *Maranta arundinacea*

PLANT FAMILY *Marantaceae*

COUNTRY/REGION OF BOTANICAL ORIGIN **West Indies**

MAJOR COUNTRIES/REGIONS OF CULTIVATION **West Indies, Central America**

SEASON OF HARVEST **Year-round**

PARTS USED **Root starch**

COLOR **Pure white**

This thickening agent isn't normally considered part of the spice category, but it's integral to so many Southeast Asian mixes and New World blends that your pantry should include some for your culinary experiments. Traded to the East by traditional Atlantic spice routes, arrowroot deserves membership in the spice rack.

Six-foot-tall stalks announce the rhizomes underground that will be harvested young, pounded into a pulp, and washed repeatedly to extract the starch. Arrowroot was first derived from West Indies native tropical roots by the indigenous Arawak peoples. Poison arrows were apparently a problem in the day, and the starchy pulp was said to extract the toxin from unlucky victims—hence the name.

While the snow-white powder is almost flavorless, it does have some advantages over other thickeners like flour or cornstarch. It's a clear thickener that can do its work at comparatively lower temperatures. What really makes arrowroot unique, however, is the glistening, silky texture it can add to sauces, normally obtained only with copious amounts of butter. The biggest drawback is that its holding power as a thickener isn't the best. Overcooking will break down the amylopectins that cause the thickening in the first place and once that happens, there's no reviving it. Because of its persnickety behavior, arrowroot is usually reserved for use in sauces that must remain clear, such as dessert fruit sauces.

One day, I found myself next to one of arrowroot's biggest fans, the esteemed Graham Kerr, simmering some stock with a touch of saffron added for taste and color. Since this was destined to become a light sauce for vegetables, arrowroot was the right choice. My Scottish friend told me he didn't like the "slimy feel you get with arrowroot and milk." It's true that with dairy products, the texture that so well simulates butter elsewhere turns into a liability. In the right recipe, namely one that has little cooking time or needs fast thickening at the end, arrowroot is your biggest asset.

Today, the island of St. Vincent in the West Indies is the largest producer of arrowroot, but because there are numerous imitators, it may be hard to find out exactly which starch you have your hands on in the bulk foods section of your market. True arrowroot has several competitors from Asia and South America, including zedoary, *sago*, and *cassava*, which behave similarly. Properties of these are fairly comparable, and although some can impart different flavors, none are so strong as to cause a problem. The real question is whether the imitators have the same texture and thickening effect; some will leave a more gritty mouthfeel or require a considerably larger amount to achieve the same thickness compared with genuine arrowroot.

ASAFETIDA

ALTERNATE NAMES Asafoetida, Hing powder, Devil's dung

BOTANICAL NAME OF CULINARY SPECIES *Ferula asafoetida*

PLANT FAMILY Parsley *(Umbelliferae)*

COUNTRY/REGION OF BOTANICAL ORIGIN Persia

MAJOR COUNTRIES/REGIONS OF CULTIVATION India, Pakistan, Egypt

SEASON OF HARVEST Fall

PARTS USED Resin

COLORS Light putty to dark amber

There are plenty of things in the spice world you don't want your nose to meet in a dark alley. With a smell that's something like a cross between rotten eggs and old socks, asafetida is most certainly on top of that list.

When a broad-headed plant like the giant fennel *Ferula* is left to its own devices, it will produce quite a lot of sap internally as it pumps water and nutrients out of the soil in an attempt to increase seed production. In the case of this plant in its native Iran, the sap is harvested and allowed to dry into the hard resinous clumps known as asafetida. Ranging from light to dark brown, it has the consistency of putty when fresh but can dry to a very hard form while still holding its potency of flavor.

This same substance can be found as a dry powder (usually mixed with starch or flour as a carrier agent), and it is perhaps one of the stinkiest spices used in the world today. In fact, its name derives from the Latin *foetida*, which translates as "foul smelling." A similarly appropriate name, Devil's dung, is self-explanatory. One whiff will convince those skeptical of the aromatic reputation.

There's a good explanation for the aforementioned smell most people find noxious. Asafetida contains sulfurous compounds that give rise to the aroma. The secret of the spice's culinary use, however, is that those same compounds evaporate under only a modest amount of heat, leaving behind a wonderfully complex garlic-and-onion flavor. It's this flavor that enhances vegetarian and Ayurvedic cuisine all over the Indian subcontinent, and the distinctive smell is the key to many authentic Indian vegetable dishes.

Beans and lentils take on a new depth of taste when cooked with asafetida, as do fresh mustard greens sautéed in ghee with some of the powder. Cauliflower flash-cooked in little more than peanut oil seasoned with asafetida and turmeric makes a fabulous filling for a pita, served with a bit of chilled tomato and cucumber.

I also borrow a technique normally used for truffles to flavor foodstuffs with the aromatic asafetida, storing lumps of the resin along with other ingredients in airtight containers for several days to impart the flavor. This works well with rice, dal, nuts, and even eggs (in the shell). The frugal cook in India can use the same batch of asafetida for quite some time, continually reaping the taste rewards.

Cauliflower and Asafetida Pitas

Although the aroma of asafetida is unpleasant at best when uncooked, a quick trip through the wok vaporizes the bad smell and unleashes its characteristic rich garlic-and-onion-like flavor. The cauliflower can be eaten as a side dish or, as here, rolled into pitas and dressed, for the perfect picnic food. **SERVES 6**

1 medium head cauliflower, cored and separated into small florets	1 teaspoon fine sea salt
1 teaspoon ground turmeric	6 pita breads
15 saffron threads	Approximately 1 cup Baba Ganoush (page 86)
1 cup chicken or vegetable stock	1 cup chopped tomatoes
2 tablespoons olive oil	1 cup diced unpeeled cucumber
2 teaspoons ground asafetida	½ cup plain yogurt
2 tablespoons finely chopped fresh cilantro	

Steam the cauliflower over boiling water until barely fork-tender, 12 to 14 minutes. Remove and allow to cool completely.

Meanwhile, in a small bowl, stir the turmeric and saffron into the stock, and allow to sit for 15 minutes.

Heat a wok over high heat. Add the oil, then the cauliflower and asafetida, and cook, stirring constantly, for 3 minutes. Add the chicken stock mixture, cover, reduce the heat to medium, and simmer for 10 minutes, or until the cauliflower is very soft. Remove the cover and cook, stirring and mashing the cauliflower slightly, until the sauce reduces and the cauliflower breaks up into a coarse puree, 5 to 8 minutes. Remove from the heat, toss with the cilantro, and season with the salt.

Spread each pita with a heaping tablespoon of baba ganoush, and top with the cauliflower. Garnish with the tomatoes, cucumber, and yogurt, and roll up the pitas to enclose all. For travel, wrap each sandwich in a square of wax paper or parchment paper, twisting the ends to seal. (The assembled sandwiches can be refrigerated for up to 4 hours.)

AVOCADO LEAF

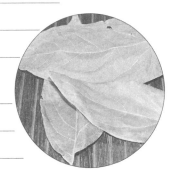

ALTERNATE NAME *Hoja del aguacate* (Spanish)

BOTANICAL NAME OF CULINARY SPECIES *Persea americana*

PLANT FAMILY Laurel *(Lauraceae)*

COUNTRY/REGION OF BOTANICAL ORIGIN Southern Mexico

MAJOR COUNTRIES/REGIONS OF CULTIVATION Southern Mexico, Central America

SEASON OF HARVEST Year-round

PARTS USED Leaves

COLOR Pale green

This dried leaf gave me some trouble when I first started experimenting, because I had missed a key trick: toasting. Without that, you'll get something that tastes like a musty attic, but with proper prep, you'll have a subtle flavor that hints at fennel and gives your Latin cuisine that authentic twist so often missed in translation.

I was clued into my mistake by a chef who explained that a toasting stage prior to use changes the flavor and vaporizes the taste you'd normally associate with fall lawn care. A dry pan or low oven will work fine for this light toasting, just long enough so the aroma begins to suggest a hint of licorice.

Avocado's very large paper-thin leaves are typically twice the size of your hand. They are as light in weight-to-volume as bay leaf, but colored a darker mottled olive green. The stems are fairly hard, but that's not a bother, since, after toasting, they're ground down to a fine powder before use.

On rare occasions, you can find the leaves fresh and use them as is, but the flavor is so mild that I actually prefer the dried versions, which seem to be concentrated in flavor. If you have the fresh leaves at hand, wrap fish or pork with them and grill quickly. Latin versions of seasoned rice can also be used to stuff the fresh leaves, which are rolled and baked to completion.

The flavor of avocado leaf is a combination of fennel and anise but much more subtle than either. Toasting brings out this character, thus giving Latin American foods a bit of delicacy in an otherwise bold, chile-laden cuisine. Anything with *queso fresco* or another mild, soft cheese will benefit from blending in ground toasted avocado leaf. Even cold dips and salsas can use its flavor, if allowed to sit and infuse for a time.

For me, the most common experience of avocado leaf has been mixed with *cojita* (a fresh white Mexican cheese) and chile powder as a stuffing for classic chiles *rellenos* from southern Mexico. Proportions for the mix are strictly the cook's choice, but once it is piped into whole fresh chiles, breaded or battered, and deep-fried, you'll have the genuine article ready as an appetizer, side, or even entrée. Accent the dish with a rich sauce like *mole*, which, conveniently, will use toasted avocado leaf for its seasoning as well.

Chiles Rellenos with Avocado Leaf

A real stuffed chile in Mexico isn't a hot affair. The large, fleshy poblano chiles are closer in heat to a mild bell pepper than a fiery pequín, and the seasoning is similarly delicate, perhaps best exemplified by the light fennel perfume of the toasted avocado leaf. Chiles rellenos can be baked or deep-fried, and they make a nice start to a meal. This recipe could easily be modified with the addition of some ground meat and served with a *mole* or chile sauce. **SERVES 4**

A handful of dried avocado leaves (approximately 25 large leaves)

2 cups soft *cojita* (Mexican fresh cheese) or ricotta cheese

1 teaspoon finely ground cumin seeds

1½ teaspoons fine sea salt

1 teaspoon freshly ground black pepper

2 cups plain bread crumbs

3 tablespoons dried Mexican oregano, crushed

1 teaspoon red chile flakes (optional)

4 poblano chiles

2 tablespoons corn oil

1 lime, quartered

Preheat the oven to 250°F. Spread the avocado leaves on a baking sheet, and toast in the oven until very crisp and fragrant, 10 to 15 minutes. Remove and grind into a fine powder (you will have about 1 tablespoon).

In a medium bowl, mix the cheese with the avocado leaf, cumin, 1 teaspoon of the salt, and pepper; cover, and refrigerate the filling for at least 1 hour, or as long as overnight.

Preheat the oven to 400°F. Mix the bread crumbs, oregano, chile flakes, and remaining ½ teaspoon salt. Carefully cut out the stems and cores of the poblanos, keeping the opening as small as possible. Shake out any seeds, and clean the interiors of webbing and white ribs.

Using a pastry bag, pipe one-quarter of the cheese filling into each chile. Rub the chiles with the oil, roll in the seasoned bread crumbs, and place in a greased baking dish. Bake for 30 minutes, or until the chile flesh is easily pierced and the filling is fully melted and hot. Serve with a squeeze of lime juice over each chile.

BARBERRY

ALTERNATE NAMES **Thornberries,** *Zereshk* **(Iran)**

BOTANICAL NAME OF CULINARY SPECIES *Berberis vulgaris*

PLANT FAMILY *Berberidaceae*

COUNTRY/REGION OF BOTANICAL ORIGIN **Central Asia**

MAJOR COUNTRIES/REGIONS OF CULTIVATION **Persia, Europe, North America**

SEASON OF HARVEST **Late summer to early fall**

PARTS USED **Fruits**

COLOR **Red-orange**

I first found these berries far from their Middle Eastern origins, in, of all places, Canada. It was at the home of a textile merchant who had brought them back from his native Iran as one of the "hard to find" spices he missed from his childhood.

The inch-long oblong red fruits grow in dense clusters on spiked branches and look quite like currants. They have a sweet, tart character that is intensified during sun-drying to almost jaw-locking intensity. The berries are used whole or ground in Middle Eastern spice blends like *ras el hanout* and Chinese mixes for soup stocks. They lend a piquant, sour zing much like dried cranberries, and they can even be eaten as a snack. Look for berries that are still pliable and brilliant red in color, not darkened to a brown brick color. That comes with age, and while the berries may remain tart, they will lack some of their original complexity.

In Iran, barberries are pounded with other spices to make a semi-dry rub for lamb and game meats destined for the grill. A simple version uses only salt and cumin in addition to the berries, but more elaborate recipes can have up to twenty ingredients, relying on the tartness of the berries almost exclusively for the sour quarter of the sweet-bitter-salty-sour balance. Their potency can stand up to the most complex of blends easily.

Barberries can also be made into a refreshing jelly and in the same vein were included in older mincemeat recipes. The early settlers in America, taking a cue from Northern European cultures, frequently brewed the berries into fruit wine that was sweetened heavily to balance the tart taste.

Some important horticultural notes are in order. Barberry shrubs can play host to particularly virulent stem rust that threatens grain crops. (The berries themselves do not pose a risk to crops, but rather the bushes they may spawn.) Extensive campaigns were waged in the early twentieth century to eradicate the bushes that had spread across Middle America, originally brought to the States by early European settlers. As the supply dwindled, of course, the berries became much more of an exotic import crop. Therefore, you may still only find them imported from the Middle East or Europe.

Be aware that several species of *Berberis* are grown for landscaping. They produce similar berries, but some of these species are poisonous and care should be taken to properly identify your shrubbery before you run out from the kitchen in a harvesting frenzy.

Chinese Mountain Duck Soup

Deceptively simple, amazingly good. I was able to convince the kind cooks at the White Swan restaurant on the road from Xiamen to Dehua, little more than a roadside stand, to share the secrets of this most sublime soup. The chefs were warm, genuine, and excited to share with a spice traveler from the West. I sat and watched a nameless stream roll by the back window as the soup cooked, the glorious smells building every minute. After twenty-seven hours en route from the States, it was the first meal I had, and I couldn't have asked for a better welcome to China. **SERVES 4 TO 6**

2 tablespoons canola oil

One 4½- to 5-pound fresh duck, cut into serving pieces

3 tablespoons Chinese Stock Spices (page 399), in a linen steeping bag or tied in a square of cheesecloth

1 cup whole dried Chinese mushrooms, rinsed

2 cups coarsely chopped Chinese cabbage (bok choy or Napa)

½ cup chopped scallions

Soy sauce

Heat the oil in a Dutch oven or other large flameproof casserole over medium-high heat. Add the duck pieces and cook, turning occasionally, until they are browned and beginning to render thin fat, 8 to 10 minutes. Add the spice bag and 8 cups water. Bring to a boil, reduce the heat to low, and simmer, partially covered, until the duck is very tender, about 2 hours. Add water as necessary to keep the duck covered. Add the dried mushrooms and cabbage and simmer until the mushrooms are tender, 10 to 20 minutes. Remove the bag of spices.

Using tongs, transfer the duck to serving bowls. Ladle the soup into the bowls, garnish with the scallions, and add a splash of soy sauce to each serving.

BASIL

ALTERNATE NAMES **Sweet basil, _Tulsi_ (holy basil)**

BOTANICAL NAMES OF CULINARY SPECIES **_Ocimum basilicum, Ocimum sanctum_ (holy basil), numerous hybrids**

PLANT FAMILY **Mint (_Lamiaceae_)**

COUNTRY/REGION OF BOTANICAL ORIGIN **India**

MAJOR COUNTRIES/REGIONS OF CULTIVATION **Egypt, Turkey, America, widely**

SEASONS OF HARVEST **Summer and early fall**

PARTS USED **Leaves**

COLORS **Mottled greens to deep purple**

Some four thousand years ago, basil left its native India and spread far and wide across the Old World. For centuries, its rumored powers have run the gamut from protection to poison, but thankfully, it landed successfully in modern kitchens as an essential herb for our cuisine.

The Italians, like cooks in most Mediterranean cultures, use the leaf both fresh and dry for its slightly bitter, slightly sweet, and seriously aromatic qualities. There are even old Italian tales of women planting basil on the window sill to attract men and men bequeathing basil sprigs to women to keep them faithful. Leave it to the Italians to intermingle food and love. Culinarily speaking, basil combines well with tomatoes in sauces throughout the region and, of course, it is the basis for pestos, mixed with nuts, garlic, and hard cheeses and pounded or blended to a smooth paste.

Much milder than oregano, but with a flavor profile comparable to oregano and sweet mint combined, basil may also have peppery tones included in the mix. I've noticed great variation in flavor, coloring, and leaf size in different cultivating regions, presumably stemming from soil and climatic conditions. The hotter regions of Egypt and Morocco seem to favor the peppery versions, and the cooler climates of Italy and North America tend toward the sweeter.

Basil's popularity as a garden herb has led to numerous hybrids, including lemon, cinnamon, and anise basil, each exhibiting the flavors of its namesake. There's also a vast array of leaf shapes and colors, from mammoth species whose leaves can reach full hand size, to jagged-edged ruffled varieties whose color ranges from maroon to lime green. These hybrids are not typically cultivated commercially to be dried, so look for them as specialty, produce-quality herbs, or take a trip to your local nursery and go into herb farming for yourself. Greenhouse or in-kitchen cultivation is simple and typically successful with only a modest amount of effort.

It's a shame to see such a marvelous flavor as basil languish in the spice rack until all its potency is lost. Its ubiquitous availability has been its undoing in that regard. Thankfully, a new generation of gardeners has brought basil back to the forefront as a fresh herb, straight from the garden or greenhouse to the kitchen. This isn't to say that dried basil doesn't have a place in the spice rack, but that the cook should be especially sensitive to the freshness factor when selecting it. Brilliance of color and vibrancy of aroma when rubbed or crumbled are the best indicators of a freshly dried crop. Of course, drying your own would be an assurance of quality, but be sure to dry the leaves quickly and evenly to preserve the most flavor. Dried properly, basil can give you a more potent version of the fresh flavor profile, the process typically accenting any underlying peppery notes and bringing an almost menthol taste to the forefront.

Asian cultures have their own species and uses of basil. Fancy purple or opal basil adds herbaceous character to stir-fries and stocks all over Thailand. A chiffonade of fresh leaves can perk up Asian soups, and frequently flowering buds that show particular pungency are used to impart impressively strong herbal character. With the Asian affinity for unusual textures, there is even a coconut-based drink with black basil seeds for a slight peppery kick. The oddity comes when you first taste the seeds that have swollen and become chewy: it looks and feels as if you're drinking

PESTO TECHNIQUES

Pesto is the original seasoning paste of Italy. As far back as the ancient Romans, herbs were pounded together with oil to create a paste. In more modern times, Liguria has become known as the center of the classic pesto universe because the tender, sweet basil that its microclimate produces makes for the most flavorful version of the now-famous seasoning. Many there can tell you the points that make the preparation special. Commissions in the region set out mandates detailing the acceptable ingredient list (a short one, not to be modified) and equipment of choice (mortar and pestle, never a machine).

Classic pesto is simply fresh basil leaves pounded with a bit of salt, a handful of pignoli (pine nuts), some grated hard cheese, and some richly flavored olive oil. Purists would stop there and have great success, but taking this time-honored technique to a wider variety of herbs and added ingredients makes perfect sense for a gardener facing a bumper crop of, say, marjoram or oregano. Almost any herb can be mixed in the same fashion, but remember that the fresh flavor is intensified in the process of macerating the leaves, so avoid those that would become bitter or unpleasantly intense.

To make classic pesto, use these simple ratios, and pound everything in a mortar and pestle to be traditional, or blend in a food processor to be convenient. Use 4 parts (by volume) fresh herbs, 1 part oil, 1 part nuts, ½ part grated hard cheese, and ⅛ part sea salt. Again, for the Italian classic you would fill in the blanks with basil, extra virgin olive oil, pine nuts, Parmesan cheese, and local sea salt. I hope that this kind of open-ended recipe will inspire you to substitute other oils, cheeses, and, of course, herbs, depending on what's seasonally available.

---

mucilaginous tadpole eggs. Not my favorite feeling in a beverage, but it continues to be popular in Southeast Asia.

In its birthplace of India, the wide leaves of *tulsi*, or "holy basil," specifically *Ocimum sanctum*, can still be seen packed with salt in large urns, to be drawn upon as needed for both cuisine and ceremony. In fact, this species is held as sacred and can be seen planted around the temples to Krishna as a great protection and offering to the divine. It is this species that migrated to Indonesia and Malaysia, where it is called for as a particularly pungent, almost chile-hot flavor that shows layers of mint and pepper on top of familiar basil tastes.

I once had a French intern use the phrase *semer le basilic*, "sowing the basil," to describe my ranting and raving about various topics. According to Rodale's *Illus-*

trated Encyclopedia of Herbs, this saying comes from the ancient Greek and Roman conviction that one must scream and curse at basil seeds when planting to ensure a good crop. I'm of the opinion that it's not necessary, but it certainly couldn't hurt the plants. Besides, it's likely to keep the neighbors out of your herb garden for a minimum of a few weeks and to keep them guessing about your mental health come harvest time.

According to the same reference, there are conflicting origins of the word "basil." During the time when basil was feared as poisonous, there was an Italian legend about the Basilisk, a serpent that could kill with one look, which might seem to have given rise to the name. Yet earlier, the Greek word for king was *basileus*, so perhaps that was the origin—further proof that this herb has been, and will continue to be, held in high regard in the kitchens of the world.

BAY LEAF, TURKISH

ALTERNATE NAMES **Bay laurel, Roman laurel, Sweet bay, Poet's laurel**

BOTANICAL NAME OF CULINARY SPECIES *Laurelus nobilis*

PLANT FAMILY **Laurel *(Lauraceae)***

COUNTRY/REGION OF BOTANICAL ORIGIN **Asia**

MAJOR COUNTRIES/REGIONS OF CULTIVATION **Turkey, Egypt, Mediterranean; widely**

SEASON OF HARVEST **Year-round**

PARTS USED **Leaves**

COLOR **Medium green**

The laurel family gives us a savory note and a bittering component essential to both Indian and Anglo cuisines. When a cook reaches for bay, he's laying a foundation of flavor upon which to build a full array of tastes.

The dried leaves of the Turkish bay laurel, *Laurelus nobilis*, are the most commonplace variety in the kitchen. Characterized by a rounder, wider shape than other species, these are sold in many different grades, from "hand select" down to "industrial," based on factors such as appearance, aroma, and oil content. Lower grades are destined for the grinder and commercial food processing. A condensed-soup manufacturer told me that a ten-pound box, roughly three cubic feet of leaves, is dumped into each one-thousand-gallon batch of tomato soup. Unless you have a serious cold, I suggest a smaller pot and better-quality bay.

The best grades will have only a few broken or discolored leaves in each handful, and the overall color will be a consistent olive green, not bleached out or irregular. The most important guide for the cook, however, is the distinctive aroma. If the signature bay scent of mild pine and camphor that has inspired everything from crab boils to aftershave isn't immediately obvious upon opening the tin, you've found old leaves not worthy of your effort; move on to a fresher crop.

The leaves had a good deal of respect in ancient times, seen in the famous laurel crowns bestowed upon emperors and champions of the coliseum alike as a sign of wisdom and triumph. Mythical tales of love, deception, and conquest all seem to feature laurel, and Homer often wove the leaves into his tales.

Fresh leaves regularly show up at my shop during the pruning season, donations from well-meaning customers. My staff once took to weaving crowns of the fresh leaves and reciting poetry in Latin on those days someone bequeathed us a massive bagful (you have to get your humor anywhere you can in the spice trade, I suppose). Because the dry leaves and their concentrated flavors work better in the kitchen, I carefully lay out the fresh leaves in a single layer on a spare screen door and point warm fans in their direction for a few days until the leaves are crisp. If you dry your own, store them quickly once crisp, discarding any that show signs of pests or mildew, usually in the form of black spotting or lacy webbing.

Despite popular belief, the leaf *can* be consumed directly, and removal before serving a soup or sauce prepared with them is strictly for the sake of convenience and aesthetics. While they won't harm you, no one wants to bite down on the relatively thick, leathery leaves, even after they've been simmered into submission.

The Turkish leaves, while not as intensely aromatic as some in the laurel family at the start, tend to time-release their flavor better than others, which makes them the bay of choice for long cooking times: e.g., stocks, soups, and stewed sauces like marinara. It's also perfectly acceptable to grind these leaves into a powder, although that's easier said than done. Since the leaves are so voluminous, traditional blade grinders can be less than effective, as the broken bits tend to fly about the mill, avoiding the whirling blades. One trick is to add a tiny amount of inert material, like dry rice or bread crumbs, to act as a pulverizer. The extra material won't interfere with your recipe, since the amount of ground bay typically used in any given dish is very small: 1 teaspoon of ground bay may equal a dozen whole leaves.

Rarely, the small grape-sized fruits of the bay tree are harvested for culinary use. With much more potent bay character, and typically almost double the oil, these are most commonly processed for commercial applications rather than home cooking.

Liquid seafood-boil concentrates use the overly potent oil, their producers knowing that the mix will be thinned with plenty of water. Since the flavor profile found in the fruit is the same as in the leaf, I'd advise using the latter in all but the most intense preparations of pickles or chutneys.

Bay is one of my favorite examples of the price gouging that takes place in the retail marketplace. Large spice brands may sell a small vial with perhaps a dozen leaves for the price a smart shopper would pay for a sack's worth in bulk. The reason they can get away with this pricing trick is that, compared to other spices, bay leaves dry to a remarkably light weight-to-volume ratio. Just three ounces will fill a quart jar to the brim—and there's no reason it should cost you more than a bowl of soup. Forget the cute glass bottles and seek out bulk merchants for bay. Buy a gallon jar of leaves for ten bucks and use the extra as packing peanuts at holiday time if you simply must get rid of the surplus.

There are too many recipes that use bay laurel to list, but some that simply have to have the very best leaf come to mind. French beef bourguignon, American crab boils, and any chicken stock of respect all must have bay included to be taken seriously. Simmering for at least twenty minutes, preferably longer, will release all the savory character into your stock. Bay is also included in many of the signature herb blends of Europe. *Bouquets garnis* from France need bay for bittering, and Italian tomato sauces take some savory humility from bay laurel. On the Indian subcontinent, the leaves get ground into *garam masala*, and across Turkey, they perfume rice and grain dishes.

BAY LEAF, CALIFORNIAN

ALTERNATE NAME **Californian laurel**

BOTANICAL NAME OF CULINARY SPECIES *Umbellularia californica*

PLANT FAMILY **Laurel (*Lauraceae*)**

COUNTRY/REGION OF BOTANICAL ORIGIN **California**

MAJOR COUNTRIES/REGIONS OF CULTIVATION **Western North America**

SEASONS OF HARVEST **Summer and fall**

PARTS USED **Leaves**

COLOR **Dark olive green**

The Californian bay laurel, *Umbellularia californica*, is not as closely related to genuine bay as the common name might imply. It has a much more elongated leaf shape and a decidedly stronger flavor than other bay species. The color is a deeper green and the long pointed leaves have a serious menthol aroma on top of a more traditional bay scent. Still, the flavor makes an excellent base, with the tastes of thyme and celery at the core.

The problem with these more aromatic leaves is that the character that makes them so impressive in the tin cooks away quickly with even moderate heat, leaving behind an overpowering camphorous, medicinal taste. They are a better choice for dishes and blends that will either cook quickly, say less than twenty minutes, or not at all, as with cold marinades and infusions of oil. The leaves can also be ground into blends that will be added directly to various dishes, but remember each teaspoon of ground spice is equal to roughly twelve bay leaves, so use sparingly. They are probably best reserved, however, for their aromatic properties, i.e., in potpourri.

If you have long gift lists at the holidays, steep light wine vinegar with Californian bay and other herbs like tarragon or rosemary, a few juniper or allspice berries, and perhaps a whole chile or two. Make a ten-gallon batch in July, set it aside in a cool, dark place, and bottle it in December after the flavors have melded together with age. With the rich infusion of bay and spice flavor, a salad dressing becomes a terribly simple affair—and experience shows that people never seem to get tired of presents with six months of forethought in them.

One of the simplest kitchen tricks for showing off the brilliance of this brightly flavored leaf comes via a simple baked potato. Before cooking, make a slice in each raw potato large enough to slip in two or three leaves, then seal tightly in foil and bake as usual. The rapidly dissipating aromatics will quickly infuse the flesh of the potatoes with savory flavor. Only a hint of butter and sea salt will finish this into a side dish worthy of the heftiest of steaks.

The first batch of Californian bay I ever received was in the form of a massive three-foot Christmas wreath made of fresh leaves, with the berries, tufted yellow flowers, and branches intact. Even before the figgy pudding had cooled, I had pulled some off to flavor the Yorkshire pudding and mull some wine for the season. But I was warned not to cook with the decorations again, unless I planned on buying a wreath explicitly for the kitchen. Ever since, I dry my *extra* wreath each December, and it easily keeps me supplied until July.

BAY LEAF, INDIAN

ALTERNATE NAMES **Cinnamon leaf, Tejpat leaf**

BOTANICAL NAMES OF CULINARY SPECIES *Cinnamomum tamala*

PLANT FAMILY **Laurel (*Lauraceae*)**

COUNTRY/REGION OF BOTANICAL ORIGIN **North India**

MAJOR COUNTRIES/REGIONS OF CULTIVATION **North India**

SEASON OF HARVEST **Year-round**

PARTS USED **Leaves**

COLOR **Pale gray-green**

Here's another example of spice-naming confusion at its worst. While this leaf is related to bay laurel botanically, the cook would be better directed toward cinnamon to find it on Western shelves. The intrepid spice shopper should also be warned that very few shops outside India have ever seen these leaves.

Wider and flatter than bay laurel, *Cinnamomum tamala* can be identified by multiple, rather than single, veins running down the length of the leaf. The leaves dry poorly to a gray green color and only weakly mimic the mild cassia-cinnamon aroma found in the fresh version. Best found fresh in the Himalayan foothills of northern India, they add a unique twist to the local sweet masalas and seem to contribute more delicate perfume than any significant flavor.

This species has never been cultivated outside the region in any quantity, and as such, a substitution of bay and cassia-cinnamon is best advised for the chef who wants to re-create the authentic tastes in *kormas* and Kashmir curries. Use in southern Indian dishes will probably be fruitless, as any reasonably potent taste—pepper, cumin, etc.—will overpower the taste of the genuine leaves.

BAY LEAF, INDONESIAN

ALTERNATE NAMES **Asian bay leaf, *Daun salam, Salaam* leaf (Indonesia)**

BOTANICAL NAME OF CULINARY SPECIES ***Eugenia polyantha***

PLANT FAMILY **Myrtle *(Myrtaceae)***

COUNTRY/REGION OF BOTANICAL ORIGIN **Indonesia**

MAJOR COUNTRIES/REGIONS OF CULTIVATION **Indonesian, Malaysia**

SEASON OF HARVEST **Year-round**

PARTS USED **Leaves**

COLOR **Matte green**

Yet another unrelated species that borrows the word "bay" as part of its name, this leaf, known in the local dialect as *daun salam*, permeates cuisines in its native South Pacific island countries liberally but tends to stay local rather than travel to the West. It's a shame because, especially in fresh form, it imparts lovely, savory, floral hints, with a suggestion of anise.

There is little or no correlation to other species of bay in flavor despite recommendations in several Western cookbooks to use those as a substitute. A better suggestion comes from a cooking school in Bali, which recommends a small squeeze of lime juice and a few fresh curry leaves to stimulate the slightly tart, slightly nutty flavor. As a last resort, use the dried leaf.

Indonesian bay leaf is used as widely as its Western counterpart for marinades, sauces, and stews. Also like its Western namesakes, drying seems to concentrate the flavors to a more useful potency, giving a decidedly cedar scent and a moderately tart flavor, making the dried leaf the preferred form almost exclusively. In some cases, recipes call for frying the dry leaves before use to further this concentration.

BLACK LEMON

ALTERNATE NAMES **Dried lime, Black lime,** *Loomi* **(Arabian Peninsula),** *Lumi* **(Arabian Peninsula)**

BOTANICAL NAME OF CULINARY SPECIES *Citrus aurantifolia*

PLANT FAMILY *Citrus (Rutaceae)*

COUNTRY/REGION OF BOTANICAL ORIGIN **Southeast Asia**

MAJOR COUNTRIES/REGIONS OF CULTIVATION **Widely across tropical regions**

SEASON OF HARVEST **Year-round**

PARTS USED **Fruits**

COLORS **Mottled brown to tan**

There is a great tendency in cuisine to improvise with whatever you have available in your local pantry. The cuisines of the Arab peninsula are no exception, and this misnomer of an ingredient is the product of just such ingenuity. If you have a surplus of citrus and searingly hot desert sunshine outside your back door, why not try putting the two together? So why is the name confusing? Because this seasoning starts life as a fresh lime, not a lemon. Perhaps you'd be better off asking for it in the local dialects, *loomi* or *lumi*.

The limes are boiled in saltwater and dried in the sun until the inside flesh turns jet black and all but dissolves. The outer skin caves in on itself slightly and turns a mottled brown. Some propose burying the limes to dry them, but for my effort, the quicker above-ground drying is the better choice. I make my own dried limes in a convenient sunny window with no problems, skipping the boiling stage entirely. Just keep in mind that speed of drying is necessary to avoid mold.

If you do find whole black limes in Arabic and other Middle Eastern markets, buy them rather than the powdered spice to preserve the potency, but know that most uses will call for them to be ground. Crack them into smaller pieces with your mortar and pestle, remove any obvious seeds, and grind to a powder in your coffee mill. At the minimum, they should be cracked open before addition to soup and stock so the inner pith is exposed and can release its flavor.

The taste is surprisingly sweeter than expected and reminds me of those sweet-tart candies from my Halloween trick-or-treating days. They're strong enough to be the only tart component in many recipes, and Arabs take advantage of them liberally, in part because of their extended shelf life. I've used year-old black lemons with plenty of punch left in them to add acid to soups.

Hashu is a blend made by cooking onions and raisins spiced with cardamom, pepper, and black lemons. It makes a traditional crust for meats, with the tart of the black lemons meshing perfectly with the sweet caramelized onions and raisins. Other applications blend the spice into yogurt-based condiments and a whole array of drinks.

Arabic Chicken Kabsa

The stewed chicken dishes of the Middle East look, at first glance, to all be the same; you start with sautéed onions, add chicken and spices, and simmer. Well, what is lacking in "stylistic" differences is made up for with that one key word in there, spices. If the kitchen equipment and the main ingredients stay the same, the real flair of cooking lies in how these ingenious cooks vary the spices.

In this dish, it's the black lemons, *loomi,* that take a simple chicken and rice dish to new heights. The beginnings of this recipe were kindly scribbled for me on a scrap of paper and shoved into the flap of a box of black lemons shipped to me from overseas. I had asked the merchant for a good suggestion for how to use his wares, and he apparently obliged while standing in the post office, waiting in line. After a bit of deciphering, I think I've gotten his intent down to a useful form.   **SERVES 6**

1 large onion, thinly sliced	1½ teaspoons ground ginger
2 tablespoons *ghee,* or unsalted butter	½ teaspoon cardamon seeds
6 chicken legs, skin removed	¼ teaspoon freshly ground cloves
1 tablespoon ground turmeric	2 medium tomatoes, seeded and chopped
1 tablespoon cumin seeds	1 chicken bouillon cube
1 tablespoon freshly ground Central Indian-style *Garam Masala* (page 388)	3 whole black lemons, cracked open
1½ teaspoons coriander seeds	1½ cups long-grain white rice
1½ teaspoons fennel seeds	Coarse sea salt, if needed

In a large heavy pot, sauté the onion in the ghee over medium-high heat until translucent. Add the chicken and cook, turning occasionally, until browned on all sides.

Meanwhile, grind the turmeric, cumin seeds, *garam masala*, coriander seeds, fennel seeds, ginger, cardamon seeds, and cloves together in a coffee mill. Add the spices to the chicken and stir to coat. Add the tomatoes, 3 cups water, the bouillon cube, and the black lemons. Reduce the heat, cover, and simmer for 30 minutes.

Add the rice and cover; cook until the rice is tender and all the liquid is absorbed, about 20 minutes. The bouillon cube should have added enough salt, but taste and adjust as needed.

BLACK SALT

ALTERNATE NAME	*Kala namak* (India)
BOTANICAL NAME OF CULINARY SPECIES	N/A
PLANT FAMILY	N/A
COUNTRY/REGION OF ORIGIN	India
MAJOR COUNTRIES/REGIONS OF PRODUCTION	India, Middle East
SEASON OF HARVEST	Year-round
PARTS USED	N/A
COLORS	Light pink to grayish purple

Actually a complex mineral compound with salt as only one component, black salt doesn't come from the Black Sea, as is frequently assumed. In fact, it's not even really black, but ranges in color from gray to pink to purple. Produced widely across the Middle East and India, it shows up in the cuisines of the same regions. It has a fetid aroma much like asafetida, from the sulfur that is inevitably part of the makeup of most batches. The flavor includes a multitude of minerals but a decidedly smoky and earthy taste, more potent than even the deepest of sea salts, comes to the surface.

Black salt has been used as a preserving agent as well as a seasoning since biblical times. A curious use from medieval times suggests that it can repel annoying neighbors, but in my opinion, it's best used in the kitchen to add a rich mineral taste—perhaps having the opposite effect on your neighbors if they smell dinner cooking.

Ayurvedic cuisine calls for black salt as an *ushna* or "hot" energy with a salty taste, and no batch of *chat masala* is complete without its base flavor and strong aroma. Because of the sulfur content, I try to cook black salt for at least a short time to evaporate the acrid aroma, although it is certainly used as a condiment salt in some ethnic cuisines. I suspect that this is an acquired taste I've yet to acquire.

BOLDINA LEAF

ALTERNATE NAME **Boldo**

BOTANICAL NAME OF CULINARY SPECIES *Boldea fragrans*

PLANT FAMILY *Monimiaceae*

COUNTRY/REGION OF BOTANICAL ORIGIN **Chile, Argentina**

MAJOR COUNTRIES/REGIONS OF CULTIVATION **Brazil, Argentina**

SEASON OF HARVEST **Year-round**

PARTS USED **Leaves**

COLOR **Waxy green**

If the Andes were a bit more accessible, we would all know the leaves of the *Boldea fragrans* tree in the kitchen. Considering how popular bay leaves are in global cuisine, the rich, savory taste of boldina could easily impress chefs the world over in similar fashion.

As potent as the California laurel in aroma, boldina leaves have a similar camphor character with leanings toward more cinnamon sweetness and peppery heat. Fresh on the tree, they can give off a very mild petroleum scent, but this, fortunately, disappears with cooking or drying, and in the freshest batches a mild mint aroma comes to the surface.

The tree is native to the highlands of Chile and Argentina, but test plantings in other regions show promise for this relative newcomer to the spice world. Most notably, Mediterranean regions have begun to plant the leaf with success, and already African cuisines have begun to call for it as a potent substitute for bay. I'm lucky enough to have a customer living in the Andes who sent me a batch stuffed in with payment for the last supply of tea I had shipped to his remote home. Hopefully, with new plantings around the world, supplies will become a bit more consistent.

The leaves of boldina are larger than bay, sometimes approaching double the width, slightly irregular in shape, and thicker than its laurel cousins. In its native

Chile, the tiny fruits of the tree are harvested and dried to use as a pepperlike spice, but the more pleasing complexity of taste comes through in the leaves.

Stories are told of medicinal properties discovered by shepherds who noticed that sheep grazing on the plants were healthier. Cooks will more appreciate the ability of the leaves to flavor meats, such as lamb, as a wrap for slow-roasting, or in accompanying sauces.

BORAGE

ALTERNATE NAMES **Bee bread, Herbs of gladness**

BOTANICAL NAME OF CULINARY SPECIES *Borago officinalis*

PLANT FAMILY **Borage** *(Boraginaceae)*

COUNTRY/REGION OF BOTANICAL ORIGIN **Asia Minor, possibly Persia**

MAJOR COUNTRIES/REGIONS OF CULTIVATION **Widely across Northern Hemisphere**

SEASON OF HARVEST **Summer to early fall**

PARTS USED **Leaves, Flowers, Stems**

COLORS **Green-gray (leaves and stems), Purple (flowers)**

like anything that's low maintenance, brings me courage, and instills a sense of happiness, but then, who doesn't? It's almost what a bachelor spice merchant shops for in a girlfriend, but I'll have to settle for borage.

When I stumbled across borage for the first time in a friend's garden, I had to read up on whether or not it was edible, since she told me she hadn't touched that plot for years and just let the plant seed and grow itself. When you read about borage in ancient or modern texts, three things become clearly associated with it: courage, convenience, and cucumbers. The last comes from the unique fresh flavor it can add to salads, dips, soups, and cocktails.

The beautiful plants have droopy, fuzzy leaves with delicate purple star-shaped flowers punctuated by black anthers that come in midsummer. It does tend to migrate to opportunistic spaces in the garden all by itself, making it a perfect quick harvest for salads and salsas. Hairs develop early on the leaves and can be a bit chewy, so rub them off fresh leaves, or simply chop the leaves very fine. The stems are edible, as are the flowers, and both are seen candied for use in confections. While the leaves can be dried carefully at home, fresh is really the preferred choice for the cleanest flavor of cucumber and mint. Borage is rarely sold commercially, even more rarely dried, but local herb farms are good candidates to check if you cannot spare the garden space yourself.

Historically, the courage portion of the borage legend came at the hands of numerous scholars calling for wine and mead brewed with borage as a confidence builder and generally euphoric tonic. Soldiers naturally started taking the drink as standard practice and in the Middle Ages, or so the story goes, a less-than-eager groom would be dosed with the wine to urge him to the altar. The seeds were carried far and wide across Europe by the Romans, so you can now see massive fields of borage in the countrysides of England, as readily as in modern-day Persia (Iran), all regions offering honey made with bees grazing on those gardens.

Beyond its use as a salad green, fresh borage can be pounded into a paste with plain yogurt for a delicate sauce for poached fish. That same muddling technique can be used at the bar for crisp cocktails made with Pernod or vermouth, and I've slipped it under shrimp cocktail with pleasantly delicate results. Blended with cream cheese, it's a spread for dainty tea sandwiches made with cucumber and cress, and anything with dill can take borage in equal measure, particularly poached fish and delicate vegetable dishes.

However you taste borage, it's bound to improve your mood—if not for some mystical property discovered by Celtic warriors, at least for its crisp, clean flavor that brightens any dish.

BREAD CLOVER

ALTERNATE NAMES Sweet trefoil, Blue fenugreek, Curb herb

BOTANICAL NAME OF CULINARY SPECIES *Trigonella caerulea*

PLANT FAMILY Bean *(Fabaceae)*

COUNTRY/REGION OF BOTANICAL ORIGIN Central Europe

MAJOR COUNTRIES/REGIONS OF CULTIVATION Northern Italy, Switzerland

SEASON OF HARVEST Summer

PARTS USED Leaves

COLOR Green

This micro-crop from the Alps is one of those little regional secrets you'd never know about unless you hung around groceries reading labels. For me, it was specifically a cheese shop, and what came of some translation efforts was the discovery of a delicate herb little known outside Switzerland.

The cheese in question was being sold as "Swiss herb cheese," which naturally presented the question, "What herb?" After the merchant and I looked at the label in puzzlement for some time, we figured out that the secret ingredient that gave the hard *Schabzigerkäse* cheese its delicate green cast and lightly nutty flavor was bread clover. Related to fenugreek of Indian fame, it has a similar taste and subtle caramel aroma with tiny hints of pepper or mint.

In the Tyrol regions of Switzerland and Northern Italy, the clover is harvested and used in the black rye breads, flavored spaetzle, and potato cakes and casseroles so popular there. While these dishes frequently call for heavy flavors like caraway and dill, bread clover serves to lighten and add herbal character. Like other delicate herbs, it doesn't hold up well to long cooking time and so is most often added near the end of preparation.

Since the herb doesn't dry well and isn't cultivated widely, your best chance at tasting its flavor is in prepared foods imported from its native area. While I'd like to think I could use the excuse to get to the Alps for a bit of snowboarding, I think I'll have to settle for imported cheese.

BUSH TOMATO

ALTERNATE NAMES **Desert raisin,** *Akatyerre* **(Aboriginal dialect),** *Akudjura* **(Aboriginal dialect)**

BOTANICAL NAME OF CULINARY SPECIES *Solanum centrale*

PLANT FAMILY *Solanaceae*

COUNTRY/REGION OF BOTANICAL ORIGIN **Australia**

MAJOR COUNTRIES/REGIONS OF CULTIVATION **Australia**

SEASON OF HARVEST **Year-round**

PARTS USED **Fruits**

COLORS **Deep yellow to dark red**

If there's a brave new frontier in the spice trade, it's most certainly in Australia. Wild-crafted spices like bush tomato and mountain pepper are the newest things to hit spice shelves in years. Funny thing is, though, the Aboriginal peoples' spice racks may predate those of the rest of the world by millennia.

Entrepreneurs in the spice trade discovered the potent bush tomato Down Under while investigating the Aboriginal diet. With a taste that starts as sun-dried tomato but ends sharper and less sweet, the bush tomato was historically seen as a staple, not a specialty spice, by the indigenous population. Some samples can even taste like caramelized sugar or dried fruit, but the finish typically brings it back to the savory end of the spectrum.

The fruits are harvested only after they dry naturally on the bush, reducing harmful alkaloids, which account for the tart flavor, and intensifying the bright tomato character. Since they're not cultivated per se, their color can range widely, from a sandy brown to purple red, depending on the growing conditions of each individual plot.

Now, with building demand for the fruit, the pungency makes most Western-ers think about bold meat rubs and savory breads. A blending of several "new" native Aussie flavors—lemon myrtle, mountain pepper, and bush tomato—makes a fine start, but the flavors also round out nicely with cinnamon and cardamom. Rubbed on game meats and slow-cooked, the mix will release all the complexities within.

A savory bread flavored with bold herbs—rosemary and thyme, for example—can marry well with bush tomato, either baked within or soaked and used as a topping. Even a spread made with olives and garlic can take advantage of the strong, raisin-like character that blooms from ground bush tomato. That treatment on grilled bread, served with pungent cheeses and a deep, fruity Australian Shiraz, was enough to cause some friends to plan an expedition to the outback. The hardest part was convincing them to leave at least one bottle of wine behind on their return, to make room in the suitcase for my next bush tomato supply.

Shrimp with New Australian Spice Dust

As mentioned above, Australia is really the new frontier in the spice trade. Indigenous species of plants are now being wild-crafted or even cultivated to satisfy a burgeoning demand. Combining these new tastes, I find a natural balance that seems to be inherent in the plants growing on the continent. **SERVES 4**

1 tablespoon brown mustard seeds	½ pound (2 sticks) unsalted butter
1 teaspoon freshly ground dried lemon myrtle	1 tablespoon shredded fresh ginger
2 teaspoon chopped dried garlic	1½ pounds large shrimp, peeled but tails left on, deveined
1 teaspoon ground mountain pepper	Juice of 1 lime
¾ teaspoon freshly ground bush tomato	

Prepare a hot fire in an outdoor grill. Grind all the mustard seeds, lemon myrtle, dried garlic, mountain pepper, and bush tomato together in a coffee mill. Melt the butter in a small pan and add the ginger; remove from the heat. Transfer ¼ cup of the ginger butter to a small bowl and set aside in a warm place.

The shrimp can be skewered or placed in a barbecue basket to facilitate flipping. Brush with the remaining ginger butter and dust with the spice blend. Grill for 2 to 3 minutes on each side, until the spices form a light crust and the shrimp are opaque throughout. Mix the lime juice with the reserved ginger butter and serve as dipping sauce.

CANDLENUT

ALTERNATE NAME Kemiri nut

BOTANICAL NAME OF CULINARY SPECIES *Aleurites moluccana*

PLANT FAMILY *Euphorbiaceae*

COUNTRY/REGION OF BOTANICAL ORIGIN Malaysia, especially the Moluccas

MAJOR COUNTRIES/REGIONS OF CULTIVATION South Pacific Islands and Australia

SEASON OF HARVEST Year-round

PARTS USED Inner nuts

COLORS Waxy white to pale yellow

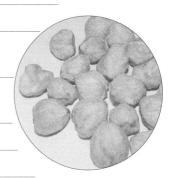

One of the original treasures brought back to Spain by the early explorers of the Moluccas, candlenuts are rich in oil and exude a creamy nut aroma that can be the start of a fabulous curry or the topping to a rich rice pudding.

I was originally sent on a quest for these nuts by an unlikely customer, a Catalan master chef who had tasted them on holiday half a world away from his homeland. After several queries that resulted, erroneously, in shipments of macadamia nuts, I finally found the genuine article in just as curious a place. On a brief layover in Hong Kong, I found that the airport gift shop was selling a trinket labeled "natural nut candles" that consisted of waxy nuts with wicks shoved into the top. Indeed, they burned a fair time, but the "not for consumption" label on the back kept me from cooking with that particular batch.

The nuts are actually toxic when raw and should be toasted before use, no matter what the label might say about "precooked." The high oil content makes them as rich as almond or coconut, and in fact they can produce a milky paste when pounded with other ingredients like cilantro, kaffir, or chiles at the beginning of a Malay curry. Add ginger, pepper, galangal, and cardamom to round out the flavor, and store the paste for up to three days under refrigeration. Because of the oil content, rancidity can set in if kept any longer.

Roasted and crushed, the nuts make their way up the Asian peninsula as toppings on sweet milk desserts and braised greens, much as Western tastes use almonds. As with crushing or grinding, toasting starts the release of oils and shouldn't be done until shortly before use. Macadamia nuts are in fact a very acceptable substitute, although they have less intensity of flavor than candlenuts.

CARAWAY

ALTERNATE NAME **Roman cumin**

BOTANICAL NAME OF CULINARY SPECIES ***Carum carvi***

PLANT FAMILY **Parsley (*Umbelliferae*)**

COUNTRY/REGION OF BOTANICAL ORIGIN **Southern Europe into Asia**

MAJOR COUNTRIES/REGIONS OF CULTIVATION **Netherlands, Canada, Russian, widely**

SEASONS OF HARVEST **Late summer and fall**

PARTS USED **Seed-fruits**

COLOR **Dark brown**

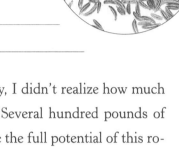

When I started doing business with a local bakery, I didn't realize how much caraway would soon pass through my hands. Several hundred pounds of seeds and countless baking experiments later, I now see the full potential of this robustly flavored spice to lend depth of character to all sorts of foods, not the least of which is rye bread.

Not to minimize the baking that introduces most people to this wonderfully heady seed, however, caraway suffers from typecasting in most spice cabinets. It can be much, much more than bread. Please let your caraway roam outside the bread dough and into more interesting applications, like sauerkrauts and root vegetable stews or anywhere you need a bold spice statement with menthol punch married to a subtly sour base.

The taste is certainly savory, but if you happen to have the luxury of sticking your head into a fifty-kilo sack of caraway, the aromas come across as seriously acrid, certainly a result of concentration of the volatile oil carvone, a component found in similarly large concentrations in dill seed. Caraway's flavor echoes this, along with the flavors of mint and thyme.

Northern Europe produces most of the world's caraway, from fields that look snow-covered when millions of tiny white flowers bloom announcing the impending spice harvest. The plant is in the parsley family, and what most people think of as a seed is actually a fruit. Elongated like cumin seed but darker brown, each fruit has small ridges down its length, much as you find in fennel. Dutch caraway is historically regarded as the best, but upstart producers everywhere are challenging that norm from Canada to Russia. Indeed, Russian distilleries have long added small amounts of caraway to their specialty vodka recipes to impart a subtle spice undercurrent to their cherished national drink. Even more famously, throughout Scandinavia, aquavit is distilled via recipes heavy in caraway.

I've toasted a lot of caraway in my time for the aforementioned bakery customer, and from light to dark roast, the seed takes on all manner of intensities. A mild heating in a dry pan will bring more of the oils to the surface and hence more intensity. Fine grinding will have a similar effect, but at some point with either process, you begin to lose more oil than you save. However, with the potency of caraway, this may be a desirable loss, depending on the dish, ultimately achieving a milder taste on the palate in, say, lighter dumplings and sauces.

Caraway seeds certainly have their advocates outside the bakery, but, as they can polarize the palate to an extreme, they usually need tempering in the dish. Milk buffers their effect when the seeds are added whole to specialty cheeses of northern Europe. Caraway makes its way across the Mediterranean to North Africa and shows up in the signature fiery paste of the region, *harissa*, where chile heat helps to level the flavor playing field.

Overnight Coleslaw

Vinegar brings out the flavors of all the spices here and makes for a great dressing on cabbage. Overnight marination begins to pickle the vegetable, but after such a relatively short time and under refrigeration, it should stay crisp and interesting, unlike many prepackaged slaws. In the South, a vinegar-based coleslaw is traditional as a topping on pulled barbecue sandwiches, on the plate of catfish and hushpuppies, or served alongside tangy ribs and potatoes.

SERVES 6

1 tablespoon yellow mustard seeds

1 tablespoon celery seeds, cracked

1 teaspoon paprika

½ teaspoon finely ground caraway seeds

½ teaspoon finely ground cumin seeds

4 allspice berries, finely ground

2 cups granulated sugar

1½ cups cider vinegar

3 cups shredded green cabbage

3 cups shredded purple cabbage

1 red bell pepper, diced

2 carrots, shredded

2 celery stalks, shredded

½ cup diced white onion

¼ cup diced pimientos

Combine the mustard seeds, celery seeds, paprika, caraway, cumin, allspice, sugar, and vinegar in a large bowl, and stir to dissolve the sugar. Add the remaining ingredients, stirring to mix. Cover tightly, and refrigerate for at least 12 hours, preferably 24, stirring occasionally. (Tightly covered, the coleslaw will keep for several days, but it will gradually lose its crisp texture.)

CARDAMOM, GREEN AND WHITE

ALTERNATE NAMES Green cardamom (unprocessed), White cardamom (bleached), Decorticated cardamom (seeds only)

BOTANICAL NAME OF CULINARY SPECIES *Elettaria cardamomum*

PLANT FAMILY Ginger *(Zingiberaceae)*

COUNTRY/REGION OF BOTANICAL ORIGIN Asia Minor

MAJOR COUNTRIES/REGIONS OF CULTIVATION India, Guatemala

SEASONS OF HARVEST Summer and fall

PARTS USED Seeds, Seed pods

COLORS Green (pods), Black (inner seeds)

It's a shame that these fabulously potent pods have gotten a reputation of being too costly. Much as with saffron and vanilla, the potent flavor more than justifies some of the daunting costs-per-pound charged at retail outlets in the West. Where else could you get the whole of India in a convenient little green package at any cost?

The half-inch-long pods look something like miniature ears of corn at first glance and exude a strong camphor aroma that hints at the flavor within. Once each pod is crushed open, you'll find roughly twenty-five jet-black seeds held together in clusters by a paper-thin membrane and a sticky residue. These seeds, and the resin coating them, which indicates freshness, provide a taste sensation that recalls the flavor of clove, pepper, sassafras, and allspice all at once. The freshest batches will impart a certain heat, again like pepper, but with a unique sweetness and aroma that is matched nowhere else on the spice rack.

A shrub in the ginger family, cardamom produces pods that are harvested at a brilliant green stage, just before they would open if left on the bush. Large wicker trays are filled to the brim with the fresh pods, which have the look and shape of olives or caper berries. They're painstakingly sorted by hand according to size, with "extra fancy" being the cream of the crop. As they're laid out on mats to sun-dry,

TURKISH COFFEE

This brew isn't so much a recipe as it is a technique, from the cultures of Turkey, Morocco, and the entire North African tier. Exceedingly strong coffee is the norm across the region, but cooks continue to mystify Westerners with the flavor. What they've picked up the habit of adding to the beans, it is revealed, is a pungent dose of green cardamom pods. Simply add the whole pods, roughly in a one-to-six ratio, to your coffee beans when grinding them to start your morning routine. Brew to your normal preference, but remember that traditionally the finished product is brewed strong in a French press and sweetened heavily enough to remove the polish from your spoon.

---

the air is filled with their distinctive scent. Walking through the rows of drying pods recalls brilliant curries, aromatic chai, and only the most fragrant of breads.

The Turks have embraced cardamom in several regional blends, like *baharat* and *zhug*, but they are most famous for their treatment of dangerously strong coffee brewed with cardamom. Whole pods are ground with the beans and steeped or percolated into an intense drink that's typically heavily sweetened. It's served in small demitasse cups, and a few of them will keep you and your taste buds on edge for hours.

Rice perfumed with a few cardamom pods during cooking is a staple of most Indian tables. Half a dozen pods for a two-cup batch of grain are more than enough, and the trick works equally well with quinoa and lentils. For texture reasons, however, most dishes will call for only the inner seeds. As nature has provided the perfect shipping container to preserve freshness, namely the tough outer husks, extraction of the seeds should be done right at the stove, not before.

Curries from the south of India especially feature cardamom seeds for their sweetness and subtle peppery bite. Creamy *kormas*, thick with lamb and legumes, tend not to have chiles for heat; rather, cardamom replaces that texture in the overall mouthfeel while simultaneously delivering a sharp floral aroma. The dairy included in most *korma* recipes seems to infuse completely with cardamom and hold the essence well, even with extended cooking.

In Scandinavia, white seems to be the norm—not in just the Arctic landscape but also in the food. Cardamom pods are no exception. White cardamom is the preferred version in the northern latitudes, where it's found in pastries, meatballs, and the classic mulled wine, glogg. Simply green pods that have been artificially bleached, usually with sulfur dioxide, the white form is less sharp than the natural green. The bleaching process seems to dull the strongest menthol qualities of the aroma and lets a different, slightly sweeter character come to the front. The extra processing makes for an expensive indulgence, sometimes as much as three times the cost of even the best green pods, which is probably the main reason you wouldn't want to replace green pods wholesale in your recipe. However, if you find green cardamom too astringent or overpowering, e.g., in baking, then white pods might be the best choice.

Mulled Cranberry Sauce

If you still buy canned cranberry sauce, even if only for the sentimental value from your childhood, I beg you to try making it from scratch just once. If there was ever an easier contribution to holiday meals, I can't image what it would be. The twist here is to flavor the cooking water with spices, taking a cue from rice or polenta cooks. **MAKES ABOUT 3 CUPS**

2 tablespoons Mulling Spices (page 367), crushed

1 tablespoon whole green cardamom pods, crushed to open husks

1 cup granulated sugar

One 12-ounce package fresh cranberries

Combine 2 cups water and the mulling spices and crushed cardamom pods in a medium saucepan, and simmer uncovered over medium-high heat until reduced to just over 1 cup of liquid.

Strain into a clean saucepan (discard the spices) and add the sugar and cranberries. Bring to a boil, stirring to dissolve the sugar, and cook, stirring occasionally, until the cranberries begin to pop. Lower the heat to medium and simmer, stirring occasionally, until the sauce begins to thicken, about 7 minutes. Transfer to a serving bowl, let cool, cover, and refrigerate until cold.

Mavrou

From the Cape of South Africa, this savory steak dish is part of the heritage of the Malay workers who migrated to the country to serve the Dutch settlers' households. Cardamom seed adds a pungent note to Capetown *Masala* that is the heart and heat of this dish. The combination of fresh and dried spices is well balanced on the palate. Serve the meat on a platter of saffron rice. **SERVES 4**

¼ cup freshly ground Capetown *Masala* (page 395)

1 teaspoon fine sea salt, or to taste

2 tablespoons grated fresh ginger

3 garlic cloves, minced

1 pound cube steak, cut into large pieces

2 large onions, sliced

2 tablespoons sunflower oil or other vegetable oil

2 cups chicken stock

1 large tomato, seeded and diced

Combine the *masala*, salt, ginger, and garlic in a medium bowl. Add the meat, tossing to coat, and allow to stand 20 minutes.

Preheat the oven to 350°F. In a Dutch oven or other casserole, cook the onions in the oil over medium-high heat, stirring, until translucent, 3 to 5 minutes. Add the seasoned meat and sear briefly on all sides. Add the stock, cover, and simmer for 20 minutes.

Stir in the tomato, transfer to the oven, and bake, uncovered, for 20 minutes longer, or until the meat is tender. Serve over rice.

CARDAMOM, THAI

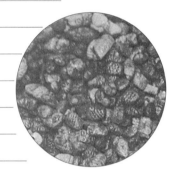

ALTERNATE NAME **Round cardamom**

BOTANICAL NAME OF CULINARY SPECIES *Amomum krervanh*

PLANT FAMILY **Ginger (*Zingiberaceae*)**

COUNTRY/REGION OF BOTANICAL ORIGIN **Southeast Asia**

MAJOR COUNTRIES/REGIONS OF CULTIVATION **Southeast Asia**

SEASON OF HARVEST **Summer into fall**

PARTS USED **Seedpods**

COLOR **Yellow-white**

Species of cardamom from Southeast Asia have the same pepper and allspice character of their green cousins, but the pods look drastically different. They are smaller and perfectly round, about the size of a large pea, and turn yellow-white when dried. Growing in the wild, the pods develop in spiked clusters at ground level, below wide-leafed foilage.

The flavor is similar to that of green cardamom, with camphor and mint notes. If there is any real difference, it's that the Thai species will lean more toward the peppery aspects, which mesh well with the ginger-laced cuisines of Thailand and Indonesia beyond. Since the crop is very small and not usually sourced widely in the West, however, substitution with the green is a more than reasonable compromise.

In a small batch I procured from my local Chinatown apothecary, I noticed that the husks were more porous than other cardamoms' and that the flavors, no doubt as a result, seemed generally less potent. The cost was not outlandish, but I suspect that the absolute freshest crops from this small harvest could command a higher price. Given the similarities in taste, I can't recommend that you spend your spice budget on Thai cardamom unless you happen to be standing on an island in the South Seas and can get painfully fresh pods.

CARDAMOM, BLACK

ALTERNATE NAMES **Brown cardamom, Nepalese cardamom, False cardamom, Winged cardamom**

BOTANICAL NAME OF CULINARY SPECIES *Afromomum subulatum*

PLANT FAMILY **Ginger (*Zingiberaceae*)**

COUNTRY/REGION OF BOTANICAL ORIGIN **Northern India**

MAJOR COUNTRIES/REGIONS OF CULTIVATION **India, Pakistan**

SEASON OF HARVEST **Summer**

PARTS USED **Seeds**

COLORS **Brown (pods), Black (seeds)**

If spices were barflies, you'd find black cardamom at your local pub ordering scotch and cigars every night. Its smoky aroma slaps you in the face and the flavor isn't far behind, waiting to assault your taste buds. While it shares a name with green cardamom, it has a wholly different potency and astringency. Its flavor says pepper, smoke, and caraway simultaneously at first and only lightly falls into more traditional camphor and sweet mint later in the palate. Substitution of one for the other is not advised, especially in anything even remotely delicate.

The pods, like those of other cardamoms, are tough and ridged, each holding about forty sticky seeds. Its one- or two-inch-long brown husks are thicker and more irregularly shaped than those of green cardamom. Typically seeds are extracted from the pods for use, since the husks can impart a bitter taste. The avid barbecue chef can reserve the husks and soak them in water for smoking fodder.

The intense nature of black cardamom makes it a less likely candidate for experimentation, but it does seem to work well in the desert cuisines of North Africa and the roasted dishes of India and the Middle East. A favorite of mine is to grind some for blending into baba ganoush, roasted eggplant dip.

Baba Ganoush

One of the first spreads you see in any respectable North African or Middle Eastern eatery is this classic roasted eggplant dish. Although the basic method remains the same, secret twists and turns to the preparation and spicing make each version different. Here the smoky taste of black cardamom underlines the already intense flavor from the roasting process. Spread into pitas, served as a dip, or used to top your favorite sandwich, baba ganoush will become a staple in your repertoire. **MAKES 2 TO 3 CUPS**

2 large purple eggplants or 4 large Asian eggplants, peeled and cut into ½-inch-thick slices

¼ cup coarse sea salt

3 tablespoons extra-virgin olive oil

Juice of 2 lemons

6 black cardamom pods, seeds finely ground

½ cup tahini (sesame paste)

6 garlic cloves, minced

¼ cup minced fresh cilantro

2 tablespoons white sesame seeds

Fine sea salt, to taste

Rinse the eggplant, then toss with the coarse salt in a colander. Allow to stand in the sink or on a deep plate for 20 minutes to exude moisture.

Preheat the broiler. Rinse the eggplant, pat dry, and spread a single layer on a baking sheet. Brush on both sides with 2 tablespoons of the olive oil. Broil 4 inches from the heat just until beginning to char, about 5 minutes. Remove the pan from the broiler and reduce the oven temperature to 350°F. Turn the eggplant, and bake on the center rack of the oven until very soft, about 20 minutes.

Combine the roasted eggplant, lemon juice, black cardamom, tahini, garlic, and cilantro in a food processor, in batches if necessary, and blend until smooth, adding water by the tablespoon if necessary. Transfer to a bowl and stir in the sesame seeds and sea salt. Cover and refrigerate for at least 1 hour, or as long as overnight.

To serve, transfer the baba ganoush to a deep platter or a serving dish, and drizzle the remaining tablespoon of olive oil over the top.

CATNIP

ALTERNATE NAME **Catmint**

BOTANICAL NAME OF CULINARY SPECIES *Nepata cataria*

PLANT FAMILY **Mint (Lamiaceae)**

COUNTRY/REGION OF BOTANICAL ORIGIN **Southern Europe**

MAJOR COUNTRIES/REGIONS OF CULTIVATION **Widely across Northern Hemisphere**

SEASONS OF HARVEST **Summer and fall**

PARTS USED **Leaves**

COLOR **Pale green-gray**

Normally I wouldn't call for catnip in the kitchen, but at the urging of the co-founder of my shop, a cat named Hobbes, I decided to experiment. Despite his urgings to blend it with fresh tuna steaks every time I was in the kitchen, I managed to find that catnip really does offer a flavor worthy of the effort.

Related to mint, catnip when fresh has a pleasantly peppery tone set amid a strong mint flavor. It finishes in a way, however, that can be bitter like celery seed or dill. Long used as a base for tea, it can make the transition into pestos and strewing herb blends successfully, especially in concert with other fresh herbs. The green leaves are moderately fuzzy, on reddish green stems that are edible as long as they are tender young shoots, not the older, more woody samples.

For those of you turning the pages with your paws, it's the *nepetalone* in the herb that gives you such a high while you're rolling around in the leaves; the reaction is actually inherent in some cats, and not in others. Catnip can induce both stimulant and sedative effects, depending again on genetics. You may see some cats chew on the herb as much as smell it, but it is the olfactory sense that processes the oils physiologically. Cats, of course, know that taste and smell are inextricably linked.

Cats also have a knack for demolishing a garden patch of the stuff just minutes before you planned to harvest it. At my house, we've noticed that there is a great difference in quality of dried leaves, so try to dry your own or, at minimum, crumble some leaves before offering them. If there is none of the savory mint aroma, you have gotten some of the industrial product that is widely sold to appease the cat-toy business. Instead, try to find some of the wild-crafted product sold in premium shops, or dedicate a garden patch and fence it off from nighttime prowlers.

Catnip was much more commonly cultivated in ancient times. The Romans ate the fresh greens and used it as medicine. It followed them on their conquests of Europe and Britain and stayed behind there in the herbal texts of the Middle Ages. One text proposes a sort of egg salad made with copious amounts, and at the urging of a certain furry member of my household, I find that it goes equally well in tuna salad.

CELERY

ALTERNATE NAMES **Celery seed, Smallage**

BOTANICAL NAMES OF CULINARY SPECIES *Apium graveolens*

PLANT FAMILY **Parsley** *(Umbelliferae)*

COUNTRY/REGION OF BOTANICAL ORIGIN **Southern Europe**

MAJOR COUNTRIES/REGIONS OF CULTIVATION **Widely**

SEASON OF HARVEST **Year-round**

PARTS USED **Seeds, Stalks, Leaves, Roots**

COLORS **Pale brown (seeds), Pale green (stalks and leaves), Off-white (roots)**

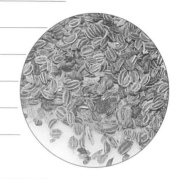

What do pickles, Worcestershire sauce, and a Bloody Mary all have in common? The bitter truth of the answer comes from tiny celery seeds. The same plant that gives us celery stalks, allowed to go to seed, gives us a crop of one of the most bitter spices on the shelf. Frequently used for their potent oil, the tiny seeds also find their way into a plethora of prepared foods ranging from ketchup to coleslaw. Minuscule in size, with as many as two thousand seeds to the gram, they are added whole or ground in small doses and impart a bite that keys singularly on the bitter regions of the palate.

The species of plant cultivated today is Mediterranean in origin, with its more pungent ancestors dating back to early Roman times, when it was held in as high esteem in ceremonial circles as in the kitchen. Selective cropping has mellowed the flavor, primarily in the stalk and root, but the seeds have maintained a potent character. What strikes me most about the taste is that it is a clean flavor that doesn't tend to interfere with other ingredients. Admittedly, it is easily identified in recipes, but not in a way that covers or obscures.

Celery is an import crop across the entire globe, with the stalks sold as a commodity vegetable. With some species, *Apium graveolens "rapaceum,"* or, commonly, celeriac, the root is harvested similarly as a vegetable, but in all species some portion of the harvest is allowed to seed. Little taste variation is detected among the different species when harvested as a seed-spice, but the seed trade seems to concentrate on more northerly latitudes, with Russia and Canada being major producers.

Acadian cuisines in Louisiana have embraced celery seeds as vital to the spice blends that are their foundation. These almost universally include celery seed, mustard, bay, and thyme in their makeup, most probably because these have all been easily grown as local peasant crops in Cajun/Creole country.

As a food professional who firmly believes in the principles of the Slow Food Movement, a doctrine that denounces overprocessed, packaged foodstuffs, I really shouldn't admit that I have an affinity for a famous brand of ready-made stuffing. Mind you, I love making the genuine corn bread version from scratch (see page 279), but there is something in the flavor of this boxed stuff that appeals to me. Since it wasn't in the aging bread cubes they include in the box, I looked in the "seasoning packet" to try and duplicate the taste I liked. As it turns out, the secret ingredient is dried celery leaf and stalk. Something about the dehydration process concentrates the flavor to something more akin to that of sweet vegetable stock and, in my opinion, a spice-like potency. I've taken to getting this in bulk and including it in my own sauces based on mushroom, beef, or onion. Now if I could only find rock-hard bread cubes in bulk, I could satisfy my addiction.

CHERVIL

ALTERNATE NAME **French parsley**

BOTANICAL NAME OF CULINARY SPECIES *Anthriscus cerefolium*

PLANT FAMILY **Parsley (*Umbelliferae*)**

COUNTRY/REGION OF BOTANICAL ORIGIN **Southern Europe**

MAJOR COUNTRIES/REGIONS OF CULTIVATION **France, Turkey, Egypt, California**

SEASON OF HARVEST **Summer**

PARTS USED **Leaves**

COLOR **Green**

I'm frequently amazed at how many people have never been directly introduced to this delicate herb that the French have so taken to heart. When you want a light touch of Provence, reach for chervil or one of the blends that use it liberally, such as *herbes de Provence* and *fines herbes*. Tasting something like rich parsley gently blended with mild tarragon, chervil seems almost custom-made for delicate sauces based on butter and white wine.

Like parsley, chervil is prone to significant flavor loss when dried, so choose the fresh whenever possible. Commercially processed dried leaves will offer some taste, but home gardeners lack the equipment to lock in the mild flavor. Use your crops of chervil fresh all summer with lighter vegetables like squash and cucumbers as they come from the garden. Buy your dry chervil commercially to overwinter in heavier bean and legume soups.

Looking very much like a sparse parsley, chervil goes to flower relatively early in the season. The flavor seems to be concentrated in the leaf, so pinch off the seed heads as they form to encourage leaf production. The unopened pods can be simmered in stock in a steeping bag and removed once they give up their flavor, which is similar to the leaf but slightly more bitter.

In Central Europe, a pesto-like sauce using fresh chervil, parsley, and chives is prepared as a delicate accompaniment to fish. Indeed, fish dishes in general take to gentle seasoning from chervil, well suited to the shorter cooking times expected with seafood. As the flavor is prone to breakdown, long stewing or intense roasting will completely vaporize the herb's character. One possible exception to this rule is a classic chervil soup that has a religious heritage. Christians came to believe that chervil symbolized new life, and some still make a traditional soup at Easter with little more than stock and copious amounts of the chopped leaf.

Provençal Roast Chicken and Potatoes

It amazes me how many people don't know how easy it is to roast a chicken. Five minutes of preparation with the chicken, and it's into the oven. By the time I've settled from the day and opened a bottle of wine, roast chicken is coming out of the oven, and the kitchen smells like the South of France.

Potatoes are always on hand, but the technique works with any convenient root vegetable you may have. Carrots are also a particular favorite of mine. The beauty of the idea is that the seasoning is already ready for you from the roasting of the bird. Vertical roasting frames that allow a chicken to sit above its drippings are ideal. If you don't have one, insert an empty aluminum soda can into the cavity of the bird and stand it on end in the roasting pan. **SERVES 4**

One 4½- to 5-pound roasting chicken, rinsed

1 tablespoon olive oil

1 tablespoon *sel gris* (Brittany sea salt)

¼ cup *Herbes de* Provence (page 368), crushed

2 tablespoons dried chervil

2 scrubbed lemons, quartered and seeded

6 medium Yukon Gold potatoes, washed and cut into 2-inch chunks, or 1½ pounds baby red potatoes, washed and halved if large

Preheat the oven to 400°F. Coat the chicken inside and out with the oil and sea salt. Similarly, coat with the herb blend and chervil all over, rubbing it between your fingers to release the fragrance and patting it onto the skin. Stuff the lemon quarters inside the chicken. Place in a roasting pan and roast until the juices run clear when the thigh is pierced, about 1¼ to 1½ hours, depending on the size of the bird. Transfer to a platter (set the roasting pan aside), cover loosely, and allow to sit for at least 10 minutes to redistribute the juices. (Leave the oven on.)

Meanwhile, cook the potatoes in a large saucepan of boiling salted water until almost fork-tender, 15 to 20 minutes. Drain.

Add the potatoes to the roasting pan and toss to coat completely with the drippings. Roast for 5 to 10 minutes, or until tender. If desired, turn on the broiler for 1 last minute or so to give the potatoes a crispier texture.

Remove the lemons from the chicken and carve the bird. Serve with the potatoes.

CHICORY

ALTERNATE NAMES **Belgian endive, Succory**

BOTANICAL NAME OF CULINARY SPECIES *Cichorium intybus*

PLANT FAMILY *Compositae*

COUNTRY/REGION OF BOTANICAL ORIGIN **Northern Mediterranean**

MAJOR COUNTRIES/REGIONS OF CULTIVATION **Southern Europe, southern United States**

SEASONS OF HARVEST **Summer and fall**

PARTS USED **Leaves, Roots**

COLORS **White-green (leaves), Flat brown (roots)**

In the United States, few people other than ardent gardeners have heard of chicory unless they've visited New Orleans. There its roasted roots are mixed with coffee in generous amounts and served with plates of deep-fried *beignets*. Café du Monde serves this concoction all night long, and it could well be the most popular drink that doesn't contain rum in that wonderful city thick with debauchery.

For the roots, however, it's rather impractical to grow your own, given the lengthy commercial stripping and roasting process. Buy it as a pure vacuum-canned product and mix your own favorite ratio with coffee—typically around five parts bean to one part root—to brew as you would normally. In the nineteenth century, the peasant communities of the U.S. South brewed chicory root alone as a cheap substitute for expensive and scarce coffee, a practice begun a century earlier in western Europe.

But chicory is now used as a specialty salad green in Italy, France, and Belgium, although the leaves as well as the roots have that coffee-like bitterness. Some liken the taste of the greens to mustard or chard. Indeed, there's almost no sweetness to the leaves, and cooking doesn't temper the bitterness as you'd expect. For my taste, I use them fresh and then only sparingly mixed with other sweeter greens.

ALTERNATE NAMES **Chile peppers, Pepperpods**

BOTANICAL NAMES OF CULINARY SPECIES *Capsicum annum, Capsicum frutescens, Capsicum chinense, Capsicum pubescens, Capsicum baccatum*

PLANT FAMILY **Nightshade (Solanaceae)**

COUNTRY/REGION OF BOTANICAL ORIGIN **Central and South America**

MAJOR COUNTRIES/REGIONS OF CULTIVATION **Mexico, Southwest United States, Caribbean, India, other equatorial regions**

SEASON OF HARVEST **Year-round, especially late summer**

PARTS USED **Fruits**

COLORS **Wide-ranging, from green (immature) to red/orange/yellow (mature); numerous unique varietals of all colors**

Chiles, or chile peppers, evoke something primeval in the mind and on the palate. Nothing can stir the senses in quite the same way, and chile heads the world over have raised these culinary gems to cult status. They have a unique ability to chemically wake our taste buds and, in the process, jolt the senses with a hot slap across the tongue.

Chiles are fruits that contain the very special compound capsicum, the chemical that causes the palate to perceive "heat." The ancient Aztecs knew of this quality and used them for everything from highly spiced hot chocolate to ritual practices that induced a sense of euphoria from the pain-induced endorphin rush.

While there are plenty of Texans out there wearing large hats and boasting of how many pickled jalapeños they can eat at halftime, I much prefer to concentrate on subtleties of flavor rather than going only for heat. Flavors are the more interesting component of chiles, and the heat levels are simply bonus side effects. Chiles have a wonderfully diverse range of flavor, from the plum-like fruit of the mild ancho to the smoky sharpness of the *pico de pajardo,* from the clean, simple zip of cayenne to the considerably more complex and dark-flavored *chilhuacle negro.*

Chiles come in all sorts of shapes and sizes, fresh and dried. The dried may be ground to a powder, either pure or blended. Generally, the closer to its natural form a dried chile is, the better its staying power on the shelf. I especially recommend the whole pods for the larger, fleshier chiles, as their flavors can be milder compared to their smaller cousins, and grinding or chopping seems to speed the demise of their flavor. Whole dried chiles can easily be ground at home, although a little work with a pair of kitchen shears may be needed to get them into your coffee mill. A light toasting makes them pliable and enhances the flavors of some chiles, but, as with any widely diverse range of flavors, this must be decided on a case-by-case basis. If needed, toast only as much as you will use immediately in a low oven until slightly crisp.

The naming conventions employed are confusing at best. Dry and fresh chiles of the same type frequently get different names. Furthermore, the same chile can have several regional names, or the same name can mean two entirely different species on either side of a border, and even from one town to the next. Blended ground chiles can also join the confusion, and while "chile" typically means a pure pod of one type, and "chili" usually means a blended powder, consistency is never assured. Add the spice industry norm to use "chili" as a name for a spice blend that merely contains chile pods among other ingredients like salt, pepper, and cumin, and you can see that the only real guide is taste, no matter how you spell it.

All species are believed to have descended from the same original South American strains. Botanically, *Capsicum annum* and *Capsicum frutescens* yield most of the peppers cultivated across the globe, with *C. chinense, C. pubescens,* and *C. baccatum* accounting for the other species. There are well over three hundred different subspecies cultivated today, ranging across all heat, flavor, color, and shape spectra, whose details could easily fill several volumes.

You can, however, make the reasonable assumption that the smaller chiles, generally *C. frutescens,* are both hotter and simpler in flavor, while the larger chiles, typically *C. annum,* tend to be milder and more complex in taste, as well as thicker fleshed. There are, of course, certainly exceptions to these rules. But all experts tend to agree that the heat is concentrated in the seeds and webbing (sometimes called "ribs" in cookbooks) found within each chile pod. Careful removal of these can substantially reduce the perceived heat and, in the case of the seeds themselves, minimize bitter qualities that can detract from the flavors of the chile flesh.

For any type, look for pods that are whole and intact, stem on, with flesh that is a consistent color and not sun-bleached. Each species of chile will have quality characteristics unique to itself: e.g., mulatos should have pliable thick flesh of a dark brown-black, pequins should be brilliant red with no dimpling to the smooth skin, and so forth.

What is interesting to remember is that "heat" is a texture on the palate, not a flavor: a tingle, a twinge, or that little something you can't wrap your taste buds around. Is it a flavor you sense when you bite into the *relleno* or is it a combination of flavor and texture? Great chefs of the U.S. Southwest, the full range of Mexico, and into South America all know that you don't need to clobber a dish with heat to get this effect. Certainly there are the intensely hot dishes of the Caribbean—such as jerk pork and the hot sauce condiments of Dominica—but the effect of texture on the palate can happen with much lower doses.

A favorite example of this texture is the combination of sweet fruit and tiny amounts of ground chile pods, a trick employed by many top chefs. On the coasts of Guatemala, breakfast can be as simple as a half dozen fresh papayas sliced and splayed out upon a grand wooden platter. The local treatment is simply a generous squeeze of lime juice and a dusting of pure ground chiles. The heat marries so well with the sweet papaya and tart citrus that I could eat this dish every morning for weeks.

Arguably the most important spice contribution of the New World to Europe and the Far East, chiles had been cultivated by all the cultures of the West Indies and Americas for centuries before Columbus even set foot on North American soil. They've been documented by findings at Mayan and Aztec ruins to as far back as the second century B.C., but it was the Spanish conquest that carried them across the Atlantic, alongside the plunders of gold and silver, ultimately, to the rest of the world.

India adopted them quickly and has become the leading volume producer in the world. Asia certainly has a taste for the hot fruit, and there is a small amount of debate as to whether they existed in China before being introduced from the West.

Aji and Rocoto

UNLIKE THEIR AGRICULTURALLY PROLIFIC COUSINS to the north, the less common species of chiles tend to thrive in the native soils of South America. Several exotics find their way into the chile-obsessed marketplaces of America, but certain notable examples stand out.

Aji is an old term applied to several types of chiles from the highlands of South America and the Caribbean Islands. One of the most impressive of these, called *aji mirasol,* has become a perennial favorite of mine, eagerly anticipated each fall. The seven-inch-long pods are a brilliant orange color when freshly dried and taste so much like dried fruit, apricots specifically, that I often make chutneys and relishes with only them and no other fruit included. *Aji ceraza, aji amarillo,* and *rocoto* chiles also come from these regions and have become wonderfully complex additions to the local cuisines.

Aleppo Pepper (Near East Pepper)

WHEN A SHIPMENT OF ALEPPO PEPPER was delayed for almost a month and I ran out of stock, I really began to see how much of a following it had gained in our culinary circles as an all-purpose, "just right" chile. One chef began to ask what time my daily shipments arrived, so he could call minutes later to check on whether his beloved spice had made it in the delivery. I knew I had a spice on my hands that was borderline addictive.

What makes this particular chile so interesting is its complexity of flavor on the palate. It begins as a slow, gentle heat with considerable sweetness and progresses (sequentially) to a more solid and intense heat, followed by a pleasant warmth and lingering tinge of sweet and sour. Named for the city and region it hails from in Syria,

Wilbur Scoville was an early-twentieth-century scientist who was intrigued by the properties of capsicum. As any good scientist will tell you, meaningful measurements are everything in the lab, so he devised a scale that directly measures this heat-causing component of chiles. The scale starts at zero for no heat, as with bell peppers, and goes to the high point of 280,000 Scoville Units (SU) for chiles like the habanero. A good reference point for us mere chile mortals is the common jalapeño, at roughly 50,000 SU. Even though higher concentrations have been achieved in medical circles and a few insane chile sauces, the human palate shuts down at approximately 200,000 SU, so anything beyond that is simply bragging rights for a chile fanatic.

---

it has several cousins in the spice world, including uurd pepper and the more generically sourced Syrian pepper, all of which exhibit similar but subtle differences. The city Aleppo itself lies in a bowl of a valley just east of the Turkish border and enjoys a microclimate that must be in no small part responsible for the unique flavor profile. The pepper is now cultivated successfully in a much wider region and with similar flavor results.

Ancho

ANCHOS ARE THE BIG HEART-SHAPED DRIED chiles that result from drying fresh poblano pods. Deep red to almost black, they're mild and fruity, smelling and feeling like prunes when very fresh. They should be tender and pliable, not brittle, and preferably with their stems intact. When broken open, they should be clean and uniform in color on the inside.

Since the skins are conveniently thin, most uses for anchos call for them to be soaked and blended into a sauce or otherwise macerated. In some cases, you will want to toast them first to bloom out of the flavors, and this is always necessary if you want to grind them into a powder, since moist pods will wreak havoc with most home grinders.

A closely related chile is the dried *mulato* pod. These are, in fact, next to impossible to differentiate from anchos on all fronts and can be substituted in almost any case.

For the chile aficionado who wants positive identification, I use a trick from my chile suppliers in New Mexico: Hold the opened pods up to the light and inspect the color and thickness. Anchos will be redder and thinner fleshed, and you can see through them, while mulatos will all but block the light with their thicker skin and darker color.

Cayenne

IT'S ALMOST UNTHINKABLE TO HAVE AN Indian meal without chiles and the heat they bring, but until the New World explorations brought them to the subcontinent, culinary heat came largely from peppercorns and the like, not from chiles as we know them today. The complexity of the Indian cuisine had developed well before the introduction of New World ingredients, and so the chile's flavor complexity seems to be less important to the cuisine than the sheer heating ability of most species cultivated in India. Cayenne is widely grown to satisfy this specific niche.

The heat of cayenne peppers can range widely, from as mild as 30,000 SU in Indian crops to as much as 100,000 SU in the African varieties. Flavor varies little from source to source and remains crisp, even tart, in character.

Cayenne is also a favorite chile among cooks in the American South because of its clean, simple heat. It's easy to cultivate and is frequently the choice for commercial uses because of its predictable nature and easy propagation. It's the base chile in Tabasco® brand pepper sauce, made into a mash with vinegar and salt and aged in barrels until the flavor develops. Its famous makers on Louisiana's McIlhenny Island attest to its local popularity by including a small bottle with every factory worker's paycheck.

Guajillo

GUAJILLOS ARE REAL WORKHORSE CHILES IN the kitchen. They are heavy enough to start thick sauces and bright enough to make blended chile powders interesting. Six to eight inches long and smooth-skinned, they're distinctly brick red and two fingers wide. The stems are easily popped off the top when dry, and a cook can quickly stir up a simple chile sauce by heating them in stock, whirring them in a blender, and then straining to remove the thick skins. The taste of a *guajillo* is less sweet than an ancho and less hot than a jalapeño. It's this middle ground that makes these chiles so versatile and useful as a base to more complex recipes.

Habanero

THIS LITTLE BEAST IS THE STUFF of legend in the chile world, the hottest chile that occurs naturally. It ripens to the most brilliant orange color, nature's first way of saying "Look out with this one!" Just one of the quarter-sized chiles has given a two-gallon batch of my fresh salsa almost too much heat to bear. If Mother Nature had warning labels, this would be the first to get one. I recommend wearing rubber gloves when you work with them, and by all means, don't touch any part of your lips, eyes, or face. They will get you a free ride to the emergency room if you're not careful.

Both legend and labs agree that the Red Savina variety of habanero is the hottest chile on the face of the planet. Following in the heat race are Scotch bonnets, Bolivian rainbows, and several other colorfully named subspecies. Copious investments of national pride are associated with chile heat, and so reports of others with higher potency from India and China, and various chile-production newcomers, must be taken with a grain of salt. Although there may well be hotter species coming onto the culinary scene, any discerning cook will be more interested in their flavor than some esoteric Scoville rating number from a lab test. I'll just settle for the habanero on the heat front and not worry much beyond that.

My real interest lies in its flavor, which is as unique as its heat. It's a perfect foil to acid-charged sauces and salsas, and I find mixing it with citrus of any sort is always a success. As with any chile, try to temper the heat in the context of the overall flavor. In the case of habanero, that means both using less and, by all means, using only the outer flesh, not the inner seeds and membranes, which contain dangerous levels of heat.

Piments d'Espelette

THESE DELICATELY FLAVORED CHILES WERE PROBABLY the first to get their own *Appellation Contrôlée*, just like the finest wines from Bordeaux. Both Spain and France produce the chiles, and both claim bragging rights to their original plantings after migration from the New World, but it seems that France was first to get its marketing act together and actually name them for the village of Espelette in the Nive Valley. Regardless, the entire Basque country celebrates them as one of their legendary food traditions.

This pride is understandable when you realize that the unique flavor comes from the specific *terroir* of the region, which is probably impossible to re-create elsewhere. The taste has a mild heat that hints at peach mixed with sea brine. The ground dried spice is increasingly available here; if you find yourself near Espelette, buy some from a local farmer and sprinkle it on a simple sandwich of creamy French Brie or smoky Spanish cheese, drizzled with bright, young olive oil from the same hillsides.

Smoked Chiles

IN MEXICO, THEY'VE DISCOVERED THAT THE flesh of chiles can carry the flavors of the smokehouse incredibly well, and chiles of all varieties are laid out in long, wood-fired houses set among the fields. A few specific varieties have made the process famous and popular around the world. Chipotles are simply smoked jalapeño peppers. Fully ripe red jalapeños are smoked to produce the *morita* varieties, two-inch-long peppers that are mottled deep red–black in color. Less mature jalapeños are smoked to give the "brown" varieties, which are twice as long and a uniform pale tan. Chipotles are often sold canned in a tomato sauce base which is infused with the smoky flavors. If you must use these rather than the "pure" chiles, remember that a significant portion of the flavor is in the canning liquid, so save it to add to your recipes.

Around the hills of Oaxaca in southern Mexico, they toss long, ripe *pasilla* chiles onto the smokers to get the pasilla Oaxaca, a smoked chile with half the heat of chipotle but with double the smoke character. A few of these tossed into a pot of black beans will make your dinner guests think you added ham hocks for flavor.

Thai and other Asian Chiles

KNOWN FOR THEIR BLAZING HEAT, THE chile species cultivated commonly in Southeast Asia are generally more simplistic in flavor. The cuisines of the region reflect this by calling for complexity via other ingredients, including lemongrass, garlic, and cilantro, and relying on the chiles for pure heat.

Some botanists make a case for the existence of chiles in Asia long before their export from the New World by fifteenth-century explorers. If this is indeed proven true, it will have been the *C. chinense* species that was cultivated, the species responsible for some of the sharpest, most tart flavors in the chile world. There is, however, no doubt that other species have now been introduced to Asia and been fully integrated to the cuisine. The Asian taste for chiles, perhaps in deference to the past, is aimed toward the upper end of the heat scale.

Large bags of generically labeled "Chinese chiles" can be had for next to nothing in the markets of Hong Kong. Exported from the mainland to feed the appetite of dim sum houses and crab shacks, they are typically *japonés* or Thai chiles, roughly two-inch-long specimens that will perfectly heat up a tofu stir-fry as well as kung pao chicken.

Simplified Pork Mole

Moles are incredibly complex sauces, based on various chiles in season, from south and central Mexico, used both as a stewing sauce and condiment of sorts. Relying on flavor layering to make the most of what's locally available, cooks of the region may simmer their *moles* for hours or days to build a taste sensation that continues to surprise you with its ongoing, changing palate. They call on various roasting and toasting techniques for the many ingredients, which range from sesame seeds to avocado leaf. *Moles* don't always include chocolate, as is popularly thought, but it is incorporated in some incarnations.

The main goal in putting together a *mole* is to get the flavors to come together successfully. Accepting that most people today won't take the time to nurse a sauce for forty-eight hours, I concocted a spice blend that attempts to come close to this flavor. Looking at the *mole* powder recipe on page 358, you see that the complexity of several chiles is included therein. If the spice blend can be made a day ahead, you both reduce your workload in the kitchen for the meal itself and give the spices time to coalesce into something greater than the sum of the parts. Serve this savory stew with rice or posole. **SERVES 4**

2 tablespoons corn oil, or as needed

1 pound boneless lean pork, cut into 1-inch cubes

1 onion, coarsely chopped

1 bell pepper, cored, seeded, and coarsely chopped

¼ cup freshly ground *Mole* Powder (page 358)

2 cups chicken stock

One 14½-ounce can diced tomatoes, with their juice

2 tablespoons *masa harina*

Heat the oil in a small pot over medium-high heat. Add the pork and cook, stirring occasionally, until browned on all sides, about 7 minutes. Transfer the pork to a plate and set aside. Add the onion and bell pepper and cook, stirring, until the onion is softened, about 3 minutes. Return the meat to the pot and add the *mole* powder, stirring to coat the meat completely. Add the stock and tomatoes with their juices. Bring to a boil, reduce the heat to low, and simmer, uncovered, for 45 minutes, or until the meat is very tender.

Just before serving, whisk the *masa harina* together with ½ cup water to make a thick paste. Add this to the *mole* and stir until the sauce is thickened.

Tex-Mex Chile Corn Bread

How do you make corn bread more than just a lump on the side of your plate? Spices, of course. By reaching for a spice rack laden with chiles, cumin, and local herbs, the locals in the southern United States and northern border regions of Mexico have made such staples as corn, beans, and rice into interesting cuisine.

I like to embrace Tex-Mex as its own unique trend rather than some bastardization of authentic Mexican food. The two are different but equally valid in my mind, although many "food types" would lead you to believe Tex-Mex is the illegitimate stepchild in the relationship. Comfort food in Texas and New Mexico has just as much right to be on the menu as anywhere else, and there's no better example than the old standby corn bread, which comes alive near the border to match up with giant cauldrons of chili and heaping plates of barbecue. **SERVES 8**

---

3 to 4 assorted/dried mild chiles, such as ancho, *mulatto*, and *guajillo*

1 tablespoon corn oil

3 ears of yellow corn, kernels cut off the cobs

¼ cup finely diced red bell pepper

¼ cup finely diced green bell pepper

2 jalapeño chiles, stemmed and minced (optional)

10 tablespoons (1 ¼ sticks) unsalted butter, softened

1 cup fine yellow cornmeal

1 cup all-purpose flour

1 tablespoon granulated sugar

1 teaspoon fine sea salt

2 teaspoons baking powder

1 teaspoon baking soda

1 teaspoon finely ground cumin seeds

½ teaspoon freshly ground dried Mexican oregano

1 cup buttermilk

1 large egg, beaten

1 cup shredded sharp cheddar cheese

Place the dried chiles in a bowl, add water to cover, and let soak for 1 hour. Remove the chiles, reserving the liquid. Scrape the flesh from inside tough-skinned varieties; finely chop soft-skinned varieties. Set aside.

Preheat the broiler. Heat the oil in a large ovenproof skillet (preferably cast iron) over medium-high heat. Add the corn kernels, bell peppers, and optional jalapeños and cook, stirring, until slightly softened, about 5 minutes. Spread the vegetables evenly in the pan and broil 4 inches from the heat until the edges begin to char, about 5 minutes. Remove from the broiler, and turn the oven to 350°F.

Place the butter in a 10-inch cast-iron skillet and put in the oven to melt. Sift together the cornmeal, flour, sugar, salt, baking powder, baking soda, cumin, and oregano into a bowl.

Pour the buttermilk into a small bowl and stir in the chile flesh, along with the beaten egg. Add the buttermilk mixture to the dry ingredients. Add the melted butter, being sure to coat the inside of the skillet with a swirl of the pan as you do so. Fold the roasted vegetables and cheese into the batter. Stir to mix, adding some of the chile soaking liquid as needed (typically no more than ¼ cup) to make a very thick but pourable batter.

Pour the batter into the hot buttered skillet and bake for 50 minutes, or until a knife inserted in the center comes out clean. Serve from the skillet.

CHIVES

ALTERNATE NAME Onion grass

BOTANICAL NAMES OF CULINARY SPECIES *Allium schoenoprasum*
(onion chives), *Allium tuberosum* (garlic chives)

PLANT FAMILY Onion *(Liliaceae)*

COUNTRIES/REGIONS OF BOTANICAL ORIGIN Central Europe
(onion chives), Central Asia (garlic chives)

MAJOR COUNTRIES/REGIONS OF CULTIVATION Widely in
northern latitudes

SEASON OF HARVEST Early summer through early fall

PARTS USED Leaves, Flowers

COLORS Bright Green (leaves), Purple (flowers)

Garlic, onions, and the like are all wonderful aromatics. Sometimes, however, they can be too much of a good thing on the taste buds. That's where their mild-mannered cousins, chives, can come in and impart the same impression of taste without running wild down the hill of potency.

The bright green color of fresh chives gives some indication of what's to follow on the palate. They are rich in a grassy-green onion flavor but mild enough not to seem bitter or harsh. I taste only hints of pepper and get much more smoothness than raw garlic can offer, even though I'm reminded of it with the first bite.

The leaves of the plant, actually hollow tubes barely thicker than a toothpick, are what's used as a spice and herb. Their delicate flavor evaporates soon after cutting, and they're prone to rapid decay in the sunlight. Don't waste your time trying to dry any from the garden. Use them fresh, or rely on commercially prepared dried versions to provide a hint of the delicacy they had originally. Keep in mind, though, that only the very best, and most expensive, freeze-drying processes are appropriate for chives, which are typically cut into ringlets first.

There are two major species of chives. The common garden chive, or onion chive, has a mild sweetness compared with its Asian cousin, the garlic chive. As its name implies, the latter is stronger and less sweet, with hints of peppery heat. This makes it a wonderful choice with the classic double-cooked pork made with paper-thin slices of fatty pork belly, first boiled and then sautéed with Chinese chili paste. I've seen chefs prepare the pork in a hot wok and then fill it literally to the brim with freshly chopped chives and green onions to cook down into a wonderful sauté-meet-stew, which is eaten as is or stuffed into *hom bow*, the classic baked pastry served for *dim sum*.

A particularly interesting treat for the home gardener or cook is to harvest chives when just beginning to flower, before seeds form. Purple fuzzy pom-poms crest the top of tall stalks that seem barely suited to supporting the load. The taste of the flower itself is more intense than the leaves, giving more of a garlic-meets-onion taste with a slight bittering. I use them as topping on morning omelets or chopped and cooked with my hash browns.

Zicil P'ak

An ingenious dip from southern Mexico, made with a base of pumpkin seeds and copious amounts of fresh herbs. The consistency mirrors the pestos of Italy, but the flavor is completely different. Serve as a dip or spread on tacos and tostadas. **MAKES ABOUT 3 CUPS**

2 tomatoes, diced	1 teaspoon finely ground cumin seeds
3 cups pumpkin seeds, toasted	3 tablespoons olive oil or corn oil
2 to 4 jalapeños, seeded and diced	1 cup chicken or vegetable stock
1 cup finely chopped fresh chives	1 teaspoon fine sea salt
1 cup finely chopped fresh cilantro	

Preheat the broiler. Spread the tomatoes on a baking sheet. Broil 4 inches from the heat until the edges are well charred, 5 to 8 minutes.

Combine the tomatoes, pumpkin seeds, optional jalapeños, chives, cilantro, and cumin in a food processor and process until thoroughly blended. With the processor on, drizzle in the oil and then just enough of the stock to reach a smooth consistency. Add the salt and pulse to mix. (The dip can be covered and refrigerated for up to 3 days; bring to room temperature before serving.)

CICELY

ALTERNATE NAMES Sweet cicely, Anise fern, Giant chervil

BOTANICAL NAMES OF CULINARY SPECIES *Myrrhis odorata* (European), *Osmorhiza longistylis* (American)

PLANT FAMILY Parsley *(Umbelliferae)*

COUNTRY/REGION OF BOTANICAL ORIGIN Central Europe

MAJOR COUNTRIES/REGIONS OF CULTIVATION Widely across Northern Hemisphere

SEASON OF HARVEST Late spring through early fall

PARTS USED Leaves, Seeds, Roots

COLORS Green (leaves), Tan (seeds), Pale yellow (roots)

If you like the sweetness of fennel but find it otherwise overpowering, cicely may be the answer to your herb dreams. It faintly mimics fennel and anise but then swings round the palate with a sweet flavor much closer to basil or even carrot.

Wide fernlike fronds fan out from the plant, but the leaf shape itself is closer to cilantro. The stems are not tough and can be chopped fine for use in all manner of herbal applications. After a wash of tiny white flowers, pointed inch-long seed pods appear in upright fingers. These can be harvested green and used for a lighter version of the flavor or allowed to develop to a ripe dark brown and opened to reveal the few seeds in each. The seeds have a stronger anise taste than the leaves, with a tiny amount of camphor, but stop short of bitter. Even the roots of this useful plant can be harvested and cooked for a different twist on dinner's standby potatoes.

Sweet cicely, as it's commonly known, dates back to Roman times but has always been hidden in the back of the garden to some extent. The European and American species exhibit similar flavors, uses, and garden behavior, differentiated only by the broader divided leaves of the latter. Although it's difficult to start, once established, cicely self-seeds annually, making for a low-maintenance crop of sweet leaves. Harvest the young lower leaves all through summer, but forget trying to dry any, as that destroys the taste. Rather, dry the seeds and/or pickle the roots if you want to enjoy the flavors over the winter.

In Belgium, the seeds have been used for centuries as a base for distilled liqueurs and the leaves pounded into sugars for baking. Farther east, in Germany, the roots are steamed with turnips and parsnips and mashed for a filling piped into dumplings or simply served as a side dish with a touch of butter. One recipe from Russia calls for cicely seeds as the only spice in pickled beets, and a Norwegian cookbook mentions cicely leaf and currant tarts as the perfect accompaniment to afternoon tea. The ability to both sweeten and flavor makes it obvious how versatile this plant really can be.

CILANTRO

ALTERNATE NAMES **Coriander leaf, Chinese parsley**

BOTANICAL NAME OF CULINARY SPECIES *Coriandrum sativum*

PLANT FAMILY **Parsley (*Umbelliferae*)**

COUNTRY/REGION OF BOTANICAL ORIGIN **Central Asia**

MAJOR COUNTRIES/REGIONS OF CULTIVATION **Widely**

SEASON OF HARVEST **Year-round**

PARTS USED **Leaves, Stems, Roots**

COLOR **Bright green**

The leaf forms of *Coriandrum sativum*, commonly known as coriander, go by various names, including Chinese parsley, an unfortunate misname, since the two are not related. No matter what you call it, it's indispensable in Latin and Asian cuisines. The same plant gives us a seed (see page 129) that imparts a lemon-meets-mustard flavor in curries and masalas, but the leaf has that plus an intensity of citrus zest and chlorophyll green the seed cannot hope to match.

Thai cooking draws upon cilantro for its herbaceous character as frequently as it does Thai basil, *kaffir* leaf, and lemongrass. Any or all of these can marry together in the fresh curry pastes of the region with great success. Recipes vary from home to home, hut to hut, but any or all of these fresh spices are pounded in tall narrow mortars with chiles, garlic, or shrimp paste, just to name a few, resulting in the red, green, yellow, and other classic curries of the region.

In the West, from Texas south all the way to the tip of South America, cilantro enhances both cooked dishes like beans and stews and cold preparations like salsas. With a distinctive flavor that lingers, it's frequently called upon to be the sole herbal character of a dish, acting to lighten chile- and cumin-heavy dishes.

One of my favorite delis happens to be a Vietnamese spot that has gotten me addicted to their sandwiches. Remembering the French influence in their country's past, they make a baguette filled with roasted pork and lightly spiced vegetables called a *bahn mi*. They always add fresh cilantro leaf to these sandwiches, as we would add lettuce to a BLT. Copious amounts give a zest that perks up the usual mix of cucumber, pickled onion, and carrot.

Some people have a very strong distaste for cilantro. To this group, the flavor comes across as soapy or bitter, a result of their taste buds' interpretation of the herb's essential oils. The chemical compounds that give cilantro and other pungent leaf herbs their punch are actually perceived differently by these individuals. Cooking can change this interpretation on the palate for the better, so those people unlucky enough to have this trait will want to avoid it raw.

Georgian Spiced Bean Balls

The Georgian region of Russia has access to some of the most ancient spice resources in the world. Its proximity to India, China, and the Middle East means that there's a treasure trove of flavors meeting conveniently in the neighborhood.

I have a wonderful friend from the region, Dr. Marina Serednitskaia, who shared some of her recipes she remembered from the Old Country. While she's a nuclear scientist by profession, you can see that it doesn't take quite that level of skill to make this flavorful appetizer. The spicing echoes influences from all directions from Georgia, taking the best fresh herbs from the east, rich cinnamon and cloves from the south, paprika and savory herbs from the north, and treasured saffron from the west. **SERVES 6**

1 pound dried flageolet beans, soaked overnight in water to cover and drained	½ teaspoon dried thyme
1½ cups walnuts, finely chopped	¼ teaspoon cassia-cinnamon
2 garlic cloves, minced	¼ teaspoon freshly ground cloves
2 teaspoons sweet Hungarian paprika	15 saffron threads
1 teaspoon fine sea salt	1 cup finely minced sweet onions, such as Vidalia
¼ cup finely chopped fresh parsley	1 cup finely minced red onion
¼ cup finely chopped fresh cilantro	3 tablespoons olive oil
1 teaspoon dried basil	Freshly ground black pepper, to taste

Put the beans in a large saucepan, add water to cover by 2 inches, and bring to a boil. Simmer for 1 hour, or until tender; drain.

Mix the walnuts with the garlic, paprika, and salt in a bowl. Stir in the parsley, cilantro, basil, thyme, cinnamon, cloves, and saffron until well mixed, then stir in the onions. Place the beans in a medium bowl and stir in the spice mixture and olive oil, mixing well and mashing the beans slightly. Season with additional salt and pepper to taste, cover, and refrigerate until thoroughly chilled.

Shape the mixture into balls the size of large walnuts. Serve as an appetizer, dusted with more parsley, cilantro, and paprika as desired.

NOTE: For a hot version, these can be deep-fried briefly. Serve with mustard or sour cream.

In my experience, there are some spices that can only be described as crowd pleasers. Along these lines, I rarely hear the phrase "I don't like cinnamon." No surprise if you think of the powerful remembrances of holiday mulling, marvelous sweet pastries, and the most complex of curries, all of which owe some of their character to one or another form of the *Cinnamomum* genus of plants.

All of the subvarieties come from the laurel family, and it is the bark of the tree that is most commonly harvested to give flavor to uncountable recipes in kitchens around the globe. From India to Iowa, cinnamon has integrated itself into all the cultures it has touched—but clarification of exactly which cinnamon you're accustomed to using probably has to do with which hemisphere you shop in, rather than a choice based on taste merits.

The history of cinnamon is almost as rich as its taste. As far back as biblical times, the bark was traded across the longest, most convoluted of routes. Arab merchants spun tales of wild beasts and perilous journeys standing between their customers and the spice supply, no doubt an effort to raise the price, but the stories helped to build cinnamon's reputation to new heights. Egyptian pharaohs ordered expeditions to remote wildernesses on cinnamon quests. Indonesians conquered other suitable climates to extend their native productions. Crusaders brought it back en masse from the Holy Land, making it a staple in the medieval kitchen. And Spaniards sailed the seven seas looking as much for cinnamon as for gold. In short, the ultimate web of supply woven around the various species of *Cinnamomum* is a tangled one at best, and the various species have become mingled in historical references.

TRUE CINNAMON

ALTERNATE NAMES Baker's cinnamon, Ceylon cinnamon, Soft stick cinnamon

BOTANICAL NAMES OF CULINARY SPECIES *Cinnamomum zeylanicum, Cinnamomum verum*

PLANT FAMILY Laurel *(Lauraceae)*

COUNTRY/REGION OF BOTANICAL ORIGIN Sri Lanka

MAJOR COUNTRIES/REGIONS OF CULTIVATION Sri Lanka, Maldives

SEASONS OF HARVEST Spring

PARTS USED Inner bark

COLOR Pale tan

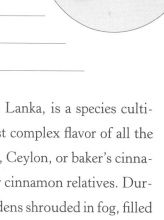

*C*innamomum zeylanicum, almost exclusively from Sri Lanka, is a species cultivated for the spice trade, and it has perhaps the most complex flavor of all the cinnamons grown worldwide. Commonly called soft stick, Ceylon, or baker's cinnamon, it is distinctly different in taste compared with other cinnamon relatives. During the rainy season on the island, the mornings reveal gardens shrouded in fog, filled with harvest workers carefully selecting tender young branches of just the right size that will become the long sticks of cinnamon prized for their aroma and taste. True cinnamon has always been able to captivate people's imaginations with images of exotic lands and equally exotic cuisines.

Typically no more than two inches in diameter, the branches are moist at harvest from the rains during the recent monsoon season, and thick with tender new growth, which helps the peeling process. Indeed, the skills needed to peel cinnamon have become so time-honored that in the strict caste system of India, cinnamon workers have their own rank. Entire families carry on the skill and provide their labor to farmers, sometimes under decades-old agreements. Younger workers learn from older, with the more experienced labor commanding top price from growers who know their abilities can measurably increase the value of their crop.

The freshly cut branches are rubbed with rods to loosen the bark, then cut with special knives designed for the process. The outermost bark is removed, yielding sheets of inner bark that will be dried gently in huts to a thin, brittle consistency. Intact pieces of this dried bark are made into cigar-shaped rolls of several sheets for each stick. They're exported in any number of cut lengths, but the uncut bales of cinnamon can be quite impressive, with stick lengths up to four feet in the fanciest examples.

Since the bark of true cinnamon is relatively thin, it can easily be ground into a fine powder at home using a coffee mill. The oils are very complex in taste and aroma and seem to deteriorate more rapidly than those of most other spices, so the extra step of grinding is well worth the effort here. A fine sifting after grinding will ensure that no small pieces of bark make it into your baking.

Because true cinnamon sticks, also called *quills*, are physically more delicate in nature than cassia, processing produces quite a lot of broken pieces and shreds, called *quillings*. These are usually destined for the grinder but are sometimes used to fill out lower grades of whole sticks. *Featherings* are other bits of the tree, unpeelable branches and twigs, which are mostly unusable except in the essential-oil industry.

There is a confusing grading system employed in Sri Lanka that is related to the quality of flavor, the thickness of the bark, and the overall appearance of a finished quill. Categories include Continental, Mexican, and Hamburg, none of which has anything to do with its associated geographic namesake. Within each category are number grades based on a variety of variables such as thickness, color, oil content, etc. There is little standardization of the system, so one estate's "Continental 5" may be equivalent to another one's "Mexican 5." Some ratings indicate a direct correlation between the number and the thickness of the bark, but examination of various lots has told me that this isn't always the case. I rely on the number grade as relative to each producer's product line rather than as a universal comparative. Typically each producer will attach the term "special" to the very best production, and thus "Continental 5 special" can be taken as the best they have to offer.

Rather than bog down in the industry's nomenclature, I suggest a simple visual inspection of the quills, looking for those with the fewest blemishes and an overall color that is consistently a light brown. Darker brown spots come from surface knots in the cinnamon branches and sometimes bring "off" flavors into the taste. Indeed, the pristine inner bark is the most desirable true cinnamon, for its flavor, potency, and appearance, and, as such, commands the higher price commensurate with its more labor-intensive harvest. Rougher bark has a relatively lower oil content and hence less taste, but it is obviously easier to obtain and the price reflects this fact.

In all cases, taste should be the real test of quality. If you chew a small piece, it should quickly take on a complex nature as a few seconds in your mouth rehydrate the essential oils. Essences of orange and cedar should come to the surface, followed by a distinctive heat reminiscent of clove or mild pepper. This bloom of complexity is the best indicator of quality, regardless of shape or form, and tells the buyer that he has found a fresh crop that's been properly harvested.

Other micro-crops found in the Maldives, coastal India, and Madagascar are also thought to be *C. zeylanicum*. In most cases, however, these alternative sources are considered inferior in quality and so find themselves primarily relegated to the essential-oil trade. Some small effort is also put into the production of cinnamon leaf oil, a commodity not usually associated with the food industry.

On the Indian subcontinent, it's true cinnamon that perfumes the curries of the south, flavors the rice and dal dishes of the north, and even finds its way into the tea called *chai* when served spiced and milked. Blended into spice classics like *garam masala*—the name meaning simply "sweet mix"—it provides a sweet flavor and mild heat.

The French fell in love, as they are apt to do, with true cinnamon following the Crusades, which led them into spice territory. Boulangeries quickly concocted *pain d'épices*, a spiced bread that took advantage of all the en vogue spices of the day: cinnamon, nutmeg, mace, and clove. Not simply relegated to sweet pastries as is common in modern times, cinnamon made its way into English savory meat pies, peppery condiments, and even the spiced wine known as *hypocras*.

The near nonexistence of true cinnamon in the American market for decades has led to a recent reawakening of interest, with new global consumers testing it in everything from cinnamon rolls to barbecue sauces. Where the typical cassia-cinnamon sold in America lent potency, true cinnamon lends complexity. Substitution between the two is done at equal ratios but gives pleasantly different results. Some cooks even aim for the best of both worlds and use a mix of the two.

INDONESIAN CASSIA-CINNAMON

ALTERNATE NAME **Sumatra cinnamon**

BOTANICAL NAME OF CULINARY SPECIES **Cinnamomum burmannii**

PLANT FAMILY **Laurel (Lauraceae)**

COUNTRY/REGION OF BOTANICAL ORIGIN **South Pacific**

MAJOR COUNTRIES/REGIONS OF CULTIVATION **Indonesia**

SEASONS OF HARVEST **Spring and fall**

PARTS USED **Bark**

COLOR **Medium to dark brown**

CHINESE CASSIA-CINNAMON

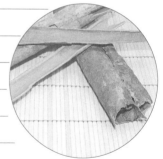

ALTERNATE NAME **Bastard cinnamon**

BOTANICAL NAMES OF CULINARY SPECIES **Cinnamomum cassia, Cinnamomum loureirii (Saigon cinnamon)**

PLANT FAMILY **Laurel (Lauraceae)**

COUNTRY/REGION OF BOTANICAL ORIGIN **Central Asia**

MAJOR COUNTRIES/REGIONS OF CULTIVATION **China, Vietnam**

SEASONS OF HARVEST **Spring and summer**

PARTS USED **Bark**

COLOR **Dark red-brown**

Cassias are the most commonly harvested cinnamon species from all over Indochina and account for something near half of the *Cinnamomum* crop worldwide. Cassia is sold in America generically as cinnamon and typically has a relatively high oil content, ranging from two to four percent. The flavor is both more simplistic and more intense than that of true cinnamon, but that does not lessen its culinary value. In fact, the intensity can work better than true cinnamons in complex curries or in dishes where the spice is featured prominently.

Each of the fancy whole sticks of all the cultivated cassia species starts as a square of bark cut from mature trees. The ends of this single layer curl back upon themselves to make a thick scroll-like stick, easily recognized as cassia rather than the collection of thinner sheets that make up true cinnamon sticks. Cassia is also sold as preground powder, a necessary evil because the superfine, flourlike consistency preferred by cooks is nearly impossible to achieve with home grinding. All cassia-cinnamon forms have a decidedly darker brown color than other species.

In America, cassia-cinnamons have been sold simply as "cinnamon" for decades to the exclusion of other species. Probably because of their relatively low cost, spice companies made the switch somewhere in the past, and now Americans know cassia better than true cinnamon. Yet, again, this is not to say that cassia is better or worse than true cinnamon, simply that it's different. When I want punch and potency, I reach for cassia; for complexity and subtlety, I grab the true cinnamon.

Indonesia, specifically the Korinjte coastal region of Sumatra, produces perhaps the best-known cassia, *Cinnamomum burmannii*, which has more savory character than others. The sticks are groomed more than those of their Chinese counterpart, *Cinnamomum cassia*, with the outer layer of bark peeled away in most cases. In comparison, the Chinese leave their harvest in a thicker, rough cut of bark with the outer bark still intact. And while the Chinese version does tend toward a sweeter character and the Indonesian toward a more savory one, this is a subtle difference at best, making substitution between the two a reasonable prospect in all but the most particular of recipes.

Vietnam, by comparison, produces a cassia-cinnamon, *Cinnamomum loureirii*, frequently termed Saigon cinnamon, that has a particularly high oil content—sometimes approaching eight percent—which, by its very intensity, changes the flavor somewhat. Its potency has gained it some degree of fame, but in tasting, the intensity can be overwhelming, and the flavor actually offers little difference from the Chinese sources, just more punch of the same flavor base.

From cinnamon toast to cola drinks, cassia-cinnamon has left its mark on the pop food culture. A stroll down the grocery aisles tells you that cinnamon has market appeal. I stopped counting references on packages somewhere between the breakfast cereals and the rice cakes, but anyone in the food business will tell you that cinnamon sells. And the range of products resulting from the eating public's love affair with the flavor proves that cinnamon can be incredibly versatile.

One lesser-known pairing that befits cassia-cinnamon is marriage with tomato sauces. A touch added to a pasta sauce brings warmth and richness in a hard-to-pinpoint fashion. Similarly, it's often the "secret" ingredient in Cincinnati-style chili and Kansas barbecue sauces.

Meat rubs from the Middle East have adopted cassia as much as they have true cinnamon. And, married with mint and pepper, cassia lends a rounding character that bridges the herbaceous with the heat in many of the regional spice mixes, such as *baharat* and *qalat daqqa*.

I discovered that it can be dangerous to leave cinnamon rolls made with the freshest cassia sitting out in your kitchen, especially with the windows open. Granted, if I need some painting or lawn work done on a Saturday morning, it's a good way to attract free labor. Those captivating aromatics are one of cassia's best assets, and the wise cook will take advantage of them as much as he uses the flavor. I frequently toss a few whole sticks into wine for poaching fruit, with excellent aroma results.

One of the more elusive parts of the cassia tree are its springtime buds. Looking like small caper berries, they're harvested just before they open in the spring. A portion of the stem is left intact on the end of the egg-shaped bud, and they are dried to a dark brown in the sun. They certainly have the cassia character, but they also lend an allspice and pepper taste to pickles and the like.

Triple-Rise Cinnamon Rolls

Anyone who has seen my baking efforts knows that I'm "challenged" in this department. I lack the precision pastry chefs possess. The only problem is that I also have a serious addiction to cinnamon rolls. When I first confronted the problem, I had the help of another member of "Bad Bakers Anonymous" who told me I just needed some successes in the kitchen to bolster my pastry confidence. He and I embarked on the quest for the perfect cinnamon roll, using a recipe that was more forgiving than some of the delicate versions we had both attempted before. What we found after far too many underwhelming tests was this version that relies on three rises, which help cover any dough-handling mistakes you might have made.

Cinnamon-flavored breads are nothing uncommon in the world, but sticky-sweet rolls flavored heavily with cinnamon are truly an American classic. I rely on a mix of cassia-cinnamon and true cinnamon for the spicing here, to gain the benefits of both. And while the recipe can be successfully cut in half, there will be no lack of interested parties, so I suggest you bake the full batch every time. You'll be sure to make new friends with any extras. **MAKES 24 ROLLS**

DOUGH

7 cups bread flour

4 packets of fast-rise dry yeast

1 cup granulated sugar

1 teaspoon fine sea salt

½ pound (2 sticks) unsalted butter, softened

2½ cups whole milk, heated until warm (115°F)

2 large eggs

FILLING

1 cup dark raisins

½ cup pecans, coarsely chopped (optional)

¾ cup granulated sugar

2 tablespoons ground cassia-cinnamon

1 tablespoon ground true cinnamon

½ teaspoon fine sea salt

GLAZE

One 1-pound box confectioners' sugar

1 teaspoon fine sea salt

½ cup hot water, or as needed

½ teaspoon pure vanilla extract

3 drops of orange oil (optional)

To make the dough, in the bowl of a stand mixer, combine half the flour, the yeast, sugar, salt, and butter, and mix with the paddle attachment. With the mixer on low speed, slowly add the milk and eggs. Switch to the dough hook and add the remaining flour. Knead for 9 minutes. Increase the speed to medium/medium-high and mix for 1 minute longer, to add lift to the dough.

Transfer the dough to a buttered bowl at least three times the volume of the dough. Cover with a towel and let rise in a warm location free of drafts until doubled in size, about 1½ hours.

Gently punch down the dough, cover, and let rise until doubled again, 1¼ to 1½ hours.

Meanwhile, to make the filling, soak the raisins in warm water for 10 to 20 minutes until plumped. Drain well. Combine the pecans, sugar, both cinnamons, and salt in a bowl and mix well. Add the raisins, and toss to mix.

Punch the dough down gently. Roll it out on a floured surface into a rectangle roughly 18 inches by 24 inches; avoid overworking the dough. With a pastry brush, brush off any excess flour. Mist the dough with water and spread the filling evenly over it; work quickly to preserve the life in the dough. Starting on a long side of the rectangle, roll the dough up evenly into a log, and pinch the seam to close. Cut the dough into 1-inch slices. Place slices on a greased 12-by-18-inch baking sheet, close but not touching. Cover the pan with a towel and allow to rise until the rolls touch each other, roughly 45 minutes.

Preheat the oven to 375°F. Bake the rolls for 15 to 20 minutes, until golden brown.

Meanwhile, to make the glaze, mix together in a bowl the confectioners' sugar, salt, hot water, vanilla, and orange oil, if using, until smooth; it should be the consistency of a thin paste. Remove the rolls from the oven, and brush with the glaze while they are still warm. Let cool on a rack, and serve warm or at room temperature.

Spiced Bananas Foster

This incredibly simple dish tends to impress dinner dates and dinner parties equally well. I had eaten the dessert on far too many a long night in my college days, wandering the streets of New Orleans, but didn't know how to make it for myself. A former employee of Brennan's restaurant, the establishment that made it famous as part of their fabulous brunch, came north to Seattle to open his own place specializing in New Orleans fare, and one day he wandered into my store. Since Southern drawls are easy to spot up here, we began chatting, discovered each other's roots, and ultimately got around to talking food.

The story goes that bananas were coming into the port of New Orleans like crazy back in the 1950s, and Mr. Brennan wanted to take advantage of them. Mr. Foster, a locally prominent businessman and frequent restaurant patron, came back from a trip to the "islands" and asked Mr. Brennan to have his chef "make something up" like he had eaten while abroad. Having recently obliged a magazine with the banana recipe, Mr. Brennan gave Mr. Foster this dish and the honor of having his name attached to the now-famous dessert.

Now that I can all but make this in my sleep, I frequently take liberties with proportions and spice ingredients. Friends regularly show up on my doorstep with bananas in hand and sheepish grins on their faces, the perfect excuse to try adding some fresh ginger, a bit of chile pepper, or even a small measure of mint. I've made this for two over a camp stove at ten thousand feet and for forty in a paella pan on a barbecue grill. Needless to say, butter, sugar, bananas, and rum taste good just about any way you can get them together. This is simply a spicier version of the classic as told to me. **SERVES 4**

4 generous scoops of vanilla ice cream

1 cup packed light brown sugar

1 teaspoon ground cassia-cinnamon

½ teaspoon cayenne

¼ teaspoon fine sea salt

2 teaspoons very finely minced fresh ginger

4 tablespoons unsalted butter

4 bananas, split lengthwise and halved

¼ cup banana liqueur

¼ cup dark rum

Place the ice cream in serving bowls and return to the freezer.

Combine the sugar, cassia-cinnamon, cayenne, sea salt, and ginger in a bowl and mix well. Place the butter in the center of a nonstick skillet and mound the sugar mixture on top. Set over medium heat and allow the butter to melt under the sugar; avoid stirring unless absolutely necessary. Once the butter has melted, stir constantly until the sugar foams over the top of the mixture, 2 to 3 minutes. Add the bananas cut side up. Carefully add the liqueur and rum and use a long kitchen match to ignite them. Once the flames have died down, turn the bananas in the sauce with long tongs and cook for 2 minutes longer.

Spoon the hot bananas and sauce over the ice cream and serve instantly.

CINNAMON, WHITE

ALTERNATE NAME **Canela (Spanish)**

BOTANICAL NAME OF CULINARY SPECIES **Cinnamomum alba**

PLANT FAMILY **Laurel (Lauraceae)**

COUNTRY/REGION OF BOTANICAL ORIGIN **West Indies**

MAJOR COUNTRIES/REGIONS OF CULTIVATION **Caribbean, Mexico, Central America**

SEASON OF HARVEST **Spring**

PARTS USED **Bark**

COLOR **Tan**

Early Spaniards thought they'd hit the cinnamon jackpot when they discovered *Cinnamomum alba* growing in the Americas. It looked like, smelled like, and tasted like cinnamon—who can blame them for naming it "white cinnamon" and loading their ships to the brim for the voyage back to Europe?

This species is generally held to be a native of the West Indies, and it was indeed used culinarily by the indigenous peoples. The bark is thin, soft, and pliable like true cinnamon, with a white outer layer, hence the name. The flavor, however, is rougher than true cinnamon, with little complexity and a lower concentration of oil than the Asian cassias. While traded on the world markets, white cinnamon represents a much smaller portion of the global supply than cassias and true cinnamons.

The Spanish word for cinnamon, *canela*, is frequently used interchangeably for both true cinnamon and white cinnamon, given their common appearance. And their substitution makes sense in the kitchen, although the quantities may need to be adjusted in the context of the dish. While Chinese or Indonesian cassia could be used in place of white cinnamon, you will get different, more pungent results with the former two.

CLOVES

BOTANICAL NAME OF CULINARY SPECIES **Eugenia caryophyllus**

PLANT FAMILY **Myrtaceae**

COUNTRY/REGION OF BOTANICAL ORIGIN **Molucca Islands**

MAJOR COUNTRIES/REGIONS OF CULTIVATION **Madagascar, Zanzibar, India, Sri Lanka, Spice Islands**

SEASON OF HARVEST **Spring to early summer**

PARTS USED **Unopened buds**

COLOR **Dark brown, with creamy orange heads**

If it were not for the lure of cloves, the Portuguese, Dutch, and Spanish explorers of the fifteenth century might simply have stayed home, the Americas might not have been discovered by the Europeans, and Great Britain might not have built a global empire.

The spice trade motivated what became the first successful circumnavigation of the globe in 1522 by Magellan, or rather by what was left of his expedition after his death in the Philippines. Specifically, the Spanish king wanted to confirm in whose territory the Moluccas lay, as the spice riches they produced could determine the balance of power back in Europe. Cloves and nutmeg from the twin islands of Ternate and Tidore became the jewel every crown desired. Lucrative monopolies by the Portuguese, the Spanish, the Dutch, and, ultimately, the English resulted in some of the greatest fortunes, bloodiest battles, and eventually the exploration of the entire globe.

On the more pungent end of the taste spectrum, cloves can actually be intense enough to "burn" the palate unless well blended in a dish, and even then in sparing amounts. The taste is similar to the peppery, sweet heat of allspice but with an even more edgy bite.

Actually the unopened bud of the clove tree, cloves are harvested painstakingly by hand just as they are turning pink, nature's indication of peak flavor and aroma.

Each looks like some tiny tubular undersea creature, with four prongs at the tip holding each of the immature flower petals; these will ultimately make the rounded "head" of the dried clove. They're sun-dried to the familiar dark brown stem color in the open air over three to four days, turned by hand to encourage the process. The best grade of cloves will have an intact, rounded tip of a lighter orange beige. Avoid samples where this head is as dark as the stem, or with excessive breakage of the rounded portion, which happens as the cloves become more brittle with age. The important flavoring oils rapidly dissipate as well, leaving behind only the strongest bite with none of the corresponding sweetness of a freshly dried batch.

The "great spice race" of the 1400s was to find the ocean path from Europe, where a small cargo of cloves could buy you a lordship and a very nice little castle in the countryside, to the source in the South Pacific, the Molucca Islands in the Indonesian Archipelago, whose treasure had only been supplied overland via Chinese, Indian, Turkish, and Venetian trade routes. The mere idea of this lucrative trade brought on a fever pitch of exploration rivaling the biggest gold rush or space race of modern times. Brave seamen risked up to an eighty percent mortality rate from scurvy, rough seas, or even pirates during voyages that could take from two to ten years.

Today's leading producers of cloves are Madagascar, Sri Lanka, and Zanzibar, as well as India. Just setting foot on the islands gives a visitor a sense of what treasures lie throughout the countryside. The trees emit enough clove essence and aroma naturally to perfume the hillsides liberally. New pinkish foliage matures to large waxy green leaves that magically scent the air when rustled by even the slightest of winds. Even rubbing the bark of a tree releases the characteristic clove smell. It's no wonder this olfactory landscape caused the first explorers to abandon their ships and simply retire amidst the beauty and serenity there.

Clove oil, extracted commercially, has numbing intensity. It's so strong that it's been used historically as a painkiller. It was this potency that allowed it to become a globally traded commodity during the era before overnight delivery. Even with several years of aging in transit, cloves could continue to impart flavor thousands of miles away from their source. Their geographic cousin nutmeg had similar holding power, and together the two propelled the Banda Islands of the South Seas into trading fame (and fortune).

Back in the kitchen, cloves have been relegated to sweets in the West but are beginning to re-emerge in savory dishes. The rest of the world has never forgotten their power in meat rubs, curries, and picklings. Certainly they can work well in sweet mixes with nutmeg and cinnamon, but matching them with savory herbs like sage or peppery blends accomplishes the often-elusive balance between sweet and heat. Canadian meat pies, a favorite, call upon cloves as a top note amidst spices that would otherwise be dark and heavy.

As potent as they are, cloves can keep well for upwards of a year when whole, but, as with any spice, they lose their punch when ground. Since it takes very little of them to impress their flavor, I like to grind my cloves with other ingredients to make them easier to measure into a recipe. It's easier to add 2 teaspoons of pumpkin pie spice than ⅛ teaspoon of pure cloves.

A holiday tradition in the Northern Hemisphere calls for an orange to be studded with cloves over its whole surface. These pomanders can be fragrant and beautiful but a real pain on your thumbs when you make them. Pre-drill holes in the orange peel with a toothpick before you start and use thimbles on your thumb and fingers, and you'll have an easier time.

CORIANDER, EUROPEAN

ALTERNATE NAME **See Cilantro, page 111**

BOTANICAL NAME OF CULINARY SPECIES *Coriandrum sativum*

PLANT FAMILY **Parsley (*Umbelliferae*)**

COUNTRIES/REGIONS OF BOTANICAL ORIGIN **Baltic regions**

MAJOR COUNTRIES/REGIONS OF CULTIVATION **Egypt, India, Canada**

SEASON OF HARVEST **Year-round**

PARTS USED **Seeds**

COLOR **Yellow-brown**

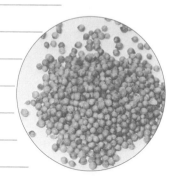

Coriander is one of the unsung heroes of the spice world. The undercurrent of flavor in everything from crab boils to curries, it gives the cook a savory base to work from and a bright top note to which to aspire.

For the seed forms of *Coriandrum sativum*, freshness is of paramount importance but perhaps one of the hardest things to judge when staring at the spice shelves in your local grocery. The problem is that the appearance of the seed changes very little over time. In the European species, the lightly ridged seeds are almost perfectly round and roughly the same size as peppercorns. Color is your first appraisal criterion, although not a perfect gauge. Look for a yellowish brown that isn't washed out or bleached, which would be a sign of age that comes from exposure to light. Perhaps the more important and reliable way to judge is to grind a small amount and smell. While they tend to frown on your doing this in the grocery aisle, it truly is the only way to tell if coriander is worth the price. What you should smell in the freshly crushed seeds can only be described as lemon-zest sharpness. These are the volatile oils coming back to life once you've released them with the grinder.

It's this lemonlike aroma and flavor in both the European and Indian species that has been used as a base for almost all curries, a sharp "pop" of flavor in picklings, and a key flavor enhancer in crab boils. Its ability to give simultaneously a bottom and top note to the palate makes it the perfect framework to which you can add, say, in the case of curry, doses of cinnamon, cardamom, and peppers. The coriander will manage to show through just enough without obscuring the other, more diverse flavors.

The seeds can be used whole in stocks or "boils," where straining will take place after cooking, or in spice "solutions" like corned beef brine, where there will be plenty of opportunity to get the tough seeds out of your way. Whether you pickle cucumbers or melon rinds, whole coriander will be part of the mix, along with mustard seeds, celery seeds, and peppercorns at minimum.

For the ground spice, always grind fresh when possible, but with coriander, the outer "husks" of the seeds can be a bit of a problem. They manage to elude the grinding blades in all but the most industrial of processes, so at home, I'd suggest a fine sifting of the just-ground product. Since coriander is inexpensive, don't drive yourself nuts trying to regrind the leftover husks. Just grind about ten percent more than the recipe calls for and discard any tough bits left in the sifter.

Once you've ground the seeds, you're ready to embark on any of several long paths in spice blending. Curries and masalas, barbecue rubs, and most Middle Eastern blends all begin with a base of coriander. It has the ability to intertwine with any number of other, brighter flavors like cinnamon, cardamom, and clove. At the other end of the flavor spectrum, it plays well with peppercorns, chiles, and mustard. This is the beauty of basing your recipes on coriander; it's next to impossible to make a mistake.

CORIANDER, INDIAN

BOTANICAL NAME OF CULINARY SPECIES *Coriandrum sativum, spp. Oblechum*

PLANT FAMILY **Parsley (*Umbelliferae*)**

COUNTRY/REGION OF BOTANICAL ORIGIN **India**

MAJOR COUNTRIES/REGIONS OF CULTIVATION **India, Pakistan**

SEASONS OF HARVEST **Summer and fall**

PARTS USED **Seeds**

COLOR **Greenish-yellow**

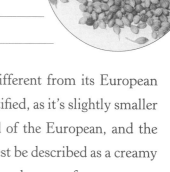

The Indian species of coriander seed looks slightly different from its European counterpart and has a less edgy taste. It's readily identified, as it's slightly smaller and distinctly egg-shaped rather than the perfect round of the European, and the color has more yellow-green hues. It exhibits what can best be described as a creamy quality of flavor. When chewing on a new shipment sample, one of my crew exclaimed, "Lemon Creamsicle," which prompted several coriander experiments at the neighborhood gelato shop.

I like the Indian varieties as much as the European in curries, but where they can really show their own is in the more delicate *kormas* and *birianyi* of the Kashmir. Their creamy character blends better and plays well with the fresh cheese, or *paneer*, often called for in the region.

Root Vegetable Curry

There are two secrets to a great curry: the cooking time must be long and slow, and the ingredients, especially the spices, must be painfully fresh. Grind the curry powder just before it goes into the pot so that the release of flavors occurs in the pot, not in the spice jar.

In this dish, the potato actually breaks down and acts as a thickener, whereas the other root vegetables hold their form, even with the extended cooking time. As with all curries, the flavors come together over time, so leftovers are a real treat. In fact, I actually cook my more complex curries a day before I plan to serve them to allow this melding of tastes. **SERVES 4**

3 tablespoons peanut oil

2 teaspoons ground Indian coriander

1 cup peeled, diced turnips

1 cup peeled, diced carrots

1 cup peeled, diced parsnips

1 cup diced yellow onions

2 tablespoons freshly ground Madras-style curry powder (see page 385), or more to taste

2 cups chicken or vegetable stock

1 cup diced potato

1 tablespoon finely diced fresh hot red chiles (optional)

Hot cooked rice, for serving

Minced scallions, for garnish (optional)

Minced cilantro, for garnish (oprional)

Yogurt, for serving (optional)

Heat the oil and coriander in a medium saucepan over medium-high heat. Add the turnips, carrots, parsnips, and onions, and cook, stirring, until slightly caramelized, 6 to 8 minutes. Add the curry powder and cook, stirring, until the curry coats the vegetables. Add enough water to cover, and simmer over low heat for 2 hours, adding more water as needed to keep the ingredients covered.

Add the stock, potato, and chile peppers, if using. Simmer for about 1 hour more, until the liquid reduces and the potatoes break apart and thicken the dish. Serve over rice, garnished with the scallions or cilantro, if using, and plain yogurt, if using, to cool the heat.

NOTE: For an extra treat, cook the rice with a few green cardamom pods, a cinnamon stick, or a few threads of saffron to impart a delicate perfume and light flavor that will offset the heavier curry.

CORIANDER, VIETNAMESE

ALTERNATE NAMES **Vietnamese Mint, Smartweed, Laksa plant, *Rau ram* (Vietnamese), *Daun kesom* (Malay)**

BOTANICAL NAME OF CULINARY SPECIES ***Persicaria odorata***

PLANT FAMILY **Buckwheat (*Polygonaceae*)**

COUNTRY/REGION OF BOTANICAL ORIGIN: **Southeast Asia**

MAJOR COUNTRIES/REGIONS OF CULTIVATION **Widely over Indochina**

SEASON OF HARVEST **Year-round**

PARTS USED **Leaves**

COLORS **Green, or green variegated with purple and red**

This leaf is sold in large bundles that might lead you to believe it's to be used as a vegetable rather than a spice. In fact, the bundles are simply the result of the volume of consumption in the kitchens of Vietnam, where it is most popular. Once you start using Vietnamese coriander, sometimes called Vietnamese mint, you might find yourself asking for it in bulk as well.

It's actually completely unrelated to European coriander or mint, but it exhibits the same citrus flavors as coriander leaf (cilantro) but with a crisper character that doesn't muddle the tastes of dishes. Almost a cross between cilantro and galangal in flavor, it mixes well in Asian recipes heavy in ginger.

Given its various regional labels, naming confusion might be the biggest obstacle to obtaining the genuine article. *Laksa,* for example, is the name of a noodle dish that calls for the leaves, and so *"laksa* herb" might be found in the Malay market, where next door at the Vietnamese grocery, they'd call it *rau ram*. If you're far from any Asian market, substituting ordinary cilantro won't ruin your cooking, it will simply be a bit further from authentic. Fresh cilantro would be a much better substitute than dried Vietnamese coriander, since the drying process destroys all the unique flavor.

A typical Vietnamese condiment incorporates the leaf in a sort of pesto technique with candlenuts, garlic, and galangal. Proportions vary according to taste, but the pounded paste is set out to perk up anything that comes to the table. You might expect chiles to be added, given the cuisine's propensity toward heat, but since Vietnamese coriander has its own peppery bite, none are really necessary.

CREAM OF TARTAR

ALTERNATE NAMES **Tartaric acid**

BOTANICAL NAME OF CULINARY SPECIES **N/A**

PLANT FAMILY **N/A**

COUNTRY/REGION OF BOTANICAL ORIGIN **N/A**

MAJOR COUNTRIES/REGIONS OF PRODUCTION **France, United States**

AVAILABILITY **Year-round**

PARTS USED **N/A**

COLOR **Pure white**

Again on the quest for tart, the French noticed something while pursuing their great passion, wine. On the inside of aging casks, a white crystalline substance, tartaric acid, formed as a natural by-product of the winemaking (and aging) process. The mystery substance was found to be as tart as lemon juice and was quickly pressed into service in French kitchens.

Another curious side effect came up in the French bakeries when meringues were being made. It seems that this magical substance had the ability to give lift to and stabilize the delicate whipped egg whites. Cream of tartar isn't used so much as a flavoring as it is for its stabilizing effects, especially considering the small amounts typically called for in recipes. While it will add a tiny amount of sour taste, added sugar in most recipes for, say, snickerdoodle cookies, will obscure any sourness it may impart. Chemically speaking, it's potassium bitartrate, derived from the impure form, sometimes called argol, that originally formed back in the wineries. This weak acid is used in making baking powder, but in the purer form it more noticeably stabilizes by forming complex molecules with proteins, like those found in egg whites. These altered molecules do a better job of entrapping air, and thus give more volume to soufflés and other dishes that rely on the egg whites staying aloft.

CUBEB

ALTERNATE NAME **Tailed pepper**

BOTANICAL NAME OF CULINARY SPECIES *Piper cubeba*

PLANT FAMILY **Pepper (*Piperaceae*)**

COUNTRY/REGION OF BOTANICAL ORIGIN **India**

MAJOR COUNTRIES/REGIONS OF CULTIVATION **Central Africa, India**

SEASON OF HARVEST **Year-round**

PARTS USED **Bud fruits**

COLOR **Black-brown**

Cubeb is one of the "ancient" spices that has found a new home in only the most adventurous modern kitchens of the West. Overshadowed by the more common black peppercorn when trade routes to India were established, *cubeb* deserves a place in the modern pantry for its remarkable intensity of flavor.

Before what we know as peppercorns became widely available in the Middle Ages, there were several other spices found in Europe and the Middle East that had the same peppery bite, but with a slightly different character. In the case of *cubeb*, there are hints of ginger and allspice alongside the familiar pepper taste.

Tiny round black buds, each with its own "tail" of a stem, give off a unique aroma and impart an earthy bite to dishes from the Middle East and North Africa, its primary area of cultivation. Used in Chinese herbal remedies, *cubeb* is noted for its warming properties. The astute cook can use this with great effect as he would clove or allspice.

There is another species found in Africa called Ashanti pepper, which has a less bitter character but as much of the peppery bite as in true *cubebs*. This species can be easily differentiated by its curved rather than straight "tail" and a more oval shape than true *cubeb*'s round body.

When I first started learning my way around spice exotica, I came across *cubeb* in texts but had the nagging feeling you get when you can't place a name. I knew I had seen it before, but for years couldn't figure out where it had crossed my path. I drove my friends nuts talking about my mystery *cubeb* reference until one sunny afternoon, sitting on a café balcony, I got into a debate about, of all things, the best-quality gin. Four gin and tonics into the discussion, we asked the barman to bring us the bottles to settle the argument about this or that producer and there, etched artfully into the side of a Bombay Sapphire bottle, was mystery *cubeb* along with grains of paradise and juniper. It has been part of their premium recipe for decades.

CULANTRO

ALTERNATE NAMES Long coriander, Mexican coriander, Spiny coriander, Sawleaf

BOTANICAL NAME OF CULINARY SPECIES *Eryngium foetidum*

PLANT FAMILY Parsley (*Umbelliferae*)

COUNTRY/REGION OF BOTANICAL ORIGIN Caribbean

MAJOR COUNTRIES/REGIONS OF CULTIVATION Southern Mexico, Caribbean, Southeast Asia

SEASON OF HARVEST Year-round

PARTS USED Leaves

COLOR Matte green

A cousin to the common coriander plant, culantro is one of those herb mysteries that Caribbean cultures have spun into legend for touring cooks. It has all the zest of cilantro leaves but with a unique bitter pepper twist born of the sun-drenched island communities that embrace it in their unique cuisines.

The leaf looks much like Californian bay, but it has a characteristic serrated edge and isn't nearly as thick. When rubbed between your fingers, it will give a uniquely lemon aroma, but a quick taste suggests something closer to celery. It's a flavor comparable to cilantro and echoes some of the same herbaceous peaks on the palate.

Culantro makes its way into the American markets via the South Florida communities that have ties to Cuba. Many grow it in their own gardens there, but it's rare as a dried product and then usually disguised with any of its many alternate names or even mislabeled as cilantro. Look for the unique leaf shape and ignore anything else you might find inscribed on the label.

In all its native Caribbean Island communities, you'll see culantro as a base "pesto" made with garlic and chiles, used to start any number of dishes. It is also shredded fine and stirred into salsas and cold soups to infuse flavor. The leaves can be quickly deep-fried and ground to crust or garnish fish and seafood.

Vietnamese markets also sell bundles of the herb, with frilly tufts of new growth at the tips. It has integrated itself into Southeast Asian cuisines to the extent that it is as common as cilantro, whether by design or by simple opportunity, given that it grows widely in the area. Typically added to meat dishes and soups, it's almost always used fresh.

CUMIN, BROWN

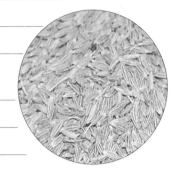

ALTERNATE NAMES *Shah jeera* (India), **White cumin**

BOTANICAL NAME OF CULINARY SPECIES *Cuminum cyminum*

PLANT FAMILY Parsley (*Umbelliferae*)

COUNTRY/REGION OF BOTANICAL ORIGIN Middle East

MAJOR COUNTRIES/REGIONS OF CULTIVATION India, widely across Middle East, Africa, Mexico, Canada

SEASON OF HARVEST Late summer into fall

PARTS USED Seeds

COLOR Light yellow-brown

Cumin in the wild is a less than impressive-looking plant. Even the giant fields of it that you see in Mexico and India look very much like overgrown garden patches. The extra-thin branches seem very weedlike and the flowers, while a beautiful purple white, are few and short-lived. It's the seeds that form soon after flowering that have made this plant, originally from the river deltas of Egypt, one of the most universally accepted spice flavors.

The pods form in clusters, and at harvest they are thrashed to release the yellowish seeds. They dry quickly to more of a green brown, and it's this color the buyer should look for instead of the older washed-brown color of aging seeds. Certainly an aroma akin to fresh cilantro should be present in a fresh supply, and a quick rub of the seeds between your palms should bring this scent back readily.

Found in ancient Egypt, cumin may very well be the original cultivated seed-spice. Used then both for ritual practices in the temple and for dinner practices in the mortar, it later made its way across Africa with the Moors on their romps up through Spain. Explorers from Iberia and traders from Africa took the spice to the New World. Eastward, Ottoman Turks adopted the flavor and sent it all through the Indian peninsula and even to the reaches of Southeast Asia. All of these cultures have made it a staple spice and, thus, a signature flavor in dishes from curry to *mole*. The flavor lingers on the tongue and can overpower when freshly harvested, so longer cooking in more complex blends seems to fit well, from *garam masala* in India to chili powders in America.

In India, there is some naming confusion that can be misleading. Cumin, or *shah jeera*, looks very much like other tiny ridged seeds including caraway, fennel, and ajwain, all of which have been mistranslated as the same. To confuse matters more, there is *kala jeera*, or black cumin, which has a different flavor profile from the "regular" cumin we know. Curiously, this entire family of spices can be intermingled with frequent success, albeit with wholly different results.

The seeds are used in baking, cheese making, countless curries and *masalas*, and even, sparingly, in fresh salsas. In some cases, a toasting to begin the release of flavor is advisable but, again, the cook's choice is the real guide. I rather like to toast a portion for the earthy component and leave some raw for the greener character.

I remember one bleary morning in my college days that left me staring into a stranger's pantry and finding only two items: eggs and a tin of ground cumin. It actually worked well, and I've since slipped bits of cumin into many of my egg dishes. I have, however, made it a point to check the pantry before I get myself into an all-night poker game.

Beets Roasted with Cumin

Cumin is one of those seeds whose flavor changes with roasting. While I like both "versions" of cumin taste, the heady character it takes on under intense heat is perfectly matched to the sweetness of beets in this treatment. To borrow the opening lines of Tom Robbins' *Jitterbug Perfume*, "The beet is the most intense of vegetables . . . the beet is deadly serious." Roasted cumin may not be as serious but I'd rather not meet it in a dark alley late at night. **SERVES 4 AS A SIDE DISH**

1 tablespoon whole cumin seeds

1½ pounds fresh beets, washed, peeled, and cut into 1-inch dice

1 tablespoon freshly ground cumin seed

2 tablespoons olive oil

2 tablespoons melted butter

In a dry skillet over medium heat, lightly toast the whole cumin seeds for 1 to 2 minutes, and allow to cool. Grind the cumin seeds in a coffee mill.

Cook the beets in a pot of boiling water until barely softened, about 5 minutes. Drain and toss the beets with the oil, butter, and ground cumin. Spread on a sheet pan and sprinkle with whole cumin seeds. Place under broiler and roast, tossing occasionally, until fork tender, but allowing some charred edges to form, about 15 minutes.

CUMIN, BLACK

ALTERNATE NAME *Kala jeera* (India)

BOTANICAL NAME OF CULINARY SPECIES *Bunium persicum*

PLANT FAMILY Parsley (*Umbelliferae*)

COUNTRY/REGION OF BOTANICAL ORIGIN Northern India

MAJOR COUNTRIES/REGIONS OF CULTIVATION Northern India

SEASON OF HARVEST Fall

PARTS USED Seeds

COLOR Brown black, with almost white ridges

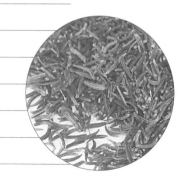

People often forget how big a country India is. The northern Kashmir regions can be like night and day compared with those of the south. In the cuisine, this difference shows up in subtle but important ways, and black cumin is a perfect example, being commonplace in the north but only rarely used in the south.

A relative of brown cumin, the plant produces seeds in the same fashion but with a much thinner shape and sweeter character. The spice is frequently mistranslated as *nigella*, black onion seed, which has a jet-black color and an altogether different shape. To differentiate, "black" cumin seeds are actually dark brown and of an elongated, ridged shape like fennel or caraway.

Musty in character with grassy hay aromas, black cumin makes its way into some of the more exotic blends of North India, Persia, and the Middle East. Cream-based *kormas* often call for its gentle sweetness instead of the potentially overpowering "white" cumin. These seeds are more prone to losing their flavor than regular cumin, so use them quickly and sniff them before buying to make sure they don't have a dusty, stale aroma.

CURRY LEAF

ALTERNATE NAMES *Neem* (India), *Kari patta* (India), *Kari pincha* (Sri Lanka), *Bai karee* (Thailand)

BOTANICAL NAME OF CULINARY SPECIES *Murraya koenigii*

PLANT FAMILY **Citrus** *(Rutaceae)*

COUNTRY/REGION OF BOTANICAL ORIGIN **India**

MAJOR COUNTRIES/REGIONS OF CULTIVATION **India, Sri Lanka, Southeast Asia, widely throughout tropical regions**

SEASON OF HARVEST **Year-round, especially spring**

PARTS USED **Leaves**

COLOR **Matte green**

I wish these wonderfully delicate leaves had a different name. The amount of confusion their common name causes can be maddening for cooks (and spice merchants), and in fact very few classic recipes for curry, the dish, call for them.

What the fresh leaves offer is a nutty fragrance and flavor best held for lighter fare or used as an aromatic complement. When they are crushed in the palm of my hand, the smell reminds me of fresh nuts, but it dissipates rapidly to leave behind a mildly bitter taste. The dried leaves, in my experience, hold little of the original flavor, and thus curry leaf should really be sought fresh in the produce sections of Indian and Asian groceries. The pointed leaves are half the size of bay laurel and more elongated. The younger shoots have more potency, and they can be beaten into a paste as in the condiments and curry pastes of southern India and Southeast Asia.

Curry leaves are sold both as intact branches and as "destemmed" leaves; I prefer the former, as they seem to give you a bit more shelf life. The leaves tend to curl upon themselves as they dry, so look for entirely flat leaves and a consistent matte green color throughout. Darkening blotches are a sign of decay, and such leaves should be avoided.

The curry plant is a heat lover, and while its main harvests come from the Indian subcontinent, Asia, and the Middle East, it's cultivated, albeit on a much smaller scale, just about anywhere that has a warm climate. Growers in the United States are mostly in Southern California, but hothouse cultivation allows most major urban markets to have a nearby source. My home-gardening friends tell me that once started, the plants are prolific enough to make a useful-sized crop for their own kitchens.

Perhaps the most common use of curry leaf is as a finishing aromatic component (rather than a base ingredient) in the curries of Central and South India. In those same kitchens, you see it used as Western cooks would bay leaf, in stocks and soups. One of the nicest illustrations of curry leaf, however, is in the tandoor oven, as both an additive to the dough and a topping on *naan*, the classic flatbread served with almost every meal in India. Vegetarian cuisines from the same regions use the leaf heavily, as the flavor melds well with the lighter fare. Classic dishes using peas, *dal*, lentils, and even homemade *paneer* cheese all find curry leaf introduced to lift the accompanying gravies and sauces out of the mundane and into the lighter, more complex palate.

Since aromatics are important in what curry leaves bring your dish, they should typically be added late in the cooking process to preserve that character. More rarely, you may want to gain the bitter character by cooking longer, but this will be at the expense of the aroma. It's not uncommon for stocks and soups to call for two measures of curry leaf, one "for the boil" and one "for the finish." Removal of the spent leaf after cooking is at the cook's discretion and is strictly an aesthetic choice.

One of the best descriptions of curry leaf I've heard came from a young customer one summer afternoon. A girl of perhaps five years of age had turned her nose up at just about every smell in the shop, but at the prompting of her mother to sniff curry leaves, she exclaimed, "It's a peanut butter plant!" I can't possibly improve on that assessment.

DILL

ALTERNATE NAMES	**Dill weed, Dill seed**
BOTANICAL NAME(S) OF CULINARY SPECIES	***Anethum graveolen* (European), *Anethum sowa* (Indian)**
PLANT FAMILY	**Parsley (*Umbelliferae*)**
COUNTRY/REGION OF BOTANICAL ORIGIN	**Northern Europe and Russia**
MAJOR COUNTRIES/REGIONS OF CULTIVATION	**Northern Hemisphere, notably Russia, Poland, Scandinavia, Turkey, and Canada**
SEASONS OF HARVEST	**Summer and early fall (dill weed), Late summer and fall (dill seed)**
PARTS USED	**Leaves, Seeds, Flowers**
COLORS	**Deep green (leaves), Beige-brown (seeds), Yellow flowers**

The dill plant gives us two tools in the spice cabinet. Both its leaf and its seed are common ingredients, but which of the two you use comes to a question of intensity. The leaf is a delicate form that dances on the herbal palate, lightly hinting at sour, while the seed is more intense and punches through in robust fare fit for the heartiest of appetites.

Dried dill weed has impressions of an incredibly mild vinegar mixed with a light herb like chervil. This very subtle sour character is what most people recognize as "dill," but there is a corresponding mild sweetness that only comes with very fresh or recently dried sources. It's this balance of sweet and tart that makes dill weed a flavor that can stand alone in dishes or simply raise the bar of taste in a more complex preparation.

Dill seed, by comparison, has little aroma until crushed or ground. It reminds me more of its seed-cousins, caraway, anise, and celery seed, in taste. There's even more of the sour flavor than in the leaf, but the herbaceous character is left behind and replaced with a hint of stinging bite on the tongue.

The "weed" is simply the leaf portion of the plant that grows in wispy branches along tall slender stalks, sometimes reaching as high as four feet. These tiny leaves are stripped from tougher stalks when fresh and are best dried in commercial processes that can capture the most flavor. Brilliant green in color, the dried leaves hold their flavor for only a few months at best, so frequent turnover of your stock should be standard protocol.

The seed is obtained from the plants late in the growing season, after large umbels with hundreds of tiny yellow flowers mature. Flattened and ridged, the beige-colored seeds are ringed with a lighter border and have relatively sharp edges. They will drop from the head when ripe, even after it's been cut. Old harvesting techniques simply hung the cut flowers over cloth to catch the seeds, but modern techniques thrash the nearly ripe seeds from the flower heads by machine.

Some small species variance is found in India with *Anethum sowa*, but this is cultivated on a much smaller scale than the dill of Europe and exhibits only a mildly different taste. The seeds look similar in color and have a slightly more elongated shape than the more common European varieties. Substitution between the species is easily done.

As for selection of quality leaves, if there's any grayish color and/or no pungent "pickle" smell, you should pass and look for a fresher batch. Similarly, look for whole leaves, as tiny as they are, instead of broken or powdered versions. Seeds can prove more difficult to grade, but look for unbroken seeds that release a pungent smell when lightly crushed.

Fresh dill weed is now more common year-round thanks to a growing hydroponics cultivation for the specialty fresh herb markets in the West. Later summer harvests from the traditional fields can also yield entire branches of fresh dill in local markets. Treat them as you would fresh flowers and keep the ends immersed in water to help extend the life. Snip off the leaf tips or simply strip entire branches with your fingers. As the stalks begin to wilt, strip off the leaves and dry or freeze them to get a few more weeks of flavor out of them. Entire heads of late-season dill can also be used in making pickles by simply lopping off the tougher lower stalks and immersing the remaining tips in vinegar or your pickling brine to infuse flavor. Conveniently, the whole plant cuttings appear in markets just as an abundance of cucumbers and other pickling fodder start to arrive.

Native to Northern Europe and Russia, dill makes an appearance in all the cuisines of these regions. Its name comes from the Nordic *dilla*, meaning "to lull," because of its calming effects. Its medicinal use dates back to the third century B.C. More familiarly, it's seen in the sour cream- and yogurt-based sauces of Scandinavia and the borscht of Russia, as well as being a perfectly adaptable taste for the wild variety of fish from the Black and Caspian seas. In these latter Baltic regions, both leaf and seed are strewn about the cuisine liberally. Anything with root vegetables gets dill, and even flavored salts of the region get some of their sour character from grinding the seed together with other spices of the region (see Svanetti Salt, page 375).

Taken back to Rome very early with the empire's expansion and easy overland trade routes, dill was used first medicinally as a mild sedative and digestive aid, only later gaining favor as an all-around seasoning. Seen as a plant "of good omen," it was baked into breads and celebrated as a taste of the gods at the same time that laurels of the flowers were used to crown returning soldiers in victory.

Dill was, in turn, propagated extensively across the entire Northern Hemisphere, first by early European settlers and much later by American pioneers, who planted it with other fall crops such as cabbage and cucumbers. Naturally, dishes incorporated these commonly harvested flavors together, giving rise to the ubiquitous picklings in anticipation of the winter season.

A simple sauce of plain yogurt, dill weed, and sea salt, all to personal taste, can be made even days ahead as a complement to poached or smoked salmon, and a cold preparation such as this will preserve more of the weed's flavor. In hot dishes, be sure to add the herb toward the end of cooking to avoid vaporizing the delicate herbal taste. The seeds have enough intensity to support crushing, grinding, and heating in all sorts of dishes that need savory or bitter tones. Some rye bread recipes call for as much dill seed as caraway, and most seafood boils will use the seeds in whole or crushed forms and allow the cooking process to release the flavor within.

Oven-blasted Cauliflower with Dill and Lemon

A favorite bar run by some expatriate Bulgarians made this simple cauliflower dish, whose only spice flavors are the sour of dill weed married to the sour of lemon juice. They tell me the technique is used in their home country on any strongly flavored vegetable, including turnips or cabbage, but always with only a single, abundant vegetable that is in full harvest at the time. True peasant food! Curiously, I discovered it went well with my occasional after-work Scotch, another dense flavor they just happen to have at the bar. **SERVES 4**

1 head cauliflower, stemmed and broken into fist-sized pieces

1 cup fruity white wine

1 tablespoon vodka

Juice of 1 lemon

1 tablespoon dried dill weed

Fine sea salt, to taste

2 tablespoons heavy whipping cream

2 tablespoons shredded Parmigiano-Reggiano cheese

Pita bread, for serving

Preheat the oven to 450°F. Steam the cauliflower over boiling water until the thickest part can be pierced easily with a sharp knife. Transfer to a baking dish.

Mix the wine, vodka, lemon juice, dill, and salt together in a bowl. Drizzle the mixture over the cauliflower. Bake for 15 minutes, basting occasionally with the pan juices. Remove and add the cream to the juices, stirring well. Top the cauliflower with the cheese and return to oven for 2 minutes to melt the cheese. Serve hot, with pita bread for dipping in the pan juices.

EPAZOTE

ALTERNATE NAMES **Skunk weed, Wormseed, Pigweed, Goosefoot**

BOTANICAL NAME OF CULINARY SPECIES *Chenopodium ambrosioides*

PLANT FAMILY *Chenopodiaceae*

COUNTRY/REGION OF BOTANICAL ORIGIN **Southern Mexico**

MAJOR COUNTRIES/REGIONS OF CULTIVATION **Mexico and southern United States**

SEASONS OF HARVEST **Summer and early fall**

PARTS USED **Leaves**

COLOR **Dark green**

All across Mexico and the southern United States, you can find epazote growing wild in just about every ditch or riverside. It can be so prolific that eradication efforts are waged yearly with little success. Perhaps everyone should just cook more beans and eat it all.

With a very acrid, petroleum aroma when its serrated leaves are freshly rubbed, the plant is key to the authentic regional preparations of beans and legumes in the hotter climates of North America. The fresh fronds of the tall bush are used whole and simmered with the beans for hours to impart flavor. The spent stalks are quite woody and fibrous and thus are removed once the dish is ready to eat. Beans are certainly the best place to use epazote, perhaps partly because it has rumored anti-gaseous effects on the body. Apart from being a good carrier for an otherwise strong flavor, beans can survive the long cooking times best applied to the herb, mellowing its character to a pleasant bitterness much like mustard greens mixed with pepper, caraway, and thyme.

Farther north, the colder climates stop the plant's spread, and its availability as a fresh herb is more erratic. If using the dried, cut product with its woody stems, wrap it in a piece of cheesecloth or a linen bag, toss it in your pot for the full duration of cooking, and remove it at the end. As the flavor is potent, remember to use it sparingly in any application so you don't overpower the dish.

A local Seattle friend who traveled across the Cascades regularly to the desert climate to the east once asked if I wanted some epazote. In he walked the next week with an entire dry plant, five feet tall, wrapped in a garbage bag. "Just shake this in your garden next spring," he said. Not ready to think about it for six months, I tossed it out in the back corner of my lot. If it weren't for the cold weather that I get in my valley, I might have single-handedly been responsible for epazote taking over the whole of western Washington the next summer. The plant's ability to seed at the drop of a hat should be encouraging news for home herb gardeners. And needless to say, I'm eating lots of beans these days.

Cuban Black Beans

The flavor of Cuba's culture is deep and smoky, and that is echoed in its cuisine perhaps nowhere better than in the ubiquitous black beans simmered with epazote and culantro and served over rice, in tortillas, or all by themselves. The savory herb flavors are perhaps the only ones that can hold up to the smoky flavors, typically from a smoked ham hock, but here given by the smoked pasilla Oaxaca chile. **SERVES 4**

2 tablespoons dried epazote, or ½ cup fresh epazote leaves

2 cups (1 pound) dried black beans, soaked overnight in water to cover and drained

3 smoked pasilla Oaxaca chiles, stems removed

2 cups chicken stock

1 small onion, diced

2 tablespoons chopped fresh culantro, or cilantro

1 carrot, peeled and diced

2 teaspoons finely ground cumin seeds

1 teaspoon freshly ground black pepper

Coarse sea salt, to taste

If using dried epazote, place it in a linen steeping bag or wrap in a square of cheesecloth. In a large pot, combine the beans, the dried epazote (not the fresh, if using), chiles, and stock. Bring to a simmer, reduce the heat to low, partially cover, and simmer until the beans are barely fork-tender, 1½ to 2 hours; add water as needed to keep the beans covered.

Remove the epazote sachet, if you used it. Add the remaining ingredients, including the fresh epazote, if using, and cook until the beans are soft, 15 to 30 minutes longer. Remove the chiles and discard. If desired, partially mash the beans with an immersion blender or a wooden spoon before serving.

ALTERNATE NAMES **Sweet fennel (seeds and leaves), Florence fennel (root bulb), Finocchico (root bulb),** *Saunf* **(seeds; India)**

BOTANICAL NAMES OF CULINARY SPECIES *Foeniculum vulgare* **(seeds and leaves),** *Spp.* **Dulce (root bulb)**

PLANT FAMILY **Parsley (***Umbelliferae***)**

COUNTRY/REGION OF BOTANICAL ORIGIN **Southern Europe**

MAJOR COUNTRIES/REGIONS OF CULTIVATION **Widely, mostly Northern Hemisphere**

SEASON OF HARVEST **Late summer to fall**

PARTS USED **Seeds, Leaves, Roots (specific species)**

COLORS **Pale green (seeds), Brilliant green (leaves), Pale greenish-white (roots)**

If you eat Italian sausage, you will recognize the flavor of fennel seed without fail. It has a unique ability to hit both sweet and savory notes simultaneously, and that makes it a perfect seasoning for dry-cured meats and fresh salami. Thankfully for us, the possibilities don't stop there.

The wispy fronds of leaves look like feathery dill in appearance, but the base has the ridged tubular stalk of celery. All it takes is one rub of the leaves, however, to tell that it's different from both in taste. It's much sweeter in all of its usable parts—leaves, seeds, and root-stalk—and it tastes more of mint, mild cardamom, and, most definitely, licorice.

The seeds make the savory-sweet bridge in Chinese five-spice, a blend that is ubiquitous in the cuisine but especially good in my mind as a dry rub for duck. Move west to India and you'll get fennel seeds in everything from Kashmir curries to Madras potato stews. It's used as widely as, and frequently in concert with, cumin seeds. The northern regions have a particular affinity for the flavor, especially Bengal, where you see it in *panch phoran*, the seed mix that gets added as often as pepper to the local dishes. You'll even find them candied as a breath mint, for a mild digestive at the end of dinner.

Continuing west, the northern Mediterranean cultures as far back as ancient Rome have made fennel a symbol of prosperity and good health. The seeds and root both were documented in the cuisine by Pliny the Elder, one of the earliest culinary authors, who called for them to be chewed upon to wake the mind and relieve flatulence—quite a combination for any spice. The root was simmered in Roman kitchens as a broth with other herbs such as thyme and oregano, for example, and served as first course to ramp up the appetite.

In modern Italy, fennel seed is perhaps the most common spice, after peppercorn, in cured meats. It can hold potency and flavor well when preserved in the fatty meats and doesn't suffer when combined with larger-than-normal amounts of salts, as lighter spices sometimes can. Many curing salt recipes, in fact, call for the seeds to be crushed together with strong herbs like rosemary and then stored in crocks for up to a year to allow the flavors to meld. The results are well worth the patience and make fine condiments if you're not of the salami-making mindset.

Recently mankind has taken a cue from nature once again and started collecting the pollen from several species of spice plants—just as the bees have done for ages. Gathering pollen gives the cook a subtle interpretation of the parent plant and makes for a delicate taste sensation in cuisine. Perhaps the most widely collected, fennel pollen is a greenish yellow crop that is popular among the sausage makers of Italy and commands a price sometimes in line with saffron. For my taste buds, this wonderfully delicate flavor is worth a good price, but perhaps it is not potent enough to command the value set by the gourmet market. If you're in Italy, or even in the upstart fields of California, and can get a less expensive batch, it's worth the experiment. If you'd be paying a hundred dollars an ounce, as I've seen in some boutique shops, save your money instead for a good bottle of Italian balsamico.

Bakeries have included fennel seeds in "multigrain" bread recipes for some time, but a baker friend tells me that he pounds all his seeds—fennel, poppy, sesame, and caraway—into a paste that he adds to the dough. This releases the flavor into the bread better, although he still tosses in a handful of whole seeds for texture and appearance as well.

A classic antipasto from Italy that is rich in fennel is deceptively simple. It calls for asparagus and fresh fennel to be sautéed with olive oil, garlic, and crushed fennel seeds (see the version on page 156). It can be served hot or cold, and it graces practically every café menu in Italy. One such roadside bistro near Florence has offered this dish for over three hundred years! You almost expect centurions to traipse in and order a batch to go for the march to Hadrian's Wall.

Scotch Eggs

Pub fare isn't supposed to be healthy. Nowhere is this more evident than in the "locals" of England, where they're fond of an appetizer that will make your cardiologist cringe, made by wrapping a hard-boiled egg in spicy seasoned meat and frying or baking until crisp. (Some versions use pickled eggs in place of hard-boiled.) One Scotch egg is enough to satisfy the most hearty of appetites at any time of day. They're almost a meal in themselves, and their portability means they're popular with the "on-the-go set" of sheep farmers in the north of Wales. Scotch eggs have been around British pubs as long as stout, and while they're not going to help your waistline, no one will notice after the third pint. **SERVES 6**

1 pound ground pork	6 hard-boiled eggs, peeled
2 tablespoons Farm Sausage Spice (page 353)	1 large raw egg
3 tablespoons finely chopped fresh parsley	2 tablespoons water
2 tablespoons finely minced onion	1½ cups fine, plain bread crumbs
1 teaspoon finely minced garlic	Peanut oil, for deep-frying (optional)
½ teaspoon freshly ground allspice berries	

In a medium bowl, combine the pork, sausage spice, parsley, onion, garlic, and allspice. Mix well. Form into 6 equal patties, and place a hard-boiled egg on top of each. Using wet fingers, wrap each patty around the egg, enclosing it completely.

Beat the egg in a shallow bowl, then stir in the water to make a wash. Dip each wrapped egg in the egg wash to coat, then roll in the bread crumbs, pressing the bread crumbs so they form a solid crust; repeat the dipping process if needed.

In a large deep pot or a deep fryer, heat the oil to 360°F; alternatively, preheat the oven to 375°F.

Deep fry the eggs, turning occasionally, for 3 to 4 minutes, or until the meat is well browned. Transfer to paper towels to drain. Or place the eggs on a small baking sheet and bake for 20 to 25 minutes, until browned. Serve with a mild mustard or malt vinegar.

Fennel and Asparagus Antipasto

In Italy, antipasto can be as varied as *dim sum* in China or tapas in Spain, but one classic that seems to pop up consistently takes advantage of two species of fennel. Whether served hot from the pan or cold, the flavors are simultaneously savory and sweet. They are enhanced even further with the precious liquid gold of Italy, *balsamico tradizionale*, the vinegar made in a manner that concentrates the flavors a hundredfold over the common balsamic vinegars found on grocery shelves. Look for it in specialty Italian groceries or gourmet shops, and don't panic when you see the $100 per five-ounce price; just remember it's used drop by drop. I use it daily and a bottle lasts for almost a year. **SERVES 4**

2 garlic cloves, minced

3 tablespoons olive oil

2 cups thinly sliced fennel

½ pound asparagus, trimmed

Juice of 1 lemon

1 tablespoon fennel seeds, cracked and lightly toasted

1 teaspoon coarse sea salt

½ teaspoon freshly ground white pepper

Good-quality balsamic vinegar, for drizzling

In a large ovenproof skillet, cook the garlic in the oil over medium heat, stirring, just until fragrant, about 1 minute. Add the sliced fennel and cook, stirring, until barely tender, 8 to 10 minutes. Meanwhile steam the asparagus over boiling water until a brilliant green and barely tender, 6 to 10 minutes, depending on the size.

Preheat the broiler. Add the asparagus to the fennel and toss with the lemon juice, fennel seeds, salt, and pepper. Spread evenly in the pan and broil 4 inches from the heat for 2 to 3 minutes, or until the aroma is irresistible. Serve hot or cold, with a few drops of vinegar drizzled over each serving.

FENUGREEK

ALTERNATE NAMES Greek hayseed, Goat's horn, *Methi* (leaf; India)

BOTANICAL NAME OF CULINARY SPECIES *Trigonella foenum-graecum*

PLANT FAMILY Bean (*Fabaceae*)

COUNTRY/REGION OF BOTANICAL ORIGIN Eastern Mediterranean

MAJOR COUNTRIES/REGIONS OF CULTIVATION India, Turkey, Baltic region, South America

SEASON OF HARVEST Fall

PARTS USED Seeds, Leaves

COLORS Caramel yellow (seeds), Dull green (leaves)

Fenugreek seeds confound most people. They're odd looking, have little smell when whole, and are hard enough to chip a tooth, yet spice rack companies have been including an allotment of them in just about every prepacked rack for decades.

The bewilderment over these slightly nutty, slightly bitter seeds starts with the almost unusable whole form that is usually sold. The rectangular, caramel-colored seeds are so brutally hard that tasting the dry seed is an exercise in futility. They absolutely must be ground to release flavor, either dry whole seeds in a mill or a batch that has been soaked for hours to soften. Once ground, they release the aroma of sweet nuts and butterscotch, but a taste will give you more bitterness than the smell would lead you to believe is present—still nutty on the palate but with a celery seed connotation. Most people will identify the taste with curry powder before any other flavor.

Long seedpods sprout oddly from the main stalk of the plant, giving rise to the name "goat's horn," almost as if they wanted nothing to do with the leaves and round white flowers elsewhere on the bush. The foliage reminds me of pea vines and is quite sweet when tender and young. Curiously, the greens have become fashionable as a "new" crop for Asian markets, especially Japan, and are in vogue even in the sushi houses of Tokyo.

Grown like most any grain, fenugreek is threshed to release the seeds at harvest in the fall after the cut bundles or uprooted plants have been dried in the sun. The plant was actually grown as a cover crop and as animal feed in early times, but it now holds a solid spot as a widely traded spice commodity. Its use in curry powders alone could account for its inclusion in spice traders' lists.

Historically, this spice-meets-hay crop gets mentioned all the way back to ancient Egypt, and it has always followed herders of cattle, sheep, and goats. Thus, any cuisine heavy in beef and lamb has found ways to incorporate the taste into its blends, the stews of Persia and Moorish Africa being main examples. As a member of the bean family, fenugreek has also crossed over as an important protein grain in the vegetarian cuisines of India and Pakistan. Certainly part of *sambhars* and *masalas*, it also gets ground into flour and incorporated into flatbreads that are conveniently seasoned by the leaves of the same plant, *methi*, and into potato and spinach fillings.

Back in Egypt, the same technique is used, with the fenugreek flour serving more as a thickener for stews or cooked as a base for dips, much as you see hummus or baba ganoush. Seasoned with tart sumac and olive oil, it is spread on pita bread or simply eaten directly from your fingers.

Toasting the seeds will bring some of the natural sugars to the surface, caramelizing them nicely into something that recalls burnt sugar and maple. However, this accelerates the decay of flavor and should only be done as needed, or you'll be left with just a stale, bitter taste.

The ingenious cook can sprout fresh seeds that haven't been treated to the contrary. Soak them in water overnight and then put them in a moist, closed environment, such as a jar covered with a wet paper towel for a few days, until tiny green shoots with rounded leaf tips appear. The sprouts make an excellent peppery, spiced green in avocado sandwiches and mixed green salads.

Like the seed, fenugreek leaf has a decidedly nutty smell and taste, more like peanut butter or fresh curry leaf. It lacks most of the seed's bitterness and is commonly used in lighter dishes in India. Mixed with *paneer*, the fresh Indian cheese, or baked into *naan* flatbreads with caramelized onions, it shows its sweet character easily and must not be overcooked into a pale shadow of itself. In some Indian communities, the leaf is consumed as a fresh vegetable, but it's more frequently sold dried to be used like a spice for its pleasant grassy aroma. As long as its flavor isn't completely cooked away, *methi* can be used as both ingredient and condiment with great success. Indian sauces can be started with *methi* soaked in water or milk to infuse flavor and reconstitute the leaf, or it can be hand-rubbed or crumbled as a flavorful garnish for lentil soups or sharp tomato-based stews.

Russian White Beans with Vinegar and Walnuts

My inspiration for these beans was a recipe from Russian Georgia as relayed by my good friends Masha and Omar. When Masha, whose family comes from the area, opened a tin of our freshly made *khmeli-suneli* seasoning, she exclaimed, "my mother's beans!" The nutty perfume of the fenugreek leaf in the blend perfectly matches the savory caraway in the seasoning salt.

SERVES 6

1 pound dried large white beans, soaked overnight in water to cover and drained

GARNISH

1 medium sweet onion, such as Vidalia, very thinly sliced

2 tablespoons wine vinegar

1 tablespoon sherry

15 saffron threads

1 tablespoon white wine vinegar

1 cup walnuts, finely chopped

2 garlic cloves, chopped

2 teaspoons sweet Hungarian paprika

Finely ground Svanetti Salt (page 375), to taste

¾ cup chopped fresh parsley

4 teaspoon freshly ground *Khmeli-Suneli* (page 374)

1 tablespoon freshly crushed dried fenugreek (*methi*) leaves

3 tablespoons olive oil

Freshly ground black pepper, to taste

Put the soaked beans in a large saucepan, add water to cover by 2 inches, and bring to a boil. Reduce the heat and simmer until tender, approximately 1 hour; drain.

Meanwhile, for the garnish, stir the onions, vinegar, and sherry together in a bowl, cover, and let stand, tightly covered, in the refrigerator for at least 15 minutes, preferably longer (the garnish can be made up to a day ahead). Crumble the saffron into the vinegar and let stand for at least 15 minutes. In a medium bowl, mix the walnuts with the garlic, paprika, and a little Svanetti salt, then stir in the parsley, *Khmeli-Suneli*, fenugreek, and the saffron/vinegar mix.

Place the cooked beans in a medium bowl and stir in the walnut mixture and olive oil, mixing well. Season with additional Svanetti salt and pepper to taste. Serve at room temperature, garnished with the drained seasoned onions.

FINGER ROOT

ALTERNATE NAME	**Chinese keys**
BOTANICAL NAME OF CULINARY SPECIES	***Kaempferia pandurata***
PLANT FAMILY	**Ginger (*Zingiberaceae*)**
COUNTRY/REGION OF BOTANICAL ORIGIN	**Indonesia**
MAJOR COUNTRIES/REGIONS OF CULTIVATION	**Southeast Asia**
SEASON OF HARVEST	**Summer to fall**
PARTS USED	**Roots**
COLOR	**Orange-brown**

In Thai produce stalls, you can find something that looks like long orange fingers clustered together like a bunch of bananas. Waiting within is a taste that has the benefits of ginger, citrus, and pepper all at once.

Most common in soup stocks of Southeast Asia and southern China, finger root is sold dried or fresh, but generally in whole form. This helps to differentiate it from other rhizomes like ginger and galangal and, more important, allows it to be steeped in stock and then removed, the typical treatment in the kitchen. Only seldom is finger root ground, since its potency doesn't dry in any useful concentration like its ginger cousins.

With its lighter taste, you get little of the heat you'd expect with ginger, so most recipes call for the root to be complemented with pepper, chiles, or cardamom. Especially in Vietnam, white peppercorn's lingering heat plays well in *phõ*, the famous broth soup that can call for finger root and all of its cousins, ginger, greater galangal, and kencur, simultaneously.

When buying the fresh roots, look for each "finger" to be intact, and apply a simple test for freshness when the shopkeeper has his head turned: hold each end of one root and bend it quickly; it should snap in half like a fresh carrot rather than curve or warp. This crisp texture coupled with its mild flavor makes finger root nice for grating fresh as a garnish on top of noodle dishes and earthy mushroom soups.

GALANGAL, GREATER

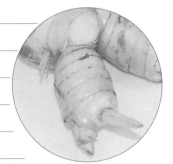

ALTERNATE NAME Laos root, Galanga

BOTANICAL NAMES OF CULINARY SPECIES Alpina galanga

PLANT FAMILY Ginger (Zingiberaceae)

COUNTRY/REGION OF BOTANICAL ORIGIN Indonesia

MAJOR COUNTRIES/REGIONS OF CULTIVATION Southeast Asia, widely

SEASON OF HARVEST Late spring through fall

PARTS USED Roots

COLOR Yellow-white, with dark brown rings

Standing in the markets of Dehua, China, I confused this rhizome with ginger at first glance. Underneath a multitude of makeshift tents in the middle of a mountain downpour (which the locals blamed on me, being from Seattle), there were countless local stands set up by farmers who had come from the countryside with their surplus crops to make a few extra yuan. Scanning the farmers' tables quickly convinced me that my confusion was only beginning.

Of all the plants in the ginger family that get the name galangal, this one is the most commonly found fresh and dried in the shops of Asia. It has, by some counts, twenty close relatives that are harvested for the kitchen, making a trip to the market stalls something akin to a research project. But this variety is recognizable as one of the larger roots, and it will be the most commonly available after ginger. The colors remind me of giant cooked shrimp more than roots, with a polished pale yellow-orange skin and darker brown bands every few centimeters down its length. Tender pink shoots poke out from the top in the freshest forms, and the root exhibits a fibrous inner flesh like ginger but of a lighter creamy color.

As the name implies, it's typically a larger plant than lesser galangal but still shy of the potent king of the family, ginger. To differentiate the taste from ginger, galangal is milder in heat and zest with more of a mustard flavor and dull citrus tone. It's more like older ginger than the vibrant young spring crop, and it can have a starchy character if a particularly large root is selected.

Where you can use galangal is in practically the same circles as ginger, albeit with very different results. The gentle warming of galangal won't clobber your taste buds as ginger can, but leaves you with a more casual back-of-the-palate feeling. *Phõ*, the Vietnamese soup, relies heavily on it, with smaller amounts of strong ginger, *kaffir* lime leaf, and peppercorn. The root is mild enough to be pounded into a pulp for curry pastes in Thailand and Malaysia, and in that instance becomes the base note to build upon with chiles, cilantro, coriander, and turmeric.

A seviche of sorts is made with lime juice and shredded galangal root that's allowed to steep together overnight before adding the seafood. This mix is particularly good for shrimp and lighter fish and even makes a wonderfully delicate marinade if you'd rather head to the grill with, say, seasoned scallops. Dust with some freshly minced coriander leaf, and you'll think you're back in Bangkok.

If fresh roots from Thailand represent too much of a commute for you, then the dry can certainly be substituted in stocks and soups, but it is not acceptable for fresh pastes. Make sure to choose the sliced dry roots, with more of the inner flesh exposed; whole dried roots won't let go of their flavor without hours of simmering. Powdered forms are also available, but my tests have shown that almost all the flavor dissipates within a few weeks after grinding. Avoid them if you can.

Spiced Whitefish in Lotus Leaf

Using various leaves to hold in the perfume of spices while cooking is a time-honored technique all over Asia. Chinese dim sum uses leaf wrappers both to hold in flavors and to impart the flavor of the leaves themselves. In the mountains of Dehua, China, I saw a chef collecting fresh lotus leaves from his local pond one afternoon. Neither of us spoke a word of the other's language, but he could tell I was curious as to what he was up to with the leaves. Not twenty feet away, he had a steamer set up over a fire and his fresh-caught lunch on the line. His spicing included slipping a slice of ginger and pinch of salt into each packet before steaming. I took his idea and merely expanded it a bit with some more select spices from the Pacific.

SERVES 8 AS AN APPETIZER, 4 AS AN ENTRÉE

8 fresh lotus leaves (available in Chinese markets)

2 tablespoons vegetable oil

1 lemon, halved

8 *kaffir* lime leaves

Eight 4-ounce whitefish fillets, or substitute any firm white-fleshed fish

2 tablespoons shredded fresh ginger

2 tablespoons shredded fresh galangal

1 teaspoon freshly ground white pepper

1 teaspoon alaea sea salt (Hawaiian red sea salt)

1 teaspoon white sesame seeds

1 teaspoon black sesame seeds

¼ cup soy sauce

¼ cup pineapple juice

1 teaspoon wasabi powder

Blanch the lotus leaves briefly in boiling water to soften; drain and pat dry. On a large work surface, lay out all the lotus leaves and brush with the oil. Squeeze the lemon juice over all and place 1 kaffir leaf in the center of each lotus leaf. Carefully set a fish fillet on top of each leaf set. Distribute the ginger and galangal shreds equally over the fish. Dust with the white pepper, salt, and white and black sesame seeds, one ingredient at a time. Carefully fold the leaves over to enclose each fish in a packet.

Place the packets, seam side down, in a bamboo steamer. Steam over rapidly boiling water for 12 to 15 minutes, depending upon the thickness of the fillets. The fish should be completely opaque. Meanwhile, combine the soy sauce and pineapple juice, and mix in the wasabi. Serve the fish with individual small bowls of the dipping sauce.

GALANGAL, LESSER

ALTERNATE NAME China root

BOTANICAL NAME OF CULINARY SPECIES *Alpina officinarum*

PLANT FAMILY Ginger (*Zingiberaceae*)

COUNTRY/REGION OF BOTANICAL ORIGIN China

MAJOR COUNTRIES/REGIONS OF CULTIVATION China

SEASON OF HARVEST Late summer

PARTS USED Roots, Seedpods (rarely)

COLORS Dark brown (skin), Pale pink (flesh), Tan seeds inside darker brown pods

Lesser galangal probably suffers from naming envy. Like rival siblings, the smaller plant tries to make up for it on the palate with a hotter, bolder interpretation. More peppery punch and less sweetness will help you differentiate lesser galangal from all its ginger cousins.

As with all the culinary entries from the ginger family, you can expect some tart flavor, slightly numbing heat, and a citrus-meets-camphor aroma. Lesser galangal, like greater, adds some mustard tones, but with more intensity. You can recognize the physical differences immediately, however, as the roots look more like turmeric fingers than greater galangal or ginger. With rough brown skin encasing a deeper pink-brown flesh, it again spites its brother with lighter rings every few centimeters, the opposite color scheme from greater galangal.

Lesser galangal is most probably the *galingale* called for by medieval cooks, who were introduced initially to the flavor by Arab traders. Later, the crusades of the thirteenth century made it more popular than ever, even giving rise to the cultivation of European galangale, *Cyperus longus*, a plant with a similar taste but ultimately more prized for its medicinal applications in the period. One can surmise that lesser galangal's simple, potent flavor survived the overland trip better than any of the other varieties.

Where you find this piquant root most effective in the kitchen is in stocks and broths where long cooking times can release the flavor fully. Both fresh and dry roots are sold, with the latter being far more common. One chef in Hong Kong told me that he calls the pounded fresh roots "pepper paste" and adds it as liberally as peppercorn everywhere. Teas are infused with slices of the fresh root where it's cultivated locally, but finding the fresh version outside the region is nearly impossible. Rather, look back to the pinnacle of its popularity in the Middle Ages, where you'll see the dried root in mulled wines, duck soups, and even fermented cordials.

Rarely, you may find the whole seedpods of lesser galangal sold as a version of cardamom. Indeed, I once thought I was buying black cardamom pods rather than galangal because the appearance of the inch-long ridged fruits is almost identical. To differentiate, galangal pods have a mild melon and camphor flavor in much more ir-regularly shaped brown seeds, whereas black cardamom has a stronger smoky taste. Generally, galangal pods will also be larger by double than any of the authentic car-damoms. Still, interesting results are to be had when you substitute one for the other.

GALE

ALTERNATE NAME **Sweet gale, Bog myrtle, Badge of the Campbells**

BOTANICAL NAME OF CULINARY SPECIES ***Myrica gale***

PLANT FAMILY **Gale (*Myricaceae*)**

COUNTRY/REGION OF BOTANICAL ORIGIN **Northern Europe**

MAJOR COUNTRIES/REGIONS OF CULTIVATION **Northern latitudes, sporadically**

SEASONS OF HARVEST **Spring and early summer**

PARTS USED **Young leaves**

COLOR **Emerald green**

Necessity truly is the mother of invention, especially in the kitchen. When the Belgian beer-brewing monks of the Middle Ages found themselves in a supply pinch for hops, they went looking for something else to add bitter flavor and preserve their wares. What they found growing in the peaty bogs to satisfy the demand was an evergreen shrub called gale.

This leafy bush had long been used in Europe when bay laurel wasn't easily available. A quick search of medieval recipes shows it called for in everything from fish stock to mutton stew. The waxy berries of the plant were used along with the similarly shiny leaves to impart a sweet bay character with subtle camphor overtones. The related bayberry tree, *Myrica cerifera*, was also used, but more emphasis was placed on the wax gleaned from its berries for candles and such. Good idea when you notice that modern science has proven it mildly toxic.

The flavor of fresh gale starts as bitter juniper meets bay but mellows rapidly in the face of heat. Sweetness not unlike fennel comes around in the nose, and in some batches I've played with in beer brewing, I've tasted sage flavors coming to the surface. Home brewers have almost single-handedly kept this herb available in its dry forms, and any reasonable home-brew store can sell you a small packet with branch, leaves, and waxy berries intact.

True flavor addicts will seek out the fresh leaves in the north woods of America or the Scottish moors, where it has the name "badge of the Campbells," no doubt due to its abundance there and presumed subsequent use by the family to have one heck of a beer festival.

Already in a pub mood from brewing, I decided a proper leek and cabbage soup was in order and tossed the extra sweet gale into the broth in place of bay. Fifteen minutes of infusion gave me its heady perfume, and it needed only a touch of salt and pepper for complete flavor. With one pub success under my belt, I stewed beef tips with gale leaves for a shepherd's pie and even tossed some into the boiling russets used to make the classic mashed potato top crust. I suspect that there's plenty more pub fare where gale will combine nicely. Buy some extra next time you are making a batch of Scottish ale.

GARLIC

BOTANICAL NAME OF CULINARY SPECIES *Allium sativum*, with numerous subspecies

PLANT FAMILY Onion (*Alliaceae*)

COUNTRY/REGION OF BOTANICAL ORIGIN: Asia

MAJOR COUNTRIES/REGIONS OF CULTIVATION Warmer climates, widely

SEASONS OF HARVEST Late summer (bulbs), Late spring (leaves)

PARTS USED Bulbs, Leaves

COLORS Pale yellow flesh, widely varied outer skins (bulbs), Green (leaves)

Garlic is one of the most widely distributed, seriously pungent flavors on the face of the planet. Whether it's a bit minced to perfume oil for sautéing, copious amounts roasted into a rich sauce, or used for the current designer flavor of potato chips, garlic is always well received by the masses. "Too much" and "garlic" rarely appear together in kitchen conversations. Garlic means instant success for prepackaged foods, and it can make even the novice cook's dishes taste like the pro's. As the most potent member of the onion family, it's grown widely across the globe, but the most impressive sources are in the Mediterranean, China, and the United States, specifically the valleys of central California.

When you drive into Gilroy, California, you start to notice that the locals are a bit insane when it comes to garlic. It has become one of those crops that evoke pride, like wine in Italy, cheese in France, and beef in Argentina—rightfully so in my opinion, since the quality and potency of California garlic is rivaled by none of the world's other producers. A yearly harvest festival there has a carnival atmosphere—with everything from garlic spreads to garlic ice cream to garlic-shaped hats. It seems that the same mindset lingers there year-round, and farmers take full advantage of garlic's sheer versatility and popularity among the culinary elite.

Spring announces the underground treasure, grown just like an onion, with tender, tubular shoots that look like giant chives, their milder cousin. A delicacy not to be missed is a light soup or an Asian stir-fry with these garlic "tops" cut and prepared like any other green. Even deep-fried and used to top casseroles, they are a gentle reminder of the flavor yet to come from the fully developed bulbs in late summer.

The flavor is hot and . . . well, tastes like garlic. It's so universally known that any flavor reference falls short of the genuine article. Asian varieties tend toward the hotter, simpler end of the spectrum, Mediterranean toward the sweeter, and American pleasantly in the middle, with what can be described as a "greener" flavor. Granted, it depends on which species you grow, but the climatic impact of each region certainly plays a part in the end: yet another difference to be embraced rather than set one against another.

The flavors of garlic are susceptible to unpleasant bitterness if overcooked, as we've all done when the phone rang while starting a sauté in olive oil. Even ten seconds too long, and you've ruined what's in the pan. Start over rather than just trying to strain the oil, another mistake many of us have made when down to our last head of garlic.

Garlic terminology is simple. The entire underground bulb is called a head of garlic and each of the segments is called a clove. With the numerous subspecies cultivated, heads of garlic take on any number of colors in their papery outer skins. In my local farmers' market, the growers from the desert valley start appearing around August with truckloads of strands braided from the fresh tops of the plants. Brilliant purple, delicate pink, snow white, and the more common pale yellow colors populate the stalls in a parade of varieties. Similarly, the heads can range from tiny specimens the size of a golf ball to giant monsters weighing over a pound.

I'm lucky enough to have a local backyard garlic producer who shows up with a few braids in tow to barter for his semiannual store of spices. Which species will grow best in your area is a question for the local nursery, but all are propagated from cloves saved from past harvests. Just as winter is departing, garlic "sets" will appear for sale to anyone with a growing season's worth of forethought. My going rate, if you're curious, is a pound of peppercorn for twelve inches of garlic braid.

Dried garlic isn't to be immediately demonized, in my opinion. Removal of the moisture through modern commercial processing can actually concentrate the flavors pleasantly. The real caveat is the old problem of shelf life that plagues so many spices. Properly dried garlic, no matter the form, should be a cornmeal yellow and have an aroma that really smells like garlic, not a pale memory—a full-on, in-your-face pungency that makes you step back and dream of Italian tomato sauce or American barbecue rubs.

It should be noted, however, that dried garlic has far too many industrial names. The size of the piece when cut—fresh, before drying—is what gives the final name to the product. Flaked garlic starts as slices of garlic at the full size of the clove. Chopped dried garlic is typically ½-inch pieces, and minced is ¼-inch pieces cut from the fresh cloves. What is usually labeled garlic powder at the supermarket is known in the industry as granulated; what the trade designates as the powdered form has a fine, flourlike consistency.

As far back the third century B.C., garlic was cultivated in the Middle East, having migrated from its (presumed) origins in Asia. It propagated easily, making it cheap and available to even the poorest of cooks. Protection from evil spirits and disease was commonly ascribed to the potent cloves, solidifying its position in every cupboard from Egyptian times forward. Even among the daily rations of wine, cured meat, and way bread was a head of garlic for each Roman centurion, on the premise that it made for a strong fighting force. Whether it was their swords or their breath, you'd have a hard time convincing the Macedonians otherwise. Every culture that garlic has touched has taken it to heart—literally, according to modern medical research focusing on its health benefits. Indian souks and English lords all grew garlic once traders introduced it to local gardens.

At the risk of writing a book within a book, the uses of garlic are manyfold. To begin, the flavor when raw can be overwhelming to some, so for timid palates, just rubbing a split clove on the inside of a salad bowl can be enough to flavor a Caesar dressing—although plenty of fans will have you mince the clove and toss it in as well. Pounded fresh for a curry paste or run through a juicer to start a soup stock, garlic has enough depth and pungency to show through the murkiest of flavor combinations.

Whole heads of garlic can be roasted into submission, transforming the hot bite of the fresh cloves into an almost candied sweetness. Shear whole heads flat of their bottom root, brush with oil, and place cut side down in a baking dish. After twenty minutes at 400°F, the cloves will break apart easily from their paper-thin skins, allowing you to squeeze the roasted flesh onto crusty bread all by itself or into an olive and goat cheese mix that will grace any antipasto plate with style.

Whole peeled cloves of garlic find their way into olives destined for designer martinis and pop up in the mix of pickled onions, artichoke, sun-dried tomato, and olive oil that tops the Italian-inspired muffelatas of New Orleans and the smoked mozzarella sandwiches of New York City's Little Italy. Fresh cloves of garlic are best peeled at home as needed rather than purchased pre-cleaned, or worse still, minced and jarred in oil. Such processes can only hasten the demise of the flavor.

Softened butter can be pounded with garlic and strong herbs to make a compound butter that can be used to start both classic French omelets and cream sauces with equal flair. If kept under refrigeration, the butter's flavors only develop as time passes, and your biggest problem will be keeping other hands out of the crock. Louisiana's French-inspired Creole cuisine also takes a heavy hand when it comes to garlic. In fact, it would come to a screeching halt without garlic, whether gently simmered for gumbos or minced for remoulade.

Lebanese chefs have long made *tzatziki*, a sauce for dipping *dolmas* or for dressing rich lamb-filled pita breads. Generous amounts of raw garlic are minced into plain yogurt and shredded cucumber, then allowed to sit for a few hours while the flavor develops. I keep a batch of this percolating away in my refrigerator at all times and pull it out for all manner of roasted meats, to spread onto flat breads with hummus, and even to cool my hottest curries from India, where a similar sauce would be called a *raita*.

Almost every dish in China makes use of the trilogy of garlic, ginger, and soy sauce somewhere in its preparation. Simple *chow mein* noodles or pork *shou mei* dumplings, for example, rely on garlic to partner with the sweet heat of ginger and the salty intensity of the soy.

Whether it's the punch of raw, the mellow sweetness of roasted, or the delightful green of everything in between, you're sure to have success wherever you add garlic.

Portobellos with Garlic Cream

When interesting varieties of garlic hit my local market in late summer, I promptly grab a few heads and roast them, simply brushed with oil, for a quick appetizer of the resulting puree spread on toast. That same harvest also gives me a key ingredient for a simple dish that has become popular with my guests. The marriage of port and mushrooms is particularly good when sown together with lots of fresh garlic. Each flavor holds up the other and becomes greater than the sum of the parts. Serve as an appetizer with plenty of crusty bread for dipping into the garlicky sauce. **SERVES 4**

1 tablespoon unsalted butter

1 tablespoon extra virgin olive oil

8 large garlic cloves, chopped

1 large portobello mushroom, trimmed and cut into ¾-inch-thick slices

½ cup tawny port

1 cup whole milk

1 cup half-and-half

1 teaspoon fine sea salt

½ teaspoon cracked black peppercorns

2 tablespoons finely chopped fresh parsley, for garnish

In a large deep skillet, melt the butter with the oil over medium heat. Add the garlic and cook, stirring, until softened, approximately 2 minutes. Add the portobello slices in a single layer and cook for 4 minutes. Turn the slices and sauté until slightly softened, approximately 4 minutes longer. Add the port, then add the milk and half-and-half, stirring constantly. Cook, stirring, until the sauce thickens and coats the back of a spoon. Add the salt and pepper and stir well.

Transfer to a serving dish and garnish with the parsley.

GINGER

ALTERNATE NAME **Ginger root**, *Sushoga* **(pickled; Japan)**, *Adrak* **(fresh; India)**, *Saunth* **(dried; India)**, *Gan jiang* **(dried; China)**, *Sheng jhang* **(fresh; China)**

BOTANICAL NAME OF CULINARY SPECIES *Zingiber officinalis*

PLANT FAMILY **Ginger (*Zingiberaceae*)**

COUNTRY/REGION OF BOTANICAL ORIGIN **China**

MAJOR COUNTRIES/REGIONS OF CULTIVATION **China, India, Australia, Jamaica, widely across tropical regions**

SEASON OF HARVEST **Year-round**

PARTS USED **Roots**

COLOR **Yellow-brown (skin), Yellow-gold (flesh)**

Ginger is a spice that knows no bounds. It can start your meal in an appetizer, add zest to your entrée, and finish in your dessert, each time transforming into something different on the taste buds. A "hand" of ginger, so named because of the shape of the root's main branch and sidelong "fingers," can be used fresh, dried, crystallized (cooked in sugar), preserved (packed in sugar syrup), or even pickled. While these many forms are all sold for culinary use, each has the distinctive ginger flavor that is a combination of lemon-like zest, peppery heat, and herbal sweetness. Each style imparts a unique character, so substitutes shouldn't be made between types. Note that the term "stem ginger" has been applied to both crystallized and preserved forms with little standardization. Care should be taken to read it in the context of your recipe.

Ginger's fresh versions emphasize a bright citrus note, while drying the root subdues that to bring the sharp bite to the forefront. Pliny himself called for the "heat of passion to come forth" in dried uses, but fresh young ginger is one of the few flavors able to cut through the intense chile pastes of Southeast Asia. The taste of the crystallized style can be cloyingly sweet, but better versions of this balance the syrup with the root in proportions that yield plenty of ginger character without overwhelming sweetness. The pickled versions have the expected tartness but with some mild sweetness and all of the heat you'd get from wasabi or peppercorn.

Dried and cut forms of ginger are the best choice for infusions into teas, something the Chinese have done for centuries with tea leaf, the Indians with *chai*, and even the Americans of the New West in herbal tisanes. As the drying process seems to concentrate and close the flavors, a hot water infusion with plenty of steeping time is recommended to bring aroma and flavor back successfully. The dried root is also pulverized into a flour consistency, familiar to any baker who ever made gingerbread or gingersnaps. For this form, more mature roots are washed repeatedly in a warm water bath, sun-dried, and pulverized in massive roller mills.

A rhizome at the top of its own family, *Zingiber*, ginger looks like a wide-bladed grass or miniature bamboo plant above ground, with the edible roots lying just underground and branching out horizontally. The crop is propagated in rows from the previous year's root cuttings that have been allowed to sprout—something ginger is apt to do even in the home cupboard if left alone in the dark. If the three-foot plants are allowed to flower, there will be a delicate purple and yellow affair set upon a singular shoot. Bulbous root stems form off the main branch, which is some two to four inches in diameter, and a very smooth outer skin develops, looking something like polished metal in the freshest specimens. This should be peeled away whenever the root will be consumed.

When shopping for the fresh root, look for firm flesh and shiny, unwrinkled skin. Age and moisture loss will cause the root to shrivel, leaving behind little of the top-note flavors and more of the strong heat. If the surface of the root is lightly scratched, there should still be a distinct lemon aroma. Also avoid any with sprouts forming on the hands. Powdered dry ginger should still exhibit a brilliant yellow color, not dull brown, and one sniff should give the aroma of mild pepper.

Crystallized ginger should still be pliable and soft, not dried to a hardened stage. It can be found either with or without a sugar crystal coating. Australia's Queensland region has become a leading producer of crystallized, sometimes called "candied," ginger. The plants are harvested at an early stage in growth, without the fibrous threads that tend to develop in the older plants. The young shoots are peeled and cooked in a sugar bath to intensify, sweeten, and, to some extent, preserve the flavor. China is another major source. The Chinese and Australian versions can vary a bit in flavor, with the latter being a bit sweeter and the former having more of the characteristic heat. Both are fine choices, for different reasons, as long as you select the best quality of the many grades each region produces.

Cultivated easily, ginger is widely distributed over all the world's tropical regions, most notably China, Australia, India, and the Caribbean. There is even a limited microproduction of high-quality ginger on the island of Hawaii, but those producers seem more geared toward the numerous medicinal applications of the roots and extracts. The plant can be harvested at a number of stages: the younger roots lack the fibrous internal threads found characteristically in older plants; while it can still be potent at older stages, the sweetness wanes, to be replaced by more heat. "Spring ginger" can sometimes be found fresh in Asian markets and comes, as the name implies, from the early-year harvest when the plant grows exceptionally quickly. Its roots are often half the size of older specimens and the skin is underdeveloped to the point that peeling often isn't necessary.

Ginger was probably the West's introduction to Asian flavors, as it was easily transported over land routes and via the Mediterranean. References to it can be found in ancient Roman and Egyptian texts. Indeed, the name derives from the Sanskrit word meaning "horn shape," and it was traded by the Phoenicians. As the plant is very adaptable in tropical climates, it was rapidly cultivated along the trade routes and became a relatively inexpensive commodity. Rumored to have aphrodisiac properties, it was being traded to the West in the first century, but it became the fashion all over Europe during the Middle Ages, even making frequent appearances as a condiment alongside the then-more-expensive peppercorn. Taxes were levied against ginger in all the European centers from Roman times forward, but perhaps one of the more interesting exchange rates was in England, where three pounds of ginger was the going rate for one head of cattle. Personally, I'd rather deal with storing the ginger than the cow.

To uncover this root's origins, I went to the mountains of China and made a discovery that shook my ginger foundations. I'm always preaching about freshness, but even I hadn't tasted ginger so vibrant and alive as that harvested from these remote regions. The intensity was certainly stronger, but the flavor was also broader, giving more of the pleasantly hot bite and subtle sweetness than anything I had ever tasted in the States. My culinary host for the evening was the White Swan restaurant on the road from Xiamen to Dehua in Fujian Province, a tiny place found only with the expert help of my guides, who obviously made it a regular stop on their travels. All the dishes were laced with peeled and shredded "mountain ginger," simply local cultivated ginger harvested as needed, that had a deep yellow tone to the flesh. A quick experiment (sneaking some back in my luggage only to find that the color had paled on the flight home) tells me this color came from its unmistakable freshness. The one thing that changed my opinion of ginger permanently, however, was the duck soup, a painfully simple "hot pot" preparation of duck, water, and spices, yet the ginger married its heat to cassia-cinnamon twigs, clove, and tamarind to create a full engagement of my palate—it truly carried the dish. Granted, the duck was incredibly fresh and the water came from the most pristine of mountain streams, but it was this spice combination held together by the ginger that made the dish unforgettable.

Even today there are shops in Hong Kong that make their entire trade in ginger. Massive pottery urns hold pieces of the peeled root preserved in a sugar syrup. In the crystallized section, every shape, from natural slices to perfectly square cubes, can be found. And mounds of fresh hands, from central China down to southwestern Australia, are set out for the consumer to inspect, some specific "estate" varieties commanding prices more typically associated with precious metals.

The British took ginger into their hearts, making it a staple in fruit conserves and orange marmalade, not to mention drawing it into their sacred afternoon tea through myriad crumpets, biscuits, and savory cakes. Perhaps their best-known culinary adaptations, however, are ginger ale and ginger beer. The latter is a brewed beverage, sometimes alcoholic, sometimes not, with a strong ginger-pepper bite. The former is more common today as a carbonated soft drink that only hints at heat while delivering the characteristic fresh ginger-citrus flavor.

The Japanese too have adopted ginger in their cuisine, most notably in the pickled form known to sushi and sashimi connoisseurs as a tart, hot condiment. The paper-thin slices range in color from a "natural" yellow or pink hue to artificially colored red or orange. There are broad ranges in quality, primarily a result of the root they pickle and secondarily the quality of the process itself. Preservative-laden shelf-stable versions should be avoided, as these have a "plastic" texture. Shop instead for the fresh-made in quality Japanese grocers (it will be kept in the refrigerated section), which will be almost as pungent as the wasabi found at its side during sushi service.

If you're lucky enough to have a high-quality juicing machine, green apple and lemon with a small piece of fresh ginger makes a better boost than any prepackaged "energy" drink. That same machine can be used to juice ginger with vegetables for a flavorful soup base. Ginger, celery, carrot, and garlic juice start all of my pan-Asian stocks.

A favorite fishmonger of mine will deeply score the flesh of whatever fresh catch of the day is on hand, stuff the slits with fresh ginger shreds and sliced garlic cloves, and steam the whole fish to perfection. Drizzling sizzling-hot ginger and garlic oil over the top brings another layer of spice flavor to his preparation, so much so that it barely makes it to the table before it's devoured.

Malay Citrus Atjar

Atjar is a sort of preserved vegetable or fruit relish common in Malaysia. Often heavily spiced, it's used as either a condiment or an ingredient in more complex dishes. The only difficult part is to be sure to make it ahead of time to allow the flavors to come together. Do be very picky when selecting the fruits or vegetables you intend to use, since you'll be adding the whole thing, peel and all. Citrus fruits of any kind are traditional, but the technique is also seen with squashes, cucumbers, carrots, and even star fruit as the idea is exported to an audience beyond Malaysia. **MAKES 1 QUART**

1 pound lemons, scrubbed

½ pound oranges, scrubbed

4 cups distilled white vinegar

Two ¼-inch-thick slices fresh ginger

½ cup coarse sea salt

¼ cup granulated sugar

1 cup olive, peanut, or safflower oil

3 tablespoons freshly ground *Berberé* (page 392)

Slice off the ends of the lemons and oranges and discard. Cut the fruit into 1-inch wedges.

Combine the vinegar, ginger slices, salt, and sugar in a large bowl, stirring until the salt and sugar are completely dissolved. Add the fruit wedges and let stand in a cool dark place for 48 hours, stirring occasionally.

Drain the fruit and return to the bowl. Add the oil and spice blend, and mix well. Pack into a large glass jar and refrigerate for at least 1 day, or up to 3 weeks.

GOLPAR

ALTERNATE NAMES Giant hogweed, Russian hogweed

BOTANICAL NAME OF CULINARY SPECIES *Heracleum mantegazzianum*

PLANT FAMILY Parsley (*Umbelliferae*)

COUNTRY/REGION OF BOTANICAL ORIGIN Central Asia, Caucasus

MAJOR COUNTRIES/REGIONS OF CULTIVATION Persia

SEASON OF HARVEST Summer to fall

PARTS USED Seeds

COLOR Yellow-brown

Iranian markets can supply you with golpar seeds, but even they might not know what they actually have on hand. The reason for the confusion in the United States is that the genuine article has been banned as a noxious weed, and therefore simple basil or angelica seeds are commonly substituted. The genuine plant, a purple-stemmed monster that can reach fifteen feet high, produces a sap that can cause painful blisters on the skin and even blindness if it touches the eyes. As such, it is a less than popular spice for obvious reasons.

The whole papery pods contain two seeds each, and those are sold much as you would see mustard or poppy seeds, to be ground into various recipes, soaked and blended into a paste, or used whole in breads and pastries. The flavor has bittering components, though not as strong as celery seed, and an interesting sweetness in the front of the palate. Golpar is commonly ground as a condiment for fruit, most notably pomegranates from Iran, or cooked, like cumin or ajwain, into bean dishes. As a substitute, I've had success with a combination of ground celery and anise seeds. Not quite the genuine article, but much less likely to cause bodily harm in the garden.

GRAINS OF PARADISE

ALTERNATE NAMES **Melegueta pepper, Guinea pepper, Africa pepper**

BOTANICAL NAME OF CULINARY SPECIES *Aframomum melegueta*

PLANT FAMILY **Ginger (*Zingiberaceae*)**

COUNTRY/REGION OF BOTANICAL ORIGIN **West Africa**

MAJOR COUNTRIES/REGIONS OF CULTIVATION **Ghana, West and Central Africa**

SEASONS OF HARVEST **Summer and fall**

PARTS USED **Seeds**

COLOR **Polished brown**

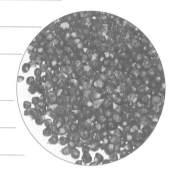

In medieval times, anything that had a peppery bite was seen as a culinary treasure. To serve such exotica from far-off lands meant you were aristocracy; it elevated your status and it showed you had arrived on the scene in style. Contemporary chefs, culinary re-creationists focused upon duplicating authentic foods from that era, first brought grains of paradise to my attention. I've felt like part of the enlightened crowd ever since.

Frequently mistranslated as cardamom seeds because of both its flavor and appearance, this spice comes from a tough leathery husk that looks like a giant brown cardamom pod. Each pod contains about eighty seeds of a slightly angular shape with a tiny nib on one end, much like a corn kernel in shape but a quarter of the size. The fresh seeds have a polished brown color and emit little aroma until cracked or ground, when a milky white core is revealed.

Historically, grains of paradise were cultivated inland from the Gold Coast of Africa—sometimes even called the Pepper Coast—and taken overland to ports on the coast, destined for Europe, specifically Portugal, France, and Italy. This was certainly more convenient than the extended overland and ocean trade routes that supplied peppercorns. Grains of paradise became a fashionable substitute for the more expensive pepper, and with good reason. Their flavor has both pepper and ginger character with an undercurrent of clove or cardamom. As such, grains of paradise were introduced into a wide variety of cuisines across the spice-starved European countries, but they were later replaced by peppercorn for the most part, as trade routes became more accessible. There has been a resurgence of popularity of the spice in modern times. It's now used in everything from beer brewing to confections. Certainly the flavor has potency worthy of such experiments, but I think that part of its popularity must come from its exotic name. The title originated back in the medieval days of export from Africa, when tales of the mystical lands that spawned the seeds were woven to entice traders and increase sales to the European markets. (Deepest, darkest Africa was a bit deeper and darker back then, so who can blame the farmers for taking a few liberties in spinning tales of inland Edens.) You may not be able to visit paradise, but for only a few coins, you can taste a bit of it.

Practically, cooks can use grains of paradise anywhere peppercorn is appropriate, but with pleasantly different results. In its native lands, the Tunisian five-spice blend, *qalat daqqa*, uses grains of paradise as its base, and medieval *poudres* (spice powders) incorporate grains of paradise to lend a touch of heat and pungency. Mixes like these have been integrated into pastries since the Middle Ages, and they were also considered pantry staples for use in savory dishes like braised meat or vegetable pies.

Perhaps part of the "paradise" with this spice is its apparent affinity for alcoholic potions. It's one of several exotic ingredients in top-shelf gin recipes, and modern-day brewers add them to their wort to bring a crisp zest, not unlike mild cloves or allspice, to spiced ales. Sack, a spiced wine typically served hot, historically calls upon grains of paradise to perk up the flavors, as does *hippocras*, a medieval libation infused with spices. Even Scandinavian countries still incorporate it into recipes for aquavit.

No matter what context you take grains of paradise in, its reputation of old is deserving of revival. The bright pop of heat and flavor is every bit as interesting as peppercorn, with even more complexity. I think if the world's farmers brought production up to global levels to make the price more affordable, cooks would once again justify the exotic tales told by traders of old.

Paradise Pepper Steak

My Southern grandmother never imagined that a spice from half a world away would grace her pepper steak, but considering the wonderful ginger-meets-pepper flavor of grains of paradise, it's a natural match. Black peppercorn, cayenne, or chile flakes are all traditional in the recipe; the spice brings a similar bite but its own signature.   **SERVES 4**

1 cup all-purpose flour

1 teaspoon fine sea salt

Four ½-pound cube steaks

2 tablespoons finely ground grains of paradise

2 tablespoons corn oil

2 tablespoons unsalted butter

4 scallions, finely chopped

½ cup dry white wine

Mix the flour and salt on a plate. Rinse the steaks briefly, dust with the grains of paradise, and dredge in the flour.

Heat the oil and butter in a large skillet over medium-high heat until hot. Add the steaks and cook until a crust forms on the bottom, approximately 4 minutes. Flip the steaks and cook until a crust forms on the second side and the meat is cooked to your liking, about 4 minutes more for medium-rare. Transfer to a platter and set aside in a warm spot.

Add the scallions to the pan and cook, stirring, just until wilted, about 2 minutes. Add the wine and cook, stirring up the browned bits in the bottom of the pan. Simmer until the sauce is reduced by half and slightly thickened, and spoon over the steaks to serve.

HORSERADISH

ALTERNATE NAMES Mountain radish, Red cole, Horse root

BOTANICAL NAME OF CULINARY SPECIES *Armoracia Rusticana*

PLANT FAMILY *Cruciferae*

COUNTRY/REGION OF BOTANICAL ORIGIN Eastern Europe

MAJOR COUNTRIES/REGIONS OF CULTIVATION Russia, Asia, widely across Northern Hemisphere

SEASONS OF HARVEST Late fall into winter (roots), Late spring (leaves)

PARTS USED Roots, Young leaves

COLORS Pale white (root flesh), Pea green (leaves)

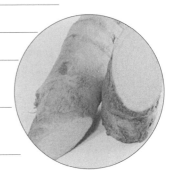

I remember coming in from snowy days in my youth for a quick sandwich of last night's cold roast beef. Given the climate, a stuffy nose was the norm, so I'd reach for my secret culinary weapon, horseradish sauce, as my winter condiment of choice. The mind-clearing pungency and heat worked as many wonders on my nose as it did on my taste buds.

Horseradish root refuses to be ignored in both the garden and the kitchen. Its heat is unlike a chile, having more of the qualities of hot Chinese mustard or Japanese wasabi, typically with even more potency than either. A whiff of the freshly grated root will make your eyes water, but when it's tempered into creamy sauces or condiments, the flavor shows through with a pleasantly piquant character.

The plant can overwhelm a garden, as it propagates from countless stem roots that branch from a main taproot. It's these stem roots that are harvested at the peak of flavor, when the cold of winter is beginning to encroach. Peeled of the rough outer bark, the flesh is a pristine white wrapped around a slightly darker core. The best flavor is gained from the outer flesh, although with tender young shoots, the entire root can be grated.

Discoloration happens quickly from oxidation, but that can be arrested by submerging the just-grated root in lemon water or by simply squeezing lemon juice liberally over all. Longer soaking in water, for less than an hour in most cases, will temper the heat somewhat if desired. In sauces, lemon or vinegar can also lend flavor balance by cutting the intensity of the horseradish, with sweetening from sugar or honey completing most condiments, such as a creamy tartar sauce for fish or the tomato-based "cocktail" sauces popular for shrimp and shellfish. In any case, try to use the grated root as quickly as possible to preserve the pungency and infuse its flavor into the other ingredients.

The very early tender leaves, one of the Passover seder bitter herbs, can be harvested to give a light interpretation of the root's flavor to salads and cooked vegetables. They are particularly nice added at the end of cooking greens like mustard or collard, where they can act like pepper to enhance flavor. If leaving them uncooked, use the leaves sparingly, lest you taste nothing but horseradish.

While the fresh root is preferred, dried versions occasionally make their way into the marketplace. In my experience, powders offer little of the pungency found in the fresh, but larger granules and cut pieces can be brought back to life with a steeping in cold water or juice if they are relatively fresh, say, less than a year old. Indeed, these forms make inclusion into salad dressings and sauces more convenient but at some cost to pungency (sometimes actually a desired mellowing effect). Test your recipes with both fresh and dry to see which results are acceptable to your palate.

Alpine countries make horseradish condiments using grated tart apples or underripe pears as a base with lemon and sugar. Farther north, the Scandinavian countries add horseradish to sour cream for a bright foil to the white-fleshed fish dishes of the region. You may notice that most preparations don't involve cooking the root. This is because the flavor almost completely disintegrates with heat, leaving only a pale imitation of the original behind.

I make fresh mayonnaise with an almost imperceptible hint of horseradish to keep my guests guessing about what makes my BLTs so tasty. I also keep a small jar of a paste made with fresh garlic, olive oil, and horseradish in my refrigerator and slip a spoonful in to make the perfect mashed potatoes.

HYSSOP

BOTANICAL NAME OF CULINARY SPECIES *Hyssopus officinalis*

PLANT FAMILY **Mint (Lamiaceae)**

COUNTRY/REGION OF BOTANICAL ORIGIN **Mediterranean**

MAJOR COUNTRIES/REGIONS OF CULTIVATION **France, Italy, Morocco, Egypt, Turkey**

SEASON OF HARVEST **Summer**

PARTS USED **Leaves**

COLOR **Brilliant green**

Hyssop stretches back in history to biblical times and left its culinary mark on the Romans, Europeans, and even comparatively modern American settlers. Yet with a savory taste that melds the best character of rosemary, tarragon, and thyme, hyssop, unfortunately, gets little attention in modern kitchens.

The long, slender leaves look very similar in shape to tarragon and the branches are tipped with blue, white, or pink flowers, all of which are edible. The entire stalks are typically harvested, as the stems are tender and usable in all but the most delicate of applications.

Particularly pungent in fresh forms, hyssop gets distilled into a liqueur called *Chartreuse*, originally formulated by French monks, that shows its uniquely herbaceous character well. Sometimes included in strewing herb bundles, it flavors white beans for cassoulet and can be chopped fine for game sausages and dry-cured meats. American settlers found the potent minty flavor made a wonderful pairing with native cranberries, and as such, eighteenth-century recipes for relishes and chutneys call upon hyssop's flavor to be infused into the liquid that will ultimately cook the tart berries.

It should be noted that hyssop is usually used fresh, since drying destroys most of the rich, heady flavor. If fresh isn't available, a more suitable substitute would be combinations of dried thyme, mint, savory, and/or rosemary.

ANISE-HYSSOP

ALTERNATE NAME Licorice mint, Korean mint

BOTANICAL NAMES OF CULINARY SPECIES *Agastache foeniculum, Agastache rugosa* (Korean mint)

PLANT FAMILY Mint *(Lamiaceae)*

COUNTRIES/REGIONS OF BOTANICAL ORIGIN North America (anise hyssop), Asia (Korean mint)

MAJOR COUNTRIES/REGIONS OF CULTIVATION North America (anise hyssop), Korea, Thailand, Laos (Korean mint)

SEASONS OF HARVEST Summer and fall

PARTS USED Leaves

COLOR Brilliant green

One of the hazards of being in the spice trade is that your friends with gardens have the unnerving habit of handing you bits of plants and shouting, "Taste this!" far too frequently. Such was my unceremonious introduction to anise hyssop one spring at a local nursery, and I must admit that the taste was an eye-opener.

I had heard of the aptly named herb from cook gardeners who grew their own precious supplies. Since I've yet to see it commercially cultivated, and since it doesn't seem to retain much flavor as a dried herb, I think gardening is the only valid choice here. Not a bad visual option when you see the tall pillars of purple spiked flowers in full bloom. The taste, as you would expect from the name, has a mild licorice impression on a base of rather sweet mint. The former hits the palate first, but the sweetness lingers longer than expected, especially in cold treatments like salsas and salads.

Because it does cultivate well in its native America, you see ingenious cooks trying it in everything from pork roasts to butter cookies. The leaves impart their taste easily and can be crushed, blended, or pounded into a sweet pesto. Seafood—shrimp, for example—can be wrapped in the larger leaves that come in the fall and grilled to perfection. A particular favorite from a local herb farm is lemonade infused with anise hyssop and lavender. The savory lavender balances the sweetness, and almost no added sugar is needed.

Closely related to anise hyssop is an entry into the herb world from South Asia called Korean mint, which has an almost identical flavor and use. If you're lucky enough to have local Asian produce markets, they may be your saving grace if your gardening skills are as poor as mine.

Lavender and Anise Hyssop Lemonade

Herb infusions add special flavors to the classic summertime lemonade. While you can certainly add the herbs directly to a regular batch of the drink, the best way to get a potent taste is to prepare a flavored syrup ahead of time and use this to make the lemonade. The same technique can be used with any combination of herbs on hand. Use the syrups in dessert toppings, or head to the bar and make some flavorful martinis and cosmopolitans.

HERB SYRUP

1 cup fresh anise hyssop leaves

¼ cup (unsprayed) dried lavender flowers

2 cups water

1¼ cups granulated sugar

4 lemons

2 quarts spring water, chilled

To make the herb syrup, combine the anise hyssop, lavender flowers, and water in a blender, and blend well. Pour into a saucepan, add the sugar, and bring to a low boil. Reduce the heat and stir until the sugar completely dissolves; let cool, then strain the mix through cheesecloth or a fine strainer and pour into a bottle.

Slice the lemons, removing the seeds, and put in a glass pitcher, along with the accumulated juices. Add the spring water and sweeten with the herb syrup to taste. Refrigerate the remaining syrup for other uses. Refrigerate the lemonade until thoroughly chilled.

JUNIPER

ALTERNATE NAME **Juniper berries**

BOTANICAL NAME OF CULINARY SPECIES *Juniperus communis*

PLANT FAMILY **Cypress (*Cupressaceae*)**

COUNTRY/REGION OF BOTANICAL ORIGIN **Southern Europe**

MAJOR COUNTRIES/REGIONS OF CULTIVATION **Italy, Turkey, Slovenia**

SEASON OF HARVEST **Midsummer**

PARTS USED **Berries**

COLOR **Blue-black, with waxy white sheen**

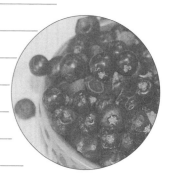

When people hear the word juniper, they think of shrubbery or gin. While I'm certainly a fan of both bonsai and a properly mixed gin and tonic, there's so much more that the culinary species of the plant can give us in the kitchen.

As might be expected, the flavor is sharp and will leave a "buzz" on the tongue if chewed directly when fresh. Showing the distinctive gin aroma in fresh batches, it can be tempered with only a modest amount of cooking heat, since the flavor compounds are particularly volatile. I like the mindset held by the ancient (and modern) Romans that juniper has a refreshing, or cleansing, character. Almost antiseptic at first taste, this will translate into lighter flavor on the palate, cutting through even the most fatty meats to add a savory, woodsy taste and aroma.

The waxy, bluish berries of the female plant are most commonly used, although I've seen some beer-brewing recipes that call for both flowers and fronds of the plant. Look for intact, undimpled berries that still exhibit signs of the natural white wax. The berries can be costly per pound, as it takes up to three years for them to mature, but the flavor is so intense that small amounts are the norm, and cost should not be a concern. One of the best regions of cultivation is Italy, and the berries can be found in Italian groceries and throughout Mediterranean cuisine. The cook-gardener is warned that only the low, shrublike culinary species of the plant, just a few of the fifty-five or so varieties in the family, should be used in the kitchen, to avoid toxic results.

One of the most common uses is in wild meat marinades. The depth of juniper's flavor combines and tempers the gamy character of venison and wild birds; it's also a natural with lamb. Crush just a few of the whole berries with coarse salt to make a seasoning salt, or cold-infuse them in oil and garlic for a few days in the refrigerator to use in searing the meats before roasting. Bolder palates might add the berries directly to garlic, sea salt, oil, and rosemary to make a paste that, slathered onto roasts, will crisp into a crust loaded with flavor.

You'll also see juniper in the picklings and krauts of eastern France and Germany. One of the most intriguing wine pairings I've ever had was a juniper-and-mustard-seed-laden sauerkraut alongside a wonderfully sweet Alsatian Pinot Gris, the sweet of the wine perfectly foiled by the berry's sharp edge.

Of course, no discussion of juniper would be complete without a nod to gin, the distilled alcohol flavored with the berries. What most people don't realize is that the recipes almost always include more than just juniper from the spice rack. Gin is one of the alcoholic beverages that vary widely from producer to producer, based on closely guarded recipes. If one isn't to your liking, try another—not just in your cocktails, but also in your cooking.

Experiment with gin in dishes where the alcohol will cook away, leaving behind traces of the juniper in its makeup. One favorite is a thin, piquant sauce made from lemon juice, capers, garlic, butter, and gin. I toss this into pasta with chopped tomato for an interestingly tart side dish anywhere I need to brighten an otherwise somewhat mundane plate.

Juniper and Mustard Sauerkraut

Sauerkraut doesn't have to be a lifeless remnant of cabbage found in the back of the fridge, left over from the last time you made Reuben sandwiches. Made fresh, it takes the underappreciated cabbage to wonderfully sour-and-sweet extremes, suitable as a side dish with pork cutlets or sausages in the German tradition. Here I start from scratch, but if you don't have a few extra weeks to make your own, purchase good-quality ready-made kraut from a local German deli and continue the recipe from there. **SERVES 4**

FOR THE KRAUT

5 pounds firm cabbage

3 tablespoons coarse sea salt, dissolved in ½ cup spring water

FOR THE DISH

3 cups prepared sauerkraut

1 tablespoon brown mustard seeds, half cracked, half left whole

1 teaspoon crushed juniper berries

½ teaspoon coarsely ground caraway seeds

2 tablespoons granulated sugar

4 slices of bacon, chopped

1 cup thinly sliced red onions or sweet onions such as Vidalia

Making kraut from scratch is simple but time-consuming, so I always make a large batch when I'm going to the trouble, but proportions are easily scaled up or down. Shred the cabbage and put in a heavy earthenware crock. Add salt water. Stir the cabbage very well, using your hands, then press it down firmly. Place the crock in a cool, dark place and place a wet towel over the surface of the cabbage, followed by a plate and a heavy weight (5 pounds or more). Let stand for 48 hours, then check to make sure enough liquid is being exuded by the cabbage to maintain a moist state throughout. Add more salted water if necessary. Let stand for up to 2 weeks, changing the towel every 48 hours and tasting the kraut occasionally to see if it has "cured." When fermentation is complete, bag or vacuum-seal the kraut, and refrigerate for up to 14 days.

For the dish, stir the 3 cups kraut together with the mustard seeds, juniper berries, caraway seeds, and sugar in a bowl, cover, and refrigerate overnight.

Cook the bacon and onion together in a large skillet over medium-high heat until the bacon renders its fat and begins to crisp slightly, about 3 minutes. Stir in the kraut and heat through. Serve as a side dish, or use as a condiment on sandwiches and sausages. Store, covered, in the refrigerator for up to 5 days.

KAFFIR LIME

ALTERNATE NAMES **Wild lime, Indonesian lime**

BOTANICAL NAME OF CULINARY SPECIES *Citrus hystrix*

PLANT FAMILY **Citrus *(Rutaceae)***

COUNTRY/REGION OF BOTANICAL ORIGIN **Southeast Asia**

MAJOR COUNTRIES/REGIONS OF CULTIVATION **Thailand, Malaysia, Southeast Asia**

SEASONS OF HARVEST **Year-round (leaves), Summer and fall (fruits)**

PARTS USED **Leaves, Fruit**

COLOR **Emerald green**

Every culture has some signature flavors that define its cuisine. For Southeast Asian populations, you cannot get more authentic than *kaffir* lime. The electric perfume of the fresh plants is unique to the roadside stalls serving soups and curries everywhere, and the taste is something not readily duplicated with any substitute.

The zest of the dimpled fruit, as well as its juice, is used in regional cuisine, but both take a back seat to the leaf. The flavor of the leaves, both fresh and dried, is a tart citrus-lime that hints of lemongrass sweetness throughout. In fact, it's an intensity you expect from the zest of more familiar members of the citrus family.

Drying the leaves is possible at home, but depending on humidity and speed of drying, you can get results ranging from the proper brilliant green of the fresh leaf to a pale yellow brown, which means you've lost most of the flavor. The thickness of the leaves you start with has much to do with your success, but all my experiments say it's also a matter of luck. Lay the leaves out on a flat counter in a single layer and aim strong lights in their direction. I have not had good luck with low ovens or dehydrators, as these tend to leach out more flavors than they save with this plant.

The plant itself looks like a joke. A thick stalk grows up with evenly spaced, waxy green leaves springing out. The first oddity is at the tip of each leaf, where another leaf

CITRIX FAMILY IMPORT BAN

There's one problem to contend with in America as of this writing. The *kaffir* lime plant, being of the citrus family, has succumbed to a citrus canker in many parts of the world. While not harmful to humans, the blight could affect other citrus crops and, as such, has been banned for *import* to the United States. Fortunately, this ban has prompted some industrious farmers here to turn to its production, and so sources for the fresh *kaffir* leaf, while more scarce than in the past, still exist. The laws of supply and demand tell us that that makes for a more expensive crop—and, unfortunately, there is no substitute in my mind for this unique flavor.

In the same family, Sichuan peppercorns are also banned, and since they don't cultivate well in the Americas, the only option for the cook is to procure their much more expensive cousin, *sansho*, from Japan. It will stretch your wallet, but at least you'll be adding the intended flavors to your cooking.

---

of the same size grows out as if someone had come along and glued them in place just to throw the casual observer an askew visual. The almost perfectly round fruit of the tree is dimpled and crinkled as if it had been partially dehydrated while still on the tree, and it's firmly planted at the end of a stalk rather than hanging from a stem. To round out its goofy appearance, there are sharp thorns about two inches long up the entire length of the short tree. Mother Nature was having quite an day when she thought up this one.

Look for a brilliant green color in both the leaves and the fruit, if you are lucky enough to come across it, not a brown or yellow tinge. More important, smell them: when you open a container of kaffir leaves, the aroma should almost knock you back with a lime punch, not leave you wondering about a hint of miscellaneous citrus.

The plant thrives in tropical climates, but it has not been widely planted outside the Southeast Asian peninsula. With the U.S. import ban (see box above), cultivation has begun in California on a limited scale, and my guess is that ingenious farmers in Australia will follow suit soon to meet the growing demand here. As *kaffir* lime is not used in Latin cuisine, the middle Americas have yet to capitalize on their ideal climate, but economics may well pressure them into the *kaffir* game too.

Phở, the classic Vietnamese broth soup, can be as simple as chicken stock and *kaffir*, or it can be complemented with galangal, garlic, and lemongrass, to name just a few variations. *Kaffir*, however, is essential for the genuine article, and I've never seen a *phở* recipe that didn't include some form of the plant. In any Vietnamese community, bragging rights are held by whoever produces the best bowl, judged not just for a jolt of flavor, but also for balance and roundness of character. *Kaffir* can contribute to this balancing act on both the sweet and sour fronts.

Pounded in tall mortars, Thai curry pastes often use a base of the lime leaf along with other fresh ingredients like garlic, cilantro, and chiles. The tart *kaffir* can cut through the stronger flavors and bring the other more disparate tastes together.

Thai Curried Beef

Once you've made your daily ration of curry paste, the rest is just assembly. For this dish, you call upon complex red Thai paste, heavy with *kaffir*, to bring the bulk of the flavor. Fresh bamboo shoots and water chestnuts are a far cry from the canned versions and really should be hunted down for this recipe; look for them in Asian markets. The cooking goes quickly, so have everything at the ready when you start. For a variation, cook cubes of fresh tofu separately in peanut oil until puffed and golden (see Ma Pua Do Fu, page 302), and add with the scallions. Serve with steamed jasmine or sticky rice. **SERVES 3 TO 4**

2 tablespoons peanut oil

1 pound boneless lean beef, such as bottom round, thinly sliced

¼ cup Thai Red Curry Paste (page 398)

2 tablespoons palm sugar, or dark brown sugar

1 cup water

4 fresh water chestnuts, peeled and thinly sliced

1 cup fresh bamboo shoots, cut into short wide ribbons, cooked in boiling water for 5 minutes (see Note)

6 scallions, trimmed and cut into 3-inch pieces

Heat a wok over medium-high heat. Add the oil and heat until very hot. Add the beef and cook, stirring, until lightly browned, about 2 minutes. Add the curry paste, palm sugar, and only enough water (about ¾ cup) to mix well. Toss in the water chestnuts and bamboo shoots and cook until heated through. Add the scallions, along with 2 tablespoons water, cover instantly, and steam until the beef is cooked to medium-rare, about 2 minutes longer.

NOTE: Most fresh bamboo shoots contain a bitter toxin, so they must always be parboiled before using.

KENCUR

ALTERNATE NAMES **Resurrection lily, Cekur**

BOTANICAL NAME OF CULINARY SPECIES *Kaempferia galanga*

PLANT FAMILY **Ginger *(Zingiberaceae)***

COUNTRY/REGION OF BOTANICAL ORIGIN **Southeast Asia**

MAJOR COUNTRIES/REGIONS OF CULTIVATION **Thailand, Indonesia, Malaysia**

SEASON OF HARVEST **Year-round**

PARTS USED **Roots, Lower stalks**

COLORS **Pale orange-yellow (roots), Green (stalks)**

With all the confusion surrounding the species of galangal offered in the spice trade, it's good fortune that *Kaempferia galanga* finally broke away and got its own name, *kencur*. This naming convention makes sense given that its properties straddle the middle ground between galangal and its cousin ginger more evenly than other related plants.

Visually, *kencur* looks most like young spring ginger. Its pale white-yellow roots are usually smaller, no more than three inches long, and less knobby than other rhizomes harvested for the kitchen. The bright green leaf shoots that grow from the top of the roots are also eaten like spring onions with various dishes of the Malay Peninsula and across the Indian Ocean to Sri Lanka and India proper.

The taste of the root is decidedly more like cardamom than galangal, with a strong aroma of menthol-meets-ginger. The mustard tones you expect from galangal are almost nonexistent, giving way to more of a citrus heat, like that in the freshest ginger.

Spicy Shrimp Toast

One of my earliest introductions to dim sum, the classic array of appetizer-sized dishes served in teahouses across China, was in British Columbia, at the age of six. A less likely venue couldn't have been conjured up, as my family had taken a day trip north of the border from Washington State, only to find ourselves in the middle of nowhere asking for directions at the first gas station in miles. It was run by a recently immigrated family from Hunan Province who, in addition to re-fueling our RV and pointing us in the right direction, offered to share their lunch. They were amazed that we actually had a dining room on wheels, and we were amazed at the array of steamers and woks, not to mention the plethora of ingredients, they had assembled for their midday meal. I remember steamed buns filled with pork, little baskets of potato with chicken and rice, and, my favorite, shrimp toast. That day planted the seed in my mind to try and re-create this most artful of culinary endeavors. And after years of miserable attempts, I finally got a proper recipe on a trip overseas to Thailand, farther south from the original but just as good as in my memory.

The shrimp flavor holds up nicely when mixed with the *Basa Genep* and tamari, while the pork adds depth. And when fried quickly at the proper temperature, the toasts are delicate and not at all greasy. You might want to make up more than you need, as they tend to disappear quickly. **SERVES 8**

---

1 pound shrimp, peeled, deveined, and chopped

2 tablespoons minced lean pork

1 tablespoon minced pork fat

1 scallion, finely minced

2 teaspoon red chile flakes (optional)

3 tablespoons *Basa Genep* (page 397) or Thai Red Curry Paste (page 398)

1 tablespoon cornstarch

2 teaspoons tamari soy sauce

8 thin slices of firm white bread

Peanut oil, for deep-frying

Combine all the ingredients except the bread and oil in a bowl and mix together with your fingers until thoroughly blended.

Trim each slice of bread to a crustless 4-inch square, and spread thickly with the shrimp mixture. Cover with plastic wrap and refrigerate for 30 minutes.

In a deep skillet or pot, or a deep fryer, add the oil to a depth of about 2 inches, and heat to 360°F. Add the toasts in batches, shrimp side down if using a skillet, and cook until the bread is golden brown. Remove to paper towels to drain, and serve warm.

KOKUM

ALTERNATE NAMES **Black mangosteen, Amsul, Sour rind**

BOTANICAL NAMES OF CULINARY SPECIES *Garcinia indica* (Indian), *Garcinia atroviridis* (Asian)

PLANT FAMILY **Mangosteen (Guttiferea)**

COUNTRY/REGION OF BOTANICAL ORIGIN **Southern India**

MAJOR COUNTRIES/REGIONS OF CULTIVATION **India, China**

SEASON OF HARVEST **Late spring to early summer**

PARTS USED **Fruits**

COLOR **Deep reddish-brown**

Here's an oddity of the spice world that's little known outside southern India's coastal regions. The sticky-sweet dried, sometimes salted, rinds of a fruit related to the mangosteen are sold packed in tiny bales. Soaked, they will yield a sweet-tart souring agent like tamarind that is used in everything from flavored ices to lentil dishes.

The tiny fruits, usually no more than two inches in diameter and with a purple-black skin, look like passion fruit at first glance. Concealed within are a dozen or so painfully hard seeds with lighter inner flesh, reminiscent of dried citrus in appearance and aroma. Recipes call for a number of "skins," which typically means fruit halves that have been opened to expose the pulp for dehydration. The seeds can be readily plucked from the skins as they rehydrate in a soaking liquid and gradually let go of the flesh. The liquid should also be conserved, to be used in various dishes or, as is the custom in the blazing-hot climates of southern India, whipped into a cooling beverage with other fruit juices and jaggery sugar. Coconut milk infused with *kokum* is a particular favorite of mine, and it can be had as a bottled beverage in most Indian and some Asian grocery stores.

This cooling effect is well documented, much as with aloe vera, and *"kokum butter"* made from various parts is marketed as a skin treatment—it is *not* a culinary product. Check the label closely to be sure what you are eating.

In bean and lentil dishes, the tartness of *kokum* blends well with more bitter components like ajwain and cumin, but it also plays nicely with sweet mixes like *garam masala*. Infusing butter with soaked *kokum* pulp to start fish curries is very traditional, and sautéing onions in *kokum* liquid makes a savory-tart base to build upon with potatoes and root vegetables. More elaborate pastes called *saars* are made with *kokum* and can include chiles, cumin, pepper, garlic, ginger, cilantro, and coriander.

The dried skins are sometimes commercially soaked and distilled into a paste or liquid that can be conveniently added to dishes for a tart flavor. Sold like tamarind pulp, this is a perfectly good product in most cases, so long as the sugar content hasn't been elevated to ridiculous levels. Remember that in all uses of *kokum,* you'll be adding both significant color and flavor with only a small dose, so plan accordingly.

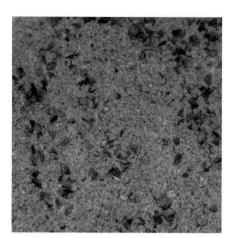

1 Adobo

2 Ajwain

3 Allspice

4 Amchoor

5 Amchoor, whole

6 Ancho Chili Powder

7 Angelica, root

8 Anise, brown

9 Anise-Hyssop, fresh

10 Annatto, seeds

11 Arrowroot

12 Asafetida

13 Avocado Leaf

14 Barberry

15 Basil, dried

16 Basil, mammoth

17 Basil, Thai

18 Bay Leaf, California

19 Bay Leaf, Indian

20 Bay Leaf, Turkish

21 Bay Seasoning

22 Beale Street Barbecue Rub

23 Berberé

24 Black Lemon

25 Black Salt

26 Borage

27 Bush Tomato

28 Cajun Blackening

29 Candlenut

30 Capetown Masala

31 Caraway, seeds

32 Cardamom, black, pods

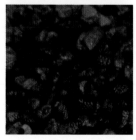

33 Cardamom, green, pods
Cardamom, white, pods
Cardamom, seeds, decorticated

34 Cassia-Cinnamon,
Chinese

35 Cassia-Cinnamon, Indonesian, chips

36 Cassia-Cinnamon Sticks

37 Catnip

38 Celery, seeds

39 Chai Spice

40 Chervil, fresh

41 Chicory, roasted

42 Chile, Aleppo Pepper

43 Chile, Ancho

44 Chile, Chinese

45 Chile, Guajillo

46 Chile, Habanero

47 Chile, Habanero, flakes

48 Chile, India, red

49 Chile, Pasilla Oaxaca

50 Chile, pequin

51 Chinese Five-Spice

52 Chinese Mushrooms, red

53 Chinese Stock Spices

54 Chives, dried (left)
Chives, fresh (right)

55 Cilantro

56 Cinnamon Sticks, True

57 Cloves

58 Coriander and Cilantro

59 Coriander, European

60 Coriander, Indian

61 Coriander, Vietnamese

62 Cubeb

63 Cumin Seeds, black

64 Cumin Seeds, black and brown

65 Curry Leaf

66 Curry, Madras

67 Curry, Pakistani

68 Curry, Sri Lanka

69 Dill Seeds

70 Dill Weed, dried

71 Dill Weed, fresh

72 Duqqa

73 Epazote, dried

74 Epazote, fresh

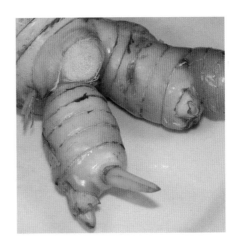

75 Fajita Taco Spice

76 Fennel, bulb

77 Fennel, seeds

78 Fenugreek, seed and leaf

79 Fines Herbs

80 Galangal, Greater

81 Garam Masala, Indian

82 Garam Masala, Kashmiri

83 Garlic

84 Ginger, crystallized

85 Ginger, dried and cut

86 Ginger, Hand

87 Ginger, Spring

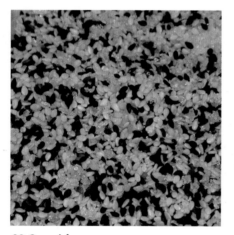

88 Gomaisho

89 Grains of Paradise

90 Gumbo

91 Hawaij

92 Herbs de la Garrique

93 Herbes de Provence

94 Horseradish, fresh

95 Hyssop, fresh

96 Juniper Berry

97 Kaffir Lime Leaf, fresh

98 Kala Masala

99 Kharcho

100 Khmeli Suneli

101 Kokum

102 Lavender Flowers

103 Lemongrass, leaf

104 Lemongrass, stalk

105 Lemon Myrtle

106 Lemon Verbena

107 Licorice Root

108 Mace

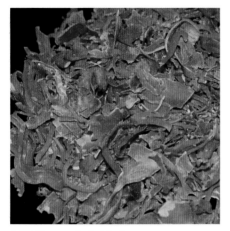

109 Mace, whole blades

110 Mahleb

111 Marjoram, dried

112 Marjoram, fresh

113 Medieval English Beef Rub

114 Mélange Classique

115 Methi

116 Mitsuba, fresh

117 Mole Powder

118 Montreal Steak Spice

119 Mulling Spice

120 Mustard Powder

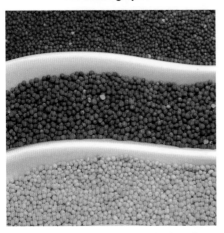

121 Mustard Seeds, brown/black/yellow

122 New Mexican Chili Powder

123 Nigella

124 Nutmeg

125 Oregano, fresh

126 Oregano, Mexican and Turkish, dried

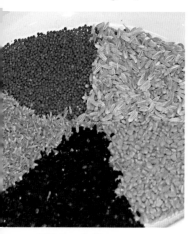

127 Panch Phoran

128 Paprika, smoked

129 Parsley, curly and flat

130 Parsley, Italian

131 Peppercorn, black

132 Peppercorn, green

133 Peppercorn, white

134 Pepper, long

135 Pepper, pink

136 Peppermint, dried

137 Pickling Spice

138 Pomegranate Seeds

139 Poppy, white and blue

140 Poultry Rub

141 Puodre Colombo

142 Quatre Epices

143 Ras el Hanout

144 Rosemary

145 Rosemary, fresh

146 Rose Petals

147 Saffron

148 Saffron Bundle

149 Sage, dried

150 Sage, fresh

151 Sage, rubbed

152 Salt, Alae

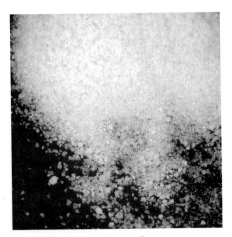

153 Salt, Kosher Diamond

154 Salt, Sel Gris

155 Sambhar

156 Sassafras Bark

157 Savory, dried

158 Savory, Winter

159 Sea Salt, Italian

160 Sea Salt, Japanese Moon

161 Sea Salt and Salt Comparative

162 Seattle Salmon Rub

163 Sesame Seeds, black/white/ natural

164 Shisho

165 Sichuan Pepper

166 Spearmint

167 Star Anise

168 Svanetti Salt

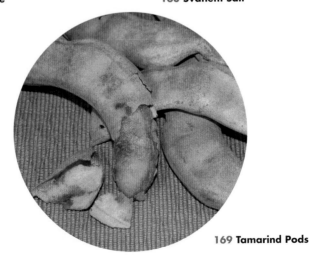

169 Tamarind Pods

170 Tandoori Spice

171 Tarragon, dried

172 Tarragon, fresh

173 Thyme, dried

174 Thyme, fresh

175 Tikka Masala

176 Togarashi

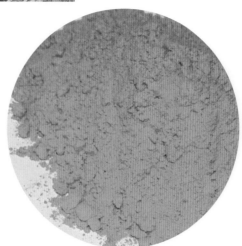

177 Turmeric, ground

178 Turmeric, root

179 Vanilla Bean

180 Wasabi

181 Yucatan Rojo Rub

182 Zahtar and Sumac

183 Zahtar, Israeli

184 Zahtar, Syrian

LAVENDER

ALTERNATE NAMES (VARIOUS SPECIES) French lavender, English lavender, Italian lavender, Spike lavender, True lavender, Fernleaf lavender, Silver sweet lavender

BOTANICAL NAMES OF CULINARY SPECIES *Lavandula officinalis.* Numerous subspecies, notably French (*L. dentate*), English (*L. angustifolia*)

PLANT FAMILY Mint (*Lamiaceae*)

COUNTRY/REGION OF BOTANICAL ORIGIN Europe

MAJOR COUNTRIES/REGIONS OF CULTIVATION France, North America

SEASON OF HARVEST Summer to early fall

PARTS USED Flowers

COLORS Various shades of purple

Lavender flowers are one of the most polarizing flavors I've found in the spice world. Either you love them or hate them—and there may be some human physiology at play that determines into which camp you fall. There is ample research to show that some people's palates interpret lavender as an unpleasant "soapy" flavor, rather than the mildly savory floral character most taste. This can be off-putting at best when you expect your dinner guests to get a savory enhancement from your herbes de Provence but get a mouthful of sudsy flavor instead. This receptor is present in only about ten percent of the population, so try an experiment to see how you perceive the flavor. A quick batch of lemonade infused with lavender, sweetened mildly, is a perfect way to test yourself on a hot summer's day.

As for the general uses of lavender, you'll see it as an integral part of the cuisine of southern France, the leading area of production, as well as in several burgeoning western U.S. styles of cooking. The newest area of significant quality production is in the upper northwest corner of Washington State, which yields plants with an interesting flavor character from the influence of the shorter growing seasons seen west of the Cascade Mountains. Lavender from French sources tends to be bolder and more savory, whereas our "home-grown" has extra sweetness on top of the traditional floral character.

With an abundance of subspecies available to the home gardener, you'll find even greater flavor swings if you grow and harvest your own lavender. The climate and soil conditions, as with most flowers, affect the final flavor significantly. Harvest—or buy from local growers—early in the season for sweetness, later in the year for the deepest, driest tastes that lavender can offer.

Lavender can be rubbed directly on meats, with a light hand, but since its potency is significant, I'd suggest incorporating it more evenly into blends by grinding. However, there's no harm in consuming the tiny purple flowers directly, other than their ability to overwhelm more subtle flavors on the palate when you bite into a whole bud.

Layering lavender flowers in plain sugar will infuse the taste in a few short weeks, for use in cookies and pastries. This perfumed sugar will flavor black tea at teatime and enhance creamy scones in the same service. A simple syrup infused with lavender can be kept on hand for making cocktails a bit later in the evening and, indeed, locals in Provence have long made infused liqueurs from their local crops. Bent into the cocktail culture of America, lavender makes a fabulous dry martini with a floral perfume unmatched elsewhere in the bar; just add several sprigs to the gin or vodka bottle and allow to steep for a few days, then strain.

I add lavender in concert with juniper to rubs for lamb and pork, as it tends to cut through fattier flavors nicely. Sautéed with the ground beef and onions to add lift to otherwise heavy meat pies, it shows its floral character well, especially when cooked with a dry red wine, which seems to bring out the best of the very classical flavor. From spiced pâté to flavored chocolate truffles, you can hardly get more French than lavender.

Lavender Shortbread

These fragrant, crumbly shortbread cookies are deceptively simple to make—the trick is getting lavender flavor into the recipe without it becoming overpowering. Making the lavender butter ahead will mellow the taste perfectly—and if you happen to make extra, your morning scones and biscuits will benefit from the effort as much as the shortbread you have for afternoon tea. **MAKES ABOUT 48 COOKIES**

¼ cup honey

2 tablespoons (unsprayed) dried lavender flowers, crushed, plus 1 teaspoon uncrushed flowers

1 pound unsalted butter, slightly softened (do not substitute margarine)

½ teaspoon fine sea salt

¾ cup granulated sugar

1 teaspoon pure vanilla extract

4 cups all-purpose flour

Combine the honey and crushed lavender in the top of a double boiler and heat over low heat for 15 minutes. Strain the honey, and discard the lavender.

Combine the butter, salt, and whole lavender flowers in a large bowl, add the honey, and beat until completely blended. Cover and refrigerate for at least 1 hour, or preferably overnight.

Bring the lavender butter to room temperature, Add the sugar and beat with an electric mixer on medium speed until light and fluffy. Beat in the vanilla. Slowly add the flour, beating just until blended. Turn the dough out onto a floured surface and shape it into a 12-inch-long log. Wrap in plastic wrap and refrigerate for at least 2 hours, or until firm enough to slice. (The dough can be refrigerated for up to 2 days.)

Preheat the oven to 350°F. Grease two cookie sheets. Slice the dough into ¼-inch rounds and place 1 inch apart on the cookie sheets.

Bake for 10 to 12 minutes, or just until the shortbread is golden brown at the edges. Let cool on the cookie sheets for 1 to 2 minutes, then, with a wide spatula, carefully remove to a rack to cool.

NOTE: The dough can also be rolled out and cut into shapes. Mix the dough, cover, and refrigerate until chilled. Roll out ½ inch thick on a floured surface and cut into desired shapes. Place 1 inch apart on greased baking sheets and bake for 12 to 15 minutes, or until golden brown at the edges.

LEMON MYRTLE

ALTERNATE NAMES **Sweet verbena, Lemon ironwood**

BOTANICAL NAME OF CULINARY SPECIES *Backhousia citriodora*

PLANT FAMILY **Myrtle (*Myrtaceae*)**

COUNTRY/REGION OF BOTANICAL ORIGIN **Australia**

MAJOR COUNTRIES/REGIONS OF CULTIVATION **Queensland**

SEASON OF HARVEST **Year-round**

PARTS USED **Leaves, Flowers, and Berries (rarely)**

COLOR **Olive green**

The Aboriginal peoples of Australia have been holding out on the rest of the spice world for centuries. The abundant plant resources from the land down under include oddities that rival the platypus in uniqueness, like wattle seed, mountain pepper, and lemon myrtle. They have all drawn the attention of cooks worldwide and spurred what is perhaps the newest frontier in the commercial spice trade.

Lemon myrtle, as the name indicates, rivals the citrus punch of lemon itself and may even be more potent, depending upon the oil concentration of the batch you're holding. Where it differs is that it has a distinct savory character underneath these top notes, akin to California bay or wintergreen.

The huge tropical trees, which range from twenty-five to fifty feet in height, are evergreens whose leaves can be harvested year-round. The dried leaves have long been used whole or ground in stuffings and rubs by the native people, but only now have found their way into the global pantry by way of industrious spice traders who recognized their potential. An industry that started around trade in citral oil, the volatile oil it shares with lemon, has now grown into a full-blown spice trade to all the other continents of the globe.

Curiously, it was a chef friend in Perth, across the continent from the producing areas of Queensland, who originally brought the leaves to my attention. He actually packed my Christmas present in the leaves to ship it to me safely and included a note that said, "By the time this gets to you, the leaves should be ready to use." The leaves, like California bay, actually need some amount of drying to concentrate the oils to more useful levels.

In the Queensland groves, some with more than a million trees, you see both ground and whole leaves packed for export globally. The ground version is not as evil a prospect as with other dried herbs, but look for sources with some gray-green color left, not the exceedingly brown tone that comes with age. As overseas production increases, I suspect that freshness of the supply will become less of a concern. Lucky locals in the production areas can even enjoy the berries and flowers of the tree, an exotic treat that doesn't currently make it out of the groves to the rest of us.

LEMON VERBENA

BOTANICAL NAME OF CULINARY SPECIES	*Aloysia triphylla*
PLANT FAMILY	**Verbena (Verbenaceae)**
COUNTRY/REGION OF BOTANICAL ORIGIN	**South America**
MAJOR COUNTRIES/REGIONS OF CULTIVATION	**France, North Africa, western United States**
SEASON OF HARVEST	**Summer through fall**
PARTS USED	**Leaves**
COLOR	**Pale olive green**

When Spanish conquistadores first found lemon verbena shrubs growing in South America, they might well have expected yellow fruit to appear in the fall. Just the waft of scent on the air would have convinced any explorer that he had found lemon groves. To get the most this plant could offer in the way of scent and flavor, however, all he would have had to do was strip some leaves from a convenient branch, sparing all that tedious work with peels and pits.

The leaves from this bush hold an essential oil that is useful in the kitchen or bath for a lemon-like essence both gentler and less acidic than real citrus. They exude so much oil, in fact, that the fresh leaves feel sticky to the touch, especially the adolescent leaves that are harvested from midsummer to early fall. For those who don't have a grove close by, the leaves generously hold their punch when properly dried.

Under ideal tropical conditions, the shrubs can grow to be sizable trees, upwards of twenty-five feet tall. More commonly, they reach something like six feet and branch out widely. With a proper sunny window, a potted version can thrive indoors even in the coldest of climates. Add a bonus of lovely clusters of purple flowers and a scent that won't stop, and you can easily justify a trip to the local specialty nursery.

If harvested frequently, the plants can still bear cutting back once or twice per year easily, even more in groomed commercial plantings, which encourage more new leaf growth. These farms' target markets may include food extract and perfume manufacturers and, perhaps most popularly, herbal tea producers. Lemon verbena has been grown widely in European gardens ever since its introduction by the Spanish, and French producers have become notable for its quality and potency—as have "upstart" growers in California and Oregon.

Frequently the plant is confused with true verbena, or verveine as it is known in the French tisane business, and while related, they have rather different flavors. Preparation as a tea is simply a matter of steeping dried leaves in hot water for around ten minutes. It's almost impossible to overbrew the leaves, as they have little if any innate bitterness.

In the kitchen, a similar infusion process can benefit milk or cream for puddings and ice cream and liqueurs for cooking or aperitifs. Fresh leaves can be added to steam baths for fish, chopped or blended into sauces and salsas, or layered into savory casseroles or batters for sweet cakes. And the flavor of the dried leaves is surprisingly potent and well preserved, not just for teas but crushed and added to stuffing, soup, or rice dishes.

The dried leaves are quite voluminous, much like bay leaf, and can present a bit of a storage problem, as you want to avoid crushing them and releasing their essential oils as much as possible. Giant zip-close plastic bags work well, and any part of the pantry—or house—you care to store them in will benefit from the scent. A wide variety of claims from medicinal to pest control are made about lemon verbena, but for my money, the real benefit is in the delicate flavor and aroma that rival lemongrass, lemon myrtle, and even real lemons.

Lemon Verbena Cheesecake

Lemon seems to lighten the heaviest of flavors. In the dessert world, it doesn't get much heavier—and richer—than cheesecake, so I called in the punch of lemon verbena. The natural sweetness of the leaves, almost more lemony than citrus itself, infuses the cake, adding an impressive aromatic component in the process. **SERVES 10 TO 12**

CRUST

1½ cups graham cracker crumbs

¼ cup packed light brown sugar

1 teaspoon ground cassia-cinnamon

½ teaspoon ground ginger

¼ teaspoon freshly grated nutmeg

¼ teaspoon ground mace

¼ teaspoon fine sea salt

8 tablespoons (1 stick) unsalted butter, melted

To make the crust, preheat the oven to 350°F. Butter a 10-inch springform pan.

Combine the graham cracker crumbs, sugar, cinnamon, ginger, nutmeg, mace, and salt in a bowl, mixing well. Add the butter, stirring until the crumbs are evenly moistened. Press the mixture into the bottom of the prepared pan. Bake for 8 minutes. Set aside to cool.

FILLING

1 cup heavy whipping cream

1 cup whole milk

1 vanilla bean, split

½ ounce dried lemon verbena (approximately 2 cups)

Three 8-ounce packages cream cheese, softened

1 cup granulated sugar

8 ounces (1 cup) sour cream

2 tablespoons all-purpose flour

3 large eggs

Fresh lemon verbena leaves, thin strips of lemon zest, and/or very thin slices of lemon for garnish (optional)

Combine the cream, milk, vanilla, and lemon verbena leaves in a saucepan, bring to a simmer, and simmer over medium-low heat until reduced by half, approximately 20 minutes. Strain, and allow to cool completely.

Preheat the oven to 350°F. Place a baking pan filled with water on the bottom oven rack and set the second rack in the middle position. (The pan of water helps to keep the oven moist and to prevent the cheese from cracking.) In the bowl of a stand mixer or another large bowl, cream together the cream cheese and sugar on medium speed until fluffy. On low speed, add the sour cream and flour, mixing thoroughly. Slowly add the milk mixture, incorporating it completely. Add the eggs one at a time, beating well after each addition.

Pour the batter into the prepared pan and bake for 1¼ to 1½ hours, until a skewer inserted in the center comes out almost clean. Add hot water if necessary to maintain the water level in the lower pan. Remove the cheesecake from the oven and let cool completely on a rack, then cover, and refrigerate overnight.

Remove the sides of the pan, and decorate the cheesecake with fresh verbena leaves, long spirals of zest, and/or lemon slices, if desired.

LEMONGRASS

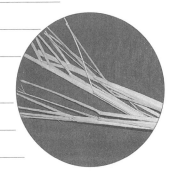

ALTERNATE NAME Citronella

BOTANICAL NAME OF CULINARY SPECIES *Cymbopogon citratus*

PLANT FAMILY *Poaceae*

COUNTRY/REGION OF BOTANICAL ORIGIN Asia

MAJOR COUNTRIES/REGIONS OF CULTIVATION Widely, especially throughout tropical regions

SEASON OF HARVEST Year-round

PARTS USED Stalks, Leaves

COLORS Pale yellow white to brilliant green

I knew lemongrass had hit mainstream America when I saw one lonely stalk hiding in the corner of my local grocery store's produce section. Although lemongrass is now commonplace all over the globe from California to Australia, and is no longer relegated to import from its native Thailand and Malaysia, it may be necessary to head to an Asian produce shop to find a recently harvested supply.

The tall stalks can reach heights of up to four feet in tropical zones but are most commonly sold as cut "bottoms," from ten to twenty inches in length, and progressing from pale yellow white to brilliant green, much like a scallion. The better-quality sources are the fresher ones that still have some green character to the tops; avoid rather dry, dull brown samples, which will have lost their potency through age. Lemongrass can be a game of inches with regard to which parts of the plant you need. When fresh, the tender middle sections of mature plants can be pounded into fabulously rich curry paste bases. The more fibrous stalk bottoms can be cut into thin ringlets, or simply pounded to infuse into stock and soup that will be strained. In younger plants, you can use more of the "green" leaves, up to the point where the stalks become too tough to be manageable. The uppermost top "greens" of the stalks are tough, razor-sharp leaves and are generally uninteresting in the kitchen, but they can be dried and used to infuse a very nice herbal tea. Try them along with ingredients like hibiscus, ginger, or citrus peel and sweeten to taste with honey.

As the name indicates, the taste is almost a perfect imitator of lemon zest and, as such, lemongrass can be used anywhere the familiar tart, sharp flavor is desired. Fish and shrimp can be easily flavored with a fine dice of the most tender shoots, and when making Asian-influenced crab boils, a stalk or two tossed into the pot will add as much aroma as flavor. If there is any difference compared with lemon, it's a slightly lesser potency and what can best be described as a mild back-of-the-palate tingle typically associated with ginger or chiles.

With the exception of herbal teas, the dried versions of lemongrass hold little interest. The volatile oils, as with lemon, evaporate quickly, and the drying process makes the various parts too tough beyond use as an infusing ingredient. Similarly, pre-ground versions have probably lost their entire flavor makeup and should be avoided completely.

Phở (Vietnamese Soup)

There is perhaps nothing more classically Vietnamese than *phở*, the brothy soup that is a source of national pride and an outlet for individual creativity. I think the people of Vietnam delight in the simplicity of the dish but also get a kick out of making theirs just a little bit different from the one at the next stall up the street.

Simmered all day long, the soup takes on a bright, acidic character from the spices, not unpleasantly so. It makes the soup refreshing and crisp rather than weighted down from too much fat or a murky mix of ingredients. The name, by the way, is pronounced "fuh." Just by taking the time to get this correct, you'll make friends at the local Vietnamese deli, where they may get a kick out of Western accents but greatly appreciate the effort/attempt, as indicated by polite giggles. **SERVES 6 TO 8**

¾ pound boneless beef, thinly sliced and cut into bite-sized pieces if necessary

1 pound beef bones, cut into 3-inch pieces (ask the butcher to cut the bones)

3 quarts water

20 *kaffir* lime leaves

2 tablespoons thinly sliced tender lemongrass

1 cup minced onions

1 tablespoon minced garlic

1 teaspoon fine sea salt, or to taste

1 teaspoon fish sauce

1 tablespoon white vinegar

2 ounces dried thin egg noodles

6 ounces firm tofu, cubed

Put the beef, bones, and water in a medium pot, and bring to a simmer. Wrap the *kaffir* leaves and lemongrass in a cheesecloth sachet and pound to crush the leaves. Toss into the pot along with the onions, garlic, and salt, reduce the heat to low, and simmer for 2 hours.

Add all the remaining ingredients, and cook until the noodles are tender. Remove and discard the sachet and beef bones. Serve piping hot.

LICORICE

ALTERNATE NAMES **Sweetroot, Sweetwood, _Orozuz_ (Spanish),
Liquirizia (Italian)**

BOTANICAL NAME OF CULINARY SPECIES **_Glycyrrhiza glabra_**

PLANT FAMILY **_Leguminosae_**

COUNTRY/REGION OF BOTANICAL ORIGIN **Turkey, Middle East**

MAJOR COUNTRIES/REGIONS OF CULTIVATION **Western United States,
southern Europe, widely across Middle East and Asia**

SEASON OF HARVEST **Late summer through winter**

PARTS USED **Roots**

COLORS **Dark brown outer skin and yellow inner flesh**

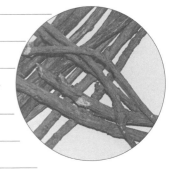

This isn't the confection familiar to the sweets shop—it's actually the branch roots of a plant in the _Leguminosae_ family. Countless medicinal benefits have been claimed over the years, but perhaps what keeps our palates interested is the naturally occurring sweetening agent, glycyrrhizin, that can compose up to one-quarter of the plant's makeup.

The roots used are a light brown color and roughly pencil thick, harvested anywhere from two to twenty inches in length. Their flavor is akin to fennel, aniseed, or star anise, and those extracts are frequently used as substitutes in southern Europe and across the Mediterranean. The Italians are particularly fond of confections made with the genuine article. A unique treatment of lamb or beef in the Basque region is a tapa of grilled marinated meat, with the peeled and sharpened roots used as skewers.

More practically in the kitchen, uses of the fibrous root are mostly limited to infusions into liquid. The texture of the roots is such that direct consumption is nearly impossible. Split the long roots lengthwise to expose the inner flesh, or purchase cut forms for the same result. Steeping licorice into cream for ice cream and sweet pastries is a proven technique, but one restaurant kitchen I know uses licorice at the other end of the spectrum: they add cut licorice and fresh ginger slices to the braising liquid for pepper-crusted pork roast. The resulting drippings are strained and thickened into a magically sweet sauce at service.

Outside the kitchen, licorice is used as a tobacco additive and in cosmetic applications. According to the ancient Greeks, it helps the body retain water and thus reduces thirst. I have had people in the midst of trying to quit smoking come and buy some to chew on for the ongoing sweetness that helps reduce craving.

Grilled Beef on Licorice Skewers

Licorice roots are strong enough, in both flavor and strength, to use as skewers for grilled meats. The sweetness permeates the meat from inside and perfumes everything cooking over the flames at the same time.

Slide the beef off the skewers into pitas or onto slices of a baguette and layer on a mild pepper puree, yogurt sauce, or mustard to highlight the licorice sweetness even more.
SERVES 6 TO 8

2 cups Rioja or other red wine

¼ cup Worcestershire sauce

5 garlic cloves, finely chopped

3 tablespoons finely ground fennel seeds

3 pounds boneless beef bottom round, cut into 1½-inch cubes

Six 8-inch-long licorice roots

2 large sweet unions, such as Vidalia, cut into 1-inch chunks

2 tablespoons regular paprika, or smoked paprika (pimentón)

In a large zip-close bag, combine the wine, Worcestershire, garlic, and fennel. Add the beef and toss to coat. Seal and refrigerate, turning occasionally, for 2 hours, preferably overnight. Meanwhile, shortly before grilling, using a vegetable peeler, peel the licorice roots, shaving them to form a point on one end. Place the peeled roots in cold water to cover for 20 minutes. If desired, soak the peelings separately to use for smoking. Prepare a hot fire in an outdoor grill.

Remove the beef from the marinade and skewer it on the licorice roots, alternating the meat with the chunks of onion. Dust with the paprika. Grill, turning regularly, for approximately 4 minutes on each side (a total of about 16 minutes), for medium-rare; or grill to desired doneness. Slide the beef and onions off the skewers onto a platter, and serve.

MACE

ALTERNATE NAME	**Blade mace**
BOTANICAL NAME OF CULINARY SPECIES	*Myristica fragrans*
PLANT FAMILY	*Myristicaceae*
COUNTRY/REGION OF BOTANICAL ORIGIN	**Banda Islands (Indonesia)**
MAJOR COUNTRIES/REGIONS OF CULTIVATION	**Grenada, Sri Lanka, Madagascar, Indonesia**
SEASONS OF HARVEST	**Summer and fall**
PARTS USED	**Nut shell covering**
COLOR	**Creamy orange to brilliant red**

Inside the bitter fruit of the nutmeg tree lie two edible treasures: the nutmeg nut, of course, but also the lacy covering around its outer shell, called mace. The brilliantly red "fingers" wrap the inner shell like a fist clenched around a ball and almost dare you to make them let go of their bounty.

When the peach-shaped fruits are first opened, you will see the leathery red mace blades wrapped around the center pit. Workers cut these blades off by hand, making separate piles of the new mace blades and the unopened nutmegs still in the shell. The blades dry quickly after harvest to a duller orange-brown or brick red color and are sold whole or commercially ground into a powder. The nutmegs are then shelled as a separate spice (see page 234). If you're lucky enough to come across intact mace blades, check to make sure they don't crumble easily between your fingers and still have some resilience. As they age and lose flavor compounds, they become very brittle.

It's almost impossible to grind fresh mace blades at home without some serious wrangling, so pick a form that best suits your cooking. Whole blades are suitable for stocks and soups where they will be removed after cooking; preground is fine for pastries and thick sauces. Those diehard freshness seekers who do attempt to grind the blades at home will do well to freeze them for a short time first to make them more grindable—but they should know that this is at a cost to flavor.

Mace can bring a burst of flavor in cream-based sauces and sweet pastries. Its inherent "heat" acts much like pepper to enhance flavor, but it's so edgy that it needs something like cream to temper the fire. Although it is different in taste from nutmeg itself, both have a burning character when tasted directly, much like clove. The flavor is powerful and even when using the more muted preground versions, small amounts are in order. The French and the Basque use mace in tandem with its sibling nutmeg to mellow the impact on the palate, a curious chemical interaction Mother Nature has left for us.

The savory aspects of mace can also be very complementary with meats and creamy cheeses. The problem of use, again, is in dosing such a potent flavor. Stirring it into fondue or adding it to basting liquids will successfully homogenize the flavor playing field, but direct application—in rubs, for example—will require more voluminous medium with mace representing no more than one-tenth, at most, of the overall measure of the blend. I frequently use coriander or fenugreek to bulk up a blend and carry the stronger flavors of mace directly to the food. I try to minimize other assertive flavors like peppercorn, cumin, or chiles that would obscure the complexity of the mace I'm looking to feature.

Steamed Spiced Fig Cake

When the holidays come around, everyone wants to get into the tradition. For pastry-impaired people like myself, it's quite a discovery when you find that there's an almost foolproof method of making a cake. Being in the food business means that people expect a cornucopia of treats to spring forth from my kitchen as winter sets in. But apart from the odd sugar cookie or apple pie, my baking efforts, especially those requiring more delicate skills, tended to be abysmal. My rescue came at the hands of English cooks who clued me into a trick that won't let you overcook or otherwise produce dry-as-a-board cake: steaming rather than baking produces a moist, rich dessert without fail. Fruit-rich and spiced in the spirit of the season, this cake will make your house smell of yuletide as it gently cooks through most of an afternoon. The only possible difficulty is easily solved by a trip to the kitchen supply store for properly sized equipment: You need a 10-inch springform pan and an ordinary bamboo steamer large enough to hold it. **SERVES 8 TO 10**

½ cup dried figs

½ cup golden raisins

1 cup sweet sherry

2 cups all-purpose flour

2 teaspoons baking powder

2 teaspoons Pumpkin Pie Spice (page 352)

½ teaspoon fine sea salt

½ cup very finely chopped walnuts

8 tablespoons (1 stick) unsalted butter, softened

¾ cup packed light brown sugar

1 tablespoon grated orange zest

2 large eggs, beaten

1 cup whole milk

Whipped cream, or ice cream, for serving (optional)

Soak the figs and raisins in the sherry for at least 30 minutes until softened; drain.

Grease and flour a 10-inch springform pan. Set up a steamer large enough to hold the pan. Whisk the flour, baking powder, Pumpkin Pie Spice, and salt together; toss with the nuts.

In a stand mixer, beat together the butter, sugar, and orange zest. Slowly add the eggs. Add the dry ingredients, alternating with the milk, beating until incorporated. Remove from the mixer and fold in the drained fruit.

Pour the batter into the springform pan, and place in the steamer over gently boiling water. Use a heatsafe plate (or aluminum foil) to cover the springform pan to prevent condensation from dripping onto the cake cover, and steam until a thin knife inserted in the center comes out clean, approximately 2½ hours; check the water level occasionally to prevent it from boiling dry.

Spoon out servings while the cake is still warm, and top with whipped cream or ice cream, if desired.

MAHLEB

ALTERNATE NAMES **Mahlab, Mahleppi, Mahlebi, St. Lucie's Cherry**

BOTANICAL NAME OF CULINARY SPECIES *Prumus mahaleb*

PLANT FAMILY *Rosaceae*

COUNTRIES/REGIONS OF BOTANICAL ORIGIN **Turkey, southern Europe**

MAJOR COUNTRIES/REGIONS OF CULTIVATION **Turkey, Syria, widely in the Mediterranean**

SEASON OF HARVEST **Midsummer**

PARTS USED **Pits of fruit**

COLOR **Pale yellow to light brown**

Why would anyone start eating the pits of cherries? If you discovered they tasted better than the fruit wrapped around them, you'd certainly consider it. This is exactly the choice the ancient Turks were faced with in the case of *mahleb*, a sour cherry that grew wild in their neighborhood.

The fruit is much smaller than your favorite Bing seen in the produce section, and the pit is similarly about half the size. Similar to "pie" cherries in sourness, the red fruit is super tart, indeed almost inedible, and thus it's harvested more for the pits. Extracted, blanched, and dried, they give us a spice that has a dry aroma reminiscent of raw almonds and mild mustard. *Mahleb* is sold whole or ground as a "flour" that becomes the nutty flavor in the classic Easter bread celebrated in Orthodox churches of Turkey. It also found its way east to Russian Georgia and west to Greece, whether via traveling chefs or Catholic expansion, and became a base flavor in slow-cooked meat and lentil dishes.

One customer who found my shop simply by searching the web for "mahleb" (apparently mine was the only listing at the time) gave me her favorite childhood recipe from Greece for a dish made with the ground flour. A simple stew of lamb shanks and tomatoes is cooked completely with peppercorns and whole branches of thyme. Water and stock levels are maintained in the pot until the very end of a long, slow stewing, then the *mahleb* flour is added to thicken it into a hearty stew. It's served with thick crusty bread, and I suppose a good Greek wine would be in order as well!

MARJORAM

ALTERNATE NAMES **Joy of the mountains, Pot marjoram, Knotted marjoram**

BOTANICAL NAME OF CULINARY SPECIES *Origanum majorana*

PLANT FAMILY **Mint (*Lamiaceae*)**

COUNTRY/REGION OF BOTANICAL ORIGIN **North Africa**

MAJOR COUNTRIES/REGIONS OF CULTIVATION **Entire Mediterranean, North America, western Asia**

SEASON OF HARVEST **Summer to early fall**

PARTS USED **Leaves**

COLORS **Widely varied greens**

A delicate cousin of oregano, this herb has found itself relegated to the supporting cast all too often in modern cuisine. The older cultures of Eastern Europe and the Mediterranean rightly elevated marjoram to a place of status on its own in everything from savory meat pies to sweet pastries.

Tasting like pillowy-soft oregano, it only starts down the path of savory, without taking too many steps. There are overtones of lavender and sage in the perfume, though never with as much punch as in the genuine articles. The herb is very light in weight-to-volume when dried, almost two cups to the ounce typically, and this seems to translate as well into lightness on the palate.

French, sweet, knotted, winter, and pot marjoram are all species cultivated for culinary purposes, and the plants can vary in appearance as much as in name. Their height and coloring are all over the map, but the flavors of each seem to be more subtle variations on the theme with an underriding delicate flavor common to all. The tiny round leaves all have a downy "fuzz" when fresh, which turns into a light dust when dried, a characteristic that is no cause for concern. Tough stems, if present, should be removed before use, but these castoffs make great fodder for the smoker and can impart the familiar sweet-meets-savory marjoram flavor into meats and fish.

The best-quality dried herb comes from the most prolific varieties and will have a green-meets-slate-gray color. Be aware that any batch that doesn't have marjoram's signature volume has been stored too long or improperly, compacting the leaves and prematurely releasing the essential oils. For the fresh herb, I always look for some of the tips to have the beginnings of growth or even flowers to tell me that I'm getting the delicate new leaves rather than the tougher old growth that will have less sweetness and more of the peppery, savory bite seen in oregano.

Marjoram species are cultivated commercially in all the herb centers of Europe, with French and Slavic regions being the most notable producers of quality. Turkish producers contribute a good, if a bit more savory, crop, and micro-producers are ranged all over the Northern Hemisphere.

Rejepolsiko Marjoram-Stuffed Duck

In Poland, marjoram, unlike other warmer-climate herbs, is plentiful, and it makes notable appearances in dishes as a featured flavor. One such dish from the Rejepolsiko region is duck breasts stuffed with ground beef seasoned heavily with marjoram. Anna, my native chef-guide, who learned the recipe from her father, tells me, "You'll think you're using too much," when you first add the two cups of dried marjoram, but when the stuffed breasts are simmered with some fruity white wine, the flavor proves that marjoram mellows when other herbs would overwhelm. **SERVES 4**

1 pound lean ground beef

2 cups dried marjoram

2 garlic cloves, minced

1 cup chicken stock

1 teaspoon fine sea salt, or to taste

1 teaspoon freshly ground black pepper, or to taste

4 skin-on boneless duck breasts

¼ cup olive oil

1 cup fruity white wine, such as Riesling

Preheat the oven to 400°F. In a large skillet, brown the beef over medium heat, stirring to break up any lumps. Drain off the excess liquid, and set aside.

Combine the marjoram, garlic, stock, salt, and pepper in a food processor and process to a paste.

Put the duck meaty side up on a cutting board. Cover with plastic wrap and, using a meat pounder or a small heavy skillet, pound the breasts to flatten them. Remove the plastic wrap, and spread the marjoram paste evenly over the meat. Spread the beef evenly over the paste, and roll each breast up to enclose the filling; secure with toothpicks.

Heat the oil in a large heavy skillet over medium-high heat. Add the duck and cook, turning occasionally, until browned all over. Transfer the duck to a baking dish and pour the wine into the pan. Bring to a boil, scraping up any brown bits on the bottom of the pan. Pour this liquid over the duck.

Transfer the duck to the oven, and bake for about 20 minutes, basting frequently with the pan juices, until thoroughly cooked. Serve the stuffed breasts whole or cut into thick slices.

MINT

BOTANICAL NAMES OF CULINARY SPECIES *Mentha spicata* (spearmint), *Mentha piperita* (peppermint)

PLANT FAMILY *Mint (Lamiaceae)*

COUNTRY/REGION OF BOTANICAL ORIGIN **Northern Mediterranean**

MAJOR COUNTRIES/REGIONS OF CULTIVATION **Widely**

SEASON OF HARVEST **Cooler months regionally**

PARTS USED **Leaves**

COLORS **Various greens**

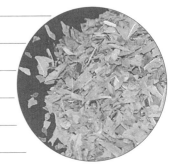

Mints of all sorts—and there are many—grow easily under the right conditions. I remember when I was a kid living in the Deep South, having, literally, to mow back a patch of mint that had sprung up on the shady end of the house to keep it from consuming the lawn. Handfuls could be picked every day, but my early spice merchant efforts proved unfruitful since everyone we knew could have bushels every day from their own patches. It's no wonder that the mint julep became the official drink of many a Southern barbecue.

Mint is one of those herbs that can surprise you with its flexibility if you let it. And when you have an almost infinite supply to work with, that's good news. Most in the West think of the herb with sweet connotations. Pastry applications start with chocolate and end with cream, all well suited to taking on mint's sweet, pungent tang. Menthol, the mint flavor constituent, infuses easily, giving as much perfume as flavor. Bruising the fresh leaves to release their oils should be a first step to ensure the most flavor. Ask any bartender how to start a mint drink and he'll tell you to "muddle" the leaves at the bottom of a glass with a (what else?) muddler—sort of an elongated pestle—usually with a small amount of sugar to better crush the leaves, and wise cooks will transfer this technique to the kitchen.

Breaking down the sweet stereotype is easily done, and in fact savory uses are more the norm for mint in Middle Eastern countries. Here the more peppery varieties are preferred, blending better with local favorites like lamb, yogurt, and beans. Moroccan and North African favorites incorporate mint, whether pure or in blends like the ubiquitous *baharat*. Both the fresh and dried leaves are used, but in either case relatively long cooking times help temper the pungency and bring a pleasantly muted version to the palate. Very commonly, dried is used for the length of cooking and a small amount of the fresh is added at the end for its aromatic quality. Fresh mint may also be introduced separately, by blending it into a yogurt or cheese condiment.

The shifts in flavor among the various species can be significant, from the "pure" mint flavors of sweet spearmint or sharper peppermint to the more exotic variations like apple mint and pineapple mint. The latter hybrids typically have more aroma of their namesakes rather than intense flavor. Since mint is the patriarch of an entire family of herbs, you'll see an almost endless array of permutations, some of which, in fact, are not closely botanically related. Examples include Korean mint (see Hyssop, anise) and Costa Rican mint (see Savory), both in the mint family but more closely related to other herbs.

Mint is a good candidate for drying, and, much like basil, gives you a concentration of flavor that changes the taste, sometimes for the better. The sweetness dims somewhat, and the "hotter," more savory notes come to the front of the palate. Substitution in recipes that call for fresh, however, is dubious at best and should generally be avoided. Where the dry leaf makes more sense is where the mint must stand up to bolder flavors. Rubs for meat with pepper and chiles, simmering with acid rich tomatoes or heavier root vegetables, and infusion into tea are all good reasons to reach for dried leaf.

Green tea mixed with mint is served strongly brewed and heavily sweetened from Turkey to Morocco, in a café culture that grew out of the trade routes from China that brought the tea westward. Normally I'd frown on a mix of "leaf" tea and herbals because of the mismatched steeping requirements, but in this particular case, the sweetness of the mint seems to mask any bitterness that comes from overbrewing the green tea. Most recipes call for a four-to-one ratio of peppermint to gunpowder green tea, steeped for about five minutes. Camels are optional.

Baharat-and-Mint-crusted Lamb

I tested this recipe with great success in front of a group of people I had never met, the friends of a new acquaintance, in a kitchen I had never set foot in. I just showed up with a lamb roast and a small cup of the spice paste I had made the night before. I mention this simply to impress on you how easy and unintimidating lamb can be. The only device you really should have for this dish is an internal probe thermometer—one with a cable attached to the probe that is inserted into the center of the roast, while the cable extends outside to the temperature indicator, so you can cook without having to open the oven door to peek. Perhaps the best fifteen dollars you'll ever spend, it will keep you from over- or under-cooking the meat, typically the biggest problem people have with lamb. My butcher tells me that a pound or so bone-in meat (before cooking) or three-quarters of a pound boneless meat per person is a good starting point for sizing your roast, allowing for generous servings (and maybe leftovers if you are lucky). I have him trim the fat to a reasonable level, leaving enough to provide natural basting.

SERVES 4 TO 8, DEPENDING ON SIZE OF ROAST (SEE ABOVE)

1 bunch fresh mint, stems removed

6 garlic cloves

Up to 1 cup extra virgin olive oil

½ cup freshly ground Baharat (page 376)

20 juniper berries, coarsely ground

One 4- to 8-pound leg of lamb, boned, rolled, and tied, or one 3- to 5-pound boned and rolled roast

Using an immersion blender, grind the mint and garlic with ¼ cup oil in a small bowl; or use a mini processor. Add the spice mix and juniper berries and continue grinding or processing, drizzling in additional oil until a thick paste forms. Cover with plastic wrap, placing it against the surface of the paste to prevent it from discoloring, and refrigerate overnight, or for up to 3 days.

Preheat the oven to 350°F. Put the roast in a roasting pan and rub generously all over with the spice paste. (If using a smaller roast, you will not need all the spice paste—the extra paste can be thinned with oil or water to make a nice table condiment.) Roast to an internal temperature of 155°F (depending on the size of the leg, this will take about 1¼ to 2 hours). Transfer the roast to a platter, cover loosely, and allow to stand for 15 minutes to help redistribute the juices before carving.

MITSUBA

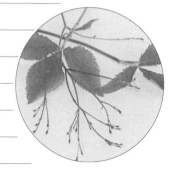

ALTERNATE NAMES Japanese parsley, Japanese chervil, Trefoil

BOTANICAL NAME OF CULINARY SPECIES *Cryptotaenia japonica*

PLANT FAMILY Mint *(Lamiaceae)*

COUNTRY/REGION OF BOTANICAL ORIGIN Japan

MAJOR COUNTRY/REGIONS OF CULTIVATION Japan

SEASONS OF HARVEST Summer (leaves), Year-round (sprouts)

PARTS USED Tender leaves, Sprouts

COLOR Pale green

I used mitsuba from my Japanese grocery store for weeks before I realized that it wasn't fresh chervil I was buying. Before I took a closer look at the leaves themselves, I thought my produce merchants had simply taken a French field trip and come back with some mild variation of that herb.

It's the three-leaf clusters that are the best clue for someone trying to find genuine mitsuba for Japanese noodle soup. The flavor, if it does vary from chervil at all, is very slightly peppery, almost as if someone had slipped in a taste of sweet allspice, but this is a very mild overtone, and cooks who cannot find the real leaves could easily substitute chervil or even flat-leaf parsley in their recipes.

Quizzing my Japanese suppliers again, I found that traditional uses beyond light broth soups include exotic mushroom preparations and egg dishes, both cases where the delicate taste will not obscure or be obscured by the other ingredients. The stems of the mature plants can be rather tough, and it's preferable to cut them away from the leaves before use. The popularity of the taste has also given rise to a thriving sprouts business, cultivated year-round in hothouses, much like alfalfa and clover. Similarly popular as a salad green or sandwich topping, the tender young shoots are harvested after just a few days' growth. Chefs make good use of mitsuba in all forms to garnish artful Japanese plates while imparting delicate flavor.

MOUNTAIN PEPPER

ALTERNATE NAMES **Tasmanian pepper, Dorrigo pepper, Mountain pepperleaf**

BOTANICAL NAME OF CULINARY SPECIES *Tasmannia lanceolata*

PLANT FAMILY *Winteraceae*

COUNTRY/REGION OF BOTANICAL ORIGIN **Southeastern Australia**

MAJOR COUNTRIES/REGIONS OF CULTIVATION **Australia**

SEASON OF HARVEST **Year-round**

PARTS USED **Leaves, Berries, Flowers (rarely)**

COLOR **Olive green (leaves), Reddish-black (berries)**

The new spice frontier of Australia offers our insatiable appetite for pepper yet more choices. Mountain pepper is botanically unrelated to "common" pepper, but it manages to satisfy in a similar, albeit more pungent, fashion. And when you tell a spice merchant that there's a "new" pepper on the market, he gets a glimmer in his eyes, knowing that the appeal of anything pepper can add to his coffers substantially.

While the verdict seems to be that only we moderns have taken advantage of mountain pepper's flavor—the Aboriginals don't seem to have tried it on their wombat steaks—it doesn't take long to appreciate the intense flavor as kitchen-worthy. And, unlike traditional *piper nigrum*, the berries aren't the only part of the plant that are dried and added to spice racks of adventurous Australian cooks. The oval leaves, smaller than bay, are dried to concentrate the flavor and used to add a relatively mild version of mountain pepper's flavor to stocks and condiments. "Relative" is the key word here, since the leaves, about half as strong as the berries themselves, are still at least double the potency of common pepper. Substituting mountain pepper for common pepper would be folly. You'd have your guests reaching for the water pitcher. The flavor of mountain pepper leans significantly toward Sichuan pepper, with a numbing effect on the palate and citrus hints that peek between the seriously peppery curtains.

The leaves seem custom-made for simmered beef dishes and add an unexpected citrus-pepper twist to classics like French beef bourguignon. Ground into a powder, they can act as a mild thickener, like *filé*, for hearty stews. And when the powder is paired with Hungarian paprika in a goulash, you begin to redraw your culinary boundaries.

The whole berries can be added in moderation wherever common pepper is appropriate, but their potency means a gentle hand is needed. Grinding gives you a sticky, oily product with the full force of mountain pepper coming to bear upon your dishes. As with Sichuan peppercorn, I prefer to temper the taste and numbing effect by mixing it with other spices like coriander or cumin.

The fine merchants of Australia have taken full advantage of their indigenous spices, blending mountain pepper with lemon myrtle, bush tomato, and wattle seed with great success. As in most regional cuisines, the natural availability of ingredients conveniently makes for good flavor combinations. Lemony myrtle, tart bush tomato, and savory wattle seeds hold up well to mountain pepper's bold nature, and such mixtures can be rubbed on local lamb or added to poaching liquid for the famous seafood that comes from the Australian coasts. Mother Nature again proves that she is perhaps the best spice merchant we know.

MUGWORT

ALTERNATE NAMES **Goose herb, Hop leaf, *Yomogi* (Japan)**

BOTANICAL NAME OF CULINARY SPECIES ***Artemisia vulgaris***

PLANT FAMILY ***Compositae***

COUNTRY/REGION OF BOTANICAL ORIGIN **Asia**

MAJOR COUNTRIES/REGIONS OF CULTIVATION **Widely across Northern Hemisphere**

SEASONS OF HARVEST **Spring and fall**

PARTS USED **Leaves**

COLOR **Flat green**

Mugwort kept popping up in my old beer-brewing texts, but as it was always followed by "substitute hops," there was never a real motivation to track it down until I saw it in a totally different context. I saw the word on a Japanese restaurant menu, listed as an ingredient in a salad. I promptly picked the salad apart until I found what looked like a tiny geranium leaf.

The curly, ornate leaves and the stems have been used in Japan as an exotic salad green for some time, but even older uses date back to Europe, where the bittering properties were used in tandem with, or to substitute for, hops. The flavor is woody and earthy, and it holds up well to cooking, especially the older specimens. A distinct mint aroma can be detected at first, which later gives way to more astringent character, much like a mellow juniper or mustard greens. The change in taste upon cooking is what makes it a useful herb in beer brewing; translating this property to the kitchen, stewing mugwort with beans or lentils would make sense.

There are well-documented uses in northern Europe, specifically Germany, of adding mugwort to roasting fatty pork or poultry, giving rise to an alternate name, goose herb. In its native Asia, there are instances of medicinal uses and even of cultural significance, such as warding off evil spirits.

MUSTARD SEEDS

BOTANICAL NAMES OF CULINARY SPECIES *Brassica hirta* **(yellow and white),** *Brassica nigra* **(black),** *Brassica juncea* **(brown)**

PLANT FAMILY *Cruciferae*

COUNTRIES/REGIONS OF BOTANICAL ORIGIN **Asia, India (brown and black), Northern Europe (yellow and white)**

MAJOR COUNTRIES/REGIONS OF CULTIVATION **Widely across central latitudes**

SEASON OF HARVEST **Late summer**

PARTS USED **Seeds**

COLORS **Yellow, Brown, Off white, Jet black**

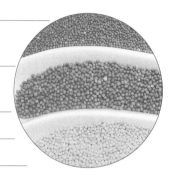

M ustard seeds can be seriously underestimated in the spice pantry because without proper treatment, they won't release their pungent treasure of taste. French Dijon, Chinese hot, or American yellow mustard can all certainly tempt the taste buds, but the whole seeds can also add depth to everything from curries to pickles.

We've all tried the prepared mustards that come with a plethora of additives from wine to honey. Even the relatively simple taste of the intensely hot Chinese condiment, typically just powder mixed with water, has become a favorite. It's the baseline of flavor, however, that the tiny seeds can add that makes them a real workhorse in the kitchen.

The four versions of whole seeds are loosely grouped botanically in pairs, black and brown together as one and yellow and white as the other. Each pair presents unique harvesting issues, but the less common species are the white and black, with the brown and yellow versions making up the bulk of global harvest. All produce what look like tiny pea pods, twenty to forty per plant, each holding four to six seeds. The yellow and white seeds are slightly larger than their brown and black counterparts, but all are perfectly round and roughly the size of a pinhead. The plants are allowed to seed, amidst a sea of tiny yellow flowers that come in June; they are harvested, dried en masse in the early fall, and threshed to release their treasures. An acre under cultivation can produce up to a ton of raw seed. They are perhaps some of the more shelf stable members of the spice world, holding good flavor for up to a year.

The difference between all the mustard seed varieties is more a question of potency than of flavor per se. The black and brown are the mildest, and almost impossible to differentiate with your eyes closed. The yellow and white have more heat and intensity. In their native India, milder versions make up the base for most curries and are usually fried in ghee to jumpstart the oil's release. Mustard in curry dishes lends a kind of heat different from peppercorn or chile while smoothing the edges between all.

In the mustard trade, innumerable proprietary recipes calling for various proportions of the different seeds can be found, remaining the secrets of each company. Several states of grind—cracked, coarse "stone-ground," and extra-fine flour—as well as the whole seeds are all employed to lend interesting textures and consistency to prepared mustards. The array is quite impressive, considering that the majority of any recipe simply consists of mustard seeds in some combination.

The famous city of Dijon, France, has become somewhat of a mustard mecca, but the name Dijon, while still an *appellation contrôlée* in France, now refers to a general style that is smooth in character, produced all over the world. While mustard was originally supported by the royalty of Burgundy as a fine luxury industry, the region's producers now make something on the order of eighty percent of all the mustard consumed in France. With the appearance of other spices via the Crusades in the fourteenth century, Dijon producers began to blend more and more complex recipes and now boast hundreds if not thousands of regional concoctions that confirm their status as the mustard center. Shops in Dijon have tastings of orange crème mustard alongside traditional smooth wine mustards, and it's not uncommon for restaurants to offer a wide selection of mustards wth every course. Even slightly sweet tarts can be flavored in varying degree with prepared mustards: a particularly odd combination from French farmhouse cookery that was unexpectedly delicious was a green apple and tomato galette that used a creamy Dijon in its potato base.

Jeremiah Colman founded the famous Colman's of Norwich brand in England around 1814, and that company continues to surpass other dry mustard powders in quality, primarily due to freshness. Their "genuine superfine" production contains a scant one percent wheat-flour stabilizer, with other versions, namely the "double superfine," having up to eighteen percent; other manufacturers may use as much as twenty-five percent in their recipes. The company's recipe, which has changed little over the years, employs both brown and white mustard seeds, harvested primarily from contract farmers in England. The seeds are processed to remove the outer bran and husks, making mustard flour or powder rather than simply ground seeds. The essential oils in most mustard powders come to life only when mixed with liquid. A few minutes after blending with water (or wine, or juice, etc.) should be allowed to let the flavors develop fully. But the same oils deteriorate quickly upon hydration, so fresh batches should be made frequently, preferably for each meal's use.

It is believed that the Romans first brought yellow and white mustard plants north through Europe. The brown and black species spread overland from their native India to meet European markets. The name derives from the Latin *ardens*, meaning "burning," and *mustum*, which is unfermented grape juice, or "must." Romans would make a combination of must and seeds as a condiment, a precursor to most modern formulas, which employ some form of vinegar to release the mustard seed oils for the base flavor of sharp heat that may be mellowed with other ingredients or simple aging.

Before modern grinding techniques were invented, pounded seeds were blended with honey, pepper, and only enough vinegar to work into putty. Small balls of the mix were formed and stored, sometimes for months, with little depreciation of taste. The cook could later pound these further into condiments or add an entire ball to simmering stock as a spicy nugget that would dissolve, leaving both heat and sweet in its wake.

The simplest recipes for prepared mustard call for seeds in various states of grind to be mixed to the desired consistency with vinegar and a pinch of salt, but more complicated versious can employ citrus juices, sherry, flavored vinegars, and countless other spices. I've had plenty of customers come back to my shop during the holidays asking for more mustard seeds as their creativity got out of control. Fortunately, mustard is forgiving and cheap, and it makes a great gift to anyone with a spare jar handy.

It's easy to see how mustard in its many forms can contribute quietly to our taste spectrum. It can wake other flavors gently or with serious punch. Certainly take advantage of exotic condiments on your corned beef or hot dog, but don't forget that simmered whole seeds and prepared powders or flours can be used to bind and bring together tastes all over the kitchen.

Blackened Chicken

This recipe is for true blackening and should only be attempted in a kitchen with adequate ventilation. Or do the cooking outside: The side burners on most gas grills work very well for this and certainly generate enough heat. Be sure to alert the neighbors so they don't call the fire department.

You want to seal in the juices with the spice crust, not just burn the outside. To accomplish this, the spice coating must completely cover the chicken and the heat must be exceedingly high. Weighting the spice-rubbed chicken also helps accomplish this, and a cast-iron skillet is really the only pan in the kitchen able to achieve the heat needed. Don't try this with boneless breasts—they'll shrivel up to nothing. **SERVES 4**

2 whole chicken breasts (bone-in), split

2 cups milk

1 cup freshly ground Cajun Blackening Spice Mix (page 344)

1 tablespoon all-purpose flour

2 teaspoons fine sea salt

Put the chicken a bowl, add the milk, and refrigerate for 1 hour.

Mix the Cajun spice, flour, and salt in a shallow pan. Drain the chicken, place in the spice mixture, and use your fingers to completely coat it. Place chicken skin side up in a baking pan and place a weighted baking sheet on top. Allow to sit in the refrigerator for another hour.

Preheat the oven to 400°F. Heat a large dry cast-iron skillet over a gas burner on high heat to the smoking point (an electric stove will not produce enough heat). Carefully place 2 breast halves at a time, skin side up, in the skillet and cook until a crust forms on the first side, about 2 minutes. Turn with long tongs and cook on the other side. Transfer to a plate and repeat with the remaining breast halves. Remove the pan from the burner and add the first 2 breast halves. Cover and place in the oven for 5 to 10 minutes, until the chicken is cooked through.

Citrus Honey Mustard

Mustard making is dreadfully simple. Use the infusion trick here to impart all manner of flavors to your homemade versions. It works well with mint, ginger, peppercorn—just about anything pungent enough to stand up to mustard's heat. **MAKES 3 CUPS**

2 tablespoons yellow mustard seeds

2 tablespoons brown mustard seeds

4 teaspoons mustard powder

2 cups dry white wine

1 orange, scrubbed

1 lemon, scrubbed

½ teaspoon fine sea salt

¼ teaspoon ground turmeric

2 tablespoons cider vinegar

½ cup honey

Grind the whole mustard seeds to a relatively fine texture in a coffee mill; stop short of a flour consistency. Mix together with the mustard powder in a small bowl, and add 3 tablespoons of the white wine. Stir well, and allow to stand, covered, for 20 minutes.

Meanwhile, using a vegetable peeler, remove 3 wide strips of orange zest and 2 of lemon zest from the fruit. Combine the zest and the remaining white wine in a small saucepan. Then add the juice from half the lemon and half the orange. Set over very low heat and simmer, covered, for 10 minutes. Remove the lid, increase the heat to a low boil, and reduce to ½ cup liquid. Remove from the heat; remove the zest.

Combine the mustard mixture, citrus juice mixture, salt, turmeric, and vinegar in a glass bowl, and stir to blend completely. Heat the honey in the microwave for 30 seconds to facilitate blending (or warm it in a small saucepan over low heat), and mix into the mustard until completely smooth. Transfer to a jar and store, refrigerated, for up to 2 months.

NIGELLA

ALTERNATE NAMES *Charnuska* (Russia), *Kalongi* (India), Sativa (Russian Georgia dialect), Black onion seed, Love in the mist seed

BOTANICAL NAME OF CULINARY SPECIES *Nigella sativa*

PLANT FAMILY *Ranunculaceae*

COUNTRY/REGION OF BOTANICAL ORIGIN Western Asia

MAJOR COUNTRIES/REGIONS OF CULTIVATION Northern Africa, Middle East, India

SEASON OF HARVEST Late summer

PARTS USED Seeds

COLOR Jet black

You have to make sure you've really got nigella in hand when you head toward the *tandoor* oven. It can be difficult to procure outside Indian groceries. Black cumin, black mustard, or even black sesame seeds are frequently found masquerading as nigella, none of which can give you the mildly bitter and dry flavor it offers. To make matters worse, there's a bucket load of common names given to this spice, including sativa, black onion seed, *charnushka*, and *kalongi*. In the United States, the plant even sometimes mistakenly gets the artistic name "love-in-the-mist," which is actually a more decorative relative not usually cultivated for its seed.

To confirm your find, look for jet-black color in a sesame-sized seed—but with a decidedly different shape. Where sesame is gently rounded, nigella is more angular, with sharp edges, and almost triangular.

Even though the seed is quite hard, it isn't typically ground as you would expect. Rather, the heat from cooking usually opens the seeds and thus releases their flavors. My friend the "cracker queen" includes nigella in some of her baking efforts. More traditionally, *naan*, the Indian flatbread cooked in searingly hot *tandoor* ovens, will have some of the tiny seeds mixed into its dough. The high heat perfectly opens the flavors into the bread and the seed adds a pleasant musty, peppery character to an otherwise simple recipe.

Multi-seed mixes from the Middle East, like *panch phoron*, incorporate nigella in whole form, sometimes pretoasted, and are sprinkled on breads, ground into pastes as a condiment, and even chewed as palate cleansers after eating a particularly strong-flavored curry.

Nigella Crackers

The stunning jet-black color of nigella seeds peppers these crackers artfully. The heat of cooking helps crack open the seeds further, releasing savory bursts of flavor into the crackers. These can be served most everywhere but they go particularly well with soft, creamy cheese like Brie and Camembert. They will keep for weeks in an airtight container, so you might want to make a double or even triple batch. You may never go back to packaged crackers.

MAKES 24 LARGE CRACKERS

¼ cup nigella seeds

1 cup all-purpose flour

½ cup whole wheat flour

½ teaspoon fine sea salt, plus 1 tablespoon for sprinkling (optional)

½ cup water

3 tablespoons olive oil

Preheat the oven to 350°F. Place the nigella seeds in a plastic zip-close bag and use a rolling pin to lightly crush them. Whisk together the flours, nigella, and ½ teaspoon sea salt in a large bowl. Add the water and olive oil and mix just until a dough forms.

Divide the dough in half. On a lightly floured surface, roll out each piece of dough into a thin rectangle about 9 by 12 inches and less than ⅛ inch thick. Place the dough on ungreased baking sheets and score lightly with a knife into 3-inch-square crackers. Dust with the remaining sea salt, if desired.

Bake for 20 minutes, or until crisp. Allow to cool completely, then break into individual crackers. Store in an airtight container.

NOTE: You can also use a pasta machine to roll out the dough, in batches, into thin strips, less than ⅛ inch thick. Let the dough rest, covered, before rolling it out.

NUTMEG

BOTANICAL NAME OF CULINARY SPECIES *Myristica fragrans*

PLANT FAMILY *Myristicaceae*

COUNTRY/REGION OF BOTANICAL ORIGIN **Banda Islands**

MAJOR COUNTRIES/REGIONS OF CULTIVATION **Indonesia, Sri Lanka, Madagascar, Grenada**

SEASON OF HARVEST **Summer though early fall**

PARTS USED **Inner nuts**

COLOR **Pale brown**

Imagine a return on your investment of 10,000 percent in three years. This was exactly the financial lure of the spice trade for the Spanish, English, and Portuguese oceangoing traders of the fifteenth century, and it was the quest for nutmeg from exotic lands that started the global spice race.

Turkish and Viennese traders first used overland routes to introduce nutmeg from the Banda Islands, a tiny chain in the Moluccas, thus giving rise to motivation to find the sea route to the legendary spice fields of the Indonesian archipelago. The first merchants who could create a gap in the trading monopoly that supplied Europe would be rewarded handsomely, and this lure enticed entire governments to take up the challenge by supporting their explorer-merchant class.

Spurred on by prices that meant a castle and lordship could be had for a small handful of the precious nuts, the English mounted the first assaults of discovery via the fabled (and as it turned out, nonexistent) routes over the North Sea, only to be stopped by the ice packs. The Portuguese and Spaniards simultaneously attempted a southern route and, via the newly established port of Malacca (modern Singapore), they ultimately discovered the riches they sought.

The tree produces a fruit that looks much like a peach, the flesh of which happens to be very bitter and mildly toxic. Inside this flesh sits a pit wrapped by an outer brown shell and blades of mace. Crack open the shell, and you get the inner nut that we know as nutmeg. Fruits are harvested from the trees with a long-handled basket tool called a *gai-gai*. Immediately after harvest, the inner nuts are soft enough to be pressed flat by your fingertips, but typical commercial operations allow the nuts to harden inside their shells before cracking them open. After the flesh of the fruit and the mace are removed by hand, the nuts are dried on great concrete platforms to a hard state, then cracked from their shells and graded based on size.

Grating the nut on a rasp reveals a mottled interior with veins of light and dark brown intermingled. Since the volatile oils evaporate quickly, avoid the preground product found commonly in stores and buy only the whole nut for fresh grinding yourself. There are other useful devices on the market that will "shave" the nut as needed, a perfectly acceptable method and one that is typically easier on your knuckles. A skin of sorts will form over the cut surface to help seal in the flavor of the remaining nut, but one stroke of the rasp or turn of the grinder will remove this oxidized layer and reveal fresh layers underneath for your next recipe. Whole or partially ground nuts can last upwards of a year. Signs of age include black spots or overall darkening from light to dark brown, at which point the nut should be discarded. Despite popular belief, nutmegs don't last forever, just longer than your average spice.

In fifteenth-century London, certain circles held fast to the idea that a handful of nutmeg "mixed with the thread of the crocus [saffron], into a full draft with hot pepper could cure death itself if administered within the moon." To my knowledge, no accounts of waking the dead were ever documented, although I'm certain there was ample profit to be made by those promoting such attempts.

More practically, grated nutmeg as a simple topping to coffee and eggnog drinks is only a hint at what this warming, mildly sweet spice can do. Cream-based sauces like the classic French *béchamel* benefit from light doses of nutmeg. The Basques use it in tandem with its mate, mace, each curiously canceling out the other's severe "burning" character on the palate. You'll find it throughout the region in savory meat rubs as often as in sweet mixes for pastry. Farther north, the Scandinavian cultures brought nutmeg in to the complex mulling of glogg, the spiced wine perfectly suited to the climate.

Early attempts to cultivate the trees outside their native lands, while initially squelched by the Dutch and Portuguese in an attempt to preserve their monopoly, ultimately succeeded in tropical climates like Grenada and Sri Lanka. Bounties were put upon viable seedlings, both by those wanting to plant them and those who wanted to see them drowned in the ocean, but it was ultimately growing conditions that regulated the very finicky plants. Fortunately for modern cooks, there are cultivations around the globe in a narrow band of opportunity that make the once-rare nuts affordable. Your rice pudding and latte will thank you if you seek out fresh nutmegs and give them a touch of spice history.

Spinach and Ricotta Gnocchi

Northern Italy has given rise to so many artisan foods—the cheeses of Reggio Emilia, the *balsamico tradizionale* of Modena, and the breads from craft bakeries that are so often copied but never duplicated—that you can't help but be drawn into a feeling of timeless tradition. One of the classics of the region is gnocchi, the small boiled dumplings usually made from potatoes, sometimes from other root vegetables. Traditionally a bold sauce accompanies the dish, with copious amounts of wine and grilled vegetables to feed the hungry vine workers after a full day in the fields. Heavy and filling, the dish is inexpensive, flexible, and able to satisfy both in volume and variety simply by changing the accompanying sauce.

In Florence, the locals call their gnocchi *topini*, which translates to "little mice," presumably from the size and shape of the hand-rolled dumplings. I was once served a dish, with some humor from the locals, which translated as "mice in the field." After assurances that no rodents were involved in its preparation, I was greeted with a large plate of gnocchi on a bed of fresh pesto. The fragrant spring basil offset the heft of the potato and was lightened further by the addition of tiny amounts of sweet anise seed in the dumplings themselves.

To continue on the path of lightening up a classic, I began to search for a technique for making fluffy, pillowy gnocchi and came across this recipe by way of a dear wine writer friend, Tom Stockley, who had traveled extensively in Tuscany. His discovery was made in an old wooden desk at a winery on the coast, and, after his translation of the recipe from Italian, I simply enhanced the flavor profile with the addition of white peppercorn, nutmeg, and mace, a regional spice trilogy I had seen in other recipes from the area.

The saucing on this dish can be a range of extremes, from a long-stewed marinara rich in tomato, wine, and spice to a simple treatment of olive oil and grated hard cheese. That's the beauty of gnocchi's ability to carry any flavor the cook desires to the palate. You might even try making them slightly larger, with different spice flavors contained in each of several batches, and serve them with no sauce as an appetizer.

Please use real Parmesan: cheese doesn't come in cardboard cylinders. Make your dinner guests grate it fresh, and if they complain, threaten to withhold the Chianti. And good Tuscan bread is a must. **SERVES 8 AS AN APPETIZER, 4 AS AN ENTRÉE**

GNOCCHI

Two 10-ounce packages chopped frozen spinach, thawed

1 tablespoon unsalted butter

¾ cup ricotta cheese

2 large eggs, beaten

¼ cup freshly grated Parmigiano-Reggiano cheese

Fine sea salt, to taste

2 teaspoons freshly ground white pepper

1 teaspoon freshly shaved or grated nutmeg

1 teaspoon ground mace

Approximately 6 tablespoons all-purpose flour, or as needed

1 tablespoon unsalted butter, melted

¼ cup freshly grated Parmigiano-Reggiano cheese

Squeeze the spinach to within an inch of its life to remove excess moisture. Melt the butter in a large deep skillet over medium-high heat. Add the spinach and cook, stirring frequently, until almost completely dry; little or no steam should rise from the pan. (It's this drying step that makes the spinach manageable in the dough; otherwise, you'll end up with a large pile of creamed spinach for dinner.) Transfer to a medium bowl and let cool.

Add the ricotta, eggs, Parmesan, salt, pepper, nutmeg, mace, and 3 tablespoons of the flour to the spinach and mix well with your fingertips. Continue to add small amounts of additional flour, mixing well, just until the dough holds together. Cover and refrigerate for 20 minutes.

Flour your hands and make small gnocchi, about the size of a walnut. Don't worry if you seem to get more dough on your hands than in the pot at first; that's all part of the preparation, and you'll develop your own dumpling-forming technique soon enough. Work in batches, using one-third of the dough each time, and drop the formed gnocchi into a deep pot of boiling salted water (it needs to be deep so that the dumplings set before hitting the bottom of the pot). After they rise to the top, boil for 3 minutes longer. Using a wire skimmer, transfer the gnocchi to a large baking dish. Meanwhile, preheat the oven to 400°F.

Drizzle the melted butter over the gnocchi and sprinkle with the Parmesan. This is most efficiently done if all are touching, then separate them in the dish so that each crisps up a bit in the oven. Bake for about 10 minutes, until golden brown on top.

OREGANO, MEDITERRANEAN

ALTERNATE NAME **Wild marjoram**

BOTANICAL NAME OF CULINARY SPECIES **Origanum vulgare, Origanum onites, Origanum heracleoticum**

FAMILY NAME **Mint (Lamiaceae)**

COUNTRY/REGION OF BOTANICAL ORIGIN **Mediterranean**

COUNTRIES/REGIONS OF CULTIVATION **Greece, Italy, Turkey, Egypt**

SEASON OF HARVEST **Spring and fall**

PARTS USED **Leaves**

COLOR **Mottled green**

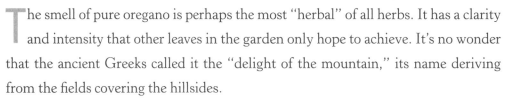

The smell of pure oregano is perhaps the most "herbal" of all herbs. It has a clarity and intensity that other leaves in the garden only hope to achieve. It's no wonder that the ancient Greeks called it the "delight of the mountain," its name deriving from the fields covering the hillsides.

In the Mediterranean varieties, which are actually specific "wild" species of marjoram, deep savory flavors come through first, followed by lighter chlorophyll tastes that end with a mild astringent bite. Many cross-species cultivars are found, adding everything from lemon to mint to the taste, but these are primarily the domain of the backyard gardener and not commercially available as a bulk commodity. The true nature of the genuine article is differentiated by its more pungent, edgy taste, which gives impressions of pepper or licorice, compared to its crossbred cousins.

Looking at the "dry" versus "fresh" forms of oregano, you discover that this herb suffers little from high-quality drying processes and may actually benefit somewhat from a mellowing of the pungency. The choice must always be made in context of the dish, but don't dismiss one or the other wholesale without tasting. While something like a complex salsa would take the pungency of the fresh well, a more delicate cream sauce may be able to handle only the toned-down dry version.

The leaves are small and round, growing low on a bushy plant. "Wild" oregano is sold still intact on the branch, but the leaves need to be removed from the fibrous, woody stems before most uses. Commercial processes that "cut and sift" are well developed and seem, on the whole, to deliver a consistent product to the marketplace. However, by the same token, this mass-marketed bulk product also can suffer from the common problem of a brief shelf life.

Cooks should look for the mottled light and dark greens that come from a combination of the new and old growth together and avoid any samples that seem to have a washed-out pale green tint throughout. The tender young leaves add a very mild sweetness, much closer to the traditional marjoram profile, while the older leaves impart the familiar pungency—needed to survive hours on the stove—that we recognize in a long, slow-cooked marinara. The leaf size or shape is of no real consequence, but they shouldn't be preground to a fine powder or overly stem laden. Rather, the leaves should be crushed between your fingertips just before use to open the flavor at the last possible moment.

Unfortunately, oregano has become one of those ubiquitous spices in the American pantry, and, through overuse and homogenization, has lost its historical flair. "Just add some to make it taste Italian" is all too common a phrase among home cooks and professionals alike. The importation of some 6,500 metric tons per year ranks it seventh among the top spice imports, according to the USDA. While that is a good, clear indicator that the herb is among the most widely used, you have to look past the fast food pizza and jarred pasta sauce industries, two of the largest consumers, to find the really interesting story of this leaf. That oregano is mundane, unspectacular, and a bulk commodity worthy only of casual use couldn't be farther from the truth.

Cultivation is certainly Mediterranean in origin—Greece, Italy, Egypt, and Turkey—but oregano made its way early to the New World via European colonists, and it is cultivated widely in myriad backyard gardens and microfarms from Washington State to Florida. There is a common belief that the Greek is the best, but in my tasting, I've found superior crops from all producing countries. As with most leaf herbs that are especially sensitive to growing conditions, the unique soil and climate of each area can yield very different results from year to year. Let your taste buds guide you, but don't render a permanent judgment on any one farm. Just expect better and worse seasons, as you would with produce or wine. The impact of *terroir*, to borrow the wine industry term, tends to overpower any small variances found in the countless different subspecies.

Rewind back in Greek and Roman history to when oregano was held high as the herb of choice in medicinal circles. My suspicion is that most ancient herbalists were as enthusiastic about what tasted good as they were about what presumably was good for your health. The specific species cultivated in ancient times, however, is unknown. And while there are various examples of oregano commercially grown around the globe, there is no consensus on exactly which species produces the best flavor. Even other herbs similar in appearance belonging to the same plant family, like marjoram, are often confused with and misidentified as true oregano. In fact, "wild marjoram" is a term still used in Italy to mean oregano.

Walking among the high hills where the slightly cooler climate makes oregano flourish, you'll see that each family in Greece has the trilogy of basil, thyme, and oregano planted—and with good reason. The sweetness of the first and the savory of the second are married perfectly in oregano, which shows both qualities. Potent bitter notes can also be detected, but not in overpowering ways. Rather, they serve to balance and come out in the finished dish well. A local farmer in a roadside cart would offer dried bundles of each of the three herbs in equal proportions, the ratios dictated by the local cuisine in the kitchen. Using oregano alone is not unheard of, but to round out the flavor with its herb cousins almost always makes culinary sense.

Fresh oregano can be used in a traditional herb pesto with good results, and bundles of oregano branches can be tossed into any stockpot. Even dropping the sprigs into a deep-fryer for a few seconds to crisp the leaves has merit, although only as a sort of condiment or a garnish, since the cooking tends to flavor the oil more than anything else.

Combined with pepper and salt, oregano can serve as the base of an herb crusting for roasted meats. Grind them all together and liberally apply to pork and beef roasts before cooking long and slow to fully develop the flavor mix.

Whether it's sprinkled as a topping or blended into a dough, baking mellows oregano's intensity, making it a good choice in breads and crackers. One of my favorite baking tricks is to blend a fine mince of fresh oregano leaf into my pizza dough, which later melds with the tomato sauce on top of the prepared pie.

Tart tomato-based sauces traditionally have a dose of oregano. For a twist, try roasting the tomatoes and oregano together on a baking tray before blending them into a sauce. The added heat blooms the tomato flavor while mellowing the oregano nicely. Even so, it will still hold up to the addition of rich red wine, or to heavy cream and butter as well, in any whimsical sauce in which the cook cares to indulge.

Overall, choose oregano when the intensity of the dish warrants it. Think in terms of stronger vinegar, pepper, or salt flavors where lighter herbs don't stand a chance of punching through. No matter what dish it finds its way into, oregano is a take-no-prisoners herb that shouldn't be relegated to the back of the spice rack, waiting for your grandmother from Rome to visit.

Spicy Italian Marinara Sauce

Within the first week of opening my spice store, I had a customer, Danny, come in and ask a very simple question: "How do I make spicy, red Italian sauce?" My technique has evolved from throwing basil into a jar of canned pasta sauce in college up to this current incarnation of a classic that truly defines central Italian cookery.

A very flexible and forgiving sauce, it really leaves the door open for personal interpretation. Change the spices with your mood, or add some seasonal vegetables. It works equally well as a sauce for gnocchi or a pizza topping.

Over the years, Danny and his family have shown up from time to time and asked if there are any new ideas for "the sauce" and whether or not I want to come to Montana for spaghetti. Someday soon we may have to meet for pasta in the Rocky Mountains. **MAKES ABOUT 3 QUARTS**

1 medium onion, finely diced

3 carrots, shredded

3 celery stalks, finely diced

4 garlic cloves, minced

¼ cup minced fresh parsley

¼ cup olive oil

2 medium tomatoes, seeded and diced

Two 28-ounce cans crushed or pureed Italian-style plum tomatoes

One 14.5-ounce can diced tomatoes

2 cups chicken stock

1 tablespoon freshly ground black pepper, or to taste

1½ cups dry Italian red wine, such as Chianti

1 tablespoon Italian Herb blend (page 371), crushed

2 teaspoons finely ground anise seeds

1 tablespoon red chile flakes, or to taste (optional)

Fine sea salt, to taste

Preheat the broiler. In a large ovenproof skillet, cook the onion, carrots, celery, garlic, and parsley in the oil over medium heat, stirring occasionally, until the vegetables are soft. Add the diced tomatoes and stir well. Place the pan under the broiler, 4 inches from the heat, and broil for about 2 minutes. Stir well, and continue to broil, stirring every 2 minutes, until the vegetables are beginning to color, about 5 minutes in all.

Transfer the vegetables to a medium pot and add all the remaining ingredients except the salt. Simmer over low heat, covered, for at least 1 hour, stirring occasionally and adding water as needed to maintain the same level of liquid. Add salt to taste, keeping in mind the salt content of the canned tomatoes (and stock).

OREGANO, MEXICAN

ALTERNATE NAME **Puerto Rican oregano**

BOTANICAL NAME OF CULINARY SPECIES *Lippia graveolens*

PLANT FAMILY **Verbena *(Verbenaceae)***

COUNTRY/REGION OF BOTANICAL ORIGIN **Latin America**

MAJOR COUNTRIES/REGIONS OF CULTIVATION **Mexico**

SEASON OF HARVEST **Year-round**

PARTS USED **Leaves**

COLOR **Green**

South of the U.S. border, they've been keeping a secret hidden under a more common name for decades. "Mexican oregano," whose lineage is completely separate from European oregano, is a delightful discovery of lime and herb character that marries perfectly with the chile and cumin-rich regional cuisine. An entirely separate species of plant, Mexican (or Puerto Rican) oregano has a flavor profile that is similar in pungency and base flavor to its Mediterranean namesake, but it is quite different in overall taste.

Where the Mediterranean sources exhibit a more savory, peppery character, the Mexican can best be described as having a citrus, even lime, connotation with less overall savory flavor. A relative of lemon verbena, it adds the herbaceous character that, in context of chiles and paprika, serves to lighten the cuisine. It enhances flavors in much the same way that salt and citrus do, heightening other flavors and drawing them together with characteristic zest. As such, it blends very well with the traditional *rojos* and *moles* of Mexico and Central America, holding up to the chile bases better than the European counterpart. Save the Greek and Italian versions for Mediterranean cuisines and others rich in olive, garlic, and tomato. The Mexican species is widely available in Latin markets and the roadside stands of the desert Southwest. With a slightly larger serrated leaf and more consistent color than the

European plant, these crops are frequently less processed and so more stems are to be expected. A grinding of leaves, stems, and all is best done just as you add it to a simmering pot of, for example, ancho or guajillo chiles and meat to make classic Tex-Mex chili. Perk up black beans or round out relleno filling in more authentic Mexican kitchens by adding the oregano with other traditional herbs like epazote or Mexican tarragon. The aromatics of this plant will fill your nose with complexity, not just leave you gasping for breath between chile jolts. Bring cumin and garlic into the fold, and you've completed the interaction on the palate born of the sun-drenched deserts from Arizona to the equator.

Wild Mushroom Fajitas

One of the great bounties of the Pacific Northwest is mushrooms. Richly flavored wild varieties spring up on the forest floors and in the local markets, just begging to be taken home for dinner. Chanterelles and oysters, morels and lobsters, all have unique tastes that are a far cry from the garden varieties you get from mass producers.

When the season hits, however, there's only so much mushroom soup and so many mushroom omelets you can stand before you start to think of the fungi in different circles. The meaty taste of the large, hand-sized chanterelles we get here in Seattle made me think that they could easily replace beef in a meal with equally satisfying results. Tortillas at the ready, I headed south of the border. **SERVES 6**

2 garlic cloves, crushed

2 teaspoons olive oil

1 pound wild mushrooms, cleaned, smaller mushrooms left whole, large ones cut into 1- to 2-inch pieces

1 pound cremini mushrooms, cleaned and quartered

½ cup chicken or vegetable stock

2 dry-packed chipotle chiles, stems removed

1 to 2 tablespoons dried Mexican oregano, crumbled

2 tablespoons freshly ground Taco and Fajita Seasoning (page 359)

½ teaspoon ground true cinnamon

1 bunch of spinach, stems removed, cleaned, and roughly chopped

Warm tortillas

In a large nonstick skillet, cook the garlic in the oil over medium heat, stirring occasionally, until fragrant and beginning to color, 3 to 5 minutes. Remove the garlic and discard. Add the mushrooms to the oil and cook, stirring frequently, until they render their juices. Drain the liquid into a medium saucepan (set the mushrooms aside in the pan) and add the stock, chiles, oregano, spice blend, and cinnamon. Cover and simmer over low heat until reduced and thickened to the consistency of a thin gravy.

Meanwhile, return the mushrooms to the heat and cook, stirring, until tender, about 10 minutes. Remove from the heat, quickly stir in the spinach, cover, and allow to sit, stirring once or twice, until the spinach has wilted.

Add the sauce to the mushrooms, and toss well. Use to fill the warmed tortillas, and top with the usual suspects—cheese, tomato, avocado, sour cream, etc.—or simply eat as is.

PAPRIKA

ALTERNATE NAME *Pimentón* (typically smoked)

BOTANICAL NAME OF CULINARY SPECIES *Capsicum annum*

PLANT FAMILY Nightshade (*Solanaceae*)

COUNTRY/REGION OF BOTANICAL ORIGIN South America

MAJOR COUNTRIES/REGIONS OF CULTIVATION Hungary, Spain

SEASON OF HARVEST Late summer

PARTS USED Fruits

COLOR Brilliant red

The farms of Hungary have captured the world's taste buds with paprika. A veritable sea of green dotted with the red flecks of the ripe fruit peeking out from underneath their leaf blankets, giving you the first clue that something wonderful hides in the fields. As the harvest season approaches, the locals are giddy with excitement despite the hard labor to come. No one else in the world takes paprika as seriously as the Hungarians.

Festivals are held during harvesttime, in the late summer, celebrating the virtues of their local bounty, and it seems that everyone gets into the act. Entire families, whether in the trade or not, come to help with the short harvest. Once the fruit is in, the real art of paprika manufacture begins. Master craftsmen will toast and blend various batches, carefully selecting which parts of the pepper are used and ultimately blending for the best flavor.

There is a range of taste that can come from paprika, starting at the sweetest, almost candy-like end and working up through several grades of more savory and subtly hot character. In American groceries, you will find a bastardization of the traditional "hot" paprika with the addition of non-paprika chiles to the mix. Less complex chiles like cayenne are mixed with paprika to get a perceivable heat on the tongue. I much prefer to mix my own ratios and avoid anything labeled "hot" in the grocery.

The very best paprika has such character and sweetness that it has spawned a rather odd local Hungarian favorite. It is mixed with lard and spread on bread alone as a sandwich. A bit more healthy interpretation is made by simply blending the chiles with oil and a touch of salt.

More famously, Hungarians have popularized the thick stew, *goulash*, that makes the most of paprika. Copious amounts of paprika give it the brilliant pink red color and depth of flavor only the freshest sources can accomplish. And in fact, it's the paprika that does most of the thickening for a dish that is little more than sautéed meats in a creamy base.

Paprika is also such an important ingredient in blended spices that it has become the fourth-most-consumed spice product in the world. Not simply used for color as some would have you believe, it is the base in chili powders and barbecue rubs, processed foods, and seasoned salts.

Smoked Paprika/*Pimentón*

HAND-SIZED CHILES LOOKING MUCH LIKE SMALL rounded bell peppers give rise to the famous smoked paprika known as *pimentón de la Vera* from the La Vera region of Spain. Harvesting them at a brilliant red stage in the fall, Spanish farmers smoke these paprika chiles over wood fires in everything from small metal baskets to long narrow smokehouses. Festivals are held each year and the patron saint of the harvest is thanked for the bounty. The unmistakable smoke fills the air, marking the coming winter season and its hefty stews that will benefit from *pimentón's* meaty, smoked flavor.

Almost all the paprika from la Vera is smoked, so much so that it's rarely labeled as "smoked" but simply as "de la Vera." Dulce (sweet), agridulce (bittersweet), and picante (hot) are subtle interpretations accomplished by seed removal (where bitter and mild heat components concentrate) and/or by addition of other hotter chiles in the grind. These smoked versions have become very popular in recent years, and now the small tins can be purchased even in mainstream groceries. As always, try to find a merchant that turns his product over regularly to avoid a bitterness that can creep in with age.

By mixing smoked paprika with other spices for a heady rub on meats, you can have a grilled taste even in the dead of winter.

Pacific Red-Crusted Chicken

One of my favorite spice mixes comes from an odd marriage of cultures: the Japanese, it seems, had a short-lived love affair with paprika from Hungary. In fact, Japanese condiment dispensers from the sixties have places for salt, pepper, and paprika. And the tastes of pepper and paprika do blend well when the absolute best quality of each is procured. The paprika should still have a pronounced sweetness, and the pepper should linger and change for several minutes. Tuscan bread, piquant green olives, and a rich Cabrales blue cheese could accompany this big, bold, red combination. **SERVES 4**

½ cup sweet Hungarian paprika

1 tablespoon coarse sea salt

1 tablespoon coarsely cracked Tellicherry peppercorns

1½ teaspoons freshly ground white pepper

2 whole bone-in chicken breasts, split

2 tablespoons extra virgin olive oil

½ cup dry red wine

½ cup heavy whipping cream (optional)

1 cup fresh or frozen peas, cooked in boiling salted water just until tender

4 cups hot cooked penne (about 8 ounces uncooked)

Preheat the broiler. Stir the paprika, sea salt, peppercorns, and pepper together and rub over the chicken breasts, coating them evenly. Place the chicken in a small roasting pan and drizzle the olive oil over it. Turn skin side down and broil 4 inches from the heat for 2 to 3 minutes, until the spices are very fragrant. Turn and broil for 2 to 3 minutes on the second side.

Turn the oven down to 375°F, move the chicken to a center rack, and bake until cooked through, about 20 minutes. Transfer the chicken to a cutting board. Add the wine, stirring up the browned bits over medium heat, and reduce until slightly thickened. (Or use a combination of the wine and cream, to temper the peppery intensity.)

Meanwhile, remove the chicken meat from the bone and thinly slice. Transfer the sauce to a large skillet and stir in the chicken and peas. Add the pasta, stir over low heat just until warmed through, and serve immediately.

Smoked Corn Chowder

When you're settled in like a bear for the kind of long, cold, rainy winters we have in the Pacific Northwest, you want something richly satisfying on the dinner table. Smoky flavors offer the satisfying comfort factor that reminds you of thick robes and warm slippers. Here, smoked paprika from Spain, called *pimentón*, does the work. It comes in hot and mild versions; the choice is up to you. **SERVES 4 TO 6**

3 cups fresh or frozen corn kernels	1 cup half-and-half
4 strips of lean bacon, cut into ½-inch-wide pieces	3 smoked pasilla Oaxaca chiles
2 tablespoons unsalted butter	1 teaspoon finely chopped fresh rosemary
1 small onion, chopped	1 teaspoon cracked black peppercorns
2 garlic cloves, crushed	1 bay leaf
1 tablespoon all-purpose flour	Fine sea salt
2 cups chicken stock	1 teaspoon smoked paprika (*pimentón*)
1 cup whole milk	1 tablespoon chopped fresh parsley

Preheat the broiler. Spread the corn kernels in a single layer on a baking sheet. Broil 4 inches from the heat, stirring once, for 3 to 5 minutes, or until spotted brown. Set aside.

In a large saucepan, cook the bacon in the butter over medium heat until it renders most of its fat, about 3 minutes. Remove with a slotted spoon, and set aside.

Add the onion and garlic to the fat in the pan, and cook, stirring occasionally, until the onion begins to color, 3 to 5 minutes. Sprinkle on the flour and cook, stirring, for 1 minute. Pour in the stock, and bring to a boil, stirring to incorporate the flour. Add the milk, half-and-half, toasted corn, smoked chiles, rosemary, cracked pepper, bay leaf, and reserved bacon. Reduce the heat, and simmer for 10 minutes. Remove and discard the chiles. Continue to simmer for 5 to 10 minutes longer. Remove and discard the bay leaf. Season with salt to taste.

Ladle the chowder into soup bowls, and top each serving with a dusting of the smoked paprika and parsley.

Hungarian Goulash

Mothers in Hungary might give a new son-in-law their daughter on the wedding day, but it's going to take a few years of proving himself before he gets the goulash recipe. The dish is as honored and revered in the southern part of the country as the paprika in its makeup. While I didn't have to marry a Hungarian woman to get this recipe, I did have to promise my Hungarian informant I would only make the recipe for people I truly love.

Technique is everything in making a goulash. Especially important is the stage where you are simultaneously deglazing the pot and caramelizing the paprika coating on the meat. Beyond that, it's a very opportunistic stew that can use cheaper cuts of beef because of the long stewing time. **SERVES 6**

¼ cup sweet Hungarian paprika, plus extra for garnish

2 teaspoons fine sea salt

1 teaspoon freshly ground black pepper

2 pounds beef stew meat, cut into 1½-inch cubes

2 onions, thinly sliced

2 garlic cloves, minced

⅓ cup olive oil

One 6-ounce can tomato paste

2 cups water

2 cups beef stock

½ cup heavy whipping cream

One 8-ounce container sour cream

¼ cup minced fresh parsley

Mix the paprika, salt, and pepper in a medium bowl. Add the meat, tossing to coat. Cover and refrigerate for 1 hour.

In a Dutch oven or other heavy pot, cook the onions and garlic in the oil over medium-high heat, stirring occasionally, until softened, 5 to 8 minutes. Add the tomato paste, stirring constantly while adding just enough of the water to prevent scorching, and cook, stirring, for 4 minutes. Add the spiced meat, stirring and continuing to add just enough water to deglaze the pot and prevent scorching, until the meat is browned.

Add the remaining water and the stock, reduce the heat to the lowest setting, and simmer, covered, for 1½ hours, or until the meat is tender, adding water as needed.

Add the heavy cream, stir well, and simmer to thicken slightly, about 5 minutes. Stir in half the sour cream and heat through (do not boil).

Serve the goulash garnished with the remaining sour cream and sprinkled with paprika and the parsley. Lots of crusty bread for dipping is also a good idea here.

PARSLEY

BOTANICAL NAMES OF CULINARY SPECIES *Petroselinum crispum* **(Curly leafed),** *Species neapolitanum* **(Flat-leafed, or Italian),** *Species tuberosum* **(Thick-rooted)**

PLANT FAMILY Parsley (*Umbelliferia*)

COUNTRY/REGION OF BOTANICAL ORIGIN Southern Europe

MAJOR COUNTRIES/REGIONS OF CULTIVATION Globally

SEASON OF HARVEST Year-round

PARTS USED Leaves

COLORS Various greens

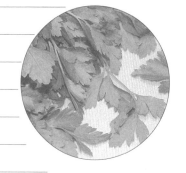

Parsley is actually the patriarch of an entire family of herbs that are useful in the kitchen. Some of the particularly curly sons, however, have given the whole family a bad name, as simply decorative in nature. Wrongly relegated to decoration alone, parsley can impart a wonderfully savory and herbaceous flavor, making it a fabulous culinary foundation. The high concentrations of chlorophyll in the fresh leaf can do wonders for a blend that needs to taste herbal without obscuring other flavors in the mix. It comes to the palate very cleanly, without the distraction of complexity.

Creole cuisine uses parsley liberally to add an herbal lift to otherwise heavy recipes. It was traditionally cheap and available in the southern United States, and so the local cuisines picked it up and found that there was indeed flavor to the unassuming leaf. Married to celery, onion, and bell pepper in fairly hefty amounts, it comprises the vegetal base to gumbos, rices, and étouffées all over Louisiana.

Italians, too, have seen the virtues of parsley, in rich tomato sauces and more delicate seafood preparations. Copious amounts can be added for extended cooking times where the leaf almost becomes a vegetable, and lighter measures can be used in conjunction with lemon and vinegar to dress salads or shrimp. The intensity of the dish will determine exactly how much to use, but typically you shouldn't be shy when adding parsley.

While there are hundreds of subspecies, three major varieties are cultivated, with the common names "curly," "flat-leaf or Italian," and "rooted." This last variety is indeed harvested with roots intact and, once washed thoroughly, can be used in its entirety just like the leaves of other versions. The problem for the cook is to discern which varieties have flavor and which have been bred in a quest for a more decorative leaf. Taste the sources you encounter for bright flavor to make your choice.

Parsley-Butter Sauce

Parsley most certainly does have flavor; it simply takes a fair amount of the fresh leaf for the flavor to come through in dishes. This sauce is easy to make and equally appropriate for tossing with pasta for a simple side dish or for serving eggs Benedict with a twist for a weekend brunch. Don't attempt this with dried parsley—it will fail miserably.   **MAKES 2 CUPS**

¼ pound (1 stick) unsalted butter, melted

½ cup finely minced fresh flat, Italian-style parsley

¼ teaspoon fine sea salt

¼ teaspoon finely ground white pepper

½ teaspoon prepared mustard powder

3 large egg yolks

Juice of ½ lemon

¼ cup semisweet white wine

In a small bowl, stir together the butter, parsley, salt, pepper, and mustard powder. In a saucepan over low heat, whisk the egg yolks with the lemon juice until very slightly thickened, about 5 minutes, being careful not to scramble the eggs. Add the wine and, whisking constantly, incorporate the butter mixture into the eggs one spoonful at a time. Continue to cook until sauce thickens, about 5 minutes more. Use immediately.

PEPPERCORNS, BLACK, GREEN, WHITE, AND "TRUE" RED

BOTANICAL NAME OF CULINARY SPECIES *Piper nigrum*

PLANT FAMILY **Pepper (*Piperaceae*)**

COUNTRY/REGION OF BOTANICAL ORIGIN **India**

MAJOR COUNTRIES/REGIONS OF CULTIVATION **India, Indonesia, South America**

SEASON OF HARVEST **Spring through fall**

PARTS USED **Fruits**

COLORS **Vary by production**

Peppercorns . . . just the word conjures up both tropical exotica and familiar comfort. Most everyone uses them daily, either while cooking or from the shaker at the table. Pepper is the ubiquitous spice for America and, in fact, for most of the world. On this side of the globe, we have to rely on overseas growers to maintain our supply. But before we get to those craftsmen, a simple pepper primer is in order.

To discover the true art of peppercorn manufacture, you must go to the pepper center of the universe, Mount Tellicherry in southwest India. The sweeping slopes of the huge mountain loom over the valley, a lush, timeless landscape. The smell of all the spices of India wafts in the air of the open markets, and the fields are rich with greenery of a different make than we're accustomed to in the West: cardamom shrubs, cassia-cinnamon trees, and, of course, the peppercorn bush. It grows wild in the countryside but is more properly trellised into bulbous mounds, some as high as eight feet, in the spice gardens, where it dangles its berry-laden tips under broad green leaves, looking something like a bushy grapevine. The soil and climate in the Nilgiri Hills of India, which lie along the Malabar Coast, produce the best pungency and intensity of flavor. When pepper is allowed to mature fully in the subcontinent sun, you get large berries that hold the most complexity and potency.

We all recognize black peppercorns, which are actually the dried berry of the *Piper nigrum* plant. It's the drying process that gives them their distinctive colors of deep brown to jet black. The almost-ripened, greenish-yellow berries are harvested from the plant in long strands of twenty to forty berries each. They are then left to oxidize in the heat of the sun, where they take on their dark color and slightly dimpled shape.

The green, unripe berries, though much less common, are also used in the kitchen. They are freeze-dried to preserve their smooth round texture and bright green color. The cost can be daunting at first glance, but remember that the freeze-drying makes them extremely light in weight. Don't let the "price-per-pound" quote scare you away, as only pennies will give you a strong punch of flavor with very little of the lingering on the palate you expect from the white or black versions. This allows the other flavors of your dish to come through without being overwhelmed.

At the other end of the continuum, the growers of old began husking the more mature peppercorns, by way of short water baths, to reveal the center of each pepper berry. The newly naked berries are dried in the sun to produce what we know as white peppercorns. They lack the initial bite of the green or black but have a wonderfully long "draw" of taste that lingers quietly on the taste buds. The Muntok regions of Indonesia are perhaps the most well regarded for this version, with a creamy color and flavor that blends perfectly in classic French cuisine.

When the berries of the *Piper nigrum* species are allowed to ripen naturally on the vines, they will mature to a brilliant red color after the initial green stage. These peppercorns, rarely seen in the West or anywhere outside the regions of production, are a wonderfully sweet and mellower version of pepper taste compared with berries at other stages. Often sold intact on the vines that spawned them, they command top prices and are best used within days of harvest. Otherwise, they will dry to dimpled peppercorns that have lost most of their sweet brilliance and, subsequently, most of their value beyond ordinary black versions.

A short aside to dispel the misconceptions of pink, long, and Sichuan peppercorns is in order (see also the individual entries). While each of these has wonderful flavors, some akin to those from peppercorns, all are different species of plant and not "true" peppercorns. Each has a unique taste and should be used only when called for specifically, not as a substitute for peppercorns.

Tellicherry has become synonymous with the top grade of peppercorns, most of which come from that mountain's region, but let the buyer beware. The size of the berries is your first clue to getting the genuine article—i.e., the bigger the better. After that, look for deep black color with tones of rich red-brown, not the dusty, almost gray color seen in the lower grades. But here's where our voracious appetite gets us into trouble. To meet demand, the lower regions of the Malabar Coast have ramped up production by way of mechanization, hybridization, and general mass production. The artisan method of peppercorn harvesting, in contrast, entails hand harvesting *only* the larger, more mature berries and curing them in the sun to preserve more of the complex flavor.

When you begin to use the better quality, you'll first notice that you need less, and soon afterward you'll realize that the flavor is actually different. The high notes are higher and the low notes lower. The time the palate regales in the rich flavor will be noticeably longer and the "heat" of the berry will be much more evident than in the stale product you're accustomed to finding on the grocery store shelf.

History has certainly taken notice of the peppercorn trade. Ransoms paid to the Ottoman Turks were often in peppercorns, and Roman taxes were paid with the same. Centurions even got a ration of peppercorns as part of their paycheck. And they certainly were on the lists of many explorer-merchants as part of the great spice races of the fifteenth century, motivating the Spanish, English, and Dutch all to seek routes to the pepper trade centers in India.

Peppercorn is the single most important crop in the spice trade today, as is obvious by its truly global use. Beyond salt and water, it is perhaps the world's most common ingredient, and the swings of the pepper trade reflect its importance in the kitchen. Any cook who can elevate the quality of just this one spice in his rack will do a great service to his cuisine.

WHY YOU SHOULDN'T BLEND PEPPERCORN VARIETIES

We're all suckers for good looks. I admit that the four-color peppercorn blends so heavily marketed in the United States tempted me when I first saw them. They are beautiful to look at, but given the flavor profiles of each, they're a waste and an unnecessary muddling of flavor.

Take first the delicate pink pepper. Sweet and fruity, it's overpowered easily by all the other true peppercorn varieties if they are fresh and still pack their peppery punch. Save the pink for use all on its own where it can be appreciated.

Note that the green and white are simply subsets of flavor of a proper black peppercorn: logical if you remember they originate from the same plant. Blending all three simply gets you to the same place on the palate, again assuming you have a fresh supply.

Where blending does make sense is with black and *either* the green or white, but not both. The point of making such a blend is an enhancement of the initial bite or lingering heat, respectively. In the French tradition, coriander or allspice would be added to such a mix to lend different flavors, but balance is always the key. The idea is to intensify the perception, not confuse the taste buds.

Steak with Pepper-Mushroom Crust

Peppercorns are one of the most ubiquitous spices in the world, but it takes a special mix of ingredients to allow their taste to shine through in dishes. Not merely a background taste in this treatment of steak, they hold up to the pungent cheese and the earthy taste of mushrooms.   **SERVES 4**

6 ounces fresh white mushrooms, cleaned

2 scallions, chopped

½ teaspoon freshly squeezed lemon juice

¼ teaspoon fine sea salt

1 tablespoon coarsely ground black pepper

3 ounces softened goat cheese

Four 8-ounce boneless sirloin steaks

In a food processor, pulse together the mushrooms and scallions until finely minced, and remove to a mixing bowl. Add the lemon juice, salt, pepper, and goat cheese and mix completely. Place in refrigerator for at least 1 hour, or overnight.

On either an indoor or outdoor grill, sear the unseasoned steaks until rare (do not cook through at this stage), typically 3 to 4 minutes on an indoor grill. Remove to a broiler-safe plate. Spread a layer of the mushroom mixture on the top of each steak, place under the broiler to cook until a crust forms, about 5 minutes, and serve. (Any extra mushroom mixture makes a fine topping for baked potatoes or spread on crusty bread.)

PEPPER, LONG

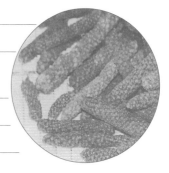

ALTERNATE NAMES Peppercones, Bengal pepper

BOTANICAL NAME OF CULINARY SPECIES *Piper longum*

PLANT FAMILY Pepper (*Piperaceae*)

COUNTRY/REGION OF BOTANICAL ORIGIN Central Africa

MAJOR COUNTRIES/REGIONS OF CULTIVATION India, Africa, eastern China

SEASON OF HARVEST Summer

PARTS USED Seed clusters

COLOR Gray-black

In the same family as the familiar round peppercorn, this pepper is actually an inch-long bud-fruit made up of hundreds of tiny seeds collected around a core stem, with a taste like pepper and mild ginger combined. Originally wild-crafted in the foothills of the Himalaya, they have traveled all across India and into Africa, but today's is only a tiny cultivation compared with the peak they experienced in the Middle Ages. It's for that reason that my culinary re-creationist friends seek them as one of the holy grails of spices for their efforts in the kitchen. Before the common *piper nigrum* was cultivated widely, long pepper found its way via the overland routes from India through Turkey and Vienna, and into the courts of France and England. Its peppery-hot taste suited the northern climates well and could be had for less than our common pepper at the time.

In light of modern supplies of common pepper, you'll be hard-pressed to find recipes that specifically call for long pepper. You can, however, take any modern recipe and substitute long pepper for its more ubiquitous cousin, albeit with different results. I particularly like to use it in sweet-hot recipes to accent the gingery undertones within. Ground to a powder and tossed with fresh fruit, added to a vinegar coleslaw, or used anywhere else that the complexities won't be cooked away are good ways to experiment.

PEPPER, NEGRO

ALTERNATE NAME Africa pepper

BOTANICAL NAME OF CULINARY SPECIES *Xylopia aethiopica*

PLANT FAMILY *Annonaceae*

COUNTRY/REGION OF BOTANICAL ORIGIN Central Africa

MAJOR COUNTRIES/REGIONS OF CULTIVATION Ghana, Malawi

SEASON OF HARVEST Fall

PARTS USED Seeds, Pods

COLOR Dark brown (dried)

If you can imagine a sea urchin with fat green spines appearing on land like something from a Dr. Seuss book, you're well on your way to picturing the negro pepper of Central Africa. Rarely found outside the continent now, it once had popularity as a peppercorn substitute.

These fruits, plucked and dried in the sun to a red-brown color, have bulbous bean pods that remind me of tiny versions of the purple-hulled peas I used to have to shell on my grandmother's back porch. Just like then, it takes a sharp knife to nip the ends of the pods and expose the inner "seeds," which hold a seriously peppery taste that once rivaled *Piper nigrum* in its use across Africa and into Europe.

Unlike other pepper substitutes, however, here the flavor is almost too much to bear. And the intensity of pepper flavor is coupled with an intense bitter character that makes it a less-than-appropriate replacement for peppercorn. Even long cooking times don't seem to relax the negro pepper into something tasty. Unless you're stuck in the Congo without a market nearby, I'd pass on these and reach for something else to spice your dinner.

PEPPER, PINK

ALTERNATE NAMES **Pepper berry, Mexican peppertree, Christmas berry**

BOTANICAL NAMES OF CULINARY SPECIES *Shinus molle, Shinus terebinthifolius* **(Christmas berry)**

PLANT FAMILY *Anacardiaceae*

COUNTRY/REGION OF BOTANICAL ORIGIN **South America**

MAJOR COUNTRIES/REGIONS OF CULTIVATION **Madagascar, Mexico, Australia**

SEASON OF HARVEST **Summer**

PARTS USED **Berries**

COLOR **Pale pink**

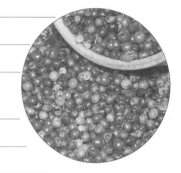

It's a real shame that someone got the idea to call these round berries peppercorns when they were discovered in the Andes of South America. It's an even bigger shame that they often get mixed in with their more potent, and mostly overpowering, namesakes.

The tiny peppercorn-sized berries are very light in weight and have a trademark pink color that is lighter than the rare red-ripened true peppercorns of southern India. Botanically speaking, they're far from the *Piper* genus, from a species called *Shinus molle*. They hint at a traditional pepper bite initially, but they have a surprise within. The paper-thin outer husks of the berry encase a hard kernel that exhibits wonderfully delicate sweetness.

Another related species, *Shinus terebinthifolius*, is cultivated on a large scale almost exclusively on the former French colony of Reunion Island, and it's the minuscule supply of the species that forces the price skyward—reason again to use the precious berries and their delicate flavor separate from the more potent true peppercorns. Look for supplies that have intact berries with little or no separated husk material at the bottom. The delicate berries break apart with age and lose their character quickly.

In the kitchen, make sure that you don't cook out the delicate flavor completely with high heat or lengthy cooking times. Some cooks choose simply to add the berries as garnish in salads or in lighter cream sauces to preserve the sweetness. In the Pacific Northwest, they blend very well in dishes with light herbs like chervil and parsley to coat local seafood, giving tiny bursts of mild pepper flavor.

ALTERNATE NAMES *Yerba santa, Huascas*

BOTANICAL NAME OF CULINARY SPECIES *Piper sanctum*

PLANT FAMILY *Pepper (Piperaceae)*

COUNTRY/REGION OF BOTANICAL ORIGIN South America

MAJOR COUNTRIES/REGIONS OF CULTIVATION Peru, Argentina

SEASON OF HARVEST Year-round

PARTS USED Leaves

COLOR Green

Being a spice merchant is like being on a global treasure hunt. The only problem is that there's no map and few guidebooks, and sometimes I don't even know what I'm looking for. Fortunately, I have customers to send me on various missions, albeit with some sketchy information at times, to keep the job interesting. One such wild goose chase was for pepperleaf from South America.

As it happened, a Peruvian woman came into my store and proceeded to tell me all about her homeland's national dish, a stew called *aheeyahko*, which had one distinctive taste that came from a spice. The spice, as she called it in her dialect, was *huascas*. I kept this on my list of spice treasures to find for years until I finally stumbled across some translations that gave me alternate names, *yerba santa* and pepperleaf. A few calls to friends in the Andes, and I had found a spice totally new to me and, indeed, to most of the rest of the world.

The broad leaves are from a bush in the pepper family; as you might surmise from the name, they have a distinctive pepper bite, but with some mellowing sweetness and character not unlike cilantro in flavor. Drying doesn't suit the leaf, so the intrepid spice hunter will need to turn to the garden for its unique flavor.

POMEGRANATE SEEDS

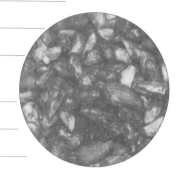

ALTERNATE NAME *Anardana* (dried seeds; India)

BOTANICAL NAME OF CULINARY SPECIES *Punica granatum*

PLANT FAMILY *Punicaceae*

COUNTRY/REGION OF BOTANICAL ORIGIN **Persia**

MAJOR COUNTRIES/REGIONS OF CULTIVATION **Middle East, Central America**

SEASON OF HARVEST **Year-round**

PARTS USED **Seeds**

COLOR **Dark red**

The hunt for souring spices continues with the pomegranate fruit. The seeds, when dried to a sticky, semi-moist state, have traditionally been used to add tart flavor to dishes and condiments where lemon or citrus in general was less available. Called *anardana* in India, their popularity has reached across the whole of the Middle East and now pomegranate is a defining taste for any respectable chutney or *tagine* that needs some sour balance.

When dried, the sweetness of the familiar fresh seeds is diminished considerably, while the seed itself becomes a bittering component. This is balanced by the outer fruit pulp, which has a raisinlike concentration of flavor. Each pomegranate has hundreds of seeds set in clumps wrapped by white pith. For drying, these must be separated from each other and laid out in a single layer to dry completely, whether in a commercial dehydrator or simply under the sun. I've achieved very good results in my homemade *anardana* tests, but because pomegranate is a fruit, the sugars and moisture raise the potential for spoilage. I used a food dehydrator in accordance with the machine's "fruit" directions, but small batches should always be the norm to ensure freshness and prevent bacterial contamination.

Since *anardana* has a fairly potent sour component, most recipes will call for very little, as a burst of flavor mid-palate. Look for it in chutney recipes and in some of the more complex spice rubs of Persia, Africa, and the Middle East. There are sporadic references to bread being made with *anardana* in the dough, but more commonly it's pounded with other spices into a condiment to be sprinkled on top, as you would crushed herbs or zahtar. Any dish that calls for sumac or lemon—e.g., hummus dip—is probably a good testing ground for dried pomegranate seeds.

I also tried a few oddball experiments with *anardana* and had good success. Crushing some into a batch of highly hopped ale I was brewing gave me sweet, tart, and malt flavors all in the same glass. Mixing some into a sesame-seed candy brittle gave a pleasant sour surprise in the middle of each sweet bite. Finally, pounding a handful in a mortar with fresh herbs and olive oil made a paste well suited for lamb destined for a long, slow roasting.

POPPY SEEDS

ALTERNATE NAME Garden poppy

BOTANICAL NAME OF CULINARY SPECIES *Papaver somniferum*

PLANT FAMILY Poppy (*Papaveraceae*)

COUNTRIES/REGIONS OF BOTANICAL ORIGIN Western Asia to Eastern Europe

MAJOR COUNTRIES/REGIONS OF CULTIVATION India, Turkey, Holland, Eastern Europe, North America, Australia, Southeast Asia

SEASON OF HARVEST Late summer through fall

PARTS USED Seeds

COLORS Blue or white

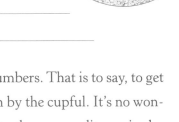

These tiny pinhead-sized seeds have found safety in numbers. That is to say, to get their real flavor, most pastry recipes will call for them by the cupful. It's no wonder they have almost migrated from the spice category to the commodity grain department.

The species most widely cultivated is a blue-black variant grown to satisfy global demand. White versions are found in India and some parts of North Africa, but they exhibit little flavor difference and, to my taste, are merely visually different. Holland has become the producer of merit, with "super-blue" grades commanding the best prices, but sources in Australia and Canada make a fine product as well, at a very reasonable cost. Perhaps the only limiting factor in poppy production is the dubious reputation it has gained from being the source of the narcotic opium. In fact, the species grown for that illicit production are not the same as those for culinary purposes, but governments are often reactionary and prefer to lump them all together.

Back in the kitchen, poppy has been used since ancient times as a savory flavor in breads and pastries. When used in large measures, it can be ground into a useful paste that carries other flavors well, especially sweets. Certain medieval recipes call for a paste of marjoram, poppy, and honey to flavor cakes and filled cookies.

Lamb Korma with Cashews

Creamy yogurt-based curries are the norm in northern and central India. Typically not as hot and cooked much more quickly than those of the south, they take advantage of more mellow spices while still delivering complexity. They can be made with any meat, but lamb is the most common. Adding nuts and seeds to a spice paste contributes fat and ultimate smoothness to the finished dish, as seen in this version with cashews. Serve with basmati rice. **SERVES 6**

1 teaspoon finely ground green cardamom seeds	½ teaspoon red chile flakes
1 cup half-and-half	2 teaspoons fine sea salt
½ cup cashews, coarsely chopped	¼ cup water
2-inch piece of true cinnamon stick, crushed	1 cup chopped onions
2 tablespoons poppy seeds	¼ cup *ghee*, or unsalted butter
1 tablespoon coriander seeds	1½ pounds lean boneless lamb, cut into 1½-inch cubes
1 tablespoon cumin seeds	½ cup plain yogurt
1 teaspoon grated fresh ginger	1 cup chicken stock
2 garlic cloves, minced	2 tablespoons minced fresh cilantro

Combine the cardamom seeds and half-and-half in a microwave container and heat in the microwave just until warm (or heat in a small saucepan over low heat). Set aside, covered.

Reserve half the cashews for garnish. Combine the rest of the nuts, the cinnamon, poppy seeds, coriander and cumin seeds, ginger, garlic, chile flakes, salt, and water in a mini processor or a blender and process to a paste.

In a Dutch oven or other flameproof casserole, cook the onions in the ghee over medium-high heat, stirring, until translucent, about 3 minutes. Add the lamb and the spice mixture, and cook, stirring, until the meat is browned and coated with the spices. Slowly stir in the yogurt and chicken stock. Reduce the heat and simmer, uncovered, for 30 to 45 minutes, or until the lamb is tender. Slowly stir in the cardamom cream and cook, stirring, until the sauce is slightly thickened. Serve garnished with the cilantro and reserved cashews.

ROSE PETALS

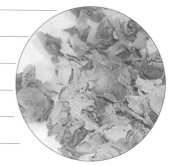

BOTANICAL NAME OF CULINARY SPECIES *Rosa spp.* **(numerous subspecies)**

PLANT FAMILY **Rose** *(Rosaceae)*

COUNTRY/REGION OF BOTANICAL ORIGIN **Asia**

MAJOR COUNTRIES/REGIONS OF CULTIVATION **Middle East**

SEASON OF HARVEST **Year-round**

PARTS USED **Petals**

COLORS **Varies, but typically pink to red**

The Middle Eastern souks that made the spice trade into an art form have long used flowers to infuse water and perfume spice blends with a sweet, dry taste. *Ras el hanout* is the classic that calls for rose petals, and pepper blends in France have called upon them similarly for a delicate undercurrent of taste.

Just about all species of rose can be used, but the common decorative varieties cultivated for appearance in the garden frequently have lighter flavors and scents than those older varieties that haven't suffered so from crossbreeding. For the spice trade, tiny "tea roses" are harvested and have their petals separated from their unpleasantly hard, bitter cores. Other commercial processes extract the flavors into water with steam to make the "rose water" sold commonly in Arabic and Indian markets.

Rose is also infused into a multitude of drinks in India and the Middle East. From teas to colas, any number of concoctions take on the dry floral character, getting as much help from the aroma as from the taste. When they are mixed with other florals like lavender or chamomile, you'll get a sweetness in herb blends that can be pleasantly hard to pinpoint, since most people associate smell rather than taste with rose petals.

ROSEMARY

ALTERNATE NAME **Old man**

BOTANICAL NAME OF CULINARY SPECIES *Rosmarinus officinalis*

PLANT FAMILY **Mint (*Lamiaceae*)**

COUNTRY/REGION OF BOTANICAL ORIGIN **Mediterranean**

MAJOR COUNTRIES/REGIONS OF CULTIVATION **Turkey, North Africa, North America**

SEASON OF HARVEST **Year-round**

PARTS USED **Leaves**

COLORS **Various greens**

have an old friend growing in a planter that has survived climatic relocation, care that would make master gardeners cringe, and the chopping off of major portions in last-minute cooking frenzies for unexpected guests. This dear old rosemary bush still never seems to stop giving, and it's this herb that I elevate to the post of "most versatile" in the kitchen.

Rosemary has one of those distinctive, strong flavors that convinces the palate that herbs aren't just delicate things reserved for dainty soups and sprinkling on baby vegetables. It takes hold of the taste buds with a woodsy flavor that reminds me of pine and sage but is buffered by a crisp herbal sweetness. It begs to be scorched and seared, as if to say, "I dare you, I can take it," and never lets you forget it's in the mix, even with other bold flavors.

And then, just when you think you've got rosemary's number, it surprises you with a subtle approach in a savory scone or crisp cracker that's had just a hint baked throughout, lightening the mood of an otherwise mundane pastry. Rosemary can dance on many stages in the kitchen, alone or in concert with other spices, but it never fails to add depth and richness.

While there are several species of culinary rosemary, most share a common flavor with little variation. The plants themselves range from tiny container-grown crawling specimens to massive upright hedgerows that have to be trimmed as frequently as the lawn. Thousands of tiny needle-like leaves grow on spidery branches, with the new growth at the tips being the most desirable. These are usually of a decidedly greener hue and slightly sweeter flavor than the older leaves, which often appear gray green and can have a harsher taste.

The stems themselves still hold some flavoring ability as skewers or smoking fodder, but the leaves have the vast majority of the essential oil and are easily stripped from the woody stems with a stroke of the hand from tip to base. While the multitude of tiny blue flowers rosemary produces in summer are beautiful, they have no real culinary value (except perhaps to beekeepers, whose charges love the stuff), and the kitchen gardener should pluck them off to encourage more leaf production.

With my own poor neglected plant doing so well in even the most desperate of climates year-round, I can easily make a case for fresh rosemary in every kitchen. There really is no excuse not to grow a small plant yourself, even if only in a convenient window or patio planter. The fresh leaf exhibits the peppery-pine scent and flavor so well that to use dried rosemary is almost a crime. The exception to this rule is its infusion into oils and vinegars, where the moisture of the fresh herb would ultimately yield rancid results. Otherwise, seek out the fresh for your pot roasts, lamb shanks, and savory breads. Avoid the stems, and always be sure to bruise, if not finely chop, the hard leaves just before they go into your dish.

Few spices have such a long list of appearances in folklore as rosemary. Ranging from your basic "wards off evil" tales from the Middle Ages to ancient stories of remembrance and love that come to the bearers of fresh sprigs, this bush truly is the stuff of legends. It surely must be its own best advocate, from the undeniable potency that comes even when simply walking by a mature plant: you can't help but be whisked away to its native Mediterranean when the perfume of lavender-meets-pine comes your way. Indeed, all the cultures of that region embrace rosemary's flavor, most notably coastal France and Italy, where the crops take on the pungency of the sea with great success. Almost all of their fresh herb bouquets and dried sachets for infusion, for everything from chicken stock to mulled wine, include rosemary sprigs for pungency and aroma.

At my local Italian grocery, they honor the ancient Roman belief that rosemary is the conveyance of friendship. All summer long there sits by the door a huge basket filled to the brim with fresh rosemary trimmings. Everyone on staff and a healthy number of customers contribute to the stock as their own prolific plants need trimming throughout the summer. The sign nearby reads simply, "Take some . . . please!" At worst it's a plea for disposal and at best, an invitation of culinary friendship I never refuse.

Skewer sticks can easily be made from some of the thicker stems of rosemary after the leaves have been stripped away. I use a vegetable peeler to slice away the outer bark on one side of the stem, to open the inner flesh to whatever you decide to skewer. Some Basque chefs have told me to soak the stems in port or sherry before using them in this fashion, but in practice, any liquid will do nicely to hydrate the essential oils and help the flavor exude into meats and hearty vegetables destined for the grill.

The most tender leaves can be pounded into sugar and stored to preserve the delicate sweetness of the new growth for use in pastry. Use a coarse sea salt for the same technique, and you can take your baking to the other end of the spectrum for crusty dinner rolls and crackers. Rosemary can work in some unexpected pastries or sweets as well. Imagine a lemon tart baked in an herb-laced crust, a sweetened crème fraîche infused with rosemary, or a rosemary caramel made from sugar that has been scented overnight with sprigs.

To tilt back to the classic, rosemary couldn't be better suited for roasting meats. Lamb is one of those foods that tend to intimidate chefs in the West, partially because of its sometimes strong flavor and partially because of the curve ball it can throw you in the spice department. What can possibly stand up to lamb in a toe-to-toe match and truly enhance rather than fight with the flavor? Rosemary with a touch of garlic and salt, as simple as it sounds, will never let you down here. The potency of rosemary stands up to lamb with ease and still manages to offer complexity, its more woody flavors mellowed with roasting and its herbaceous green remaining strong enough to show through.

Spice-crusted Pork Chops

Pork chops, made with a prepared crumb crust sold under a variety of brand names, is a classic of the Middle American meat-and-potatoes set. The idea is a sound one: adding texture and sealing in the juices of the meat. The store-bought mixes, however, lack interesting flavor and rely more on large amounts of sugar to accomplish their task. By making your own, you can layer in flavors with the spices and truly enhance pork chops rather than just covering them up.

SERVES 4

2 cups cornflake crumbs

1 cup *panko* (Japanese bread crumbs)

2 tablespoons all-purpose flour

1 tablespoon granulated sugar

2 teaspoons dried rosemary, coarsely cracked

2 teaspoons dried basil

1 tablespoon sweet Hungarian paprika

½ teaspoon ground cassia-cinnamon

⅛ teaspoon freshly ground cloves

1 teaspoon fine sea salt

1 teaspoon cracked black peppercorns

½ teaspoon freshly ground white pepper

1 large egg

Four 2-inch-thick (double-thick) pork chops

Juice of 1 lemon

Preheat the oven to 375°F. Prepare the crust coating by stirring (not grinding) the cornflake crumbs, *panko*, flour, sugar, rosemary, basil, paprika, cassia-cinnamon, cloves, salt, and peppercorns together in a bowl. Spread on a plate. Beat the egg in a shallow bowl. Rinse the pork chops and dip them into the egg, then press into the crust mix: add more or less crusting to preference, dipping in egg wash again if necessary. Place in a baking dish and bake for 50 minutes, or until an instant-read thermometer registers 160°F; sprinkle the lemon juice onto the pork halfway through cooking. Let the pork stand briefly before serving.

SAFFLOWER

ALTERNATE NAMES **Osfor (Hindi), Bastard saffron**

BOTANICAL NAME OF CULINARY SPECIES ***Carthamus tinctorius***

PLANT FAMILY **Daisy *(Asteraceae)***

COUNTRY/REGION OF BOTANICAL ORIGIN **Middle East**

MAJOR COUNTRIES/REGIONS OF CULTIVATION **India**

SEASON OF HARVEST **Summer through fall**

PARTS USED **Flower petals**

COLOR **Orange-red**

The trade in saffron look-alikes can be a profitable one if there are uneducated buyers afoot in the markets of Turkey, India, and Persia. Safflower is one of the common culprits in this bait-and-switch, so let the buyer beware.

When they are set side by side, it becomes very obvious that the petals of the safflower are much more orange in character and have a wider, more angular shape than saffron's long, wirelike threads. What it can offer with great success is a coloring very much like saffron—but without any of the corresponding flavor, of course. This coloring ability is what has kept it on the world markets since ancient times, partially for culinary efforts and partially in the textiles trade. Saffron robes are very frequently safflower robes, but since you don't normally taste your clothes, there's no harm in the switch. Cooks may care to experiment with the petals in the kitchen, but beyond color, there are no real culinary benefits.

SAFFRON

ALTERNATE NAME	*Azafrán* (Spanish)
BOTANICAL NAME OF CULINARY SPECIES	*Crocus sativus*
PLANT FAMILY	Iris *(Iridaceae)*
COUNTRY/REGION OF BOTANICAL ORIGIN	Asia
MAJOR COUNTRIES/REGIONS OF CULTIVATION	Iran, India, Spain, Mexico
SEASON OF HARVEST	Late fall
PARTS USED	Flower stigmas
COLOR	Deep red

No spice on the planet evokes such dreams of riches as saffron. Its mere mention conjures up images of opulent saffron-laced curries in the courts of India, rich bouillabaisses served to the monarch of France, *tagines* born of the widely traveled Moorish palate, and, of course, complex paellas fit for a Spanish king.

Although it's by far the most expensive spice on the globe, its cost shouldn't really be daunting, as the potency of this miraculous herb makes it literally pennies per dish—even if the average price can be in the $1,000-per-pound range. Most saffron is sold at retail in grams for less than $8, more than enough for several meals.

To be a smart buyer, you must first strip away copious amounts of national pride that seep into any saffron sales pitch. Spaniards will tell you that theirs is far superior to the Kashmir, and Iranians will scoff if La Mancha is even mentioned. Indeed, these are the major producing areas, with newcomers in New Zealand and Central Africa attempting cultivation, albeit on a microscale as yet. If you're diligent in your sampling of the different regions, you'll find that the *terroir* of each imparts its distinct effect upon the final taste. For myself, the Spanish tends toward a more savory tone while the Iranian has a sweeter character.

Saffron is the stigma of a crocus flower, and what makes it so expensive is the labor involved in harvest and the sheer acreage needed to produce even a small amount. Something like fifty thousand flowers, a football field–sized patch, must be grown to produce just one pound. During the two-week season of harvest, the flowers must be picked each morning and hand-plucked of the three stigmas in each blossom. Exactly which parts of the stigma are used varies from region to region, with the Iranians typically saving only the ruby red tips for their highest-quality production. The Spaniards usually take a longer length of the stigma, leaving some of its lighter orange-white base intact in the final product.

These lighter orange-white threads, which are actually the styles of the flower and attach the stigmas to it, should be all but nonexistent in highest-quality batches, as they contain little of the desired flavor components. Frequently some are included to bulk up the weight or to reduce the labor needed to remove them, but only a few per hundred are acceptable.

After plucking, there is a light roasting stage that dries the stigmas and fixes the flavor in the threads. This gentle step is done in the time-honored method over wood fires, tended by only the most expert of farmers. Even as little as a minute too long over the fire, and days of effort and thousands of dollars can go up in smoke.

As for each region, a look to Spain shows the potential for very fine product. The government-sponsored grading system has "First Quality" as the top grade, followed by "Quality," and then generically "Ungraded." Although locale is not strictly a quality grade, saffron is typically identified as to its state of production, with La Mancha being preferred over Rio. It's curious that Spain has exported on average some forty percent more than it has produced for the past decade, a fact that must indicate a mixing in of non-Spanish product on some level.

Iran (Persia) and the Kashmir regions of India have always been producers of significant quality, but there is no established grading system by which to judge. Quality merchants will have their lots tested in a lab to establish average amounts of the three flavoring and coloring components (see below), and price accordingly.

Whatever the region, there are a few telltale signs to guide the buyer. First, look for a vibrancy of red color rather than a duller brick red that comes with age. Also look for a moist pliability to the threads, especially around harvesttime—when the temptation to clear out last year's crop at discount prices is strong. Shake the bag or container to see if there's an accumulation of tiny broken bits in the bottom. As saffron ages and dries, these bits snap off the delicate threads.

The three compounds in saffron that give it color, flavor, and aroma are, respectively, crocin, picrocrochin, and safranal. There is great debate in the industry as to the best way to test batches and establish quality. Some merchants stand behind one or another lab result, some believe that a high number of one automatically leads to high concentrations of another, and still others will enter into a discussion of how two of these compounds degrade so fast that tests can't prove anything. An elderly farmer from La Mancha put the question to an end for me years ago. He said, "If you feel and smell something wonderful, and if you make your rice and taste all of Spain, then you have a good crop. Tests be damned, I know what I want to taste." Ever since, I have tended to agree with him and I simply taste-test my batches at the beginning of each harvest rather than bogging down in some lab-numbers debate.

Remembering that saffron is an annual harvest in all of the regions, you should use only the current year's crop, typically harvested in the late fall or early winter by all the Northern Hemisphere producers, and store it carefully to help extend its potency. Any reputable merchant or package will indicate its "season," with either the year of harvest alone or the two-year indicator of which years the harvest straddled, e.g., 2001/2002. Certainly saffron can hold some of its original flavor for years. Indeed, in Spain, the workers all take home a portion of their pickings as payment and store it as a sort of flavorful savings plan. Still, the fresher the crop, the higher the flavor and the brighter the color, so annual turnover of stock is recommended. I find that refrigeration is prudent only after the first six months and even then only in the hottest climates, as the cold will leach out more flavor than it saves when the threads are particularly fresh. Later in its life, though, refrigeration may be the lesser of two evils.

The newcomers in New Zealand offer interesting potential. Being in the Southern Hemisphere, they may in time be able to present us with a bright new crop in late June, just when the traditional producers' product is beginning to wane. Still, the costs of labor may be New Zealand's undoing, and only time will tell if these upstarts can supply any significant crop to the world market.

In terms of classical uses, the king of dishes is the Spanish paella, the rice and meat and/or seafood dish, cooked over open fires in a shallow wide pan, which is infused with saffron, the only seasoning beyond a bit of salt and pepper. Also from the Iberian Peninsula come the fish stews known as *zarvelas*, very similar to the classic bouillabaisse of nearby Mediterranean France (specifically Marseilles), both of which are delicately flavored almost exclusively with saffron.

In the Middle East and the Indian subcontinent, savory breads are flavored with saffron, giving them a distinctive yellow orange tinge and a pleasing dry, floral aroma. Historically, the most affluent of rulers would command that their curries contain "no small measure of saffron" as a sign of wealth and power, and even their royal looms would weave saffron-dyed robes to impress the locals and visitors alike. The use of saffron had social consequences on top of the obvious flavor benefit, and if you had the means to acquire saffron, you most certainly let it be known in and out of the dining room.

It's most practical to infuse freshly crumbled threads in a few tablespoons of liquid, e.g., water or sherry, to jump-start the flavor into your dish. Ten minutes of soaking time will impart a deep color to the liquid, which can then also be added to the dish. This step is particularly important in baking and in thicker sauces, to help homogenize the saffron throughout.

A word of caution is in order, however, because it's far too easy to go overboard with saffron. There can easily be too much added, considering that enough top-quality threads to coat a fingertip will, for example, flavor a gallon of stock. Resist the "more is better" temptation to avoid an overly dry, overly astringent flavor. The perfume should be noticeable but not overload your senses. The taste shouldn't leave your tongue bristling and have you wondering what else was in the soup. When in doubt, use less, since you can usually add a bit more of the saffron-infused liquid and cook a few minutes longer to get to a level that makes your taste buds comfortable. With saffron, you really *can* have too much of a good thing.

Saffron Butternut Bisque

Fall is harvesttime for saffron in Spain and the peak of squash season in the Pacific Northwest. Just because they're thousands of miles apart doesn't mean we can't share each other's bounty. Thank goodness for overnight delivery. **SERVES 4 TO 6**

1 large butternut squash, peeled, seeded, and cubed

1 large turnip, peeled and diced

¼ cup olive oil

1 teaspoon coarse sea salt

20 saffron threads

¼ cup dry sherry

1 onion, diced

2 garlic cloves, minced

2 quarts chicken stock

Fine sea salt, to taste

1 teaspoon freshly ground white pepper

1 cup heavy whipping cream

Chopped fresh chives or parsley for garnish

Preheat the broiler. In a large bowl, toss the squash and turnip with 2 tablespoons of the oil to coat. Spread on a small baking sheet and sprinkle with the kosher salt. Broil 4 inches from the heat until the edges begin to char, then stir and return to the broiler. Repeat as necessary until the vegetables are slightly charred on all sides.

Meanwhile, crumble the saffron into the sherry, and allow to stand for 15 minutes.

In a small heavy pot, cook the onion and garlic in the remaining 2 tablespoons oil over medium-high heat, stirring, until translucent, 2 to 3 minutes. Add the roasted vegetables, stock, sea salt, saffron mixture, and pepper. Bring to a simmer, reduce the heat to low, and simmer, stirring occasionally, until the vegetables are very tender, about 20 minutes. Adjust the salt as needed. Blend with an immersion blender until smooth (or transfer to a regular blender, in batches, and blend until smooth, then return to the pot). Stir in the cream and heat through. Serve garnished with fresh chives.

SAGE

BOTANICAL NAME OF CULINARY SPECIES *Salvia officinalis*

PLANT FAMILY **Mint *(Lamiaceae)***

COUNTRY/REGION OF BOTANICAL ORIGIN **Northern Europe**

MAJOR COUNTRIES/REGIONS OF CULTIVATION **Widely across Northern Hemisphere, notably Croatia**

SEASON OF HARVEST **Summer through early winter**

PARTS USED **Leaves**

COLORS **Varied greens**

I never answer the question, "What's your favorite spice?" at my shop because I think it's both too difficult to choose and too dependent upon my mood. Having thrown out that standard disclaimer and with the luxury of print to buffer my answer, it is most definitely sage.

My earliest cooking memory comes from a Thanksgiving holiday when my mother was preparing corn bread dressing for the turkey. My job was always to test the mix for spices, perhaps an omen of my career to come, and in our house, that meant simply salt, pepper, and sage. I think there must have been something genetic in our family that bent us toward sage, since all the nonfamily guests always seemed to comment on the potency of the herb in our recipes. I never gave it a second thought. Sage should be strong and assertive, and let you know it's there.

The leaves themselves have a feathery soft texture on the stem. The tender stems of fresh young sage can be chopped and used along with the leaves, but as you get older growth or switch to dried leaves, you'll need to remove stems. Named for the process that removes the stems from dried leaves, "rubbed" sage is pillowy soft and considerably fluffier than other ground herbs. If possible, for accuracy, measure by weight rather than volume, or, at minimum, remember that rubbed dry sage can take up to three times the space of an equal amount of the fresh. The dried leaves work very well, perhaps even better than fresh, as they concentrate nicely and offer the palate a more potent version of all the original flavors with no loss thereof, a problem that plagues the drying process.

The plant grows in a wide variety of hybrids. Common garden sage still remains my favorite, since it has a unique, clean taste that is simultaneously astringent, sweet, and warming. I taste less pine and cedarwood flavors than rosemary, more marjoram-like soft herbaceousness, and mild pepper woven in for good measure. Sage cultivates well in a wide range of climates, and the world's cuisines have accepted it as broadly. Perhaps most famous are the sage fields of Eastern Europe in the Dalmatia region of Croatia. Native to the borders of the Adriatic, sage here takes on a particularly complex aroma and taste with sweet mint connotations on top of the typical woody, herbal character.

Washington State and Oregon have also become champions of the sage cause. The dry desert microclimate east of the Cascade Mountains has begun to produce interesting flavors, less sweet than the European, and with a stronger pepper component on the taste buds. The unique heat of the desert surely accounts for this shift and, as with other herbs, the home gardener can expect swings in the flavor based on the specific growing conditions.

Back in Europe, you see sage used as an herb in making pesto, cooked into pastas, added to stock, and even fried as a garnish. It seems that its potency is easily regulated despite its sometimes overwhelming aroma when fresh. A specific example from Croatia uses sage leaves to wrap duck breasts that are then smoked over the herb stems. When the duck is cooked, the wrapping is removed, leaving behind the essence of sage without the strength you'd get from eating the leaves directly.

In my kitchen, I think there's no better flavor combination than sage and onion, cooked together to slightly caramelize the onion and bring the full pungency of sage to the front. I start most savory gravies and stews with this combo and even add the mix to breads, in the dough or as a topping. My sage addiction shows no sign of easing anytime soon.

Mom's Holiday Corn Bread Dressing

As I've said elsewhere, I have both dressing and sage fixations. Some would suggest counseling, but I'd have to admit these were problems before that would help. There are fewer ways more apt to give you the wonderfully heady flavor of sage without distraction than corn bread dressing.

"Casual" stuffing to me is an everyday side dish (see page 351); on major occasions, you want to take the extra effort to make the "holiday" version. One of my earliest memories of cooking was with my grandmother, who told me that it wasn't in fact "stuffing," but actually "dressing." "If you put it in the turkey, son, you'll dry the whole thing out like toast on a hot sidewalk," she said, and the message took hold. I've never put anything bready inside my poultry, no matter what you call it.

If there are any family secrets in the dressing category, it's simply in the bread makeup. I remember that the week before a holiday dinner, a brown bag of bread oddities would begin to fill up on the kitchen counter. Spare loaf ends here, extra dinner rolls there, or even the occasional hush puppy would get tossed in. Left open to the air to go a bit stale, a similar hodgepodge of baking will ultimately become the foundation for your holiday dressing bonanza. Just as with the frugal settlers who inspired bread stuffing in the American colonies, nothing goes to waste, from spare bread to the drippings of the roast turkey. **SERVES 8**

CORN BREAD

8 tablespoons (1 stick) unsalted butter

1 cup yellow fine cornmeal

1 cup all-purpose flour

3 tablespoons granulated sugar

1 teaspoon baking powder

1 teaspoon coarse sea salt

1 large egg

1 cup buttermilk

DRESSING

1 large onion, finely chopped

4 celery stalks, finely chopped

¼ cup dried sage, crushed

1 tablespoon fine sea salt, or to taste

1 tablespoon freshly ground black pepper, or to taste

2 pounds miscellaneous bread (see headnote), cut into 1-inch pieces (approximately 10 cups)

1 cup beef stock

1 cup roast poultry drippings, mostly defatted (or substitute chicken stock)

3 large eggs, beaten

Up to 4 cups chicken stock

Start by making the corn bread: Preheat the oven to 375°F. Put the butter in a 10-inch cast-iron skillet and place in the oven to melt.

Meanwhile, mix the dry ingredients together in a medium bowl. In a small bowl, lightly beat the egg with a fork and stir in the buttermilk. Add to the dry ingredients, then pour in the melted butter, swirling the butter around in the pan to coat the bottom and sides well in the process. Fold the ingredients together thoroughly. Pour into the hot buttered skillet and bake for 25 minutes, or until a knife inserted in the center comes out clean. Remove the corn bread, and leave the oven on.

To make the dressing, stir together the onion, celery, sage, salt, and pepper in an extra-large bowl. Add the bread and toss to mix. Use a knife to cut the corn bread, in the skillet, into 1-inch chunks, and add to the mixture. Add the beef stock and poultry drippings, mixing well. Stir in the eggs. Gradually add chicken stock until the consistency is of a moist, extra-thick batter (the more liquid you add, the denser the finished result).

Pour the dressing into a deep baking pan and bake for approximately 1 hour. Check for doneness by inserting a spoon into the center: the dressing should hold together but not have become overly dense.

SASSAFRAS

ALTERNATE NAME **Gumbo filé (leaves)**

BOTANICAL NAME OF CULINARY SPECIES *Sassafras albidum*

PLANT FAMILY **Laurel (*Lauraceae*)**

COUNTRY/REGION OF BOTANICAL ORIGIN **North America**

MAJOR COUNTRIES/REGIONS OF CULTIVATION **Louisiana, Mexico**

SEASON OF HARVEST **Fall**

PARTS USED **Leaves**

COLOR **Olive green**

In the French Acadia country of the Deep South, eighteenth-century cooks needed a thickener. Enter the sassafras tree, which had already proven its worth through its bark, as a beverage. On the advice of native peoples, curious cooks began to dry and grind the leaf and discovered its pleasantly mild camphor character. This flavor only hints at the "root beer" connotations of bark from the same tree.

The processing of leaves, steeped in the secrecy of old family circles, can include stages of roasting, sun-drying, rubbing, destemming, and even steaming. The more industrial treatment produces a dense powder of flour consistency that should be used sparingly. The small-scale artisan treatments can yield a fluffy product much like rubbed sage, and while it's still quite potent, its higher volume-to-weight ratio will make you feel as if you're using more.

Sassafras oil, which contains the carcinogen safrole, is outlawed in the United States because of its medical risks, but the unrefined products from the plant, the bark for teas and the leaves for the thickener filé, are deemed to be low enough in harmful concentrations as to allow their trade.

In the kitchen, there is another risk when using gumbo filé. "Son, you're gonna be havin' a big pot o'glue if you cook that anymore!" bellowed a Cajun chef friend who'd been extolling the virtues of filé at the stove one Mardi Gras afternoon. The amount used, as mentioned, is tiny, but even that measure, if cooked too long or at too high a heat, can render a dish stringy and sticky to the point of inedibility. Most Southern cooks know to add the filé last to a pot, just removed from the heat, allowing only the carryover heat to cook the spice and render its thickening and flavoring effects.

Creole Gumbo

Gumbo is a thin stew or a thick soup, depending on your perspective, traditionally rich with, well, whatever you can find down in southern Louisiana. It's opportunistic at best and made with a wide array of meats, seafood, chicken, and just about anything that moves in the bayou. I spent too many a Mardi Gras night down there, but we could always come back to a local college friend's house and count on his mom, a doctor by profession, having made some gumbo for the bleary-eyed crew in the morning. During Mardi Gras, the concepts of breakfast and dinner become a bit blurry, like everything else down there.

Everyone in New Orleans knows how to make gumbo. Of course, you can certainly see it in the restaurants as a local favorite hyped up to the tourists, but you're also just as likely to walk past someone making a batch at the back door of their office over a portable gas burner, a crew of college kids simmering a pot before the game, or a local bar giving it away to attract patrons.

The most important steps in making gumbo come at either end. You must make a proper roux to begin the dish and you must finish it with gumbo filé, powdered sassafras leaf. In between, it's much more forgiving and can be modified as desired to fit whatever you have on hand. Personally, I have the boys at the Central Market on Decatur Street, near the French Market in New Orleans, send me a care package overnight with some spicy andouille sausage and live crawfish. While they're at it, I have them toss in an authentic muffulata sandwich, just in case I get hungry while the gumbo simmers. **SERVES 6**

8 tablespoons (1 stick) unsalted butter

½ cup all-purpose flour

3 tablespoons freshly ground Creole Spice Blend (page 345)

1 onion, coarsely chopped

2 celery stalks, coarsely chopped

½ cup coarsely chopped green bell pepper

2 tablespoons tomato paste

2 cups chicken stock

½ pound andouille sausage, chopped

½ pound medium shrimp

½ pound fresh (preferably) or frozen whole crawfish

1 cup shredded, poached chicken

1 pound okra, sliced

2 cups diced, seeded tomatoes

¼ cup chopped fresh parsley

2 bay leaves

1 teaspoon fine sea salt, or to taste

1 tablespoon gumbo filé

Begin by making the roux: melt the butter in a large pot over medium heat. Add the flour, stirring constantly. Cook, stirring, until the roux is a peanut butter color and a nutty aroma comes from the pot; don't look away, or it will scorch. Add the Creole spices, onion, celery, bell pepper, tomato paste, and 2 to 3 tablespoons water, stirring to coat the vegetables with the roux and spices. Add the remaining ingredients except the gumbo filé, then add water to barely cover the ingredients. Cover and simmer over low heat for 1½ hours. Remove from the heat and add the gumbo filé, stirring constantly until thickened. Serve immediately, with white rice.

SAVORY, SUMMER AND WINTER

ALTERNATE NAMES Bean herb (summer), Pepper herb (summer), Donkey pepper (winter)

BOTANICAL NAMES OF CULINARY SPECIES *Satureja hortensis* (summer), *Satureja montana* (winter)

PLANT FAMILY Mint *(Lamiaceae)*

COUNTRIES/REGIONS OF BOTANICAL ORIGIN Turkey, Eastern Europe (summer), Mediterranean, Turkey (winter)

MAJOR COUNTRIES/REGIONS OF CULTIVATION Southern Europe (summer), Northern Europe through Mediterranean and North Africa (winter)

SEASONS OF HARVEST Summer through early fall (summer), Year-round in temperate climates (winter)

PARTS USED Leaves

COLORS Green leaves on reddish stems (summer), Darker green on yellowish stems (winter)

You'd think that more people would know how to use savory, considering that the instructions are right there in the name. The ancient Romans had a love affair with the leaf, but since then there's been a steady decline in consumption, save for a few enclaves of European cuisine that make the most of this potent flavor.

Savory makes a wonderful bridge between herb and spice, with definitive pepper notes on a classic thyme taste. In its more popular days, some would use it in place of less affordable pepper. While the intensity is much lower than peppercorns', desperate times called for stretching the spice budget in any way possible.

Summer savory is more delicate than winter savory, and it grows in a smaller, more temperate region and for a shorter season, centered around the summer months. The plant itself is a short-lived annual and that translates to the flavor in kind. The tastes are pronounced up front but linger less than you would initially expect. There is also some tinge of mint that creeps into the palate of summer savory, perhaps a flavor that is obscured by winter savory's stronger pepper bite.

Winter savory is a much more hearty plant that ranges a bit more freely. Being a perennial, it can, depending on the local climate, be harvested almost over four seasons, much like rosemary. While both savories have a punch, winter is the marathon runner and lingers more than its cousin.

The herbs can be substituted for each other with success, but choose your proportions carefully when making the switch. Just as with other herbs, I've noticed significant swings depending on the time of year and local growing conditions. So you might use equal measures of each during the tender, early season but need to cut winter savory measures in half when substituting it late in the year, as it will have developed more of the intense pepper character that made it famous in Rome.

Beans and lentils have long taken doses of savory well, given their extended cooking times. But the herb, especially winter varieties, can maintain flavor for the full duration needed. Reaching again back to its heyday in ancient times, the Romans would grind garbanzo beans into a flour with savory to make a sort of flatbread. Mixed with water and spread into a thin layer, it would bake into a dense savory biscuit that was eaten all day long.

As they were known to do with other examples, the centurions spread the popularity of this herb northward and made it a staple in German and English kitchens. Taking advantage of its prolific growth in the cooler climates, cooks made winter savory the more commonplace herb, but both are seen sporadically in the culinary documentation of the era. While its use has declined since as an "all-purpose" herb, there are ample examples of fresh sausages and dry-cured meats taking advantage of its potent flavors.

Tourtière (Spiced Meat Pie)

When you're hunting for recipes, you sometimes find them in the last place you'd expect. I have an affinity for snowy places and, as such, I spend a lot of time in my adopted second home of British Columbia. You can imagine my curiosity when I found myself at the other corner of the continent in Florida at Disney World's Epcot Center one painfully hot summer day, facing a massive pavilion sponsored by my beloved (and much cooler) Canada. The lure of snow-covered scenery and air conditioning had me through the doors almost instantly.

Once inside, I cleared the informational film and headed straight for something billed as "classic Canadian"' cuisine. What the chefs immediately told me I had to try was a *tourtière*, a stuffed meat pie that's seasoned with savory herbs and served traditionally around the holidays in the Great White North. They were kind enough to share a slice and the recipe. Years later, now that I've found numerous other variations from all over Canada, I have to say the recipe the Mouse was serving was incredibly authentic—and delicious. **SERVES 4**

¾ pound extra-lean ground beef

¼ pound ground pork

¼ cup finely diced onion

½ teaspoon minced garlic

1 tablespoon olive oil

½ cup diced potato

¼ cup finely diced carrot

¼ cup finely diced celery

Approximately ½ cup chicken stock

1 tablespoon rubbed sage

½ teaspoon freshly ground dried winter savory

½ teaspoon freshly ground black pepper

½ teaspoon freshly ground white pepper

½ teaspoon freshly ground dried thyme

½ teaspoon fine sea salt

½ teaspoon freshly ground dried rosemary

⅛ teaspoon freshly ground cloves

Top and bottom crusts for a 9-inch pie (store-bought or your favorite recipe)

Brown the ground meats together in a large skillet over medium heat, stirring occasionally. Drain off any excess liquid, and set aside.

In a small skillet, cook the onion and garlic in the oil over medium heat, stirring, until translucent, about 3 minutes. Add the potato, carrot, and celery and cook, stirring, until tender, adding stock as necessary to prevent scorching. Remove from the heat.

Grind the herbs and spices together in a coffee mill, and stir into the reserved meat. Add the vegetables, and mix well. Allow the filling to cool completely.

Meanwhile, preheat the oven to 375°F. Line a 9-inch pie plate with the bottom crust, and spoon in the cooled filling. Cover with the top crust and crimp the edges to seal. Cut 2 or 3 steam vents in the top crust. Bake for 45 minutes, or until the crust is golden brown and the filling is piping hot. Serve, along with roast vegetables spiced with the same savory herbs, to even the hungriest of hockey players.

SCREW PINE

ALTERNATE NAMES	**Pandan leaf**
BOTANICAL NAME OF CULINARY SPECIES	***Pandanus amaryllifolius***
PLANT FAMILY	**Screw pine *(Pandanaceae)***
COUNTRY/REGION OF BOTANICAL ORIGIN	**Southeast Asia**
MAJOR COUNTRIES/REGIONS OF CULTIVATION	**Asia, Indonesia**
SEASON OF HARVEST	**Year-round**
PARTS USED	**Leaves, and their essence**
COLOR	**Pale green**

The tough, spiked leaves of the screw pine plant look more like tropical landscaping than something you'd take into the kitchen. And the mature leaves are almost hard enough to use as knives—but deep inside, they have a unique flavor that has no substitute.

Screw pine leaves are used fresh to perfume rice dishes of the South Pacific and Southeast Asian peninsula, but the flavor almost completely evaporates when the leaves are dried. Although chopped dried leaves are sold, the wise cook will ignore that form and seek out instead an essence-laden water typically sold under the name *pandan* in Asian markets.

Nutty aroma is the first clue to the flavor screw pine can impart. The taste marries incredibly well with sweet coconut milk dishes and tropical fruit desserts. My favorite Vietnamese deli serves half a dozen variations on the theme, mixing screw pine–infused syrups and gelatins with rice, poached fruit, even black-eyed peas. Shredded coconut or peanuts garnish all the desserts, further underscoring nutty essence.

Screw pine is a signature flavor in the yellow rice entrées and black rice desserts of Bali. In addition to the nutty taste, it can bring a dry floral aroma not unlike lavender or rose. Just a small dose of the flavored water is added to the cooking liquid; using only *pandan* water would be overkill. Add it when about half the other cooking liquid has been absorbed, but make sure the cover is tight to hold in as much essence as possible.

Balinese Chicken Satay

Satay is becoming as mainstream as teriyaki or kebabs in American kitchens. The difference between the homogenized versions you are all too likely to encounter and the authentic article, however, is the spicy sauce used to season the skewers. A proper Indonesian version will use one of the freshly prepared *sambal* pastes that are unique to the islands.

In the West, satay is typically made with chunks of chicken, as I've done here, but it's not uncommon to see the dish prepared with ground meats, the spices mixed in and the meat pressed onto the ends of sticks of bamboo. These are grilled over coconut husks or fried in peanut oil, resulting in what look like bulbous chicken drumsticks. Because of their shape and cultural weapons connotation, only men typically prepare the dish: it seems that the male gender the world over is still enamored with cooking over fire.

Indonesian cooks use a wide variety of *sambal* pastes that call upon the spice oddities native to the South Pacific. *Pandan* leaves, Vietnamese coriander, and finger root, among others, all get blended in to make that something special you taste on the beaches. Although similar *sambals* can be purchased in your local Asian markets, those same groceries can typically supply you with all the special ingredients needed to make it fresh. The extra effort is immeasurably rewarding. **SERVES 4**

1 pound boneless, skinless chicken breasts, cut into 1-inch cubes	¼ cup finely chopped culantro or cilantro
Juice of 2 limes	1 tablespoon minced fresh finger root or galangal
2 tablespoon *pandan* (screw pine) essence	2 teaspoons minced fresh ginger
2 shallots, minced	Wooden skewers, at least 10 inches long
¼ cup Sambal Goreng (page 396)	

Place the chicken in a glass pie dish or small baking dish. Pour the lime juice and *pandan* essence over it, then toss with the shallots. Cover and refrigerate for 1 hour, turning occasionally.

Meanwhile, combine half the *sambal*, the culantro, finger root, and ginger, in a food processor or blender and process to a paste. Cover and allow to stand for 30 minutes.

Prepare a hot fire in an outdoor grill. Thread the chicken onto skewers, reserving the marinade. Spread the spice paste liberally over the chicken. Grill over hot coals, turning occasionally and drizzling the reserved marinade over once or twice, until cooked through. (Alternatively, perch the skewers over the marinade dish, using the skewers to elevate the chicken over the liquid, and bake in a preheated 425°F oven, basting once or twice with the marinade, for 10 to 12 minutes, or until cooked through.) Serve with the remaining *sambal* as a condiment.

With the abundance of reasonable sea salts, or, at minimum, interestingly textured kosher salt, there's no good reason short of de-icing your walkway to keep large boxes of table salt in your house. The fact is that table salt has almost no redeeming qualities in the kitchen. The mineral composition is sodium chloride, NaCl, nothing more—with the possible exception of iodine. This was historically added when deficiencies in the public diet warranted it, but now ample sources are found elsewhere.

Table salt's lowest common denominator of makeup robs it of anything flavorful you'd find in much more complex, chemically speaking, sea salts. For an eye-opening taste test, set any sea salt next to table salt and you'll find the harsh, metallic character clearly evident in the latter.

Sea salt holds onto more than just sodium chloride in its taste makeup. It's the natural algae, vegetation, and minerals floating in the seawater that ultimately give each ocean, and its salt, its distinctive character. In some cases, the evaporation fields themselves where the salt is harvested impart other minerals to its makeup and add even more taste. The mineral composition of sea salt can include up to fifty compounds, including zinc, magnesium, and iron. (They can be veritable multivitamins on your table.) It's these buffering minerals and organics that make sea salt a better choice over harsh processed table salt.

According to some studies, the origins of certain medical deficiencies can be shown to parallel the time when processed salt was introduced to the public on a large scale. No matter what the ultimate truth of the matter is medically, the bottom line is that salt is perhaps the most common spice in all the world's cuisines and, as such, deserves examination and culinary forethought. While there are literally hundreds of regional salts produced, a thumbnail sketch of a few commonly available ones is presented below.

Pacific Ocean salt is typically harvested from island communities and, not surprisingly, given their relatively remote locations, the flavors tend to be clean and crisp, with less organic character than others. Typically much cheaper than other sea salts, they are good for all-around kitchen use and won't break the budget in the process.

France's Brittany coast salts are among the most famous for their complex makeup and rich ocean character. *Fleur de sel*, or the "flower of the ocean," is the cream of the crop, so to speak. Originally, the salt producers in coastal France simply cracked the salt crust that naturally formed on top of their evaporation ponds and allowed it to sink back into the water, thus permitting the evaporation to continue. But chefs and cooks in the area realized that this top harvest of salt had a delicate sea flora sweetness compared with the bottom-harvested salts. These latter salts, known as *sel gris* or gray salt, are removed when the pond has evaporated completely and typically have a coarser texture. Their flavor is heavier and richer in minerals, making them better when roasting or crusting vegetables and meats. Reserve the lighter *fleur de sel* for finishing salads and other fare, rather than cooking with it.

The French also manufacture a smoked salt from the same fields that produce smoked garlic in the late summer. A large-grain sea salt is put in screened trays over fires and allowed to absorb the character of the smoking wood. As the large-grained salt is a good carrier of flavor, even small doses can impart significant character. However, this technique seems to be exclusive to the French, and the shipping costs of heavy sea salt make it a less than widely distributed product.

In Hawaii, red alaea, the natural clay mined from volcanic veins, is mixed into locally harvested sea salt. The salt's color is actually a pink hue and, as would be expected from clay, the taste is deep and earthy. This makes a very nice salt for finishing at the table or rubbing on seafood.

Many Japanese sea salts typically have a very strong zinc taste that makes them almost too harsh for everyday use. Anything from the ocean, especially sushi and raw oysters, will blend well with these, but be careful not to overuse them. One exotic version, "moon salt," is said to be harvested only during a full moon, on the presumption that certain elements of the sea are at their peak only once each lunar month. This and other specialty harvests can be wonderfully delicate, if not easily affordable, and

COOKING VERSUS FINISHING SALTS

I break down salts into two categories, cooking and finishing. The former are "simplistic" salts, to be used at the stove, and the latter are much more complex, to be used as a condiment with the finished dish. Both types are useful, but usually, if you're looking for general flavor enhancement, you'll use a simple salt at the stove. If the salt has some delicate flavors to preserve, use it at the table.

As with all spices, "to taste" means you should add some, cook, taste, and evaluate. Cooking brings the flavor up to full force and shouldn't be second-guessed. Wait for that development before adding more; it's much easier to add than to take away.

---

should be sought out for the pinnacle of Japanese cuisine. In typically intense style, Japanese chefs have a colloquial saying to the effect that only with decades of study can you master the subtle art of salt work.

Maldon salt is harvested from the coasts of England and represents the character of the North Sea. Only slightly less complex than the famous salts of Brittany, it has a stronger character and similar taste of ocean vegetation. It stands up well to fried foods as a finishing salt and easily makes the transition to all-purpose seasoning when you want the salt character to burst through. Its most unusual characteristic comes from the manufacturing process, which yields large flat crystals that look more like shredded coconut at first glance. This makes it quite popular as a condiment, and I've even seen the crystals decorating fine chocolates in the best sweets shops of London.

Sea salts come from all around the Mediterranean coast, but they tend to fall somewhat short of their neighbors to the north in both complexity and strength of flavor. Having said that, there are myriad micro productions that can import unique flavors from sweet to sharp and, therefore, should be taste-tested before passing judgment. And they make fine choices when baking fish in a hard salt crust that holds in natural juices and flavors. The shell is broken open upon serving, and the taste of the fish is only delicately salty. One Basque variation calls for baking fresh mullet on a bed of coarse sea salt over an open grill to draw out moisture and concentrate the taste of the fish into wonderful intensity.

Seaweed is a staple in so many kitchens on the planet that entire volumes on the subject could be authored easily. Well over a hundred various species are harvested for culinary use. From rolled sushi wrappers to soup thickeners, seaweed has found myriad uses in our global diets. In this text, however, it is a few specific forms and species that have made the leap into a spice context that should be mentioned. Delicate green flakes are used as a basis for Japanese condiment blends like Shichimi-Togarashi (page 401), and placed on the table in a pure form to offer extra saltiness as desired.

On a trip to the Brittany coast of France for sea salt, I noticed small piles of red, blue, yellow, and green off to the sides of the salt-leaching ponds. Curious as to what the brilliant colors were, I inquired of my salt producer, and he explained that the fishermen would collect certain fields of seaweed off the coast for him to dry on his farm. The process is a simple one; sorting, drying, and cutting to a uniform size is all that's required.

The French and Japanese have both embraced seaweed as an ingredient to be used much as you would salt, in every color of the rainbow and every flake size from powder to two-inch pieces. Having tasted all the varieties gathered, I can't discern any major differences based on color, but I do get character unique to the source ocean, just as you find with sea salts.

The flakes are used in condiment spice blends and in artful presentations as a topping or crusting. The leaves are toasted as well, seaweed being a good carrier of roasted flavors. I had a tremendous bowl of udon noodles in, of all places, the Tokyo airport on a transfer from Hong Kong. The sweetness of the broth was balanced nicely with the heavily roasted red seaweed that garnished it. While I still wouldn't recommend a food tour of the world's airports, it's good to know that even they can get some things right if the dish is simple enough.

The French don't feature seaweed quite as prominently, using it more as a flavoring in soups where the salty and vegetal connotations of the sea are desirable. Some coastal interpretations of bouillabaisse get a dose to round out the traditional saffron profile. Seaweed is known to Basque chefs by the misnomer "algae," but they also take advantage of ground seaweed as a salt substitute in the squid and mullet dishes of the region.

SESAME SEEDS

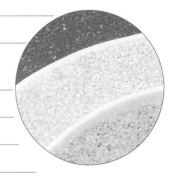

BOTANICAL NAME OF CULINARY SPECIES *Sesamum indicum*

PLANT FAMILY *Pedaliaceae*

COUNTRY/REGION OF BOTANICAL ORIGIN Northern Africa

MAJOR COUNTRIES/REGIONS OF CULTIVATION Africa, Mexico, China, Indonesia

SEASONS OF HARVEST Late summer and early fall, regionally

PARTS USED Seeds, Oil

COLORS Yellow-white or jet black, Red or brown (rarely)

Sesame seeds show up in the oddest places. Whether they're used to bulk up a spice mix, artfully strewn across a Japanese plate, or made into rock-hard candy, you can bet the nutty flavor will show up on your palate.

Both white and black varieties are cultivated for the spice trade, but there is little flavor difference between the two. What is apparent in both is a richness of flavor that comes from the oil content within. Sesame oil has long been used as a flavoring, and when you buy toasted versions, the bloom of taste can be amazing. Tasting like dry-roasted nuts, the oily seeds make any dish richer in flavor.

Some other entries into the sesame market come from Asia and North Africa, where seeds are produced in curious red and brown varieties. Again very similar in taste to their white and black cousins, they are harvested with oil production in mind. And some brown seed is actually the unhulled version of the common white seed. These are often sold as "natural" and have a slightly rougher flavor but a more fibrous texture.

Some artisan bakers use a mix of natural sesame, fennel, and poppy seeds as a topping on crusty baguettes with great success. No matter the color or form, the nutty character shows through when sesame seeds are incorporated into your dishes.

A final Note: you have to get your humor wherever you can in the retail spice trade. One slow afternoon in the shop found my crew chasing one of our younger customers, who was extolling the virtues of every jar she could reach, normally cause for alarm in a store with several hundred glass containers. They finally mesmerized her with a bag of mixed black and white sesame seeds. Not sure what she found so interesting in them, given the wide array of much more breakable things around her, someone asked if she liked the seeds. With perfect comic timing and as serious a look as a five-year-old could muster, she finally asked a simple question in reply. "If you plant these, do you get zebras?"

Sesame Brittle

Somewhere between a cookie and candy, this sweet treat graces the shelves of most Asian and Middle Eastern shops. Made fresh, it is inestimably better than the prepackaged versions, as sesame seeds, like nuts, have a fat content that makes them susceptible to spoilage. So make up a batch before your next trail hike or holiday cookie exchange. **MAKES ABOUT 30 PIECES**

1 cup granulated sugar

¾ cup honey

½ cup water

½ teaspoon coarse sea salt

1½ cup white sesame seeds

4 tablespoons (½ stick) unsalted butter, cut into pieces and softened

1 teaspoon baking soda

Grease a 12-by-18-inch rimmed baking sheet. Combine the sugar, honey, water, and salt in a large heavy saucepan and bring to a boil over medium heat, stirring to dissolve the sugar. Add the sesame seeds. Watching carefully, as foaming to triple volume is possible, cook, stirring constantly, until the mixture reaches 300°F on a candy thermometer. Remove from the heat and immediately add the butter and baking soda. Stir to incorporate, then immediately pour onto the prepared baking sheet, and carefully spread with a greased spatula into a large rectangle about 9 by 15 inches. When the brittle is partially cooled and beginning to set, score with a large heavy knife into rectangles about 3 by 1½ inches. Allow to cool completely, and break along the scored lines. Store in an airtight container.

SHISO

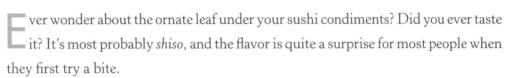

ALTERNATE NAMES Perilla, Wild sesame, Beefsteak leaf

BOTANICAL NAMES OF CULINARY SPECIES *Perilla frutescens*

PLANT FAMILY Mint *(Lamiaceae)*

COUNTRY/REGION OF BOTANICAL ORIGIN China

MAJOR COUNTRIES/REGIONS OF CULTIVATION China, Japan, Korea

SEASON OF HARVEST Summer

PARTS USED Leaves

COLORS Green or purple-red

Ever wonder about the ornate leaf under your sushi condiments? Did you ever taste it? It's most probably *shiso*, and the flavor is quite a surprise for most people when they first try a bite.

The three-inch leaves have a decorative serrated edge and come in deep green and purple-red varieties. The taste surprise is best described as a beefy, meaty flavor, giving rise to other names like "beefsteak leaf." Also called "perilla," after its botanical name, the leaf owes its popularity almost exclusively to the voracious Japanese appetite for its singular flavor. The art of Japanese cuisine also has an affinity for its aesthetic qualities, and superior grades of pristine hand-picked leaves can command surprisingly high prices.

The flavors dissipate easily with cooking, so the leaf is almost always used alone and uncooked in salads or as garnish toward the end of cooking. The Vietnamese and Thai add it shredded to noodle dishes, proving that the leaf can make an impact outside its mother country. In Australia and the West, Japanese communities have imported the leaf for their own cuisine and, in doing so, cross-pollinated their host countries. You can now see *shiso* in the bistros of New York and the cafés of London as frequently as in Tokyo, but the daunting cost of the fresh leaf keeps it in the realm of taste oddity rather than mainstream use.

The pricey market has led the industrious Japanese to devise all manner of drying and preservation techniques. Vacuum-sealed, nitro-flushed pouches promise to deliver the freshest flavor in a convenient "dry" form. While the efforts are laudable, there is still some deterioration in taste, and I urge cooks to continue to seek out the fresh form. But if anyone has the ability to successfully bring a dry version of shiso to market, it will be the Japanese, so I'd stay tuned there.

Pork Dim Sum with Shiso

With an herb as pungent as *shiso*, it's easy to ramp up the flavor of an old standby. *Shu mei*, a simple Chinese dim sum of steamed pork, is no exception. Here I simply borrow a touch of Japanese style and let *shiso* leaf do the rest. **SERVES 4 TO 6**

½ ounce fresh *shiso* leaves (approximately 12 leaves), stems removed

¾ pound ground pork

5 medium shrimp, peeled, deveined, and minced (optional)

2 scallions, finely chopped

1 tablespoon minced fresh ginger

5 garlic cloves, minced

2 teaspoons tamari soy sauce, plus extra, for dipping (optional)

1 teaspoon freshly ground Chinese Five-Spice (page 399)

½ teaspoon fine sea salt

¼ teaspoon red chile flakes (optional)

1 medium egg white

2 teaspoons arrowroot

18 to 20 round dumpling wrappers (see Note)

2 tablespoons black, white, or mixed sesame seeds

Cut the 4 largest shiso leaves into ¼-inch-wide strips, about 3½ inches long; reserve. Finely mince the remaining leaves.

Combine the pork, shrimp, if using, scallions, ginger, garlic, minced shiso, tamari, five-spice, salt, chile flakes, if using, egg white, and arrowroot in a bowl, and mix until thoroughly blended.

Oil the bottom of a bamboo steamer basket. Lay out the wonton wrappers on a work surface. Place 2 or 3 *shiso* strips across each wrapper so that they overlap and extend just beyond the edges. Place 1 tablespoon of the pork mixture in the center of each wrapper, and sprinkle the sesame seeds on top. With a cupping motion, pleat the edges of each wrapper around the filling to shape the wrapper into a small pouch with the pork mixture exposed on top.

Place the dumplings in the steamer basket, without touching. Set over boiling water, cover, and steam over medium-high heat for 30 minutes or until the filling is cooked through. Serve with additional tamari for dipping, if desired.

NOTE: Round dumpling or wonton wrappers, about 3 inches in diameter, are sometimes labeled "*gyoza* skins." If necessary, use a 3-inch biscuit cutter or other round cutter to cut rounds from the more widely available square wonton wrappers.

SICHUAN PEPPER

ALTERNATE NAMES Chinese prickly ash, Flower pepper, Fagara, Japanese pepper (*sansho*)

BOTANICAL NAMES OF CULINARY SPECIES *Zanthoxylum piperitum*, *Zanthoxylum sansho* (*sansho*)

PLANT FAMILY Citrus (*Rutaceae*)

COUNTRIES/REGIONS OF BOTANICAL ORIGIN Central China/Himalayas

MAJOR COUNTRIES/REGIONS OF CULTIVATION China, Southeast Asia, Japan (sansho)

SEASON OF HARVEST Fall

PARTS USED Seed pods, Seeds

COLOR Reddish-brown

This bush from Southeast Asia is in the citrus *Rutaceae* family and exhibits the same tartness found in lime, but with a curious twist. The bud actively engages the palate in a way that can only be described as shocking. The buzz left behind when it is chewed will have your tongue tingling and even numb, much as cloves or allspice would, but with much more electric intensity. To entice you more, the spice has a true progression of flavor, from citrus zest to numbing shock to lingering mild sweetness.

There are actually several species of Sichuan pepper cultivated for culinary use all over Indochina, with distinct versions coming from Nepal, Indonesia, and India as well as the main producer, China. All are similar in appearance, namely reddish-brown seed pods wrapped around jet-black seeds, and each maintains the citrus-meets-pepper flavor.

All but essential to Chinese five-spice, the tiny black seeds can be rather bitter and gritty. Better grades of the spice, in fact, have these removed completely, leaving only the pods; but reasonable avoidance of the seeds that collect at the bottom of the tin in lower grades is practical. There's no need to pick out each and every seed unless you have lots of free time on your hands.

The Japanese cultivate a close relative, the Japanese prickly ash, and produce *sansho* as a condiment pepper from its buds. The difference in flavor is almost imperceptible, but the difference in price will give you another sort of shock. At this writing, *sansho* was roughly twenty times more expensive, presumably because of the very limited supply being exported from Japan relative to its large Asian neighbors. Given the current ban on import from Southeast Asia, however (see "Citrix Family Import Ban," page 193), this may be the only course left for a desperate cook.

Ma Pua Do Fu

My good friend Yuen, who comes from the Yunnan Province in southwest China, gave me an education on tofu that opened my eyes. I had always cast tofu off to the side as a rubbery, tasteless medium that simply added texture to my egg drop soup. If I had continued to use the aging blocks of tofu normally found in the grocery store, I would have been right. What Yuen showed me is that tofu (or bean curd) is as sensitive to freshness as are peaches or fish. Any city with a strong Asian community will have a local tofu factory that produces fresh blocks to satisfy even the pickiest of tofu connoisseurs.

As tofu ages, the structure becomes dense and resistant to change. It will stubbornly resist advances by heat or flavor, maintaining its rubbery character. But when tofu is fresh, say less than two or three days old, it has a more porous nature that not only accepts flavors better but will actually puff up almost like egg whites when fried. This dish, whose name translates simply to "hot fried tofu," is a staple of Chinese cuisine and may be made any number of ways, with soft or firm tofu, deep-fried or simply pan-seared, but always with the characteristic hot spicing. The version Yuen taught to me is what she made in her home village, but she admitted that even over the next hill, the rules could be entirely different. I suggest a tour of your local Chinese restaurants to try the different styles. Even if it's not on the menu, I guarantee the cooks in the back will have their own version for you to try. **SERVES 3 TO 4**

SEASONING PASTE

5 garlic cloves, minced

5 fresh hot red chiles, stems removed

3 tablespoons red or black bean paste

2 teaspoon coarse sea salt

1½ cups peanut oil

One 12-ounce block firm or extra-firm tofu, as fresh as possible

2 garlic cloves, crushed

1 tablespoon minced fresh ginger

2 tablespoon chicken stock powder (available at Chinese groceries and some supermarkets)

2 tablespoons finely ground Sichuan pepper, or black pepper

15 scallions, coarsely chopped

To make the seasoning paste, blend the cloves, chiles, bean paste, and salt together in a mini food processor or a blender; add a few teaspoons of water if necessary to make a paste. Cover and allow to stand for at least 1 hour, or as long as overnight, in the refrigerator.

Heat the peanut oil in a wok or large deep skillet over high heat. Meanwhile, cut the tofu into 1-inch cubes. Have a cup of water at the ready. When the oil barely begins to smoke, carefully add the tofu and fry, turning occasionally, until golden on all sides. Drain off most of the oil, then add the garlic, ginger, chicken stock powder, pepper, and up to 3 tablespoons of the seasoning paste. Heat to desired heat level. Cook, stirring constantly, adding small splashes of water as needed to prevent scorching, until the tofu is coated with the spices, 2 to 3 minutes. Add the scallions and cook for a minute or so longer to barely wilt them. Serve hot with rice and use the remaining seasoning paste as a condiment.

STAR ANISE

ALTERNATE NAME **Chinese anise**

BOTANICAL NAME OF CULINARY SPECIES *Illicium verum*

PLANT FAMILY *Illiaceae*

COUNTRY/REGION OF BOTANICAL ORIGIN **Southern China**

MAJOR COUNTRIES/REGIONS OF CULTIVATION **China, Laos, Vietnam**

SEASON OF HARVEST **Late summer through early winter**

PARTS USED **Seed pods, Seeds**

COLOR **Dark brown, with polished tan seeds**

Essential to Chinese cuisine, the fruits of the star anise are as beautiful as they are practical. Nature makes perfectly pointed stars, each arm of which contains a shiny, polished seed, as the fruit of this evergreen tree, which has large waxy leaves and flowers that turn yellow just before fruiting. It's actually the star-shaped casing that has the most flavor, although the seeds contain some as well.

The Chinese have a version of the four-leaf-clover legend about star anise; it's widely believed that a whole intact star with more than the normal eight "arms" is very good luck. Whole stars without broken bits are quite beautiful, but in the kitchen, all that's really needed are pieces with an even coloring that still exhibit the characteristic fennel-and-anise aroma. Since the stars will either be removed after infusing or ground entirely, it's simply aesthetic concerns driving the demand for "extra fancy" grades, which can command as much as ten times the price of lesser ones, most probably due to the hand processing needed to cull them. Do avoid leaves or large woody stems, which can be present in the lowest grades, but only the most luxurious of budgets should pay the premium price for perfect stars.

Chinese Five-spiced Beef

Five-spice combinations seem to prevail throughout history, from Africa to the Middle East, from the Mediterranean to Asia. One of the most famous, though, is Chinese five-spice. It harmonizes sweet, savory, and bitter on the palate and has been documented in Chinese texts from some three thousand years ago. To use a "sand pot" or earthenware stewing pot, as I do today when preparing this dish, is similarly ancient: they've been discovered in archaeological digs dating back to the Zhou dynasty, so it's not a stretch to assume that beef cooked in this simple fashion could predate almost every other cuisine on the planet.

Given the long cooking process that will tenderize the meat, less expensive cuts of meat can be used. The cooked meat would be served as an accent to rice and steamed vegetables, not alone on the plate as in the West. **SERVES 4 TO 6**

¾ cup soy sauce

1½ cups water, preferably spring water

2 tablespoons honey

1½ tablespoons freshly ground Chinese Five-Spice (page 399)

Four ¼-inch-thick slices of fresh ginger

Two ¼-inch-thick slices of fresh galangal

4 garlic cloves, crushed

1 stalk of lemongrass, bottom 4 inches only

One 1½-pound flank steak

In a Dutch oven or other heavy flameproof casserole, combine all the ingredients except the beef and bring to a boil. Reduce the heat as low as possible and add the beef. Cover tightly and simmer for 2 to 3 hours, or until the beef is falling-apart tender, adding more water as necessary.

Remove the lemongrass, ginger, and galangal and discard. Transfer the beef to a cutting board, and cut it across the grain into thin slices. Return the beef to the pot, stir well, and heat through. Serve over rice.

SUMAC

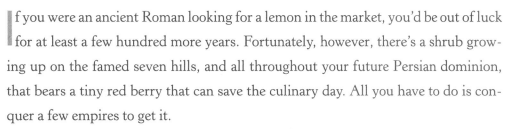

ALTERNATE NAME **Sumak**

BOTANICAL NAME OF CULINARY SPECIES *Rhus coriaria*

PLANT FAMILY **Cashew (*Anacardiaceae*)**

COUNTRY/REGION OF BOTANICAL ORIGIN **Mediterranean**

MAJOR COUNTRIES/REGIONS OF CULTIVATION **Mediterranean, Turkey, Middle East, especially Syria**

SEASONS OF HARVEST **Late summer and fall**

PARTS USED **Berries**

COLOR **Deep purple**

If you were an ancient Roman looking for a lemon in the market, you'd be out of luck for at least a few hundred more years. Fortunately, however, there's a shrub growing up on the famed seven hills, and all throughout your future Persian dominion, that bears a tiny red berry that can save the culinary day. All you have to do is conquer a few empires to get it.

Perhaps Caesar didn't have the berries of the sumac bush quite as high on the list of must-haves as cooks would like to think, but the impact of its berries is clear across all of Eastern Europe, the Middle East, and on into India. The bush produces dense clusters of pea-sized berries after flowering that, when dried, give a sour punch as strong as lemon but with a tiny touch of sweetness to mellow the impact. The berries are sun-dried in the fall after harvest and allowed to shrivel to a reddish-purple color in large stacks, still attached to the stalks. A threshing stage easily separates them once fully dried.

Sumac is seen only rarely as whole berries; its typical form is a coarse powder that exhibits the same colors and a pleasantly sour smell. Most powders have a small amount of salt added to help preserve flavor and color, as well as to prevent fermentation, so you should adjust recipes for salt content assuming that ground sumac will add some salty character.

If the whole berries are found, they will almost always be completely dried with a hard shell and warrant soaking or grinding before use. One interesting treatment seen in a London restaurant is to soak the berries in gin overnight and use the entire mix, liquid and all, as a base for a mint sauce. Fresh mint, thyme, and garlic are added, along with enough water to allow a puree to be made in the blender. The sauce is then reduced to a thicker consistency over heat and served with a wide variety of roast meats.

The kebabs of Persia are frequently dusted with sumac before roasting, with more of the spice added as a condiment later. The tart flavors hold up well to grilling over open fires, and street vendors will offer a dish of sumac-laden zahtar with your order. Infused into yogurt, sumac can brighten otherwise boring marinades for meats. Rice dishes can take on subtle interpretations of sumac's color and taste when the berries or powder are added to the cooking liquid, as with saffron or cardamom.

Hummus

Almost everyone knows hummus, the garbanzo bean-based dip from their favorite Mediterranean restaurant. Unfortunately, almost everyone knows the insipid premade versions common to the local grocery these days. When freshly made, hummus has a light, fluffy texture and a dry, brilliant blend of tart and savory flavors. I've added sumac and mint, commonly just sprinkled on top as a garnish, to lift the flavor even more. **MAKES ABOUT 3 CUPS**

Two 15-ounce cans low-salt garbanzo beans (chickpeas), drained and rinsed

2 tablespoons fresh lemon juice

8 garlic cloves, minced

2 tablespoons chopped fresh parsley

1 tablespoon chopped fresh mint

½ cup tahini (sesame paste)

¼ cup minced red onion

1 tablespoon ground sumac

½ teaspoon fine sea salt

½ teaspoon freshly ground Tellicherry black pepper

2 tablespoons extra-virgin olive oil

Pita bread, for dipping

In a food processor, combine the beans, lemon juice, garlic, parsley, mint, and tahini and process until smooth. Transfer to a bowl, and add the onion, sumac, salt, and pepper. Beat until thoroughly blended.

Spread the hummus on a serving platter, and drizzle the olive oil over the top. Serve with wedges of pita bread for dipping.

ALTERNATE NAMES **Callamus, Wild lily, Sweet grass, Myrtle grass**

BOTANICAL NAME OF CULINARY SPECIES *Acorus calamus*

PLANT FAMILY *Araceae*

COUNTRY/REGION OF BOTANICAL ORIGIN **India**

MAJOR COUNTRIES/REGIONS OF CULTIVATION **India, Pakistan**

SEASONS OF HARVEST **Summer and fall**

PARTS USED **Rhizome**

COLOR **Off white**

This rhizome native to the north of India was long called for in puddings and rice dishes of the Kashmir, but in the past few decades it has fallen into disuse because of its proven carcinogenic properties. I would suggest a substitution of cinnamon, ginger, and the tiniest amount of dill seed to simulate the bitter taste that ends an otherwise aromatic, piquant start.

SYLPHIUM

Sylphium is a hard flavor to describe, primarily because no one has tasted the herb for the past two thousand years, thanks to the ancient Romans, who consumed it to extinction. We only know of the spice because of historical accounts by Pliny and a few rare appearances in archaeological findings. Tableaus and coins of the era picture a leafy herb looking something like a broad grass.

Scholars have made good guesses as to the true nature of the mystery leaf, prized for its delicate taste, and have surmised that it could have been a subspecies of savory, tarragon, or even asafetida. Since accounts are few and far between, it's really anyone's guess as to which would be closest, but since the ancient Romans aren't knocking on the door for dinner these days, you can take some liberties with the recipes.

TAMARIND

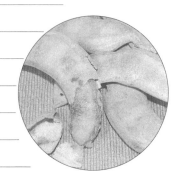

ALTERNATE NAME *Tamarindo* **(Spanish)**

BOTANICAL NAME OF CULINARY SPECIES *Tamarindus indica*

PLANT FAMILY **Bean** *(Fabaceae)*

COUNTRY/REGION OF BOTANICAL ORIGIN **East Africa**

MAJOR COUNTRIES/REGIONS OF CULTIVATION **Asia, Mexico**

SEASON OF HARVEST **Summer through late fall**

PARTS USED **Pulp from bean pods**

COLOR **Deep maroon to brown**

The large bean pods of the tamarind tree have a fuzzy teddy-bear quality to their outside skins that doesn't even begin to hint at the jaw-locking tartness waiting within. Inside the five-inch bulbous pod is a pulpy mass surrounding several exceedingly hard seeds. It's this sticky pulp that has the tartness of cranberry and the sweetness of sugarcane.

The fresh pods may be peeled and mixed with any liquid medium, as long as the finished dish will undergo some straining to remove the seeds. In Peru, I've seen children use these exceedingly hard seeds as a sort of casting stone for a game played in the dust. My throwing arm wasn't the best and I lost several pieces of gum before I decided to focus my efforts back on the pulp that is the real treasure.

More often than not, you'll find this pulp in a partially processed brick in Thai or Indian markets, with or without seeds, or, more preferably, in a commercially prepared concentrate. Modern techniques of distillation make this just as favorable a product to my mind. Processors start by drying the pods until the furry, paper-like skin falls away easily. The pulp mass is pounded and mixed with only enough water to aid in the seed removal, and then it's cooked and strained into a thick, viscous consistency much like that of a heavy syrup.

All four major components of taste on the tongue—sweet, bitter, salt, and sour—have their own "reference" flavors in modern cuisine. In the spice world, all are easily exploited with certain ingredients, but balance, as with all recipes, is the key. Traditional blends, whether by design or evolution, aim to accomplish this, and it's something for the home cook to remember when experimenting.

In the quest for flavor, we've come up with some pretty odd ways to tempt the quarter of our palate that reads "sour" in cuisine. I call it the "quest for tart," and it's a thread that runs through just about every major cuisine in the world. Certainly citrus, especially lemon, is a keynote speaker to this part of the tongue, but so is tamarind. Other contenders include amchoor, myrtle, lemongrass, sumac, and anardana (dried pomegranate seeds), and, with lesser intensity, coriander and cream of tartar.

This concentrate packs quite the sweet-tart punch, and it is a signature flavor in Thai and Mexican dishes. To use the concentrate, thin with water or another liquid to be included in the dish and add it to taste. Since each brand, and indeed each tin, can vary widely in potency, make sure to take a quick taste before adding it to dishes. Brands of lesser quality add other ingredients like sugar or vinegar to alter the taste; try to use only pure versions.

Philippine Chicken Adobo

The Philippines claim as their national dish a chicken or pork stew made with a salty, spicy broth that includes vinegar as a flavor enhancer. The spicing is traditionally garlic and pepper, but many a street vendor has a "special" spice that makes his or hers the best. Spices like annatto or turmeric are sometimes included, but typically only for their color, not for any significant flavor.

The Philippine version is not traditionally chile-hot, but the same vinegar stewing technique is sometimes encountered in Mexico, given the same name while incorporating some of the local heat. To confuse matters, the name "adobo" is also given to an all-purpose seasoning blend used in Latin American cooking.

While the traditional Philippine dish is simple from a spice perspective, the potent base flavors just beg to be enhanced with other spices. For my version, I've drawn inspiration from Southeast Asian influences to increase the complexity of the dish. In the Philippines themselves, chicken and pork are easily substituted for each other and frequently used in tandem. **SERVES 4**

6 garlic cloves, crushed

2 tablespoons peanut or corn oil

One 4½-pound chicken, cut into serving pieces and rinsed

2 cups water

½ cup distilled white or cider vinegar

2 tablespoons tamari soy sauce

1 tablespoon tamarind concentrate

1 tablespoon ground ginger

2 Thai red chiles, stems removed and seeded (optional)

Fine sea salt, to taste

1 teaspoon freshly ground white pepper

2 tablespoons light brown sugar

3 tablespoons minced fresh Thai basil

2 tablespoons white sesame seeds

In a Dutch oven or frameproof casserole, cook the garlic briefly in the oil over medium-high heat, until fragrant. Add the chicken pieces and cook, turning occasionally, until the chicken is slightly colored. Add the water, vinegar, tamari, tamarind, ginger, chiles, salt, and pepper. Cover and simmer over medium heat for 30 minutes.

Stir in the sugar, basil, and sesame seeds and cook, uncovered, for 15 minutes, or until the chicken is cooked through. Serve over white rice.

Tamarind Refreshers

Tamarind seems to invite experiments at the bar. Its punch will hold up to the alcohol in cocktails easily, and in fact can be used with most any liquor. Try tamarind whiskey sours or tart margaritas with a base of tamarind and lime, or for your next beach party, these tropical rum twisters. **MAKES ENOUGH TAMARIND BASE FOR 8 TO 12 COCKTAILS**

**TAMARIND BASE
(MAKES ABOUT 1½ CUPS)**

5 tamarind pods, peeled, or 2 tablespoons tamarind concentrate

2 cups water

½ cup granulated sugar

FOR EACH COCKTAIL

1 shot Tamarind Base

1 shot of rum (vanilla, coconut, or spiced)

Superfine sugar

½ lemon

Maraschino cherries (optional)

To make the tamarind base, combine the tamarind pods, water, and sugar in a saucepan and bring to a simmer over low heat, stirring occasionally, to dissolve the sugar. Continue to simmer, stirring occasionally, for 15 minutes.

If using fresh pods, use a wide spoon or spatula to mash and separate the pulp from the hard seeds, then strain to remove the seeds, pressing as much pulp from them as possible. Transfer to a jar, cover, and refrigerate until ready to use.

For each cocktail, shake the tamarind base and rum with ice in a cocktail shaker, and strain into a sugar-rimmed martini glass. Squeeze lemon juice to taste on top, and garnish with cherries, if desired.

TARRAGON

ALTERNATE NAMES French tarragon (*Artemisia*), Mexican tarragon (*Tagetes*), Mexican mint marigold (*Tagetes*), Winter tarragon (*Tagetes*)

BOTANICAL NAMES OF CULINARY SPECIES *Artemisia dracunculus* (French tarragon), *Tagetes lucida* (Mexican tarragon)

PLANT FAMILY Daisy (*Asteraceae*)

COUNTRIES/REGIONS OF BOTANICAL ORIGIN Central Europe (*Artemisia*), Mexico (*Tagetes*)

MAJOR COUNTRIES/REGIONS OF CULTIVATION Southern Europe, Turkey (*Artemisia*), Mexico (*Tagetes*)

SEASON OF HARVEST Midsummer to early winter

PARTS USED Leaves

COLORS Varied greens with gray-white down

Tarragon sneaks onto your taste buds with subtlety and then surprises you with its punch. The French love this sort of sneak attack in their herbs and for centuries have cultivated the best sources to include in their spice blends.

One of the "high" herbs of French cuisine, it's originally from more northerly regions, presumably the Baltic, and it has found its way into every cuisine along the way, from Scandinavia south through Germany and Belgium, ultimately landing in the fields of Provence alongside chervil, lavender, and thyme.

The fresh leaves taste like a vegetal interpretation of mild anise, but that description doesn't tell the whole story. The flavor continues to build slowly to a peppery high point that lingers behind with an almost vermouth-like perfume. It finishes with a tongue-numbing taste that brings forth memories of lavender and savory. Dried leaves have the same flavors, albeit with muted intensity. They lose more of the pepper tastes but hold onto a sweetness that is usually concealed in the fresh forms.

Each leaf is wide and slender like a blade of grass, with tender white down on the underside of the youngest leaves. With the leaves clustered densely on the stem, tarragon's overall shape reminds me of wispy beds of kelp on the sea floor. The flavor oils are very volatile, and fresh-cut is a better choice unless the dried leaves are from recent harvests. With the dried, look for a brilliant green color and unbroken whole leaves. Pale or graying color indicates age and subsequently little flavor. Infusion into vinegars and oils can hold the essence very well and, as such, these are acceptable ways to extend the useful life of dried tarragon.

The plant will flower given the chance, but the buds themselves are too acrid for use and it's advisable to harvest the most tender leaves before they reach that stage. Several species are bred to be prolific producers of leaves, but take care in plant selection, as some varieties can be much less flavorful than the preferred culinary French species. Specifically, the Russian varieties are far less potent in flavor with more coarseness to their taste and should be avoided in the kitchen.

Any fresh bouquet garni, the bundle of herbs cooked in and ultimately removed from a dish, would certainly call for tarragon alongside its "high" cousins of basil, thyme, and marjoram. The idea of infusing the fresh herbs tied in a small linen sack is common and allows the spent leaves to be removed easily after cooking. Bruise the herbs inside the pouch to help release flavor oils, but take care not to cook longer than necessary, to avoid the more bitter character that can come from the stems later in the process. Tarragon is also found in another French classic, béarnaise, which is little more than a simple butter and lemon sauce. Tarragon's lighter notes impart just the right herbal balance to the tart character of the sauce, and lingering anise bite holds up well to the intense citrus.

Across the Atlantic in Mexico, there is another species of plant that, while unrelated to true tarragon, shares many of the same flavor properties. Predictably more peppery and intense from the climate, Mexican tarragon, also called "mint marigold," looks similar in leaf shape but holds its flavor poorly. As such, it should be purchased only in fresh forms for use in salsas and Latin specialties that need herbaceous character. Anywhere fresh cilantro is called for, the cook may substitute Mexican tarragon with interestingly different results.

Leek and Potato Soup with French Herbs

French herb blends run the gamut from strong to mild, and I think the more delicate combinations are best suited to creamy soups and lighter broths. Here the milder character of the leek is well matched to the fines herbes, and a spicy surprise waits at the finish of each bowl with the Worcestershire sauce. The pops of delicate sweetness from the pink pepper berries will be unexpected to anyone who's not eaten them alone before. **SERVES 4**

3 medium leeks, sliced lengthwise in half, cut into 1-inch pieces, and thoroughly washed

2 tablespoons unsalted butter

2 shallots, minced

2 garlic cloves, minced

4 cups chicken stock

3 tablespoons Fines Herbes (page 369), crushed, plus extra for garnish

3 pounds Yukon Gold potatoes, scrubbed (or peeled if desired) and cut into 1½-inch chunks

2 teaspoons fine sea salt, or to taste

2 cups whole milk

Four ½-inch-thick slices of French bread, toasted until crisp

Worcestershire sauce

Approximately 2 teaspoons pink pepper berries for garnish

In a large soup pot, cook the leeks in the butter over medium heat, stirring occasionally, until slightly softened, about 3 minutes. Add the shallots and garlic and cook, stirring, until softened, about 2 minutes more. Add the stock, herbs, potatoes and salt, and simmer until the potatoes are tender, approximately 20 minutes.

Add the milk. Using an immersion blender, blend the soup to the desired consistency—from thick and chunky to completely smooth. Or blend the soup in a regular blender, in batches, and return to the pot. Reheat the soup if necessary.

Place a slice of toast in the bottom of each bowl and add a dash of Worcestershire sauce to each. Ladle the soup into the bowls, and garnish with more fines herbes and the pepper berries.

THYME

ALTERNATE NAME **Pebrella (Spanish wild thyme),** *Serpolet* **(French wild thyme)**

BOTANICAL NAMES OF CULINARY SPECIES *Thymus vulgaris, Thymus piperella* **(wild thyme),** *Thymus citriodorus* **(lemon thyme), Numerous subspecies**

PLANT FAMILY **Mint** *(Lamiaceae)*

COUNTRY/REGION OF BOTANICAL ORIGIN **Southern Europe**

MAJOR COUNTRIES/REGIONS OF CULTIVATION **Europe, Africa, North America**

SEASON OF HARVEST **Early summer through late fall**

PARTS USED **Leaves**

COLORS **Various greens**

Thyme is one of the older cultivars in the herb garden and it has propagated to become one of the widest families of plants used for culinary purposes. It's ubiquitous in European cuisine, with the Spanish and French being leading producers as well as consumers. Herbes de Provence wouldn't be the same without it, and you'll see the fresh sprigs in most every tapas menu.

The herb's main flavor compound, thymol, is sold as an essential oil, and the species offered for the home gardener are countless. The sheer volume of these variations, from lemon thyme to hyssop thyme to orange thyme, gives some indication of thyme's inherent ability to please the palate. It appeals to some basic wild flavor instinct founded in the earthiness of the forest vegetation but bent toward more delicate herbaceous sensitivities.

The reddish stems carry hundreds of tiny pointed leaves, each no bigger than a few millimeters in length. The leaves are stripped simply with a pull of the hand down the stem. In late summer, even the flowers of the plant can be used, for a particularly pungent version of the same basic flavor profile.

Thyme is at its best when paired with ingredients that mirror its heady impact on the palate, like game meats, root vegetables, and mushrooms. A pot growing in a kitchen garden can also be quite useful from an equipment perspective. Make an herb brush out of a tied bundle of fresh stems and place it in a large mortar to pound the leaves. Add oil, salt, and garlic, then use the "brush" to apply the flavors to your favorite roast or root vegetables. Toss the spent brush into a simmering pot of stock, and nothing has gone to waste.

Thyme serves as a mild bittering component in the Middle Eastern zahtar blends. The flavors of sources from the region tend to lean in that direction, as compared with the sweeter versions found in the United States. Morocco and Egypt are both serious producers and, as is usually the case, this means that the herb finds its way into the local cuisine of North Africa. On the braziers of Casablanca, lamb shanks are rubbed with a paste made of thyme, garlic, and oil and slow-roasted over coals to meld the flavors together.

Both Cajun and Creole ethnic dishes call on thyme, probably because of its ready availability as a wild species in the earliest days of settlement of the Louisiana territory. When it is used in conjunction with bay leaves and mustard, the peppery herbal character comes through in gumbos and jambalayas, even when Southern cooks add their trademark dose of cayenne.

Special variations of note include lemon thyme, grown widely in home gardens and just now becoming a commercially harvested product, and wild thyme, or *pebrella*, from the hills of Spain, long cultivated to take advantage of the unique microclimate in the area. As the name implies, the former layers a distinctly lemon flavor on top of the more savory base. The latter has more of a peppery bite that goes well with fatty meats and roasts, and even the classic *paella*.

As if the abundance of variations weren't enough to confound the cook trying to decipher the individual species, there is also a long-leafed version closely related to common thyme, *thymbra spicata*, grown in the Middle East. There it takes on the name *za'atar*, and those familiar with the condiment of the same name made in the area with sesame seed and sumac will recognize the deep flavors and almost juniper-like qualities, as it is frequently included in the mix as well.

Lamb Tagine with Lemon and Figs

The *tagines* of Morocco are mystical beasts. The mystery starts with the unique domed crock that's used to make them and continues all the way down to their special spicing. Anytime a dish gets its own specific equipment—for example, Spanish paella pans or French cassoulet pots—you know that the dish has reached almost cult status. After that, the inclusion of dried fruits in a meat dish, while not exclusive to *tagines*, is certainly one of the more unusual culinary pairings, which lends to its reputation as unique.

The aforementioned pot looks like a rounded pyramid lid on a relatively shallow earthenware pan. The domed lid helps to constantly baste the dish (from the internal condensation of liquid) as it cooks. A *tagine* is traditional; started in the low base over coals, once the lid is added it becomes a low-maintenance dish that tends itself until finished. If you don't have a *tagine* pot, never fear: the stew can be made with only a modest amount of extra effort in a Dutch oven or enameled stockpot. More important are the spicing and choice of ingredients.

SERVES 4

¼ cup olive oil

1 pound boneless lamb, cut into 1-inch cubes

1 cup diced onions

1 carrot, finely diced

1 cup short-grain white rice

4 teaspoon freshly ground *Mélange Classique* (page 370)

2 teaspoons ground cassia-cinnamon

1 teaspoon freshly ground black pepper

10 saffron threads

1 cup chicken stock

¾ cup dried figs, halved

½ cup diced preserved lemons (available in Middle Eastern and specialty markets)

½ cup black olives, pitted and halved

¼ cup brown, red, or yellow lentils, picked over and rinsed

4 sprigs fresh thyme, preferably lemon thyme

3 bay leaves

Preheat the oven to 325°F. Heat the oil in the bottom of a *tagine* pot or other heavy, ovenproof pot over medium-high heat. Add the lamb, onions, and carrot; cook, stirring, until the lamb is lightly browned all over. Transfer the lamb to a plate and set aside, leaving the vegetables in the pot. Add the rice to the pot and cook, stirring constantly, over medium heat for 3 minutes, or until coated with oil.

Add the spice mix, cassia-cinnamon, pepper, and saffron to the stock and stir well. Begin to add the spiced stock to the rice in small amounts, stirring until it is absorbed by the rice, repeating until all the stock is absorbed. Return the lamb to the pot and add the figs, lemons, olives, lentils, thyme, and bay. Add water to cover, stir well, and cover the pot. Place in the oven and cook for 1½ to 2 hours, stirring occasionally to prevent sticking, until the lamb is very tender. Add a little additional water if necessary, but keep in mind that the finished dish should be thicker than typical stew consistency. Remove the thyme sprigs and bay leaves before serving.

TURMERIC

ALTERNATE NAME **Indian saffron**

BOTANICAL NAME OF CULINARY SPECIES *Curcuma domestica*

PLANT FAMILY **Ginger (*Zingiberaceae*)**

COUNTRY/REGION OF BOTANICAL ORIGIN **Eastern Asia**

MAJOR COUNTRY/REGION OF CULTIVATION **India**

SEASON OF HARVEST **Summer through fall**

PARTS USED **Roots**

COLOR **Brilliant orange**

The shocking orange color of this root's inner flesh is perhaps its most striking feature, but beyond that, the flavor gives a wonderful base from which you can build the simplest of lentil dishes or the most complex of curries. Not a flavorless coloring agent as pale, aging specimens would have you believe, turmeric has a very mild mustard-ginger flavor when freshly shredded or recently dried. In the very best quality, a mild pepper note comes to the palate at the end.

A rhizome in the ginger family, turmeric dries to be as hard as concrete, so industrial grinding processes are needed to attain flour consistency. Home grinders don't stand a chance, so save your time and effort and purchase preground turmeric for your curry dishes. As long as the product still exhibits reasonable aroma, it's perfectly acceptable in the kitchen. The rare fresh roots can be used, but with significantly different results; best to save them for stocks, sauces, and spice pastes. Handling of them, apart from staining your hands a brilliant yellow orange, is done the same way as with fresh ginger: namely, peel off the outer skin and finely shred on a rasp or superfine grater.

The branch roots that stem from the main are what's harvested for culinary use. These are pencil-thin and have a rough outer skin that is peeled off after boiling or steaming, then they are dried quickly and powdered immediately to capture the most flavor. That powder is destined for everything from giant mustard factories to tiny curry houses. Incidentally, curcumin is the main flavoring compound in turmeric and has actually been shown in studies to be an antioxidant.

Turmeric is cultivated in tropical locales as widely as its cousin ginger, literally around the globe. Its native India leads the producing countries, but all of Asia, the Pacific Island countries, and even the Caribbean and South America get into the production game.

Aryuvedic culture traditionally allows the use of turmeric, and the cuisine draws heavily upon it in conjunction with sharp mustard and hing powder to impart flavor into beans and lentils. Cooking the grated fresh root in ghee, the clarified butter, is often a first step to more complex cuisines throughout India.

Turmeric's consistently strong coloring ability has kept the price low, since both the food coloring and textile dye industries' demands are consistently strong. American "hot dog" mustard relies heavily upon the spice for its coloring, as do cheeses, butters, and a myriad of chutney and pickle recipes. Even the famous saffron robes of India are often colored textiles using turmeric first to start the dying process.

And one of the first initiations my employees suffer in the spice shop is a coloring of their wardrobe via association with our curries. The running joke is that no one wears white, for even if they try, they rapidly get the "orange badge of courage" on their pockets, pants, and faces. Since turmeric in its powdered form has a magic ability to travel far and wide outside its jar, home cooks are warned to wear yellow on curry-making day.

Chicken Tikka Masala

Most people presume that chicken *tikka masala* is yet another spicy entry from the Indian sub-continent. It is a favorite national dish, but the surprise is that the country in question isn't India. Rather it's a culinary icon of England, created when Indian cooks who immigrated from British colonies on the subcontinent took inspiration from their homeland and tailored a traditional dish to their new locale. The spices are sweeter and less hot than you'd find in India, to better suit London palates. And the introduction of tomatoes is decidedly Western.

In modern-day England, tikka masala has been elevated to cult status, fit for both the finest restaurants and take-away boxes. God save the Queen (and her chefs) indeed! **SERVES 4 TO 6**

2 cups yogurt

2 tablespoons *Tikka Masala* (page 365)

2 teaspoons ground turmeric

3 tablespoons fresh lemon juice

2 pounds boneless, skinless chicken breasts

4 tablespoons (½ stick) unsalted butter

1 pound tomatoes, coarsely chopped

1½ cups tomato puree

2 tablespoons tomato paste

One 2-inch piece fresh ginger, finely chopped and pounded to a paste

6 garlic cloves, pounded to a paste

Coarse sea salt, to taste

1 tablespoon honey

Up to ½ cup heavy whipping cream (optional)

Chopped fresh parsley or chives, for garnish

Combine the yogurt, *Tikka Masala*, turmeric, and lemon juice in a small bowl and mix well. Put the chicken in a baking dish and pour the marinade over it, turning to coat. Cover and refrigerate overnight.

Preheat the oven to 350°F. Melt the butter in a large skillet over medium-high heat. Add the chicken, in batches as necessary, and cook, turning occasionally, until lightly browned on both sides. Transfer the chicken to a large baking dish. Add the tomatoes, tomato puree, tomato paste, ginger, garlic, and salt to the skillet, and cook, stirring, until thoroughly blended, about 2 minutes.

Pour the sauce over the chicken and transfer to the oven. Bake for 20 to 25 minutes, or until the chicken is cooked through. Transfer the chicken to a serving platter. Stir the honey into the sauce in the baking dish. If desired, transfer the sauce to a saucepan, stir in cream to taste, if using, and heat gently over low heat. Spoon the sauce over the chicken and garnish with parsley.

VANILLA BEAN

BOTANICAL NAME OF CULINARY SPECIES *Vanilla planifolia*

PLANT FAMILY **Orchid** *(Orchidaceae)*

COUNTRY/REGION OF BOTANICAL ORIGIN **South America**

MAJOR COUNTRIES/REGIONS OF CULTIVATION **Madagascar, Tahiti, Mexico, Central America, Central Africa**

SEASON OF HARVEST **June to July**

PARTS USED **Bean pods**

COLORS **Green (uncured), Black (cured)**

One of the most seductive flavors to cross our taste buds, vanilla beans rival saffron in intensity and cardamom in aromatic complexity, and they evoke as much universal appeal and sensory overload as cocoa and cinnamon. Vanilla comes from the New World, and the Aztecs were the first to tap into the flavor of the bean, with a primitive curing and fermenting process most probably discovered by accident in the forests of South America. Mayan cultures even used the pods for taxes and raised them ceremonially to their gods as a treasure of the forest. Not until the early sixteenth century did this delicate flavor reach the Old World, via the Spanish explorers. It quickly became the fashion in Europe and ultimately spread to gain worldwide acceptance.

The plant is actually an orchid, its long green seedpods holding unlocked flavor beneath large waxy leaves. The climbing vines are trained up and over large arched trellises with the beans, up to a foot in length, dangling below in tempting fashion. Anyone visiting top producers in Madagascar or Tahiti would be disappointed, however, if they tried to pluck the fresh pods for themselves. Looking more like fat green beans grouped in a banana bunch rather than the familiar cured black pods, they hold almost no flavor on the vine.

Tensions are as high as at any vineyard when the harvest season approaches in June. Timing of the harvest is critical to flavor development, and it only happens when the estate masters deem the pods are at the right stage, typically just before the pods would open and gain a yellow tone. The trellised setup makes for easy harvesting, so entire plantations can be harvested within a few days, critical when considering how important timing is for the crop. Then there's a lengthy process of drying needed to develop the familiar flavor we know as vanilla. The "green" harvest is typically sold at regional market auctions to processors who take up to six months to cure the beans to a rich brown black.

The complex process is steeped in mystery and tradition but typically includes a short blanching, a firing, and ultimately a series of drying stages, done on long sheets of burlap, wicker trays, or linen-lined baskets. Ovens are used in the more modern facilities initially, but even there, the beans are later spread in a single layer and rolled or twisted only after a few days of drying in the sun in the more ancient fashion. The best beans are meticulously turned and monitored, the process adjusted to get the most flavors during the months of processing. After several cycles, the beans begin to gain their familiar color and the aroma becomes unmistakable, even from miles away.

When buying vanilla beans, first a visual inspection is needed. There should be a uniform color through the whole length of the bean. As the beans age, lighter reddish ridges will develop, indicating undesirable dryness. In fact, the lower-quality beans used in the perfume industry are often called "red" beans.

In particularly fresh beans, a crystalline substance looking like tiny white threads may form on the outside of the pod. Not undesirable mold as some might guess, this is actually vanillin, the main flavor component, in high concentration, and it's a very good sign of quality. Try to conserve the crystal as much as possible in these most prized "frosted" beans.

Vanilla beans are, however, prone to a naturally occurring white mold when kept in airtight conditions. The mold will impart a sour flavor and any beans with even the slightest sign of white, spotty spores should be discarded immediately, as the mold will spread quickly to your entire stock if not held in check.

Some say that a longer bean is better, but I find little correlation between length and quality. Plumpness of the bean is a better sign of both proper curing and proper storage. Some processors artificially oil the beans to give a glossy look. While some natural oil will come to the surface of a fresh bean, avoid any that are particularly greasy. The very best guide for assessing the quality of the beans lies within the pods when split open. Inside the pulpy mass, there are hundreds of tiny black seeds that contain the highest concentrations of vanillin: the higher the seed content, the better the bean. The outer shell of the pod contains significant flavor as well and should also be conserved.

The cost of vanilla, rivaled only by saffron, can be daunting at first glance. Farmers may get as little as $10 per kilo for their green beans, but the finished product can be in the range of $500 per kilo at retail levels. This is partly because of the lengthy processing and partly because of the virtual monopoly the world's top producers hold on the market. Still, the cost to the consumer is reasonable when the potency of vanilla is considered. At an average cost of $4 per bean, even the most frugal of cooks can justify the expense when they realize that a single bean can flavor an entire pot of poached pears, a few gallons of ice cream, or pound after pound of sugar.

A recent cyclone that hit Madagascar, a major producer, showed exactly how delicate the market structure is with regard to supply and demand. The reduction of the global supply by some thirty percent from that natural disaster caused the price to triple, not just for the poor crop year, but for several years afterward as the processors tried to make up for lost time by leaving prices high.

Many uses of vanilla come in the form of an extract made from the bean. It's an easy process to master at home (see below) and almost always yields a higher-quality product than the commercial versions. Bottled concentrates are also where artificial vanilla finds a home. The high demand and cost of genuine vanilla has created a prolific market for bottled, artificial vanilla, but the home cook should avoid the latter whenever possible.

The whole beans are called for in famous desserts like crème brulée, but infusing the pods into everything from an ice cream base to port-wine poaching liquids is sure to impress diners with the sweet creamy character that is unmistakably vanilla. When using the whole beans, pound them *before* splitting and scraping the pulp. This step helps to open up the inner seeds and release the flavor into the pulp and, ultimately, your dishes.

Mexico, Madagascar, and Tahiti are traditionally the biggest vanilla producers. It took the development of artificial pollination techniques to extend the cultivation of vanilla orchids beyond their native Central America. The long vines of the plant are trellised to facilitate this hand pollination. When the timing is right, something looking like a big feather duster is flicked from bud to bud in the long, arching rows where the bean pods will ultimately hang down.

To make your own vanilla extract, pound and split one bean per pint of alcohol to be infused. Scrape the pulpy mass from inside the bean to further aid release of the flavor compounds, making sure that every last bit of the bean is saved for the bottle. Most people will tell you that plain vodka and brandy are good mediums to use, but my preference is to avoid the other flavors inherent to either and use pure grain alcohol (190 proof) for my extracts. As this is highly flammable, care must be taken to keep it away from heat sources in the kitchen.

Homemade Coffee Liqueur

It takes either time or heat to release the flavor of a vanilla bean. The conundrum is that the latter will vaporize some of the rich character, but it is usually a necessary evil for the pastry chef; a "cold" process will preserve all the nuances of flavor that make vanilla what it is, one of the most seductive tastes on the human palate, but at the cost of considerable time. In this recipe, you should wait a minimum of six months for the flavor to emerge—and longer is better. Store as you would wine, in a cool, dark place at a constant temperature. When the holidays approach, decant the mixture into smaller bottles and give as gifts to friends and family.

MAKES ONE 750-ML BOTTLE (ABOUT 3 CUPS)

2 vanilla beans

1 cup granulated or superfine sugar

1 cup pure grain alcohol (do not substitute vodka; you'll get less impressive results)

Hot strong brewed or French-press coffee

An empty 750-ml wine bottle (the size of the bottle is important here, to minimize air space)

Gently pound the whole vanilla beans with the back of a large knife or wooden mallet to mash the inner pulp and seeds. Split the beans lengthwise and cut into ¼-inch pieces, carefully conserving every last bit of the highly concentrated flavor. Add to the wine bottle, along with the sugar and alcohol, then top off with the hot coffee. Let cool, then seal the bottle tightly. (A plastic-coated cork works best, as natural corks let flavor escape.) Store in a cool, dark place for at least 6 months, shaking daily for the first month to fully mix the ingredients. The vanilla pieces will ultimately dissolve, but the liqueur may need straining if you're the impatient type and open the bottle early.

You could use this in mixed drinks (but that seems a waste if you ask me); far better to sip it after dinner, with a simple dish of vanilla-bean ice cream.

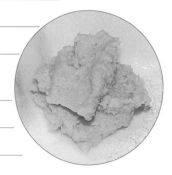

ALTERNATE NAME Japanese horseradish

BOTANICAL NAME OF CULINARY SPECIES *Wasabia japonica*

PLANT FAMILY Cabbage *(Brassicaceae)*

COUNTRY/REGION OF BOTANICAL ORIGIN Japan

MAJOR COUNTRIES/REGIONS OF CULTIVATION Japan, New Zealand, North America (rarely)

SEASON OF HARVEST Summer and fall

PARTS USED Roots

COLOR Pale green

One of the most prized crops from Japan, this pale greenish root is grown only in cold mountain streams under some of the most closely guarded growing practices in modern agriculture. Many outside Japan have gone to great lengths to duplicate its wonderfully hot flavor.

Up to a few inches thick, the root looks something like a miniature palm tree trunk, with progressive ridges from each bit of new growth. It's peeled and shredded to make the familiar condiment seen in sushi bars, with the more prized versions coming from the potent inner core rather than the tougher outer layers.

The fresh is certainly a delight, but in the West, it's more commonly a dry powder that's offered to the cooking public. Unfortunately, the highest-quality wasabi is quite expensive, and that has given rise to imitations made of horseradish, mustard, and green coloring. Admittedly, this may be unavoidable in all but the larger enclaves of Japanese-American society.

There have been some efforts in the microclimate of the Pacific Northwest to cultivate a crop for domestic consumption. Indeed, the secrets of production have slowly leaked from Japan, and crops, albeit expensive and limited, do come from a handful of producers in the United States, who are now providing both the fresh root and *pure* wasabi pastes, not to be confused with the pale imposters.

Treat the fresh root like horseradish, shredding only as much as needed into a lemon-water bath to soak out some of the harsher character. Pulsing in a food mill pure will yield a fiery paste, or it can be tempered with other ingredients to make vinaigrettes, mayonnaises, or other hot condiments. If dry is your only option, make sure to allow some time once it is rehydrated so that the flavor compounds come back to the surface. Premixed pastes are available, but I've not found a brand that can capture the intense pepper-mustard flavor well. Make your own paste from the powder or fresh root. One tip if you have no nearby Japanese groceries is to visit your favorite sushi bar. No doubt they're importing a good supply and will probably share some with aspiring home cooks.

Beet-and-Wasabi-crusted Halibut

When you remember how much sugar resides in a beet, you can start to envision the sweet-hot crust this particular combination can offer. It has been tweaked to perfection by Chef Matt Janke, who has a café above Seattle's Pike Place Market. **SERVES 4**

3 tablespoons beet powder (available at health food stores and specialty spice markets)

1 tablespoon wasabi powder

1 teaspoon coarse sea salt

1 teaspoon coarsely ground black pepper

1 cup all-purpose flour

1 teaspoon red chile flakes (optional)

½ cup *panko* (Japanese bread crumbs)

Four 6-ounce halibut fillets

2 tablespoons olive oil

¼ cup dry white wine

2 tablespoons finely chopped scallions

½ cup tamari soy sauce

Preheat the oven to 375°F. Combine the beet powder, wasabi, salt, and pepper in a coffee mill and coarsely grind. Combine with the flour and spread on a plate. Mix the chile flakes, if using, with the *panko*, and spread on another plate.

Brush the fillets with water and coat heavily in the flour mixture. Press into the *panko* to coat.

Heat a large skillet over medium-high heat. Add the oil and heat until very hot. Add the fish and cook, turning once, until golden brown on both sides. Transfer to a baking dish and pour the wine around the fish. Bake just until opaque throughout and flaky, 4 to 6 minutes.

Combine the scallions and the tamari, and serve in tiny individual bowls as a dipping sauce alongside the fish.

ALTERNATE NAMES	**Wattle, *Mulga (Acacia aneura)***
BOTANICAL NAMES OF CULINARY SPECIES	***Acacia victoriae, Acacia aneura***
PLANT FAMILY	**Bean *(Fabaceae)***
COUNTRY/REGION OF BOTANICAL ORIGIN	**Australia**
MAJOR COUNTRY/REGION OF CULTIVATION	**Australia**
SEASON OF HARVEST	**Year-round**
PARTS USED	**Seeds**
COLOR	**Dark brown**

One of the biggest oddities to come from the new spice frontier in Australia is what are actually the seeds of a tree, eaten more like a bean by the Aboriginals for sustenance. Of the hundreds of species of acacia tree, only a few produce pods that can be eaten without harm, but those few give yet another spice entry from Down Under.

Enterprising spice hunters in the outback knew of the native habit of consuming the seeds like beans, but they discovered that the underlying character of savory nuts reaches spice intensity when roasted, much like coffee. The flavor is certainly roasted as expected, but with a chicory bitterness and coffeelike nose.

Harvesting of the seeds is still a wild-craft operation done randomly in the outback, rather than any organized cultivation. Processing the seeds entails opening the pods, usually by heating them until they pop open, followed by a further roasting stage of the separated beans over direct fire to give the distinct roasted flavor. This labor-intensive process will probably keep wattle seeds off the commodity-sized export lists for some years to come.

Cooks who obtain a small measure would do well to experiment in creating blends with other Australian native herbs. Lemon myrtle and bush tomato marry perfectly, to give a deeply flavored sort of mock curry. Ground wattle seed isn't the most pleasant of textures, typically a bit coarse even after several minutes of extra grinding, so use as a condiment might not be the best idea. When I found a small amount, I got the wild idea to add it to boiling water for a few minutes and use that as a base for mushroom polenta. Needless to say, with such new spice fodder at an inventive chef's disposal, we can expect some more odd ideas to come forward before wattle seed settles into a solid position in the spice rack.

ZEDOARY

ALTERNATE NAME	**Wild turmeric**
BOTANICAL NAME OF CULINARY SPECIES	*Curcuma zedoaria*
PLANT FAMILY	**Ginger (*Zingiberaceae*)**
COUNTRY/REGION OF BOTANICAL ORIGIN	**Indonesia**
MAJOR COUNTRIES/REGIONS OF CULTIVATION	**Tropical Asia, Indonesia, India**
SEASON OF HARVEST	**Year-round**
PARTS USED	**Roots**
COLOR	**Pale yellow**

This rhizome made a bad first impression on me when I came across some dried samples. The cut pieces were stringy and unpleasant, the flavor was unpleasantly bitter and dry, and I felt as if I were chewing dry socks. When I tasted the end of a fresh root the following year in an Asian market, my opinion changed for the better—to some extent. The dry character was less intense, and I got faint remembrances of galangal root.

Indeed, other ginger family members have relegated zedoary to industrial perfume uses and occasional inclusion in regional Indonesian and Indian specialties that also include ginger and turmeric. The plant doesn't cultivate as easily as ginger, galangal, or kencur and thus lost most culinary favor after the Middle Ages, when overland routes to Europe brought it in the same shipments as galangal from India. Even then, uses in the kitchen took a back seat to medicinal applications.

I did find one odd use still employed for the root in modern times. In Southeast Asia, slices of the root are steeped in a local vodkalike distillation to impart a dry aroma. Almost no flavor is transferred in the process, but you can *feel* the dryness on the palate when you make a martini out of the infusion. Try this only with the fresh root, not the dried, unless you want your drink to taste like old laundry.

HERB
AND
SPICE
BLENDS

BAY SEASONING

Bay seasonings are an American classic in the coastal communities of the east and on into the Gulf of Mexico. The abundant cold-water crabs, lobster, and shellfish from these fishing grounds all have a bold taste that can hold up to the potent mix that starts with strongly aromatic Californian bay and leads the palate through to peppery allspice. Celery bitters the flavor enough for balance, and cinnamon and ginger bring sweet character that accents the supple flavor of the freshest seafood.

This blend is flexible enough to use as a boiling spice, for a direct-on-the-fish seasoning, or even for infusing dipping butters for lobster and shrimp. The complexity of the cardamom and clove aromatics is fabulous when coupled with the best ocean flavors, but those same oils evaporate quickly, so the last thing you want with bay seasoning is "old."

"New" Bay Seasoning MAKES ABOUT 3 CUPS

1 cup Italian or Pacific coarse sea salt

1 cup sweet Hungarian paprika

¼ cup celery seeds

2 tablespoons allspice berries

2 tablespoons black peppercorns

2 tablespoons mustard powder

2 tablespoons ground ginger

2 tablespoons ground cassia-cinnamon

2 tablespoons cayenne

1 tablespoon cardamom seeds

1 tablespoon whole cloves

20 Californian bay leaves

Combine all the ingredients, and coarsely grind together in a coffee mill as needed.

BARBECUE RUBS

Barbecue has become synonymous with America, alongside apple pie, jazz, and baseball. While the idea of cooking meats over fire can't be claimed as original, nowhere else on the planet has it reached such cult status, with contests, cooking teams, and even dedicated barbecue schools all extolling the virtues of the myriad techniques and secret ingredients that have evolved over time. If you want to start a debate among a circle of guys around the fire, just tell them your barbecue is the best. I can guarantee that at least several present will have a litany of reasons why you're wrong.

While the type of equipment, the fire, the wood fuel, and, of course, the meats all vary from region to region (if not from cook to cook), devotees all generally share one theme among them. Namely, they are barbecuing long and slowly—the real thing—averaging several hours at least over low heat, rather than grilling quickly over high heat. Part of the confusion comes from the habit of calling any outdoor event with food over the fire a barbecue. Rest assured, one of our gentlemen from the discussion will straighten you out if given the chance.

The long cooking time has given rise to another habit, of using spice rubs: sometimes simple, sometimes complex, combinations based typically in paprika, peppercorn, and garlic that are applied liberally to the surface of the meats to infuse their flavor over the extended cooking time. Technically neither a marinade nor a crusting, they lie somewhere in between, meant both to flavor the meat and to encourage a charring of the outside to hold in juices. Again, the debate has as many sides as cooks as to exactly how and what you accomplish with a spice rub, but no matter what, there is plenty of room for personal expression over the barbecue pit.

Each of the major regions of the U.S. barbecue circuit has developed an undercurrent of a theme to its flavors and techniques, based on the meats available and the local tastes. Memphis is known for pork and dry rubs, Kansas more for beef with wet, sugary treatments. Different still are the Carolinas, which mix spices with vinegars for tart versions of pork, and the desert Southwest, which embraces complex chile combinations for Tex-Mex style on everything from buffalo to lamb.

MEMPHIS-STYLE BARBECUE

When I was a kid growing up in the Deep South, Memphis was in my backyard, and a trip there wasn't complete without a taste of barbecue. I fell on the dry side of the longstanding "wet sauce" versus "dry rub" debate, and that meant mecca for me was "round back" of a building on Second Avenue at a place called Rendezvous.

Feeling like a turn-of-the-century gumshoe stalking down an alley, I'd literally follow my nose to this venerable old establishment that dry-packs their ribs with a spice rub and cooks them slowly for upward of eighteen hours. As you make your way down the steps that lead to the restaurant, you have a sense that nothing has changed, including the menu, since the old riverboat days that made cotton king just a few blocks away, on the Mississippi. The biggest barbecue contest in the United States conveniently occurs on the banks of the river in conjunction with the annual "Memphis in May" festival, and I'm fairly certain the fires of the barbecue pits in the neighborhood burn year-round. Around the famous Beale Street, barbecue is as deeply rooted as blues music and takes you back to the old days with every bite.

My rub below was inspired by years of casual research (accompanied by several pitchers of beer) at Rendezvous and later from packs kindly sent via Federal Express to whatever corner of the planet I found myself when the craving hit. The overnight carrier happens to have its main hub ten minutes from downtown Memphis, and that means that on some occasions the ribs were still warm when they landed on my desk.

For my preference, I blanch racks of pork ribs for just a few seconds in boiling salted water, then pack them heavily with the spice rub and wrap tightly in foil. A 200°F oven or barbecue pit will give you meat that falls from the bone in a mere eight hours.

Beale Street Barbecue Rub

With this rub, the real complexity of flavor develops over time in the BBQ pit. The whole seeds will add pops of flavor as they open with cooking.   **MAKES ABOUT 3 CUPS**

1 cup sweet Hungarian paprika

5 tablespoons dried Mediterranean oregano

¼ cup allspice berries

¼ cup garlic powder

¼ cup Tellicherry black peppercorns

2 tablespoons mustard powder

2 tablespoons dried Spanish thyme

2 tablespoons coarse sea salt

2 teaspoons Worcestershire powder (see page 366)

1 teaspoon Indian cayenne

½ cup packed light brown sugar

3 tablespoons yellow mustard seeds

2 tablespoons celery seeds

2 tablespoons coriander seeds

Combine the paprika, oregano, allspice, garlic powder, peppercorns, mustard powder, thyme, salt, Worcestershire powder, and cayenne. Grind together in a coffee mill. Stir the sugar into the ground spices, then stir in the seeds. Store airtight to prevent clumping, and use liberally as a rub.

KANSAS CITY-STYLE BARBECUE

In Middle America, with Kansas as the epicenter, beef is the meat of choice for barbecue. Sweeter sauces are preferred, including everything from honey to tomatoes. To balance the flavor, the spice blends are made a bit more savory and less sweet, knowing that the wet sauce will complement and round out the profile.

Kansas City Barbecue Rub
and Sauce Base   MAKES ABOUT 4 CUPS

1¼ cups sweet Hungarian paprika

½ cup garlic powder

½ cup coriander seeds

¼ cup cumin seeds

¼ cup rubbed sage

¼ cup coarse sea salt

¼ cup packed light brown sugar

3 tablespoons dried Spanish thyme

3 tablespoons mustard powder

2 tablespoons celery seeds

2 tablespoons dried Turkish oregano

2 tablespoons Tellicherry black peppercorns

1 tablespoon whole cloves

Combine all the ingredients, and grind together in a coffee mill as needed. Use as a dry rub or the base for a wet sauce. To make a sauce, in a small saucepan, dissolve 2 tablespoons of the spice in 2 cups tomato sauce and ¼ cup honey or sugar over low heat. Adjust the spice mix to taste.

CAROLINA-STYLE BARBECUE

Pork is the meat of choice for barbecue in the Carolinas, but with a decidedly different approach to the sauces from other regions. A thin, tart sauce made with vinegar is more authentic, and the relatively simple spice blends for rubbing the meat or making the sauce can just as easily be tossed into the coleslaw.

Tarheel Barbecue Rub
and Sauce Base   MAKES ABOUT 1¾ CUPS

½ cup freshly ground Ancho Chili Powder (page 357)

⅔ cup packed light brown sugar

⅓ cup sweet Hungarian paprika

3 tablespoons Tellicherry black peppercorns

1 tablespoon cumin seeds

2 tablespoons coarse sea salt

1 teaspoon cayenne

1 teaspoon whole cloves

Combine all the ingredients, and grind together in a coffee mill as needed. Use as a dry rub or a sauce base. To make a sauce, combine ¼ cup cider vinegar, 1 cup tomato sauce, and ½ cup water in a medium saucepan. Add 2 tablespoons of the spice mix, stir, and simmer over low heat for at least 20 minutes. Adjust the spice mix to taste.

POULTRY RUBS

Poultry of all sorts is great from the barbecue pit. Whole chickens, turkeys, and game hens will cook in about a quarter the time of red meats, but they need a gentler hand from the spice rack. Given the speed of cooking, you'll see many a chicken tossed into the pit at barbecue contests "to feed us while we wait for the real food."

A great trick for poultry, whether in the barbecue pit or in the oven, is to stuff the cavity of the bird with lemon or orange quarters, peel and all. They'll perfume the bird and add another layer of flavor, melding with the spices you've rubbed inside and out.

Herb Poultry Rub

Classic poultry rubs are herb-based, given the lighter nature of the bird's flavor. Salt is omitted here, since the rub isn't ground fine enough to allow even distribution. Salt the bird separately and then use the spice rub inside and out. If using cut-up poultry, dust evenly on all sides. **MAKES ABOUT 2¾ CUPS**

½ cup dried rosemary leaves

½ cup celery flakes

½ cup dried marjoram

½ cup rubbed sage

⅓ cup dried onion flakes

3 tablespoons cracked Tellicherry black peppercorns

2 tablespoons chopped dried garlic

2 tablespoons dried Spanish thyme

Combine all the ingredients. Pulse in a coffee mill as needed, just until the rosemary leaves and onion flakes are broken down a bit, and rub on poultry.

Paprika Poultry Rub

Lightened by the herbs and lemon peel, this rub is heavier than some aimed at poultry, but not so much as to interfere and mask the flavor of the meat. It's particularly nice on game birds. **MAKES ABOUT 2¾ CUPS**

¾ cup dried marjoram

½ cup sweet Hungarian paprika

¼ cup freshly ground Ancho Chili Powder (page 357)

¼ cup onion powder

¼ cup dried lemon peel

½ cup rubbed sage

2 tablespoons coarse sea salt

2 tablespoons Tellicherry black peppercorns

1 tablespoon celery seeds

Combine all the ingredients. Grind together in a coffee mill as needed, and rub on poultry.

SEAFOOD RUBS

In historic Pike Place Market, we get millions of tourists every year. We see a parade of people coming past the shop carrying boxes of fresh salmon, all looking for a different twist to the old standby paprika-based rubs. So we took an Asian spin on a classic grilled fish technique and came up with this mix. It also works quite well on other fatty fish, and even chicken headed for the grill.

Seattle Salmon Rub   MAKES 1¼ CUPS

¼ cup dried orange peel

¼ cup packed brown sugar

¼ cup Tellicherry black peppercorns

3 tablespoons coriander seeds

2 tablespoons cracked star anise

1 tablespoon cumin seeds

1 tablespoon fennel seeds

1 tablespoon sea salt

Combine all the ingredients. Grind together in a coffee mill to a semi-coarse texture as needed. Use as a dry rub, or mix with oil into a paste to coat fish or chicken.

Southern Catfish Mix

My grandfather Albert always made up a batch of this coating for his neighborhood-feeding catfish fry; he always said the trick was in the seasoning. This is equally good on seasoned French fries and hush puppies.   MAKES ABOUT 2¾ CUPS

1 cup all-purpose flour

1 cup fine yellow cornmeal

3 tablespoons fine sea salt

2 tablespoons garlic powder

2 tablespoons freshly ground dried Mexican oregano

2 tablespoons freshly ground dried rosemary

2 tablespoons coarsely ground Tellicherry black pepper

1 tablespoon cayenne

1 tablespoon sweet Hungarian paprika

Stir all the ingredients together. Use to dredge fish fillets bound for the deep-fryer.

CAJUN BLACKENING

The technique of blackening gained fame in the mid-eighties, but, in fact, most people who attempted the style never achieved its main goal. To seal in juices and form a spice crust, you must use intense heat, enough to cause copious amounts of smoke, and home cooks typically stopped well short of that for fear of destroying the kitchen. That said, the blend of spices inspired by Cajun cuisine is a perfectly good seasoning even if you don't intend to make a charred crust on the meat. Use it either way on pork chops or fish, with as intense a hand as you like.

Cajun Blackening Spice Mix   MAKES ABOUT 2¾ CUPS

15 Turkish bay leaves

1 cup sweet Hungarian paprika

½ cup dried Mexican oregano

¼ cup garlic powder

¼ cup yellow mustard seeds

3 tablespoons Tellicherry black peppercorns

2 tablespoons cumin seeds

2 tablespoons dried Spanish thyme

2 tablespoons onion flakes

1 tablespoon cayenne

2 teaspoons celery seeds

Pulse the bay leaves in a coffee mill until pulverized. Combine the remaining ingredients, and add the bay. Grind together in a coffee mill to a fine powder as needed. Use to coat meat or fish fillets heavily before searing them in hot oil over high heat until smoke appears, to form a hard crust.

CREOLE SPICES

Creole is a decidedly different cuisine from its geographic neighbor, Cajun food. Where Cajun is bold and brash, Creole is more thoughtful and reserved. It's based on the same local ingredients, but Creole cooks look for refinement from their French roots, with techniques and spicing cues from Europe. Taking advantage of the classic "trinity" of onions, bell pepper, and celery, this spice blend is a simple way to re-create the subtlety of the regional flavors. Some heat is still present, but not as pungently as others in Louisiana might prefer—adjust the heat to your own personal taste.

Creole Spice Blend   MAKES ABOUT 1¼ CUPS

¼ cup onion flakes

¼ cup celery flakes

¼ cup dried Turkish oregano

2 tablespoons dried Spanish thyme

2 tablespoons sweet Hungarian paprika

1 tablespoon garlic powder

1 tablespoon Tellicherry black peppercorns

1 tablespoon Muntok white peppercorns

2 teaspoons cayenne

Combine all the ingredients. Grind together in a coffee mill as needed, to season sauces or to stir into a roux as it cooks to start seafood and rice dishes.

MONTREAL STEAK SPICE

This combination of flavors has gained a reputation of its own and is now blended all over North America as a dusting spice for steaks and chops. The distinct character comes from the blending of traditional pepper, salt, and garlic with dried vegetable and citrus components, an idea spawned by Montreal's combined French and English heritage.

Steak Spice Blend   MAKES ABOUT 1¼ CUPS

3 tablespoons coriander seeds

3 tablespoons black peppercorns

2 tablespoons dried red bell pepper

2 tablespoons dried green bell pepper

2 tablespoons onion flakes

2 tablespoons garlic flakes

2 tablespoons dill seeds

2 tablespoons coarse sea salt

1 tablespoon caraway seeds

1 tablespoon dried thyme

2 teaspoons dried lemon peel

Combine all the ingredients. Pulse to blend in a coffee mill, in batches as necessary, leaving some texture to the blend. Dust on grilled meats or roasted potatoes.

SEAFOOD BOILS

Seafood boils are about as American as apple pie anywhere the creatures are harvested. Setting up the "long table" out back and loading the steamer with shrimp or crawfish down South, lobsters in New England, or crabs in the Pacific Northwest stir something of a kinship with the land and regional pride in each community.

A complete meal can be had in one pot by tossing in potatoes or corn, or a first course of clams and mussels. What ties all the flavors together is usually the spiced broth used to cook the whole lot. The technique is as simple as it sounds. Just crush the spices, add them to the simmering water, and let them infuse for about fifteen minutes, then add your seafood and extras. Serve everything in a huge spread on newspaper, with plenty of bibs and napkins.

Gulf Coast Shrimp Boil   MAKES 1¼ CUPS

20 Californian bay leaves

20 dried pequín chiles

¼ cup allspice berries

¼ cup European coriander seeds

2 tablespoons celery seeds

2 tablespoons yellow mustard seeds

2 tablespoons Tellicherry black peppercorns

1 tablespoon whole cloves

1 tablespoon dill seeds

Combine all the ingredients. Crush as needed into seafood cooking liquid, using roughly 1 tablespoon per quart of liquid.

Chesapeake Crab Boil   MAKES 1 ¼ CUPS

20 Turkish bay leaves

¼ cup allspice berries

¼ cup European coriander seeds

2 tablespoons celery seeds

2 tablespoons yellow mustard seeds

2 tablespoons cassia-cinnamon chips

2 tablespoons whole Tellicherry black peppercorns

1 tablespoon whole cloves

1 tablespoon dill seeds

Combine all the ingredients. Crush as needed into crab cooking liquid, using roughly 1 tablespoon per quart of liquid.

Alaskan Crab Boil   MAKES ABOUT 1 CUP

20 California bay leaves

¼ cup allspice berries

3 tablespoons Tellicherry black peppercorns

2 tablespoons celery seeds

2 tablespoons dried lemon peel

1 tablespoon dried dill weed

1 tablespoon whole cloves

1 tablespoon fennel seeds

Combine all the ingredients. Crush as needed into crab cooking liquid, using roughly 1 tablespoon per quart of liquid.

CORNED BEEF SPICES

I laugh out loud when I see the pathetic pouches of seeds packed in with cellophane-wrapped corned beef in the supermarkets of America. Not only is there barely enough spice to season the beef properly, but the quality and makeup leave plenty to be desired in the spicing department. Originally a method of tenderization and preservation, "corning" meat means simply to soak it in a brine of salt, sugar, and spices and allow chemistry to take its course. If it's done properly, you'll get a richer, more tender cut of meat that can be the centerpiece of dinner or the beginning of sandwiches to rival those of any New York deli.

Make enough solution to cover your cut of beef, preferably a round or bottom roast up to five inches thick. Choose cuts that are consistent in thickness throughout for best results. Place the meat in a nonreactive or glass container, cover with the brine, and place weights on top to keep it submerged. Refrigerate for at least 24 and up to 72 hours.

Corned Beef Spice Mix   MAKES ABOUT 1¾ CUPS

1 cup yellow mustard seeds
20 Turkish bay leaves, crumbled
¼ cup Tellicherry black peppercorns
¼ cup Muntok white peppercorns
2 tablespoons allspice berries
2 tablespoons coarsely ground celery seeds

Combine all the ingredients in a large mortar and pound with the pestle to partially open the seeds.

Corning Solution   MAKES ABOUT 1 GALLON

1 gallon water
1 cup sea salt
1 cup sugar
½ cup Corned Beef Spice Mix

Stir all the ingredients together until the salt and sugar dissolve.

PICKLING SPICES

Pickled vegetables, whether traditional cucumbers or exotic melon rinds and beets, all need a spice mix whose flavor can survive the pickling process. Here's a simple recipe from the early nineteenth century that made the most of what was available in the newly formed United States.

Pickling Spice Mix   MAKES ABOUT 1¼ CUPS

20 Turkish bay leaves, crumbled

¼ cup yellow mustard seeds

¼ cup Tellicherry black peppercorns

¼ cup Muntok white peppercorns

2 tablespoons allspice berries

2 tablespoons dill seeds

2 tablespoons coarsely ground celery seeds

Combine all the ingredients. Use freshly cracked in pickling brines or ground fine as a seasoning.

BREAD STUFFING SPICES

Use this spice mix in conjunction with some dried bread cubes to replace the boxes of stuffing that have become popular on American grocery shelves. (I have to admit that I've always liked that stuff as a quick side dish, but it drives me nuts to pay two dollars for a nickel's worth of dry bread and a tiny spice packet!) I liberate the ends of leftover bread nightly by simply cutting them up and throwing them on a pan in the cooling oven after cooking dinner. Keep big plastic bags of them in a cool dark place, next to a tin of this spice blend, and you'll always have a fast side dish available. Great with pork chops or roast chicken.

"Instant" Stuffing Spice Mix   MAKES ABOUT 1¼ CUPS

¼ cup plus 2 tablespoons celery flakes

¼ cup onion flakes

¼ cup dried marjoram

2 tablespoons rubbed sage

2 tablespoons cracked Tellicherry black peppercorns

1 tablespoon granulated sugar

2 teaspoons coarse sea salt

Combine all the ingredients, and grind together in a coffee mill as needed. To make stuffing, bring 2 cups chicken broth to a boil in a large saucepan. Add 2 tablespoons unsalted butter and 1 tablespoon of the freshly ground spice blend. Simmer over low heat for 2 minutes, and add just enough cubes of dried bread (about 2 cups) to soak up the liquid. Remove from the heat, cover, and let stand for 5 minutes.

PUMPKIN PIE SPICES

Harvesttime in the fall has given rise to an American classic, pumpkin pie, the dessert made with a puree of pumpkin and a spice blend that has found universal appeal in holiday baking. So popular is the blend that you'll see it called for in everything from apple tarts to mashed potatoes year-round.

The most important factor, as usual, is freshness of the aromatic components contained within. Make only as much as you will use immediately, whether in a pie or another recipe. If you're adventurous enough to also use freshly pureed pumpkin rather than canned, you might find yourself making pies for all the neighbors, whether you like it or not, throughout the holiday season.

Pumpkin Pie Spice   MAKES 2 TABLESPOONS

1 tablespoon ground cassia-cinnamon

1 teaspoon ground ginger

½ teaspoon freshly ground cloves

½ teaspoon freshly ground allspice berries

½ teaspoon ground mace

½ teaspoon freshly shaved or grated nutmeg

Sift the cassia and ginger together in a coffee mill to mix well and to eliminate any lumps. Stir the cloves, allspice, mace, and nutmeg together and sift with the cassia and ginger.

SAUSAGE SPICES

There are as many recipes for sausage as there are for curry or barbecue. Walking over the next hill will give you ten more opinions. Spicy-hot or not, sweetened or not, bitter or savory; the combinations are endless. This is a mix for "fresh" breakfast sausage that is simply stirred with ground pork and allowed to sit overnight in the refrigerator before being panfried. It's standard fare on the farms of Middle America, starting at about daybreak.

Farm Sausage Spice   MAKES ½ CUP

- 2 tablespoons cracked fennel seeds
- 1 tablespoon rubbed sage
- 1 tablespoon coarsely ground dried rosemary
- 1 tablespoon marjoram
- 1 tablespoon dried Turkish oregano
- 2 teaspoons red chile flakes
- 2 teaspoons coarse sea salt
- 2 teaspoons freshly ground Tellicherry black pepper

Stir all the ingredients together. Use to taste, typically 1 tablespoon per ½ pound of ground pork. (To test your pork mixture, panfry a tiny sample patty, then adjust the seasoning if necessary.)

SEASONING SALTS

Seasoning salts are one of the fastest-growing categories of spice sales in America. You might ask why, and the reason is simple: profits. The type of salt used by the food industry is relatively cheap, which makes seasoning salts as heavy with profit as with salt. They're also incredibly versatile, from a marketing perspective; you can attach just about any culinary trend to a seasoning salt. Tex-Mex, Japanese, Greek, Chinese, French, and English cuisines have all been tapped recently to become the latest flavor craze in seasoning salts.

I'm not trying to automatically demonize these catch-all flavor enhancers, but I do think even the simplest of cooks can make their *own* seasoning salts and probably get more bang for their spice buck in the process. Seasoning salts aren't hard to formulate, and the nature of salt is that these will stabilize and preserve whatever tastes you care to add to them. The blends also tend to get better over time as the flavors infuse the salt and each other. This means you can make a large batch for yourself every six months and draw from the pot as needed.

Buy good-quality sea salt in bulk, and start experimenting. For all seasoning salts, it's best to grind or crush all the spices together with the salt by running the entire batch through a coffee mill. The texture depends on your preference. Little bottles make great gifts for the neighbors and won't break the bank. Here are a few ideas to get you started.

Western Seasoning Salt   MAKES 1½ CUPS

1 cup coarse sea salt

2 tablespoons black peppercorns

2 tablespoons freshly ground coriander seeds

2 tablespoons red chile flakes

1 tablespoon garlic flakes or chopped dried garlic

1 tablespoon dried rosemary, coarsely cracked

Greek Seasoning Salt   MAKES ABOUT 1 CUP

1 cup coarse sea salt

1 tablespoon dried marjoram

1 tablespoon dried Greek oregano

1 teaspoon freshly ground celery seeds

French Seasoning Salt   MAKES 1¼ CUPS

1 cup coarse sea salt

3 tablespoons Herbes de Provence (page 368), crushed

Japanese Seasoning Salt   MAKES 1¼ CUPS

1 cup coarse sea salt

¼ cup *Shichimi-Togarashi* (page 401)

Adobo

Here the term "adobo" doesn't refer to the dish made famous in the Philippines, of course, but to the Latin American all-purpose spice mix of the same name that is strewn about on meat, beans, and even roasted vegetables. The base of garlic and onion powders also makes it a thickener of sorts, well suited to stews of local specialties.

MAKES ABOUT 1 ¼ CUPS

¼ cup garlic powder

¼ cup onion powder

3 tablespoons dried Mexican oregano

2 tablespoons cumin seeds

2 tablespoons coarse sea salt

2 tablespoons black peppercorns

1 tablespoon dried orange peel

1 tablespoon dried lemon peel

Combine all the ingredients, and grind together in a coffee mill as needed.

CHILI POWDERS

The naming confusion surrounding chiles can be daunting (see Chiles, page 95), but that doesn't minimize the importance of these powders based on the whole pods. Remember that chili powders are more than just pods ground down. They are fully rounded flavoring blends that include garlic, pepper, and paprika, among others, taking the chiles' flavors to new levels of complexity and making them more versatile in the kitchen.

Perhaps the biggest advantage of making the powders yourself rather than purchasing over-the-counter versions is control over the component ingredients. Commercial versions far too often have overloads of salt or sugar, or corn flour to bulk up the product. By making purer versions at home, you increase flavor and can actually use less.

As you would expect, chiles are still the main ingredients, and which ones you choose as the beginning of your blend should be well thought out. Heavier, sweeter chiles will need more savory help from peppercorns and herbs; sharper, hotter chiles may need sweet spices for balance. The choice of how much, if any, salt is added can also be made in context, depending on where the powder will most likely end up in cooking. The possibilities are endless, and experimentation is encouraged.

Ancho Chili Powder

Fruity, leathery ancho chiles have a plumlike sweetness that is perfect for a traditional chili made with meat and tomatoes. Some more modern camps will add beans, a source of great debate, but chili powders made with anchos as a base have enough heft to carry these well too. Remember that this is salt-free when you use it—recipes that call for commercial chili powder will need an added dose of salt. **MAKES ABOUT 1½ CUPS**

> 8 dried ancho chiles
> 4 dried *mulato* chiles
> ¼ cup sweet Hungarian paprika

3 tablespoons onion powder

3 tablespoons garlic powder

1 tablespoon cumin seeds

Remove the stems from the chiles and cut them into 1-inch pieces. Lay flat on a baking sheet and toast in a 200°F oven until slightly crisp. Combine the chiles with the rest of the ingredients, and grind together in a coffee mill as needed.

Chipotle Chili Powder

Smoked chipotle chiles make a wonderful start for chili powders destined for salsas and soups. I particularly like this one for corn chowders that use milk or cream. Dairy seems to temper the smoky edge perfectly, leaving just enough heat behind to satisfy even chile fanatics and still not scare away the masses. **MAKES ABOUT 1½ CUPS**

4 dried ancho chiles

4 dried chipotle chiles

¼ cup smoked paprika (pimentón)

3 tablespoons onion powder

3 tablespoons garlic powder

1 tablespoon cumin seeds

Remove the stems from the chiles and cut them into 1-inch pieces. Lay flat on a baking sheet and toast in a 200°F oven until slightly crisp. Combine the chiles with the rest of the ingredients, and grind together in a coffee mill as needed.

Mole Powder

The famous *mole* sauces of Central Mexico can be complex affairs at best, some involving upwards of thirty ingredients and cooked for days on end. Reasonable interpretations can be made with somewhat less effort by starting with this fairly complex chili powder, which can then be stewed with the other sauce ingredients for the final dish.
MAKES ABOUT 3 CUPS

6 dried *chihuacle negro* chiles

2 dried *mulato* chiles

2 dried *pasilla* chiles

¼ cup sesame seeds

20 dried avocado leaves (found in Mexican markets)

¼ cup sweet Hungarian paprika

¼ cup smoked paprika (*pimentón*)

3 tablespoons onion powder

3 tablespoons garlic powder

3 tablespoons light brown sugar

2 tablespoons unsweetened cocoa powder

2 tablespoons ground true cinnamon

1 tablespoon allspice berries

1 tablespoon anise seeds

1 teaspoon whole cloves

Remove the stems from the chiles and cut them into 1-inch pieces. Lay flat on a baking sheet and toast in a 200°F oven until slightly crisp. Lightly toast the sesame seeds and avocado leaves in a baking pan in the oven or in a dry skillet over medium heat. Let cool. Combine all the ingredients, and grind together in a coffee mill as needed.

Taco and Fajita Seasoning

Forget the packets of seasoning at the grocery; they're half salt and half mystery. This recipe is much more potent, so you'll want to use less, say 1 tablespoon per pound of ground beef to start. **MAKES ABOUT ¾ CUP**

¼ cup pure ancho chile powder

2 tablespoons dried Mexican oregano

2 tablespoons onion flakes

1 tablespoon garlic flakes or chopped dried garlic

1 tablespoon dried thyme

1 tablespoon dried tomato (see Note)

2 teaspoons coarse sea salt

½ teaspoon Worcestershire powder (see page 366)

Combine all the ingredients, and grind together in a coffee mill as needed.

NOTE: Dried tomato is available at natural food stores and specialty spice markets. If necessary, substitute freshly ground chopped or diced sun-dried tomato.

Central and South American Blends

Yucatan Rojo Rub

This is an interesting precursor to our modern barbecue rubs. The annatto and allspice combination makes it solidly New World in flavor and it gets a citrus base from the lemon and coriander. It's excellent as a rub for roasted poultry.   **MAKES ABOUT ¾ CUP**

> 2 tablespoons annatto seeds
>
> 2 tablespoons cumin seeds
>
> 2 tablespoons coriander seeds
>
> 2 tablespoons dried Mexican oregano
>
> 2 tablespoons coarse sea salt
>
> 2 tablespoons allspice berries
>
> 1 tablespoon chopped garlic
>
> 1 tablespoon black peppercorns
>
> 10 whole cloves
>
> 2 teaspoons dried lemon peel
>
> 2 teaspoons ground cassia-cinnamon

Combine all the ingredients, and grind together in a coffee mill as needed.

Mayan Cocoa Mix

I shared this idea with a café-owner friend in my adopted winter home of British Columbia, and it promptly gave birth to his best seller for the season. Apparently all the snowboarders found it "cool, dude," without even knowing that their newfound favorite originally came from a hemisphere away. One patron reacted by saying, "It's a buzz in my mouth," and I couldn't agree more.   **MAKES ABOUT ¾ CUP**

> ¼ cup chopped almonds
>
> 3 tablespoons unsweetened cocoa powder
>
> 2 tablespoons cocoa nibs (see Note)
>
> 2 tablespoons light brown sugar
>
> 2 teaspoons ground true cinnamon

1 teaspoon allspice berries

1 teaspoon cayenne

½ teaspoon whole cloves

Combine all the ingredients, and grind together in a coffee mill as needed. To make cocoa, infuse milk with the mix to taste by heating gently for 10 minutes, then strain and serve hot.

NOTE: Cocoa nibs, which are cracked, roasted, and hulled cocoa beans, are available at specialty gourmet markets.

In the early days of transatlantic commerce, ships crossing the newly charted ocean had a problem that importer/exporters still suffer today. Even then, the costs of operating a ship mandated a profitable venture in *both* directions of the journey. From Africa, the abhorrent slave trade of the era was no exception. With the shortest routes being from the Ivory Coast to the Caribbean Islands, ships would follow those in the first leg of a triad that then proceeded to the European ports, loaded with New World bounty, and, ultimately, back to Africa. Any captain who could load his ship with viable product in the islands could shorten his journey by months, eliminating a stop on the North American continent to find salable goods. As a result there's the direct influence of Caribbean spices on Europe, especially the coastal ports of England and Spain. Allspice, chiles, and cocoa all have those profiteers to thank for their introduction to the Old World and, ultimately, the Far East.

The slave trade also brought many crops westward with it, most notably cumin, cardamom, and, later, nutmeg. During the era of exploration, plenty of crops that were attempted in these cross-Atlantic experiments failed, but now, with modern horticultural techniques, just about anything that can grow in the "hot zone" of plus or minus 15 degrees latitude from the equator is cultivated around the entire globe.

Jerk Rub

Made famous first and foremost by its heat, this blend really does show all that the New World spice crops could offer to the cook. Traditionally used as a rub/marinade for tough meats like goat, it works perfectly well on just about any meat or poultry; or try it on fish or shrimp. Make skewers to hold small pieces of meat to ensure good coating and penetration of the flavors; if possible, marinate them overnight in the refrigerator.

MAKES ABOUT ¾ CUP

¼ cup coriander seeds

2 tablespoons onion powder

1 tablespoon garlic powder

1 tablespoon allspice berries

1 tablespoon ground ginger

1 tablespoon dried thyme

1 tablespoon black peppercorns

2 teaspoons dried chives

2 teaspoons ground cassia-cinnamon

1½ teaspoons granulated sugar

1 teaspoon freshly shaved or grated nutmeg

1 teaspoon whole cloves

1 teaspoon pure habanero chile powder

Combine all the ingredients, and grind together in a coffee mill as needed. (To use as a marinade, combine 1 tablespoon of the freshly ground spices with 1 cup dry white wine and the juice of 1 lime; increase the quantities as necessary.)

Poudre de Colombo

The workers from Sri Lanka's capitol, Colombo, emigrated all over the globe to work in various industries, including the sugarcane trade in the Caribbean. They took their curry techniques from home and applied them to locally available ingredients. Curiously, there's no heat component to the spice blend, gaining that rather from fresh chiles in the dish that it seasons. **MAKES ABOUT 1¼ CUPS**

½ cup long-grain white rice

2 tablespoons fenugreek seeds

1 teaspoon whole cloves

3 tablespoons coriander seeds

2 tablespoons brown mustard seeds

2 tablespoons ground turmeric

1 tablespoon cumin seeds

1 tablespoon black peppercorns

Toast the rice, fenugreek, and cloves in a small dry pan just until smoke appears. Add the remaining ingredients and let cool. Grind together in a coffee mill as needed.

Trinidad Curry

This is a curry mix that combines the flavors of the Caribbean and the techniques of Southeast Asia. The fresh components require that it be made only as needed, but the fresh ginger and chile make this a unique example of how curry techniques evolve around the world. **MAKES ABOUT ¾ CUP**

> 3 tablespoons coriander seeds
>
> 3 tablespoons ground turmeric
>
> 2 tablespoons black peppercorns
>
> 1 tablespoon cumin seeds
>
> 1 teaspoon allspice berries
>
> 1 teaspoon cardamom seeds
>
> 1 teaspoon freshly shaved or grated nutmeg
>
> 1 teaspoon ground cassia-cinnamon
>
> 1 tablespoon grated fresh ginger
>
> 1 habanero chile, seeded and finely minced

Combine all the ingredients except the ginger and chile, and grind together in a coffee mill. Transfer to a mortar, add the ginger and chile, and pound with the pestle to make a rough paste.

Tikka Masala

Evidence of the Indian influence can easily be seen in this blend with cardamom, chiles, cumin, and fenugreek, but the British tastes come through via sweet paprika and garlic. (See Chicken *Tikka Masala*, page 323, for the story of why this is, surprisingly, a British spice mix.)

A restaurateur who makes giant batches of chicken *tikka* for his customers once suggested that I mix a small amount of this freshly ground spice with softened butter, say 1 teaspoon per stick of unsalted butter, and keep it as a spiced reserve in my refrigerator. Adding a small pat when making the rice to accompany the traditional dish adds a delightful union to the plate, but I also find myself using the butter with omelets and potatoes when I want a little something spicy to peek through. **MAKES ABOUT 1 CUP**

5 *guajillo* chiles, stems removed, cut into 1-inch pieces

6 Turkish bay leaves

2 tablespoons sweet Hungarian paprika

2 tablespoons ground turmeric

1 tablespoon dried garlic flakes or chopped dried garlic

1 tablespoon red chile flakes

1 tablespoon black peppercorns

2 teaspoons ground ginger

2 teaspoons cumin seeds

2 teaspoons fenugreek seeds

1 teaspoon cardamom seeds

1 teaspoon caraway seeds

½ teaspoon freshly grated nutmeg

¼ teaspoon freshly ground cloves

Combine all the ingredients, and grind together in a coffee mill as needed.

WORCESTERSHIRE

I'm not proposing that you make your own Worcestershire sauce—the list of ingredients alone would make you recoil from the task. But since this English flavoring has become such a fixture in most people's pantries, it's worth mentioning as a blended spicy concoction. As the label on famous brands will tell you, it's wonderful with meats as a marinade or sauce in its liquid form, but the food industry has had a secret weapon on its shelves for years. Since it's easier to ship a two-pound box of *dry* Worcestershire than a fifty-gallon drum of the liquid, major food processors have long used Worcestershire in a powder form. Available from specialty spice purveyors, it is brutally potent, but it can be a great addition to your barbecue rubs and chile powders. Just like the liquid sauce, it contains a litany of spices as well as vinegar, tamarind, onions, molasses, garlic, soy sauce, lime, and (surprise for your vegetarian friends) anchovies.

Glogg Spices

A spiced red wine that's made with strong spices and has fruit steeped in it to release sweetness, glogg is a Scandinavian specialty around the holidays. It's frequently fortified with vodka after an initial twenty minutes of simmering and served to very happy Swedes. **MAKES ABOUT ⅓ CUP**

    10 white cardamom pods
    2 slices fresh ginger (about ⅛ inch thick)
    2 tablespoons fennel seeds
    1 tablespoon juniper berries

Combine all the ingredients in a linen steeping bag, or tie up in a square of cheesecloth, and use the side of a heavy knife or a small heavy pan to bruise the spices within. Add to simmering wine; remove after 20 minutes to avoid bitterness, and serve the wine in mugs.

Mulling Spices

Break out the Dickens, and put on a pot of mulled wine or cider around the holidays. About 2 tablespoons of this mixture per 750-ml bottle is a good starting point, but adjust to personal preference as desired. It's important to remove the spices after they've released their flavor to avoid bitterness. **MAKES ABOUT ½ CUP**

20 green cardamom pods

2 tablespoons dried orange peel

2 tablespoons cassia-cinnamon chips

1 tablespoon cracked star anise

1 tablespoon allspice berries

1½ teaspoons whole cloves

2 slices fresh ginger (about ⅛ inch thick)

Combine the dried spices together in a linen steeping bag, or tie up in a square of cheesecloth, and add to simmering wine. (This is enough spice for 4 bottles of wine or a similar measure of apple cider; reduce the quantities as appropriate for less.) Add the ginger slices to the wine, simmer for 20 minutes or so, then remove the spice bag and ginger and serve the wine in mugs.

Bouquet Garni

Almost always made with a bundle (the literal translation of the word "bouquet") of fresh herbs, this classic sachet is in every stock or soup of French origin. The mixture offers as much perfume as flavor. Although the stronger flavors of sage and rosemary are not traditionally included, I tend to add one or the other when appropriate to the dish.

MAKES 1 SACHET

1 fresh thyme branch

2 fresh marjoram sprigs

2 fresh parsley sprigs

1 fresh rosemary or sage branch (optional)

3 Turkish bay leaves

Tie all the herbs together with kitchen twine, and toss into stock. (If desired, the herbs can be placed in a steeping bag for easy removal.)

Herbes de Provence

This is perhaps the most popular herb blend from the South of France; the great debate here is the inclusion or not of lavender. While I've had experts swear that it must be included to be authentic, I've also had French grandmothers tell me the opposite. As the flavor of lavender is potent and quite polarizing—i.e., you'll love it or hate it—so I leave the choice to the cook. **MAKES ABOUT ⅔ CUP**

2 tablespoons dried chervil

2 tablespoons dried marjoram

2 tablespoons dried tarragon

2 tablespoons dried basil

1 tablespoon dried thyme

1 tablespoon dried lavender (optional)

Stir all the herbs together. Crush the herbs between your fingers to release their flavor when adding to recipes.

Herbes de la Garrique

From the French region that bears its name, this is a more savory blend than those in Provence. This deeper profile of herbs is better for flavoring heavier sauces like those made from roasted meat drippings. **MAKES ABOUT ¾ CUP**

10 Turkish bay leaves, broken

2 tablespoons dried summer savory

2 tablespoons dried marjoram

2 tablespoons dried basil

1 tablespoon dried thyme

1 tablespoon dried rosemary, cracked

1 tablespoon dried sage

1 tablespoon dried mint, preferably peppermint

2 teaspoons fennel seeds, cracked

Stir all the ingredients together. Crush the herbs between your fingers to release their flavor when adding to recipes.

Fines Herbes

This is a lighter interpretation of the French countryside than *herbes de* Provence (page 368) or *de la* Garrique (above). The delicate blend dances on top of the palate, especially with the chives, which add an incredibly mild onion and garlic flavor. **MAKES ABOUT ⅔ CUP**

2 tablespoons dried chervil

2 tablespoons dried chives

2 tablespoons dried parsley

2 tablespoons dried marjoram

2 tablespoons dried tarragon

Stir all the herbs together. Crush the herbs between your fingers to release their flavor when adding to recipes.

Mélange Classique

This peppery French blend still takes a cue from an herb base. This is seen frequently as a dusting on seafood or in white bean dishes. Cassoulet, the classic meat and bean casserole, uses this as a seasoning to pull together the flavors of its widely varied ingredient list over the extended cooking time. **MAKES ABOUT ¼ CUP**

> 4 Turkish bay leaves, broken
>
> 1 tablespoon coriander seeds
>
> 1 tablespoon white peppercorns
>
> 2 teaspoons dried marjoram
>
> 1 teaspoon dried thyme
>
> 1 teaspoon dried rosemary
>
> ¼ teaspoon freshly shaved or grated nutmeg
>
> ¼ teaspoon whole cloves
>
> ¼ teaspoon cayenne

Combine all the ingredients, and grind together in a coffee mill as needed.

Mignonette Pepper

This mix is much better at rounding out peppercorn flavor profiles than the mixed colored peppercorn blends—and you gain sweetness from the allspice and tartness from the coriander. Perfect for the table of any cuisine. **MAKES ABOUT ⅓ CUP**

> 2 tablespoons black peppercorns
>
> 2 tablespoons white peppercorns
>
> 1 tablespoon allspice berries
>
> 1 tablespoon coriander seeds

Mix the whole spices together, and fill a pepper mill for condiment use.

Quatre-Épices

This classic blend, literally translated as "four spices," is believed to have been the original combination for *pain épices*, the famous French spiced bread. The peppercorn builds slowly in the chew of the bread, leaving you with a wonderful tingle on the palate. Proportions vary from sweet to savory depending on ultimate application—e.g., more nutmeg and mace for pastry, more peppercorns if you plan to dust the spice on pâté. To preserve the potency of the nutmeg and mace, mix this in small batches as needed.

MAKES ABOUT 3 TABLESPOONS

1 tablespoon white peppercorns

1 tablespoon black peppercorns

1 teaspoon freshly shaved or grated nutmeg

1 teaspoon ground mace

Combine all the ingredients, and grind together in a coffee mill as needed.

Italian Herb Blend

The mixing of herbs in the Mediterranean is more a question of what is growing in your garden than set proportions. Typical combinations are heavier in Italy than in France because of the growing conditions and the native species. **MAKES ABOUT ⅔ CUP**

2 tablespoons dried Mediterranean oregano

2 tablespoons dried basil

2 tablespoons dried sage

2 tablespoons dried rosemary

2 tablespoons dried marjoram

Combine all the ingredients together. Crush the herbs between your fingers to release their flavor when adding to recipes.

Anne-Marie, my great "culinary re-creation" friend, tells me that any kitchen in the Middle Ages not equipped with the following three blends was in poor shape indeed. *Poudre forte* and *poudre douce*, literally "strong powder" and "sweet powder" respectively, were used as all-purpose seasonings of the day. The beef spice was used as a rub to flavor, just as we use rubs today, not to hide the taste of spoiled meat, as is commonly believed. In fact, my culinary researchers who focused on the Middle Ages tell me that the notion that spices were used to cover up rancid meat is completely baseless. While salt curings, some with interesting spice combinations included, certainly were used to preserve meats, they weren't used on foods that had already gone bad. Then, as today, that would put people at risk for sickness and disease.

Poudre Forte   MAKES ABOUT 1/3 CUP

2 tablespoons ground cassia-cinnamon

2 tablespoons black peppercorns

1 teaspoon ground ginger

1 teaspoon grains of paradise

1 teaspoon whole cloves

Combine all the ingredients, and grind together in a coffee mill as needed.

Poudre Douce   MAKES ABOUT 1/3 CUP

2 tablespoons ground cassia-cinnamon

2 tablespoons light brown sugar

1 teaspoon ground ginger

1 teaspoon allspice berries

1 teaspoon galangal powder

1 teaspoon sea salt

Combine all the ingredients, and grind together in a coffee mill as needed.

English Beef Rub   MAKES ABOUT ½ CUP

¼ cup packed light brown sugar

2 tablespoons ground cassia-cinnamon

1 tablespoon juniper berries

1 tablespoon black peppercorns

2 teaspoons allspice berries

2 teaspoons coarse sea salt

Combine all the ingredients, and grind together in a coffee mill as needed.

Two similar spice mixes from Russian Georgia, these are some of the best examples of how to use fenugreek leaf, also called *methi*, in the context of a blend. The complexity of each concoction will allow you to stew them on the stovetop with beans or to braise meats with them. Each has a nutty perfume that comes out even further with a modest amount of heat.

Kharcho   MAKES ABOUT ¾ CUP

3 tablespoons dried fenugreek leaves

3 tablespoons sweet Hungarian paprika

2 tablespoons coriander seeds

1 tablespoon dried winter savory

2 teaspoons caraway seeds

2 teaspoons chopped dried garlic

1 teaspoon black peppercorns

1 teaspoon red chile flakes

Combine all the ingredients, and grind together in a coffee mill as needed.

Khmeli-Suneli   MAKES ABOUT 1 CUP

¼ cup coriander seeds

3 tablespoons dried fenugreek leaves

3 tablespoons sweet Hungarian paprika

2 tablespoons fenugreek seeds

2 tablespoons ground turmeric

1 tablespoon dried winter savory

1 tablespoon dried basil

1 tablespoon black peppercorns

2 teaspoons dried mint, preferably peppermint

1 teaspoon whole cloves

1 teaspoon ground cassia-cinnamon

Combine all the ingredients, and grind together in a coffee mill as needed.

Svanetti Salt

This salt blend, named for the mountain ranges of Russian Georgia, has become one of my favorite seasonings. Inspired by the local taste in spices, it fits with foods found in its native lands like beets and potatoes, but it easily roams farther afield as a steak seasoning, a fish rub, or a dusting on steamed Brussels sprouts.

The sour character of the dill seed melds perfectly with the deep savory notes of the caraway. I've noticed that this blend actually improves with a bit of age. If coarsely ground a few weeks ahead of use, the salt becomes infused with the spice aromas, and the overall impact on the taste buds seems more balanced. **MAKES ABOUT 1½ CUPS**

1 cup coarse sea salt

2 tablespoons caraway seeds

2 tablespoons coriander seeds

1 tablespoon fenugreek seeds

1 tablespoon chopped dried garlic

1 tablespoon Aleppo pepper

1 tablespoon black peppercorns

2 teaspoons dill seeds

Mix all the ingredients and run through a coarse grain mill, or pulse together in a coffee mill. Store for up to 6 months.

Baharat

Baharat translates as "spice" in the Middle East, and this is one of many variations that occur from house to house. A ubiquitous seasoning, it is added to soups, mixed with fresh herb as a condiment paste, and blended with oil to coat roasted meats. I like to add fresh mint and cilantro leaves to the spice blend and rub it on lamb to be slow-cooked on the barbecue. **MAKES ABOUT ¾ CUP**

¼ cup sweet Hungarian paprika

2 tablespoons black peppercorns

2 tablespoons coriander seeds

2 tablespoons cumin seeds

1 tablespoon ground cassia-cinnamon

1 tablespoon allspice berries

1 teaspoon cardamom seeds

½ teaspoon whole cloves

¼ teaspoon freshly shaved or grated nutmeg

Combine all the ingredients, and grind together in a coffee mill as needed.

NOTE: For a Turkish variant, add 1 tablespoon dried mint.

Hawayil

This is a blend from Arabic regions that demonstrates the local infatuation with saffron. The savory character of the cumin and nigella plays very well with the dry air given by the saffron in heavy lentil dishes. At the other end of the spectrum, the sweetness of cardamom keeps the mix from becoming as arid as the deserts that spawned it.

MAKES ABOUT ¼ CUP

> 1 tablespoon black peppercorns
>
> 1 tablespoon cumin seeds
>
> 2 teaspoons nigella seeds
>
> 2 teaspoons cardamom seeds
>
> 2 teaspoons ground turmeric
>
> 2 teaspoons caraway seeds
>
> 15 saffron threads

Combine all the ingredients, and grind together thoroughly in a coffee mill to distribute the saffron evenly.

Qalat Daqqa

An Arabic variation on the Tunisian five-spice blend (see page 395), this has a similar bite but adds some mint to appease the local tastes. It's nice as a rub on heavier meats like lamb, or grind until fine and add to yogurt or cook with oil into a condiment paste.

MAKES ABOUT ⅓ CUP

> 2 tablespoons black peppercorns
>
> 1 tablespoon ground cassia-cinnamon
>
> 1 tablespoon dried mint, preferably peppermint
>
> 2 teaspoons grains of paradise
>
> 1 teaspoon whole cloves
>
> ½ teaspoon freshly shaved or grated nutmeg

Combine all the ingredients, and grind together in a coffee mill as needed.

Ras el Hanout

Ras el hanout is really a spice merchant's dream blend. The term translates as "head of the shop" and the result is simply the whimsy of the owner of your local spice bazaar. Since we spice merchants are a proud lot, we always try to show off a bit by including some of the most exotic ingredients we can find. Keeping in mind that there are hundreds of variations, this one is fairly representative of what you'd find in the Arabic countries that started the trend. Use it as a rub on roast meats, in casseroles and stews, or ground fine as a condiment. **MAKES ABOUT ¾ CUP**

3 long pepper pods

4 inches true cinnamon stick

1 tablespoon paprika

1 tablespoon coriander seeds

1 tablespoon brown mustard seeds

1 tablespoon cumin seeds

1 tablespoon black peppercorns

2 teaspoons grains of paradise

2 teaspoons dried rose petals

2 teaspoons dried lavender

2 teaspoons ground turmeric

1 teaspoon nigella seeds

1 teaspoon caraway seeds

1 teaspoon cardamom seeds

1 teaspoon anise seeds

1 teaspoon ground mace

1 teaspoon *cubeb*

1 teaspoon ground ginger

1 teaspoon galangal powder

½ teaspoon ajwain seeds

Combine all the ingredients, and grind together in a coffee mill as needed.

ZAHTAR

This famous condiment blend can have many interpretations, and the name can also be applied to certain regional species of pure herb in the thyme family; see Thyme, page 317. While there are hundreds of permutations, though, each of which seems to evoke a sense of specific spice pride from those bearing the recipe, most fall within two extremes of the flavor camp.

One end of the flavor spectrum is heavy in tart sumac, accented by simple herbs and a deeper nutty character from sesame (Syrian), and the other is considerably more herbaceous, sending the lemony punch of sumac to the background in exchange for brighter herb flavors (Israeli). Both these recipes have gotten acceptable reviews from visitors from each region, with one caveat: "but it's not as good as mine." In the Middle East, spices really do come with bragging rights.

Zahtar (the spelling also varies) is sometimes used as a dry condiment, sometimes blended with oil into a paste, but its flavor blooms with grinding as the oils of the sesame seeds come to the surface. Also found baked into dough or as a topping for flatbreads, it can be enough to make bread into an appetizer all by itself. Some will toast the spice before using, but I find this strictly optional.

Israeli Zahtar   MAKES ABOUT 1 CUP

½ cup white sesame seeds

3 tablespoons dried Turkish oregano

2 tablespoons dried thyme

1 tablespoon dried dill weed

1 tablespoon ground sumac

2 teaspoons coarse sea salt

Combine all the ingredients, and grind together in a coffee mill as needed.

Syrian Zahtar   MAKES ABOUT 1⅓ CUPS

1 cup white sesame seeds

3 tablespoons ground sumac

1 tablespoon cumin seeds

1 tablespoon coriander seeds

2 teaspoons dried lemon peel

2 teaspoons coarse sea salt

1 teaspoon anise seeds

Combine all the ingredients, and grind together in a coffee mill as needed.

Zhug

This paste from Yemen has a fresh green taste that is perfect as a grilling spice for fish and lamb. Milder versions can be used as condiment pastes at the table, but to my mind, the high heat of cooking melds the flavors together better.   MAKES ABOUT ¾ CUP

2 teaspoons cardamom seeds

2 teaspoons coriander seeds

2 teaspoons black peppercorns

4 fresh hot red chiles

1 roasted red bell pepper, peeled and seeded

¼ cup diced onion

4 garlic cloves, minced

¼ cup fresh cilantro leaves

Lightly toast the seeds and peppercorns in a small dry skillet over medium heat. Let cool, then grind together in a coffee mill. Combine the remaining ingredients in a mini food processor and process to a paste. Stir together with the ground seeds and allow to stand 4 hours at room temperature, then cover and refrigerate until ready to use.

CHAI SPICES

So you've heard the term *"chai"* bandied about lately by the coffee industry marketers. You may have even seen some of the ready-made concentrates on the shelf at the grocery in the "exotic foods" section. But what is *chai* exactly? The word simply means "tea" in Hindi, and it refers to the classic "railway tea" of India, prepared with a mix of local spices and milk in almost every train station throughout the country. It's the drink of choice all over South India and is rapidly becoming as fashionable in the West as the popular coffee-based beverages.

It will help to understand the origins of the drink if you remember that the (then) pale British palate was superimposed upon the local Nilgiri Hills population. The Brits were all about tea a few hundred years ago when they were on the subcontinent colonizing everything in sight. Tea leaf was planted far and wide, and as the ingenious locals were apt to try whatever was available, the preferred drink for everyone in the area soon became a classic cup of black tea with milk and sugar. But then the local palate for spice in everything reared its head, and an impromptu blend of regional cardamom, peppercorn, and perhaps some ginger made its way into the drink.

The "classic" process was simply to boil the whole lot (tea, milk, and spice) together in a samovar over a fire, then to keep the tea warm over low heat and dip out your cup's worth throughout the day. Sweetening could be palm sugar or honey, and since the bold spices could hold up to it, plenty was usually the norm.

If you fast-forward to modern times, you'll find the recipes have evolved along the same basic principles of spice, tea, and milk, but the variations are too numerous to count. With the classic base, everything from cassia-cinnamon, mace, clove, and nutmeg to *methi* (fenugreek) and even citrus is added. There simply are no hard-and-fast rules for your choice of flavors to blend into the tea base. Black tea is the preferred choice, although some have experimented with green tea in the mix—usually with disastrous results. The heaviness of the spice needs the deeper flavors of black tea as a base, but again, experiment to find your own preferences.

The preparations and techniques that have made classic chai so interesting have been overlooked in modern versions of the beverage. Many attempts have been made to distill these flavors into grocery concentrates for convenience of preparation, but it's tantamount to instant coffee versus fresh brewed. The concentrates are frequently oversweetened with inexpensive corn syrup, and the drinker has little control with regard to the overall finished flavor. Any process that can be made "fresh" will preserve more complexity of flavor and give you more tools to waken the palate. It's painfully simple, and there's a strong case to be made for taking the extra five minutes out of your day to make *chai*, for, if nothing else, relief from the far-too-fast pace of instant gratification.

A bit of finesse is needed at a few points in the prep. Crush the spices fresh, not ahead of time, to preserve the volatile oils. Follow my "two-stage" steeping method so that you don't either oversteep the tea or understeep the spices. This was a problem in the classic "boil it all together" method, but since the tea of the area was forgiving and generally not too complex, the harm done to the drink was minimal. Today, with such a widely varied and interesting selection of teas for you to choose from, it's advisable to take more precautions so as to give both the spices and the tea their just due in the brewing process.

Lastly, this isn't a place to skimp on the milk. There's interesting flavor chemistry that happens between the butterfat of the (nonskim) milk and the tea, so the degree of creaminess in the cup is more than the sum of the milk parts added. I keep a small bottle of whole milk in the fridge just for making *chai*, and when I want to be particularly decadent, the real cream comes out. I save the skim for my morning cereal.

Classic Sweet Chai Mix   MAKES ABOUT ⅓ CUP

1 tablespoon green cardamom pods

1 tablespoon dried orange peel

1 tablespoon chopped dried ginger (available at baking supply shops and specialty spice markets)

1 tablespoon cassia-cinnamon chips

1½ teaspoons whole cloves

Scant 1 teaspoon whole black peppercorns

Scant 1 teaspoon cracked black peppercorns

Combine all the ingredients. To use, crush in a mortar, or pulse-grind in a coffee mill until the cardamom pods open.

Roast Chai Mix   MAKES ABOUT ¼ CUP

1 tablespoon coriander seeds

1 tablespoon fennel seeds

1 tablespoon cassia-cinnamon chips

1½ teaspoons whole cloves

1½ teaspoons cumin seeds

1½ teaspoons black peppercorns

Combine all the ingredients in a dry skillet and toast just until smoke appears; let cool. To use, crush in a mortar or pulse-grind in a coffee mill until the coriander seeds open.

TO PREPARE FRESH CHAI:

For 16 ounces *chai*, add 1 heaping teaspoon of the just-crushed spice blend to a small teapot. Glass French-press-style pots work well for this method, as long as you leave the press up to give the spices and tea leaves full room to expand. Add ¾ cup of just boiling filtered water, and wait for 5 minutes while dreaming of India. Add 1 heaping teaspoon of black leaf tea, such as Assam, Nilgiri, or Yunnan, and top off with another ¾ cup boiling water. Wait a time that's right for the tea you chose, say 3 minutes. This is a good time to dream of railway stations and the markets of Delhi. Strain the whole pot into ½ cup of warmed milk and sweeten to taste with sugar or honey. Enjoy the *chai* and remind yourself why you'll never, ever go back to those nasty premade concentrates.

Chat Masala

This blend, despite some of its somewhat odorous components, gets used in India as a condiment seasoning on everything from fresh fruits to roast meats. **MAKES ABOUT ½ CUP**

1 tablespoon black peppercorns

2 teaspoons cumin seeds

2 teaspoons *amchoor* (mango powder)

2 teaspoons *anardana* (dried pomegranate seeds)

2 teaspoons dried mint, preferably peppermint

2 teaspoons black salt

2 teaspoons kosher salt

1 teaspoon cubeb

1 teaspoon ajwain seeds

1 teaspoon ground ginger

1 teaspoon asafetida powder

1 teaspoon cayenne

Combine all the ingredients, cover tightly, and allow to stand overnight before use. Grind together in a coffee mill as needed thereafter.

Char Masala

The roasting of the seeds in this simple sweet mix, seen in slow-cooked vegetarian dishes and in simple "mock" curries, makes for a push-pull effect on the palate. First the roasted flavor hits, then the sweetness of the individual spices shows through. Given cardamom's volatile nature, make only as much as you will use immediately. **MAKES 3 TABLESPOONS**

5 teaspoons cumin seeds

2 teaspoons cardamom seeds

1 teaspoon whole cloves

2 teaspoons ground cassia-cinnamon

Toast the seeds and cloves in a dry skillet or under the broiler, until very fragrant. Add the cassia-cinnamon, and grind together in a coffee mill.

CURRY POWDERS

It surprises most people to learn that curry powders as we know them in the West are almost nonexistent in India. It's not that the flavors or styles we think of as "curry" aren't present in the country that inspired them, it's just that a premixed powder for making the dish is unheard of. Cooks instead will make a powder on the fly for each particular dish as appropriate.

Given the almost innate ability of Indian cooks to spice their meals individually, we can still draw on some regional norms to make curry powders that would be typical of the many cuisines of the country. It's sometimes a game of inches in the massive subcontinent, as even a few kilometers up the road can substantially change what's found in the spice rack.

Madras-style Curry Powder

This is the classic curry powder from the southern regions of the country. Relatively complex, it is perhaps the closest thing to a "reference" curry powder for Western tastes; i.e, this style is what most of us here expect curry powder to taste like. **MAKES ABOUT ¾ CUP**

¼ cup coriander seeds

2 tablespoons brown mustard seeds

2 tablespoons ground turmeric

1 tablespoon fenugreek seeds

1 tablespoon cumin seeds

1 tablespoon red chile flakes

2 teaspoons ground ginger

2 teaspoons ground cassia-cinnamon

2 teaspoons black peppercorns

1 teaspoon cardamom seeds

Combine all the ingredients, and grind together in a coffee mill as needed.

Pakistani-Style Curry Powder

Farther to the north, there are sweet notes from anise and true cinnamon to meet the local tastes. This one is especially good with the vegetable curry dishes popular among the locals. **MAKES ABOUT ½ CUP**

4 dried *guajillo* chiles, stems removed, cut into 1-inch pieces

3 tablespoons coriander seeds

4 teaspoons sweet Hungarian paprika

1 tablespoon cumin seeds

1 tablespoon ground ginger

1 tablespoon ground true cinnamon

2 teaspoons anise seeds

2 teaspoons black peppercorns

½ teaspoon whole cloves

Combine all the ingredients, and grind together in a coffee mill as needed.

Kashmiri-Style Curry Powder

Sometimes called "royal curry" for the Moghul kings whose cooks developed the tastes, this is one of the few curries to incorporate saffron successfully. The blend is relatively simple otherwise, but it draws upon the unstoppable depth of saffron's flavor to fill in any gaps. **MAKES ABOUT ¾ CUP**

4 dried *guajillo* chiles, stems removed, cut into 1-inch pieces

¼ cup coriander seeds

2 teaspoons cardamom seeds

2 teaspoons ground cassia-cinnamon

10 whole cloves

15 saffron threads

2 tablespoons ground turmeric

1 tablespoon fennel seeds

1 tablespoon cumin seeds

Lightly toast the chiles, coriander, cardamom, cassia-cinnamon, and cloves, stirring, in a dry skillet over medium heat, until fragrant. Combine with the remaining ingredients and let cool. Grind together in a coffee mill as needed.

Sri Lankan-style Curry Powder

On the island to the southeast of the subcontinent, they have developed a taste all their own. Roasting the spices until they are intensely aromatic lends an almost toffee character to the finished product, resulting in a curry powder that meshes well with heavier meats and vegetables. **MAKES ABOUT ¾ CUP**

- ¼ **cup coriander seeds**
- 2 **tablespoons fenugreek seeds**
- 1 **tablespoon fennel seeds**
- 1 **tablespoon cumin seeds**
- 1 **tablespoon black peppercorns**
- 2 **teaspoons ground cassia-cinnamon**
- 1 **teaspoon cardamom seeds**
- 1 **teaspoon whole cloves**
- 15 **dried** *pequín* **chiles**

Toast the coriander, fenugreek, fennel seeds, cumin, and peppercorns in a dry skillet, stirring, over medium-high heat, until very fragrant; let cool. Lightly toast the cassia-cinnamon, cardamom, cloves, and chiles. Combine all the ingredients, and grind together in a coffee mill as needed.

GARAM MASALA

Literally translated, *garam masala* means "sweet mix," and a blend along this theme is as common as curry powder in cuisines all over the Indian subcontinent. Typically, garam powders can be differentiated from curry by the lack of chile heat or the usual base turmeric. Beyond that, the two categories of blends are very similar, both rich in cumin, peppercorn, and coriander.

Central Indian-style Garam Masala

The majority of recipes calling for garam can use this basic recipe. The sweet notes of the cardamom are particularly susceptible to evaporation, so be sure to grind the mix fresh when using it. **MAKES ABOUT 1 CUP**

> **20 Turkish bay leaves**
>
> **½ cup cumin seeds**
>
> **3 tablespoons coriander seeds**
>
> **2 tablespoons black peppercorns**
>
> **2 teaspoons cardamom seeds**
>
> **2 teaspoons whole cloves**
>
> **2 teaspoons ground mace**

Combine all the ingredients, and grind together in a coffee mill as needed.

Kashmiri Garam Masala   MAKES 1 CUP

> **2 tablespoons cardamom seeds**
>
> **1 tablespoon whole cloves**
>
> **15 dried mace blades or a generous pinch of ground mace**
>
> **2 teaspoons freshly grated or shaved nutmeg**
>
> **2 tablespoons black cumin seeds**
>
> **¼ cup Tellicherry black peppercorns**
>
> **6 tablespoons coriander seeds**
>
> **2 tablespoons cassia-cinnamon chips**

Toast the cardamom, cloves, and mace blades (not ground mace), stirring constantly in a dry skillet over medium-high heat, until smoke begins to appear. Transfer to a bowl, add the nutmeg and ground mace, if using, and stir well. Toast the cumin seeds and peppercorns in the same way, and add to the bowl. Toast the coriander and cassia-cinnamon, add to the bowl, and stir all together. Allow to cool completely, and grind as needed.

Kala Masala

One of the more complex, layered mixes from India, *kala*, or "black," masala gets its flavor from the deep, dark ingredients used, some of which are toasted to bloom their flavors into the blend. **MAKES ABOUT 1½ CUPS**

> 3 dried *guajillo* chiles, stems removed, and cut into 1-inch pieces
>
> 3 tablespoons coriander seeds
>
> 5 whole cloves
>
> 5 star anise
>
> 3 tablespoons unsweetened shredded coconut
>
> 8 black cardamom pods
>
> 8 Turkish bay leaves
>
> 2 tablespoons poppy seeds
>
> 2 tablespoons ground turmeric
>
> 2 tablespoons black peppercorns
>
> 1 tablespoon black sesame seeds
>
> 1 tablespoon cumin seeds
>
> 2 teaspoons black cumin seeds
>
> 2 teaspoons ground cassia-cinnamon
>
> 2 teaspoons *amchoor* (mango powder)

Lightly toast the chiles, coriander, cloves, star anise, and coconut, stirring, in a dry skillet, over medium heat, until fragrant. Remove the seeds from the cardamom pods. Combine the seeds and the remaining ingredients with the toasted spices, and grind together in a coffee mill as needed.

Sambhar Masala

Partly for seasoning and partly for texture, South Indian chefs frequently use lentils and other *dal* as thickeners and carriers of spice flavor. This combination makes sense for bean dishes and roasted vegetables, as some of the toasty character of the lentils will transfer to the dish. **MAKES ABOUT 1¼ CUPS**

½ cup brown or black lentils, picked over

2 tablespoons coriander seeds

10 dried Catarina or cascabel chiles, stems removed

2 tablespoons unsweetened shredded coconut

2 tablespoons brown mustard seeds

2 tablespoons ground turmeric

1 tablespoon cumin seeds

1 tablespoon fenugreek seeds

1 tablespoon black peppercorns

1 teaspoon asafetida powder

Lightly toast the lentils and coriander, stirring, in a dry skillet over medium heat, until fragrant. Grind the remaining ingredients to a fine powder in a coffee mill, and combine with the lentils and coriander. Grind together in a coffee mill as needed.

Panch Phoron

A visually interesting seed mix, this Bengali specialty gets tossed into bread doughs and ground into soups rich in beans and lentils. I like to crack the seeds but not grind them completely, to leave an interesting texture. Since they're usually cooked a fairly long time, they will soften to a pleasant texture. **MAKES 1¼ CUPS**

¼ cup fennel seeds

¼ cup nigella seeds

¼ cup cumin seeds

¼ cup fenugreek seeds

¼ cup brown mustard seeds

Combine all the seeds, and use whole or cracked (see headnote), as needed.

The blends of Africa all seem to pay tribute to the Moorish conquerors who swept across the continent and into Europe, leaving trails of flavor behind. Conquering armies of old truly did ride upon their stomachs, and they conveniently brought spices from their homelands to the new territories and vice versa, with the Moors being no exception across the North African tier.

The complex mixtures heavy in peppercorn, cardamom, and other Indian sub-continent natives found their way into the sun-parched cuisines of Africa. The Indian concept of long, slow stewing also came with the conquerors, and it brought those same spices to a new level of complexity, especially when combined with African locals like ajwain and cubeb. Thanks to the Moors, the *tagines* of Morocco have the sweet fruit influences of Spain and are unified to savory Middle Eastern fare with a bridge of spice. Later, the New World crops of chiles and allspice came via the established Moorish trade routes in reverse, and now they permeate the foods of these regions. If anything good came from the conflicts of old, it was on the common ground of the dinner table.

Piri-Piri

Piri-piri may be used for either a wet hot sauce, much like Tabasco, or a spice blend with tart notes of citrus and tomato acid: here is a recipe for the latter. The heat can be overpowering if used as a condiment, but if cooked into dishes, the acids in the mix temper the heat of the chiles somewhat. It still packs a punch, so use with caution. **MAKES ABOUT ½ CUP**

    ¼ cup sweet Hungarian paprika
    1 tablespoon black peppercorns
    1 tablespoon cayenne
    5 dried *pequín* chiles
    2 teaspoons dried lemon peel

Combine all the ingredients, and grind together in a coffee mill as needed.

Mint Chermoula

Moroccan cuisine uses this as both a basic flavoring paste in cooking and a spicy condiment. The bulk of the blend comes from the fresh onion base, but it calls upon the North African specialty ajwain for bittering in the background. This version adds fresh mint to lift the flavors. **MAKES ABOUT 1¼ CUPS**

1 small onion, diced

3 garlic cloves

¼ cup fresh spearmint leaves

1 tablespoon fresh cilantro

¼ cup sweet Hungarian paprika

¼ cup coriander seeds

1 tablespoon coarse sea salt

1 tablespoon black peppercorns

2 teaspoons ajwain seeds

2 teaspoons cayenne

Combine the onion, garlic, mint, and cilantro in a mini processor and blend to a paste. Grind the remaining ingredients together in a coffee mill, and stir into the paste. Allow to sit for at least 1 hour before using, and store in the refrigerator for up to 1 week.

Berberé

Berberé is perhaps one of the more complex African blends that often bewilders Westerners, first with its pronounciation ("bar-ee bar-ee"), and then with its flavor, which continues to dance on the palate even after an initial jolt of heat. The ajwain sneaks up on the bitter part of the palate and the ginger/cassia/cardamom sweetness is unexpected in the otherwise savory mix. Used to make stocks and soups, it's a bit too hot to be applied as a condiment or anywhere the heat of cooking won't mellow the flavors and bring the otherwise dissimilar array of tastes together. **MAKES ABOUT 1¼ CUPS**

¼ cup coriander seeds

¼ cup sweet Hungarian paprika

3 tablespoons ground turmeric

2 tablespoons dried *pequín* chiles

2 tablespoons black peppercorns

1 tablespoon chopped dried garlic

1 tablespoon fenugreek seeds

2 teaspoons allspice berries

2 teaspoons cardamom seeds

2 teaspoons ajwain seeds

2 teaspoons ground cassia-cinnamon

1 teaspoon whole cloves

1 teaspoon ground ginger

¼ teaspoon grated nutmeg

Combine all the ingredients, and grind together in a coffee mill as needed.

Duqqa

This has become fashionable on some Western menus as a dip for pita bread when mixed with oil, much as you would use hummus. Blended with water or another more interesting liquid, it can be served warm or cold. The spice blend is also used to thicken and flavor soups in both Africa and the Middle East, but my guess is that Western restaurateurs won't be able to resist its crossover use in any number of ways. (If nothing else, where else do you get to put two Qs together on the menu?) **MAKES ABOUT 1 ½ CUPS**

1 cup unsalted roasted chickpeas (available in Italian and specialty markets)

¼ cup sesame seeds

3 tablespoons coriander seeds

2 tablespoons cumin seeds

2 tablespoons black peppercorns

1 tablespoon dried thyme

1 tablespoon dried mint, preferably peppermint

Coarse sea salt, to taste

Toast the chickpeas and sesame seeds in a dry skillet over medium heat until the sesame seeds begin to color. Combine all the ingredients, and grind together in a coffee mill, in batches as necessary. Be careful not to oversalt, as some chickpeas come presalted. Store in an airtight container.

Harissa

A blazing-hot condiment, harissa is usually a paste made with oil. This versatile version can easily be blended with oil or simply used in its dry state.   **MAKES ABOUT 1 ¼ CUPS**

2 dried *guajillo* chiles, stems removed, cut into pieces

20 dried *pequín* chiles

¼ cup sweet Hungarian paprika

3 tablespoons coarse sea salt

2 tablespoons coriander seeds

2 tablespoons cumin seeds

1 tablespoon ground cassia-cinnamon

2 teaspoons dried lemon peel

2 teaspoons garlic flakes or chopped dried garlic

1 teaspoon caraway seeds

Combine all the ingredients, and grind together in a coffee mill as needed.

Tabil

In North Africa, they make a spice blend that shares its name with its primary ingredient, coriander. Used as a general-purpose blend, *tabil* is mixed as easily in soups as it is rubbed on meats.   **MAKES ABOUT ½ CUP**

¼ cup coriander seeds

3 tablespoons garlic flakes or chopped dried garlic

1 tablespoon red chile flakes

1 tablespoon caraway seeds

Combine all the ingredients, and grind together in a coffee mill as needed.

Tunisian Five-Spice

A spice combination that was born from the overland trading routes that brought exotica from the interior of Africa to the trading coast in the northwest, this is equally fine for roasting meats or stewing with beans and lentils.   **MAKES ABOUT ¼ CUP**

2 tablespoons white peppercorns

1 tablespoon ground cassia-cinnamon

2 teaspoons grains of paradise

1 teaspoon whole cloves

½ teaspoon freshly shaved or grated nutmeg

Combine all the ingredients, and grind together in a coffee mill as needed.

Capetown Masala

The Dutch settlers in South Africa adopted the continent's propensity toward curry techniques and ended up making a spice blend that is relatively simple but has top notes from cardamom, a nod to European tastes. It's fairly hot by tradition, but you can adjust the heat level down to your taste. The chile used is simply cayenne, again demonstrating that not all curries need to be complex.   **MAKES ABOUT 1¾ CUPS**

½ cup cayenne

½ cup sweet Hungarian paprika

¼ cup coriander seeds

3 tablespoons cardamom seeds

3 tablespoons ground turmeric

2 tablespoons cumin seeds

1 tablespoon black peppercorns

Combine all the ingredients, and grind together in a coffee mill as needed.

INDONESIAN SAMBALS

Sambal is really a catch-all term for any of several relatively simple pastes in Southeast Asia, specifically Indonesia. All are based on fresh chiles, and typically large volumes at that. Most include *trassi*, a partially fermented shrimp paste found in local groceries. Garlic, shallots, ginger, and candlenuts round out most examples, with each having a particular twist: roasted chiles in one, crunchy bits of fresh chile in another, sweet coconut milk in yet another—the sky is the limit for these condiment pastes. As an example, I've included *sambal goreng*, a version whose unique angle is the fried chile technique, which mellows the chiles slightly and blooms their flavors into the condiment.

Sambal Goreng   MAKES ABOUT 2 CUPS

1 cup minced shallots

¼ cup peanut oil

4 garlic cloves, chopped

10 fresh Thai red chiles, stems removed, chopped

1 teaspoon *trassi* (shrimp paste)

1 teaspoon fine sea salt

2 tablespoons chopped peanuts

Cook the shallots in the oil in a large skillet, stirring, until translucent, 2 to 3 minutes. Add the garlic and cook, stirring, just until fragrant, about 1 minute more. Strain the shallots and garlic from the oil, and transfer to a food processor. Return the oil to the pan, add the chiles, and cook, stirring, until soft, about 3 minutes. Transfer the chiles and oil to the processor, and add the *trassi* and salt. Blend until smooth. Transfer to a bowl and add the peanuts. Store, covered, in the refrigerator for up to a week.

Basa Genep

This is a classic flavoring paste used widely in Indonesia and specifically in Bali. The flavors perfectly mirror the palate of the region, and so, armed with this paste, you'll have your dinner guests thinking of dugout canoes and pristine beaches. **MAKES ABOUT 1 CUP**

    10 macadamia nuts or roasted candlenuts
    4 dried *pequin* chiles
    1 teaspoon white sesame seeds
    1 teaspoon coriander seeds
    1 teaspoon black peppercorns
    ¼ teaspoon freshly shaved or grated nutmeg
    8 shallots, minced
    5 garlic cloves
    3 tablespoons grated fresh galangal
    1 tablespoon grated fresh turmeric
    1 tablespoon grated fresh *kencur*
    1 tablespoon grated fresh ginger

Combine the nuts, chiles, sesame seeds, coriander, peppercorns, and nutmeg and finely grind in a coffee mill. Transfer to a food processor, add the remaining ingredients, and process until smooth, adding small amounts of water if necessary. Store, covered, in the refrigerator for up to a week.

THAI CURRY PASTES

I hear lots of requests for "red" or "green" Thai curry in my shop. I usually have to explain that these aren't dry curry powders as found in India, but rather fresh pastes that are pounded together in restaurants and home kitchens daily. A base of fresh herbs is used to bind together drier spices, much like an Italian pesto. The color, while descriptive, gives only a small clue as to the ultimate makeup, a moving target at best based on the availability of ingredients. Generally, through, red pastes are hot, and green pastes will make you forget your name from the endorphin rush. Practically, the chiles that make the color difference make up the bulk of the flavor/heat difference as well.

Thai Red Curry Paste   MAKES ABOUT 2½ CUPS

1 cup packed fresh cilantro leaves

¼ cup fresh Thai basil leaves

20 fresh *kaffir* lime leaves

5 fresh red Thai chiles, stems removed

4 garlic cloves

2 shallots, minced

2 tablespoons grated fresh ginger

2 tablespoons grated fresh galangal

2 tablespoons finely chopped tender fresh lemongrass

1 tablespoon ground coriander seeds

1 teaspoon *trassi* (shrimp paste) or fish sauce

1 teaspoon freshly ground white pepper

Vegetable oil, as needed

Blend all the ingredients in a food processor until smooth; some oil may be needed to achieve blending. (Be sure to wear a bleachable *sarong*, since the paste stains like crazy.) Store, covered, in the refrigerator until ready to use.

Chinese Five-Spice

Most everyone knows of the classic spice combination from China, but exactly *where* does one use it? The polite Chinese answer I got translated as "wherever you're hungry." This mix is so liberally strewn onto roast meats and vegetables that many believe it was the original barbecue rub. Indeed, the famous Peking duck includes it in the "bronzing" sauce made from the best soy sauce. Duck and fatty cuts especially take on the licorice intensity from the star anise and fennel. Double-cooked pork made with the fatty back cuts, called *pha rho*, gets dusted with the spice, and you're likely to taste the sweet tang of pepper and cassia-cinnamon in hot fried tofu, *Ma Pua Do Fu* (page 302).

Given the current difficulties in finding Sichuan peppercorns (see "Citrix Family Impact Ban," page 193), here you will need to substitute good-quality black peppercorns. If possible, add a squeeze of lime juice to your dish to help bridge the replacement.

MAKES ¼ CUP

1 tablespoon cracked star anise

1 tablespoon fennel seeds

1 tablespoon ground cassia-cinnamon

1½ teaspoons whole cloves

1½ teaspoons Sichuan peppercorns or black peppercorns

Combine all the ingredients, and grind together in a coffee mill as needed.

Chinese Stock Spices

This mix from the hills of Fujian is added to stock each morning and simmered all day to impart the flavors of the spices. The stock becomes the basis for everything from simple soup to elaborate wok-seared whole fish. A pot is always simmering in the background of the Chinese kitchen and gains intensity all day long. Noodles cooked in the stock take on all its complexity and can become a meal in their own right with little more preparation. The Chinese have long understood that layers of flavors gained over time can make the simplest ingredients bloom with taste. **MAKES ABOUT 1 CUP**

¼ cup thinly sliced fresh ginger

¼ cup broken cassia-cinnamon sticks

¼ cup barberries

2 tablespoons tamarind paste

5 slices fresh or dried angelica root

8 star anise

6 whole cloves

2 tablespoons sea salt

Combine all the ingredients, and refrigerate if not using immediately. If using the spices in a soup or broth that will not be strained, wrap in a linen steeping bag or a square of cheesecloth, and remove at the end of cooking.

This makes enough for 2 gallons of stock. Combine the spices with 1 pound beef or chicken bones, add 2 gallons water in a stockpot, and simmer gently for at least 4 hours, maintaining the water level as it cooks. Strain before using.

Shichimi-Togarashi

This condiment, also called "seven-spice," is usually made with *sansho*, Japanese prickly ash bush. Because of the high cost and difficulty in getting this ingredient, I substitute citric acid (available at health food stores) and increase the chile flakes a bit, with good results. Sprinkle on rice, sushi, or a Japanese noodle bowl. **MAKES ABOUT ⅔ CUP**

2 tablespoons Japanese or Chinese mild chile flakes

2 tablespoons black sesame seeds

2 tablespoons white sesame seeds

2 tablespoons poppy seeds

1 tablespoon granulated dried tangerine peel (available in Asian markets)

½ teaspoon dried lemon crystal (citric acid)

2 tablespoons seaweed flakes or crushed nori

Combine all the ingredients except the seaweed and grind very coarsely in a mortar and pestle or coffee mill. Add the seaweed flakes at the end, leaving them intact for texture.

Gomaisho

Gomaisho is one of those blends that show simplicity at its best—and the importance of selecting regionally authentic ingredients. Japanese sea salt is the key, with its sharp, almost metallic flavor that plays off the rich, oily character of the roasted sesame seeds. Toast only what you need daily and grind at the table for the best flavor this condiment can offer.

¼ cup black sesame seeds

¼ cup white sesame seeds

1½ teaspoons fine Japanese sea salt

Lightly toast the seeds, stirring, in a dry skillet over medium heat. Transfer to a nonreactive, heatproof bowl, preferably glass, and stir in the sea salt. Cover and let stand for 10 minutes to mix the flavors. Grind in a mortar and pestle or coffee mill, and use as a condiment.

Acton, Bryan, and Peter Duncan. *Making Mead.* Michigan: G. W. Kent, Inc., 1984.

Alford, Jeffrey, and Naomi Duguid. *Seductions of Rice.* New York: Artisan, 1998.

Andoh, Elizabeth. *At Home with Japanese Cookery.* New York: Alfred A. Knopf, 1980.

Basham, A. L. *The Wonder That Was India.* Calcutta: Rupa & Fontana, 1967.

Bayless, Rick. *Authentic Mexican Cooking.* London: Headline, 1989.

Blunt, Wilfrid, and Sandra Raphel. *The Illustrated Herbal.* New York: Thames & Hudson Publishing, 1979.

Brickell, Christopher, ed. in chief. *American Horticultural Society Encyclopedia of Gardening.* London: Dorling Kindersley, 1993.

Coetzee, Renata. *Funa, Foods from Africa.* Durban: Butterworth Publishers, Inc., 1982.

Corn, Charles. *The Scents of Eden.* New York: Kodansha International, 1998.

Cremo, Michael (Drutakarma Dasa). *The Higher Taste.* London: Bhaktivedanta Book Trust, 1983.

David, Elizabeth. *Is There a Nutmeg in the House?* New York: Viking Press, 2001.

Fernandez, Adela. *Traditional Mexican Cooking.* Mexico City: Panorama Publishers, 1985.

Garland, Sarah. *The Complete Book of Herbs & Spices.* London: Frances Lincoln Publishers, 1979.

———. *The Herb Garden.* New York: Pequin Books, 1984.

Giles, Milton. *Nathaniel's Nutmeg.* London: Hodder & Stoughton, 1999.

Grant, Rosamund. *Caribbean & African Cookery.* London: Virago, 1989.

Grant, Rose. *Street Food.* Freedom, CA: The Crossing Press, 1988.

Hampstead, Marilyn. *The Basil Book.* New York: Pocket Books, 1984.

Hemphill, Ian. *The Spice and Herb Bible.* Toronto: Robert Rose, 2002.

Herbst, Sharon T. *The New Food Lover's Companion,* 2nd ed. New York: Barrons Educational Series, 1995.

Holt, Geraldene. *A Taste of Herbs.* London: Conran Octopus, 1991.

Iny, Daisey. *The Best of Baghdad Cooking.* New York: Saturday Review Press, 1976.

Jaffrey, Madhur. *Madhur Jaffrey's Indian Cooking.* New York: Barrons Educational Series, 1995.

Kennedy, Diana. *The Art of Mexican Cooking.* New York: Bantam Publishing, 1989.

Kerr, Graham. *Graham Kerr's Kitchen.* New York: Berkeley Publishing Group, 1994.

———. *The Galloping Gourmet.* New York: Doubleday & Co., 1966.

———. *Graham Kerr's Swiftly Seasoned*. New York: G. P. Putman's Sons, 1996.

Kowalchick, Claire, and William Hylton, eds. *Rodale's Encyclopedia of Herbs*. Emmaus, PA: Rodale Press, 1987.

Long, Cheryl, and Heather Kibbey. *Classic Liqueurs*. Lake Oswego, OR: Culinary Arts, 1990.

Lust, John. *The Herb Book*. New York: B. Lust Publications, 1974.

Miller, Mark. *The Great Chile Book*. Berkeley, CA: Ten Speed Press, 1991.

Norman, Jill. *The Complete Book of Spices*. London: Dorling Kindersley, 1990.

———. *Herbs & Spices: The Cook's Reference*. New York: Dorling Kindersley, 2002.

Ortiz, Joe. *The Village Baker*. Berkeley, CA: Ten Speed Press, 1993.

Raichlen, Steven. *The Caribbean Pantry Cookbook*. New York: Artisan Publishing, 1995.

Rozin, Elisabeth. *Blue Corn & Chocolate*. New York: Alfred A. Knopf, 1992.

Sahni, Julie. *Classic Indian Cooking*. New York: William Morrow, 1990.

Sinclair, Kevin. *China: The Beautiful Cookbook*. Sydney: Weldon Owen, 1992.

Singh, V. S., and Kirti Singh. *Spices*. New Delhi: New Age Publishing, 1996.

Spices Board of India. *Indian Spices—a Catalog*. Cochin, 1992.

Stella, Alain. *The Book of Spices*. Paris: Flammarion, 1999.

Stellenbosch Fynproewersgilde, The. *The Way We Eat in Stellenbosch*. Pretoria, South Africa: Human & Rousseau, 1979.

Stuckey, Maggie. *The Complete Spice Book*. New York: St. Martin's Press, 1997.

Traunfeld, Jerry. *The Herbfarm Cookbook*. New York, Scribner, 2000.

Williams, Faldela. *The Cape Malay Cookbook*. Cape Town: Struik Publishers, 1988.

Williams, Sallie. *The Complete Book of Sauces*. London: Collier MacMillan Publishers, 1990.

Wolfert, Paula. *The Cooking of the Eastern Mediterranean*. New York: Harper Collins, 1994.

INDEX

(Page numbers in boldface refer to recipes; page numbers in italic refer to main entries.)